# CRISES IN THE CONTEMPORARY
# PERSIAN GULF

# CRISES
## in the
# CONTEMPORARY
# PERSIAN GULF

Edited by
BARRY RUBIN

FRANK CASS
LONDON • PORTLAND, OR

8991265

First published in 2002 in Great Britain by
FRANK CASS PUBLISHERS
Crown House, 47 Chase Side, Southgate
London N14 5BP

and in the United States of America by
FRANK CASS PUBLISHERS
c/o ISBS, 5824 N.E. Hassalo Street
Portland, Oregon, 97213-3644

Website: www.frankcass.com

British Library Cataloguing in Publication Data

Crises and quandries in the contemporary Persian Gulf. –
(BESA studies in international security)
1. National security – Persian Gulf Region  2. Persian Gulf
Region – Strategic aspects  3. Persian Gulf Region – Foreign
relations  4. Persian Gulf Region – Politics and government
I. Rubin, Barry  II. Begin-Sadat Center for Strategic Studies
953.6

ISBN 0-7146-5267-9 (cloth)
ISSN 1368-9541

Library of Congress Cataloging-in-Publication Data

Crises and quandries in the contemporary Persian Gulf / edited by Barry Rubin.
    p. cm. – (BESA studies in international security, ISSN 1368-9541)
  Includes bibliographical references and index.
  ISBN 0-7146-5267-9 (cloth)
    1. Persian Gulf Region–Strategic aspects.  2. Persian Gulf Region–Politics and
government–20th century.  3. National security–Persian Gulf Region. I. Rubin, Barry
M. II. Series
  DS326.C75 2001
  327'.09536–dc21

Typeset in 11.5/13pt Goudy Old Style with Janson
by Vitaset, Paddock Wood, Kent
Printed in Great Britain by
MPG Books Ltd, Bodmin, Cornwall

# Contents

# List of Tables

# List of Abbreviations

| | |
|---|---|
| ADNOC | Abu Dhabi National Oil Company |
| AI | Amnesty International |
| Bpd | barrels per day |
| BSIS | Bahrain Security and Intelligence Service |
| BWC | Biological Weapons Convention |
| CBW | chemical and biological weapons |
| CDLR | Committee for the Defense of Legitimate Rights |
| CENTCOM | US Central Command |
| CENTRASBAT | Central Asian Peacekeeping Battalion |
| CIA | Central Intelligence Agency |
| CWC | Chemical Weapons Convention |
| ECP | Executives of Construction Party |
| EU | European Union |
| GCC | Gulf Co-operation Council |
| GDP | Gross Domestic Product |
| GHQ | general headquarters |
| IAEA | International Atomic Energy Agency |
| ICA | Islamic Coalition Association |
| ICBM | Intercontinental-range ballistic missile |
| ICM | Islamic Cultural Movement |
| IIPP | Islamic Iran Participation Party |
| ILA | Iraq Liberation Act |
| ILSA | Iran and Libya Sanctions Act |
| IMF | International Monetary Fund |
| INA | Islamic National Alliance |
| INC | Iraqi National Congress |
| IRBM | Intermediate-range ballistic missile |
| IRGC | Islamic Revolutionary Guard Corps |
| IRIB | Islamic Republic of Islam Broadcasting |

| | |
|---|---|
| IRNA | Iranian Republic National Assembly |
| MAD | mutually assured destruction |
| MWt | Megawatt |
| MIRA | Movement for Islamic Reform in Arabia |
| MOIS | Ministry of Intelligence and Security |
| MRBM | Medium-range ballistic missile |
| NATO | North Atlantic Treaty Organization |
| NBC | nuclear, biological and chemical (weapons) |
| NPT | Nuclear Non-proliferation Treaty |
| OECD | Organization for Economic Co-operation and Development |
| OMV | ongoing monitoring and verification |
| OPEC | Organization of Petroleum Exporting Countries |
| OPCW | Organization for the Prevention of Chemical Warfare |
| P-5 | the five permanent members of the UN Security Council |
| RCC | Revolutionary Command Council |
| RL | Iraqi Regional Leadership of the Ba'th party |
| PLO | Palestinian Liberation Organization |
| SAMBA | Saudi American Bank |
| SABIC | Saudi Basic Industries Corporation |
| SLV | space launch vehicle |
| SRTI | Special Representative for Transition in Iraq |
| Tcf | trillion cubic feet |
| TEU | Twenty foot Equivalent Unit |
| UAE | United Arab Emirates |
| UN | United Nations |
| UNCIM | UN Commission on Inspection and Monitoring |
| UNCTI | UN Commission for Transition in Iraq |
| UNMOVIC | UN Monitoring, Verification and Inspection Committee |
| UNSC | UN Security Council |
| UNSCOM | United Nations Special Commission |
| WMD | weapons of mass destruction |
| WTO | World Trade Organization |

# Notes on Contributors

**Jon B. Alterman** works in the Research and Studies Program at the United States Institute of Peace, Washington, DC, where he covers issues related to the Middle East. He edited *Sadat and His Legacy: Egypt and the World, 1977–1997*.

**Amatzia Baram** is head of the Jewish–Arab Center and the Gustav Von Heinemann Middle East Institute, Haifa University. His books include *Culture, History and Ideology in the Formation of Ba'thist Iraq, 1968–1989*; *Building Toward Crisis: Saddam Husayn's Strategy for Survival*. He is co-editor of *Iraq's Road to War*.

**Daniel L. Byman** is a policy analyst with the RAND Corporation and the Research Director of RAND's Center for Middle East Public Policy. Dr Byman is the author of numerous articles and several RAND monographs, including, as co-author, *Confronting Iraq: US Policy and the Use of Force Since the Gulf*; *Political Violence and Stability in the States of the Northern Persian Gulf*; and *Air Power as a Coercive Instrument*.

**Daryl Champion** holds a PhD in political science and international relations from The Australian National University. He is a Middle East-based education and media consultant.

**Michael Eisenstadt** is a senior fellow at The Washington Institute for Near East Policy, specializing in Arab–Israeli and Persian Gulf security affairs. He is co-author, with Eliot Cohen and Andrew Bacevich, of *Knives, Tanks, and Missiles: Israel's Security Revolution* (Washington, DC: The Washington Institute, 1998).

**Sean Foley** is a PhD candidate in Georgetown University's History program, where he held the Taher Scholarship in Arab

Studies (1998–1999). He interned at the State Department's Iran desk and with the US Embassy in Abu Dhabi, UAE. He has articles in the *Dictionary of Islam* (Oxford University Press), the *Middle East Review of International Affairs (MERIA)*, and other journals.

**Shafeeq Ghabra** is a professor of political science at Kuwait University and Director of the Kuwait Information Office in Washington, DC. He is former editor of Kuwait University's *Journal of the Social Sciences* and author of *Kuwait: A Study of the Dynamics of State, Authority and Society* and *Israel and the Arabs: From the Conflict of Issues to the Peace of Interests*.

**Jerrold D. Green** is Director of International Development, and Director of the Center for Middle East Public Policy, Professor of International Studies at the RAND Graduate School (RGS), and a Senior Political Scientist at RAND in Santa Monica, CA, USA.

**Turki al-Hamad** writes on Arab politics and thought for *al-Sharq al-Awsat* and is a former professor of political science at King Saud University in Dhahran.

**Barry Rubin** is Deputy Director of the BESA Center for Strategic Studies, Bar-Ilan University. He is editor of the *Middle East Review of International Affairs (MERIA)*, and editor of the *Journal of Turkish Studies*. His books include: *The Transformation of Palestinian Politics: From Revolution to State-Building; Revolution Until Victory: The Politics and History of the PLO; Cauldron of Turmoil: America in the Middle East; Modern Dictators*; and *Paved with Good Intentions: The American Experience and Iran*. He is co-editor of *Iraq's Road to War*.

**Abbas Samii** is a regional specialist for Radio Free Europe/Radio Liberty. He is editor of *Iran Report*, and is based in Washington, DC.

**Amin Tarzi** is a senior research associate (Middle East) at the Center for Nonproliferation Studies, Monterey, CA, USA.

# Preface

The Persian Gulf area is the world's greatest paradox. Wealthy, yet economically and socially underdeveloped; traditional, yet full of the turmoil of change, it is no wonder that this area has been the focal point of so much violence, struggle and controversy in the twentieth century.

This book addresses the main strategic issues in today's Persian Gulf, a region that is arguably the most likely to produce a crisis that would draw international political and economic involvement. This estimate was fulfilled when a terrorist group, led by a Saudi and including mostly Saudi hijackers, seized four US passenger planes on 11 September 2001 and crashed them into the New York World Trade Center and the Pentagon, killing thousands of people. The echoes from this event will affect Gulf politics and stability for years to come.

Among the broader questions discussed in this book are:

- Strategic Balances: The effort to find a way to balance Iran, Iraq, the Arab monarchies – Saudi Arabia, Kuwait, the United Arab Emirates, Bahrain, Qatar and Oman – and outside powers in order to avoid war or subversion among the regional states.

- Modernization: The attempt of extremely traditional societies to transform themselves rapidly to deal with new material items and ideas.

- Internal Instability: The impact of cross-state subversion and rapid change on societies – all ruled either by monarchies or radical dictatorships – which can be highly resistant to innovation.

- Weapons of Mass Destruction: An arms race that has

1

involved nuclear weapons, missiles, and chemical and biological weapons in an already volatile situation.

- Inter-State Conflicts: Two of the biggest wars of the last half-
century resulted from Iraq's invasions of Iran and of Kuwait.

- Ethnic Rivalries: Differences between Arabs and Kurds, or
between Sunni and Shiite Muslims, are major challenges to
stability in several states.

- Oil: The Gulf area has the world's largest concentration of oil
resources and is a major center for natural gas production as
well. In other words, the Gulf is the number one location for
the world's number one strategic resource.

- The Challenge of Radical Islamism: Rapid social and other
changes in the region have been met by an upsurge in Islamist
thinking and movements. Osama bin Laden and his followers
were one of the forces generated by this ferment, leading to
a global crisis following the attack by a group of mostly Saudi
terrorists on the World Trade Center and other American
targets on 11 September 2001. The resulting 'War on Terrorism'
futher shook up the Gulf's relations with the United States,
as well as internal politics.

To discuss these and other issues, the book's chapters give
equal coverage to the Arab monarchies, Iran and Iraq. It provides a detailed analysis of developments in the most important
monarchies: Saudi Arabia (Champion, pp. 127–46); Kuwait
(Ghabra, pp. 105–23); and the United Arab Emirates (Foley,
pp. 33–67). In each of these kingdoms, national integration and
socio-economic development are fascinating processes which
face considerable barriers. Especially original is the chapter on
why, surprisingly, these countries have maintained their stability
in the face of so many challenges (Byman and Green, pp. 75–
103).

Other chapters deal with the monarchies' efforts to co-operate
against potential Iranian and Iraqi threats (Hamad, pp. 21–32)
and to seek US protection (Alterman, pp. 163–179). Throughout the 1990s the United States sought ways to pressure Iraq

into compliance with UN resolutions and to weaken Saddam Hussein. But US policy was never able to find a satisfactory and effective way of doing so (Tarzi, pp. 181–198).

The key issue regarding Iran is the struggle between radical and moderate factions in the government, each representing a very different vision of society (Samii, pp. 277–313). Despite Iran's potential oil wealth, both economic mismanagement and external pressures have created significant inflation and unemployment and, thus, pressure for change. Finally, Iran's drive to obtain weapons of mass destruction (Eisenstadt, pp. 223–256) stirs up considerable concern over Tehran's future intentions.

In Iraq's case, the continued rule of Saddam Hussein and his provocative behavior toward neighbors (Baram, pp. 199–221) has meant an enduring outcast status. Baghdad's continued efforts to hide and rebuild its military arsenal in the face of sanctions has contributed heavily to this problem. Yet Iraq also has its internal problems, especially given the dissatisfaction of the majority of Kurds and Shiite Muslims with Saddam Hussein's government.

This book provides a comprehensive, systematic picture of the region's current issues and problems.

The following chapters are reprinted with permission: Turki al-Hamad,[1] Shafeeq Ghabra[2] and Michael Eisenstadt.[3]

The editor would like to thank Linda Sharaby, Cameron Brown and Elisheva Rosman-Stollman for their production and editing assistance.

## NOTES

1. al-Hamad, T., 'Imperfect Alliances: Will the Gulf Monarchies Work Together?', *Middle East Quarterly*, 4, 1 (1997), pp. 47–53.
2. Ghabra, S., 'Kuwait and the Economics of Socio-Economic Change', *Middle East Policy*, 5, 3 (1997), pp. 358–72.
3. Eisenstadt, M., 'Living with a Nuclear Iran', *Survival*, 41, 3 (1999), pp. 124–48.

# 1

# The Persian Gulf Amid Global and Regional Crises

## BARRY RUBIN

By virtue of its oil resources and consequent income, the Persian Gulf region is one of the world's key strategic areas. Also, by virtue of its place as a location of so much rapid social change and intellectual ferment, the Gulf area has also become a focal point for global conflict and instability.

Consider the contemporary issues that arise from developments in this once-obscure backwater zone, which has also been the scene of some of the most intensive geopolitical competition and violence.

- Regarding Iraq: there are international sanctions; questions about Baghdad's development of weapons of mass destruction; the autonomous Kurdish zone in the north and that area's involvement with insurgency in Turkey; along with the whole question of Iraqi President Saddam Hussein's future and intentions. In its recent past there has been a major war with Iran, the seizure of Kuwait, Iraq's expulsion by an international coalition, and major internal revolts by Kurdish and Shiite groups.

- Regarding Iran: there are US sanctions; another high-priority program to develop weapons of mass destruction; and massive domestic battles between factions holding quite different visions of the country's future. In its recent past there has been comprehensive revolution, and an eight-year-long war with Iraq. Its government is an unprecedented experiment with Islamist rule; and each of its borders poses a different equation of potential conflict and complex diplomacy.

- Regarding Saudi Arabia: there is the story of the world's largest producer and exporter of oil; the recipient of massive wealth; and the challenge of social change in one of the world's most traditionally minded countries. In its recent past, it made the unprecedented decision to allow in US troops to throw Iraqi forces out of Kuwait. From this mix of events came Osama bin Laden, the wealthy revolutionary who was the author of the 11 September 2001 attacks on America that left thousands of people dead in the worst terrorist incident in recent history. Indeed, the majority of plane hijackers involved in this event came from Saudi Arabia.

How has the Gulf changed in this tumultuous period? What are the main features of its strategic and political problems?

## BACKGROUND AND CONTEMPORARY ISSUES

To begin with, several interlocking points should be established about the relationship between the Cold War and the Gulf area. First, despite the region's importance, it was never much of a theater in the US–USSR conflict. This was partly due to the fact that the Gulf was far more in the American, rather than the Soviet, sphere of influence. While Moscow had a close relationship with Iraq, it never really penetrated the region. There was virtually no direct Russian presence. In comparison, the United States had alliances with Iran and Saudi Arabia, and US or British influence was pre-eminent in all the smaller Arab states of the region.

Although they instituted a short-lived oil embargo in 1973, the Gulf Arab monarchies – Saudi Arabia, Kuwait, the United Arab Emirates (UAE), Qatar, Bahrain and Oman – never let themselves be influenced very much by US support for Israel or other regional policies. Their key interest was in some level of American protection against local threats from radicals, internal upheavals, or perhaps Soviet actions. At the same time, though, they did not want to provoke their own highly traditional people or militant neighbors by showing too high a profile in their relationship with the US.

This balance of simultaneously seeking a protector and appeasing potential threats basically worked for many years, from the 1940s through the 1980s. There was no need to try to obtain help from the USSR because its Middle Eastern clients – Iraq, Syria, Egypt under the rule of Gamal Abdel Nasser, and South Yemen – were the very forces threatening local regimes. The monarchies co-operated to some extent by forming the Gulf Co-operation Council (GCC) but they could never defend themselves from external attack or intimidation without outside help.

Second, local, sub-regional issues predominated in setting the agenda for the Gulf states. The underlying power dynamic was a triangle with two strong sides and one weak side. The two strong sides were Iran and Iraq, each with large populations and relatively strong armies. Both countries desired to dominate the Gulf, each in its own way, during the rule of different regimes and ideologies. Their intended victims were weaker: the six Arab monarchies. This geostrategic framework seems a given factor likely to shape the Gulf's future as it did its past.

As suggested above, the Gulf Arab monarchies dealt with this competition in various ways. One technique was to use the United States as a protector against aggressive regional powers. Another was to appease Baghdad or Tehran. Finally, the monarchies could play one of these stronger states against the other.

Third, the Cold War ended in the Gulf area earlier than in other parts of the world. Neither the Iranian revolution nor the Iran–Iraq War, much less the Iraqi invasion of Kuwait and subsequent US-led war on Iraq, were part of the Cold War. On the contrary, it was the absence of superpower competition that made these events possible. While the modern history of this region is far too complex to analyze here in any detail, it is necessary to examine briefly the main events and the periods into which they fall in order to understand the contemporary Gulf.

## Iran as Protector (1958–78)

Following the radical coup in Baghdad in 1958, Iraq became the principal local threat to the Gulf monarchies, most directly by threatening Kuwait's independence in 1961. In response, Gulf Arab monarchies forged a relationship with the United States as a protector. At the same time, these states appeased Iraq – and other radical Arab states – by expressing their support for Pan-Arab nationalist causes and by subsidizing militants who fought against Israel and the West.

This did not prevent the Gulf Arab monarchies from also developing good relations with the Shah of Iran, who sought to become the primary power in the Gulf but did not threaten the monarchies' own sovereignty. Iraq wanted to overthrow the kings while Iran only wanted to lead them. For Iran's part, it sought American help and protection regarding the threat on its northern border – the Soviet Union – and increasingly to counter the threat on its southern border from radical Arab states.

In 1971, with many of its resources tied up in the Vietnam War, the US government initiated a special relationship with Iran, intensifying the two states' previous alliance. President Richard Nixon and National Security Advisor Henry Kissinger promised the Shah three types of help: all the arms he wanted to buy – except nuclear weapons; US advisors to teach his military personnel how to use them; and assistance for the Kurdish rebellion against Iraq. With the rapid increase in oil prices after 1973, Iran became able to buy far more military equipment than anyone previously expected. The Shah was set to become the Gulf's policeman.

## The Iranian Revolution (1978–79)

Ultimately, it was not the Gulf monarchies that proved unstable but Iran itself. Iran's Islamic revolution transformed the country from a US ally and the Gulf monarchies' protector into the world's chief anti-American state as well as the principal threat to its neighbors. It became quickly apparent that there was no way to appease the new regime in Tehran.

Despite some American fears, Islamic Iran remained non-aligned and did not move closer to the USSR. Moscow was unable to exploit the Iranian revolution to spread its influence in the Gulf areas and, preoccupied with other matters, did not try very hard to do so directly. The Soviet invasion of Afghanistan to preserve the country's shaky Communist regime was related to the new power balance in the region, but proved a disastrous step whose costs and humiliations helped to bring down the Soviet regime itself.

## The Iran–Iraq War (1980–88)

Again, ironically, it was not Iran – the state threatening the GCC – but Iraq, which had become the Arab monarchies' supposed protector after Iran's revolution, which initiated a war. Iraq was motivated both by fear of Iranian subversion and by the sense of an opportunity to defeat Iran and easily dominate the Gulf. Baghdad had, of course, underestimated Iran's stability. Instead, the war lasted for eight years and resulted in a million casualties. Although Iraq won in the end, the cost was terribly high.

For the Arab Gulf monarchies, Iraq was essentially fighting as their defender against the radical Islamic threat emanating from Iran. They subsidized its war effort with billions of dollars of aid, albeit often concealed as loans, and lobbied for other countries – especially the United States – to back Iraq. After Iraq began attacking Iranian ships with French-supplied missiles, Iran started hitting tankers carrying oil from the Gulf Arab monarchies. The Kuwaitis and Saudis asked the United States to organize convoys protected by US warships under the rationale that tanker ships transporting their oil would be 're-flagged' as American vessels. The United States did so in 1987 and 1988. At times, there were small-scale clashes between US and Iranian forces. Losses on the battlefield, exhaustion, the increasingly apparent fact that the war was unwinnable and fear of American intervention, led Iran to sue for peace in 1988.

The USSR had played virtually no role in these events. It refused to supply arms to its old ally Iraq, angering Baghdad, though some weapons did come from Soviet bloc sources. The

Saudis and Kuwaitis hinted that they might ask for Soviet help in convoying tankers if the United States refused to do so, but this was a fairly obvious gambit rather than a real initiative. The United States itself, of course, did not enter the fray to counter Soviet influence but to stop the extension of Iran's power as well as to preserve regional stability and protect oil supplies.

### The Iraqi Invasion of Kuwait (1990)

While Iraq had won the war against Iran, the costs had been great and the gains few. Iraqi President Saddam Hussein faced a worsening economic situation. At the same time, his ambitions to lead the Arab world and to control the Gulf had only grown. He saw conquering Kuwait as a step toward seizing the riches of the Gulf Arab monarchies and simultaneously placing himself firmly at the head of the Arabs.

Saddam Hussein also concluded, in part due to poorly formulated American signals, that the United States would do nothing to stop him from annexing Kuwait. He also apparently believed that the Saudis and other Gulf Arab monarchies would be too afraid to retaliate. The Soviet Union was simply not a factor at all in his calculations.

### The Second Gulf War (1991)

However, Saddam had miscalculated badly. The Gulf monarchies invited Western help and a US-led coalition drove Iraq out of Kuwait. In a real sense, the monarchies took an unprecedented step by inviting foreign troops onto their soil. Yet they were also acting within the same historic framework that had prevailed during the previous two decades in order to balance the region's strategic triangle.

What had changed was the relationship between those actors. Since neither Iran nor Iraq could be trusted to balance the other – given that they both menaced the monarchies – the dependence on outside protectors was more important than ever. In this new situation, the United States became the Gulf's single protector. In their own way, the Gulf monarchies developed a policy of dual containment in the 1990s; that is, they sought to convince the United States to protect them by containing both Iran and Iraq.

But they also formulated their own interpretation on this situation. Convinced that the United States was unwilling or unable to remove Saddam Hussein, the Gulf monarchies had to look after their own future with one eye on their powerful, potentially threatening, neighbor. They supported the continuation of UN sanctions against Baghdad and were not averse to periodic American bombing attacks when Iraq refused to cooperate. At the same time, however, they did not want to endorse such attacks too openly.

They were neither ready to support a serious effort to overthrow Saddam Hussein nor did they need to appease Iraq during the 1990s. Still, they knew the day might come when a return to appeasement would be needed. Consequently, the Gulf Arab monarchies were careful about not antagonizing Saddam Hussein. Indeed, Iraqi intransigence kept them from being more flexible than they preferred. For example, the Iraqi president's January 1999 speech calling for the overthrow of other Arab regimes was one of a continuing series of signs that Iraq was still dangerous.

One option was to become engaged in the Arab–Israeli peace process. All the Gulf Arab monarchies agreed to attend the 1991 Madrid conference, involving them for the first time in face-to-face negotiations with Israel. While Saudi Arabia and Kuwait were less enthusiastic, the other monarchies took some steps toward normalization with Israel. To some extent, they viewed Israel as an additional balancing factor to deter the threat from radical regimes. Equally, the Gulf monarchies supported the Palestinian Liberation Organization (PLO) in creating a Palestinian Authority in the West Bank and Gaza Strip, as well as seeking an independent Palestinian state through negotiations with Israel. But, angry at PLO support for Saddam Hussein in the 1990–91 crisis, the Gulf Arab monarchies gave it little financial aid. Iran and Iraq both opposed the peace process.

Another option increasingly favored by the Gulf Arab monarchies in the late 1990s was opening to Iran. Tehran, engaged in at least some degree of moderation, was now seen as a lesser threat than Iraq. This new perspective brought the Gulf monarchies full circle, back to their original strategy of using Iran to balance Iraq. This policy accelerated in 1999, with Iranian President Muhammad Khatami's successful visit to Saudi Arabia, and Saudi statements supporting Iran's rearmament program.

The monarchies also continued their large-scale arms purchases from the United States and other Western countries. These proceeded at a slower pace than in the past, however, partly due to economic weakness in the Gulf's oil-producing states.

This economic factor was another important strategic consideration. While oil prices had fluctuated in the 1970s and 1980s, Iran, Iraq, Saudi Arabia, Kuwait and the UAE had made billions of dollars from petroleum exports. During the 1990s, though, oil prices remained low, and income levels dropped. Given their higher social spending and more developed infrastructure, Gulf oil producers ran into debt. Saudi Arabia, for example, borrowed money from foreign banks.

Although this situation did not bring about a crisis, the necessary belt-tightening could bring about internal unrest. Moreover, higher levels of urbanization and education among Gulf citizens would eventually bring more demands for democratization and participation. This has arguably happened first and foremost in Iran. There were also groups in the Arab monarchies that thought that modernization was proceeding too quickly and involved too much Westernization. While all these scenarios remained potential problems, the Gulf Arab monarchies continued to be quite stable.

## TRENDS FOR THE FUTURE OF THE GULF REGION

Iraq and Iran are the Middle East's main anti-status quo powers. The fact that both countries are undergoing dramatic change has major consequences for war, peace and stability in the region.

One key factor is the question of international sanctions against Iraq and US sanctions against Iran. There is an important and often misunderstood point about sanctions. While their ultimate goal may be to remove a regime or force it to alter policies, an equally important objective is to deny a government the resources to increase its power and implement its own aims – or at least to reduce the scope of its immediate ambitions. In this latter regard, the sanctions have been successful.

In Iraq's case, the key issue will be the removal of sanctions, while for Iran the central question is the internal political struggle.

## Iraq

If and when sanctions are completely – or almost completely – lifted, Baghdad will reap great advantages and face a choice between aggressive and accommodationist strategies. Several specific developments are fairly predictable:

1. Iraq will declare victory over the United States, insisting that Baghdad's own steadfastness and power brought an end to pressures. The government will thank the Arab and Islamic world, as well as such friends as China, France and Russia. In short, Iraq's escape from isolation will be interpreted as a mandate for continuing old policies rather than as a chance to prove that Iraq has learned a lesson.

2. Foreign companies will rush to invest in Iraq. Many businesses will approach Baghdad, especially with propositions to rebuild and modernize oilfields. This would, in theory, give Saddam Hussein a strong incentive to follow a moderate policy so as not to antagonize the West or scare off these new partners. Saddam will proceed cautiously, at least by his own standards, which are far more adventuresome than those of other leaders.

3. Publicly, Iraq will put the priority on reconstruction and on rebuilding its economy, at least for a while. This would be required to consolidate Iraq's gains in escaping isolation and to provide some benefits for its long-suffering citizens. No government could neglect to correct the fall in living standards and decline of services faced by Iraq since 1991. Saddam Hussein's decision to invade Kuwait in 1990 was itself conditioned on Iraq's poor economic situation and the population's bitterness following a costly eight-year war with Iran.

4. However, the pace of reconstruction could be far slower and the economic boom far smaller than expected, with disappointment arising from several factors, including:

- low oil prices – made even lower by a surge of Iraqi oil on the market;

- continuing corporate fears about risking investment or business with Iraq;

- counterproductive policies by Iraq's own government; and

- the very size of the task to return Iraqis to their 1979 living standards, from before the war with Iran.

Saddam could react to this outcome with anger – speaking of betrayal and sabotage by foreigners or his own subjects, and a more active foreign policy to obtain money – perhaps by pressuring Saudi Arabia and Kuwait.

5. The first major international initiative by Iraq would probably be the re-conquest of the north and the destruction of the Kurdish autonomous zone. This could well be done by finding a local Kurdish ally to invite in the Iraqi army. The United States and other countries are unlikely to oppose such an offensive with force. Turkey could be neutralized because a weaker Kurdish nationalist movement would make it more secure. The lack of international reaction or retaliation would further embolden Saddam.

6. Iraq would re-arm as best it could. At first, this would take place under the guise of a reasonable rebuilding of forces destroyed in 1991 and replacement of outdated equipment. Of special importance would be the restarting of efforts to obtain and build weapons of mass destruction (WMD). Again, Saddam would be emboldened to act tougher and more aggressively in future.

The argument here is not that Saddam would rush into new foreign adventures, attacking Iran, Kuwait, or Israel. Baghdad has learned at least a few lessons from past mistakes, while situations have also changed. Iraq will lack the military capacity to engage in aggression for a number of years. And even given

Saddam Hussein's worldview, it would be hard for the Iraqi leader to decide this was a desired move.

Nonetheless, Iraq will certainly be an extremist voice in the region and will engage in activities that clearly defy – to the extent possible without provoking serious retaliation – US interests, regional stability and progress towards peace.

Beyond this, Iraq will find itself with policy alternatives similar to those it faced in 1988, when the war with Iran ended. It could choose to be a good Arab citizen, roughly the policy course pursued by the current regime between 1968 and 1988. To rejoin the Arab world – and to try to regain subsidies from Saudi Arabia and Kuwait – Baghdad could toe the general Arab line. It would be especially militant in criticizing the Arab–Israeli peace process and maligning the United States, but there would be no extreme deviations from the Arab consensus. Saddam Hussein would avoid threatening the Gulf Arab states or verbally attacking other Arab leaders. He would not – at least not too loudly – repeat his ambitious claims to regional primacy, in order to avoid antagonizing Egypt, which claimed to be leader of the Arab states and usually functioned as such. Such an Iraq would avoid trouble in order to focus on rebuilding. It would mobilize not only popular Arab sympathy with its suffering but also support from other governments as well. This would seem to be the 'logical' alternative after the disasters and losses of the last decade.

But, of course, both historic experience and an examination of his more recent behavior shows that this is not necessarily the path that Saddam Hussein would choose. Saddam will not abandon his desire for revenge, while his honest belief that others are seeking to overturn or injure him often turns his perceptions into self-fulfilling prophecies.

The alternative, radical choice would be to renew Iraq's policy of the 1988–91 era. Saddam Hussein could proclaim that Iraq's struggle and 'victories' over the West demonstrate its fitness to be Arab leader. Small threats and insults could antagonize other Arab leaders beyond the point of making them willing to engage in appeasement. These could include attacks on their relations with the United States, accusations of treachery in 1991, hints of continued Iraqi claims on Kuwait, excessive efforts to intimidate neighbors into giving aid, and implications that Iraq would be a better Arab standard-bearer than Egypt.

While Iraq would certainly express various levels of antagonism – in different ways – toward Israel, Iran and Turkey, the question is whether threats might cross lines that would bring counter-threats, escalation and crisis. The quarrel with Israel is likely to remain verbal. Iraq could reconstitute its terrorist assets but these are quite limited compared to Syria or Iran.

This scenario's implication – that Saddam will once again be his own worst enemy – does provide comfort for regional stability. Such a strategy would deny Iraq potential allies, international – including Arab – aid, and foreign investment. It would handicap both rebuilding and rearming the country. No matter how many radical groups, newspapers, or Arabs in the street proclaimed Saddam to be a hero, Iraq would not derive any material benefit. Moreover, such an atmosphere could not even equal what happened in the 1988–91 period, which availed Baghdad nothing in practical terms.

Still, Iraq's posturing would lead to regional unease and undermine US leverage while encouraging radical states and forces throughout the region. If Saddam pushed too far, another war or crisis could result.

A serious international crisis is less likely, however, simply because the United States in particular, and the West in general, might be unwilling to confront Iraq's words or deeds. In the medium run, this could be the run-up to another crisis of a different – probably unforeseen – nature.

Two main scenarios should be considered here. One is Iraq's obtaining serious WMD capacity, especially nuclear weapons. The fact that Iraq lags behind Iran, and that progress is likely to be slow – whatever items Iraq has hidden away – reduces the likelihood of this event over the next five years. It would take some time for Iraq to regain 1990 levels of such equipment or technology.

The other is an Iraqi attack on some other state. Equally, Iraq's weakened armed forces and limited resources make this unlikely over the first five years after the end of sanctions.

In short, Iraq is more likely to be a nuisance rather than a menace for some time to come. Aggressive rhetoric or acts might even injure Iraq more than others. But its regional role would be negative for progress and stability, while creating serious concern in Israel, Iran, Turkey and the Arab world.

The fact that the West is even less willing now to confront or punish Saddam politically now than before will only increase his appetite for the next stage. Iraq's frustrations over economic development as well as its more ambitious wishes for leadership and regional domination are also likely to set up a new and explosive crisis if Saddam survives most of the next decade.

### Iran

Iran would be both a potential victim and a beneficiary of Iraq's revival. Tehran would gain because the Gulf Arab states and the United States already view it as a counterweight to Saddam. This attitude is playing a central role in the current *rapprochement* with Iran.

But the main factors affecting Iran's future are internal, following the election of President Muhammad Khatami in 1997 and ensuing factional dispute. Some basic points might be summarized as follows:

- Khatami is sincere about wanting to bring economic and social reforms to Iran. He knows that easing the international situation and Iran's escape from isolation will help him achieve his goals.

- He has a huge base of supporters who share his vision, though many have less patience than he does.

- These forces at present, however, lack the strength to impose their will on the radical faction, which still controls the state apparatus and military, especially the Revolutionary Guards.

The outcome of the struggle in Iran is unclear and will take a long time to resolve. It seems more likely that Khatami and his supporters will eventually win, but this historic shift could be delayed by many years.

Meanwhile, there remains the strong possibility of a trade-off or division of labor between the two factions. This could be a deliberate decision but is more likely – and equally effective – as a *de facto* arrangement. The moderates would be able to ease economic, social and cultural restrictions; the radicals would retain control, or at least veto power, over foreign policy.

This means that Iran would continue to back terrorism, express an extremely militant line on regional issues and develop WMD. At the same time, it would also be cautious about not attacking or overly antagonizing neighbors. Iran's military is in extremely bad shape and Tehran is not spending lavishly to re-equip it. To some extent, the development of missiles – and even nuclear weapons – is a cheaper substitute for a full re-stocking of conventional arms.

In short, Iran is able to follow a line roughly parallel to Saddam's more moderate policy choice. This allows Tehran to rebuild relations with Gulf Arab states, attract more foreign investment, and co-operate with several countries – though actual allies will remain scarce. Yet this will not be sufficient to bring about détente with the United States, an end to the sanctions, or even unrestricted economic and political relations with European countries.

Beyond this, everything depends on the balance of internal forces. Even if Western states agree that they want to strengthen the Iranian moderates, they do not know precisely how to do so. For example, do Western concessions to Iran prove to the masses that Khatami's policy is best or do they merely demonstrate that Iran can continue radical policies at no cost? How much does Khatami's popular support translate into actual power to make and implement decisions?

The main conclusion is that there will be no decisive outcome overnight – at least not one in Khatami's favor – no matter how promising longer-term prospects for a more moderate line are. Western countries must explore the possibilities of improving relations while carefully monitoring Iranian behavior. On the one hand, the radicals seem to have at least temporarily blocked Khatami from changing the country's course while, on the other hand, the moderates' overwhelming election victories signaled their increasing power.

There is no simple solution to this problem except for con-stant re-evaluation, flexibility, and close observation of events in Iran. At present, Iran is much less of a threat because of its weakness and internal debate. But only time will tell whether the radicals have, or think they have, such freedom of action that they can accelerate their subversion and WMD programs. No one should be locked into a preconception which makes them try to fit facts into expectations on whether Iran is unchanging or moderating. Everyone should expect difficult tests and critical situations from Iraq's reemergence from isolation.

## THE IMPACT OF WMD

An issue requiring serious consideration is the future effect of WMD in the Gulf area. Most efforts and research have been focused on anti-proliferation. However, while this is certainly important, Iran already possesses long-range missiles and will soon have a nuclear weapons' capacity. Experience has shown that without sanctions Iraq will certainly make an all-out effort to obtain these arms and will eventually succeed in doing so.

The strategic impact lies not only with the potential use of such weapons – and these two regimes are less averse to using them in principle than almost any other government on earth – but also in the political leverage that accompanies their possession. Given the historic role of appeasement in the area, the ability to threaten neighbors with WMD would greatly enhance the ability of Iran or Iraq or press the monarchies into concessions or co-operation.

An interesting feature of this situation is the fact that Iran's military budget has fallen steadily in recent years. It is quite understandable, though, if one thinks of WMD as a cheap solution to a serious problem. If Iran must decide between buying hundreds of costly planes, thousands of tanks and dozens of ships – as opposed to nuclear weapons and missiles – the latter solution is far cheaper. In effect, the atomic bomb itself has become the poor man's atomic bomb, because it provides an overwhelmingly powerful weapon at a very low cost, and is no longer out of the reach of countries like Iran or Iraq.

An especially important question is whether, and to what extent, the United States will provide a credible umbrella for the Gulf monarchies to protect them from the threat or use of such weapons. Otherwise, they will have to re-think their own strategic policies, alliances, and behavior in any future crisis.

The one thing that is certain about the Gulf area is that it will continue to be of central importance to international affairs in the coming decade. It is likely that the focus on the Gulf will involve several crises and one or more war. To a large extent, the 'war' arising from the 11 September 2001 terrorist attacks on the United States was generated by Gulf politics. Indeed, bin Laden cited as the direct reason for his revolt the presence of US forces in Saudi Arabia from 1991 on, a measure taken to repel forces from Kuwait and to ensure Gulf security thereafter.

# 2

# Imperfect Alliances: Will the Gulf Monarchies Work Together?*

## TURKI AL-HAMAD

Theoretically speaking, the Gulf Co-operation Council (GCC) is a coherent alliance; but is it in fact so?

The six GCC states – Saudi Arabia, Kuwait, Bahrain, Qatar, the United Arab Emirates, and Oman – have much in common: socio-economic and political structures, political culture and obsessions of security and threats. Although they differ in their perceptions of threats, the GCC states define security in a very narrow, one-dimensional way: as the status-quo continuity of the political regimes.

These common elements were the formal declared reasons behind formation of the GCC in 1981. Article 1 of the organization's Basic Law explains that it was established as a result of the six states' 'peculiar relations [and] shared characteristics and systems, based upon the Islamic doctrine.' Article 4 declares the council's final goal to be the complete unification of the six states.

In actuality, these motives for founding the GCC were soon forgotten, and the organization became almost exclusively security-oriented. This shift suggests that the council's nature depends less on the inner workings of its members than on the vagaries of external circumstances. Further, the council's history indicates that the common elements of the GCC states – what brought them together in the first place – have come to be sources of differences. All this matters to the United States

*This article is published with the kind permission of the *Middle East Quarterly* and originally appeared in its March 1997 issue, pp. 47–53.

because troubles in the GCC states could require another direct American military involvement.

We cover three main topics here: the circumstances that led to the council's formation; differences among the GCC states that cause misunderstanding and possible conflict; and the various views of GCC states regarding external threats. The conclusion considers what steps need to be taken for the GCC states to flourish.

## HISTORICAL BACKGROUND

The Persian Gulf region experienced no less than five profoundly important developments in the decade prior to the GCC's formation in early 1981: the British withdrawal; the oil price revolution; the Iranian Revolution; the Soviet invasion of Afghanistan; and the Iran–Iraq War.

### British Withdrawal

In 1971, Britain announced its intention to withdraw from east of Suez – including all of the Persian Gulf. In the American and Soviet view, this created a political vacuum; they responded by engaging in a wide-ranging competition, and the Gulf region became an area in the Cold War. Distrust became the name of the game. Washington considered the Gulf region vital to its interests and acted as the heir of Great Britain, while Moscow attempted to gain a foothold through South Yemen and Oman.

### Oil Price Revolution

After the October 1973 Arab–Israeli war, crude oil prices began to escalate in a dramatic fashion, moving from $3.01 on 1 October 1973, to $5.19 on 16 October 1973, to $34.41 on 1 November 1980. As some of the largest oil producers, with the largest known oil reserves in the world, the future GCC states assumed a pivotal role in the world economy. Thus did six states with a combined population of approximately 13 million become crucial to the stability of the global economy and its political order.

22

## Iranian Revolution

In 1979, Ayatollah Ruhollah Khomeini led the movement that toppled the Shah of Iran, creating – in the American view – another power vacuum in the Gulf. Iran had been seen as a buffer between the USSR and the Gulf, while the Shah served as the region's 'policeman'. To keep the Soviets out of a rapidly changing area, Washington found it imperative to establish a new regional order. That the new Iranian leadership from the start declared its intention to export the Islamic Revolution to the whole Muslim world, and to the Gulf region in particular, made this American concern all the more urgent.

In the Gulf monarchies, the export of Iran's revolution was seen as a severe security threat, and not incorrectly, for most of them have significant numbers of Twelver Shiite citizens who found the revolution's slogans especially attractive. The fall of the Shah also cast doubt on the United States as a reliable ally, leaving the monarchs wary of too great dependence on a single external power;[1] perhaps this role which had once been filled by Great Britain could not be by the United States, and not under current circumstances. Operation Desert Storm improved this reputation slightly, but still the wariness remains.

## Soviet Invasion of Afghanistan

Before December 1979, Soviet troops stood more than 1,000 km from the warm waters of the Gulf; in that month, the distance narrowed to 500 km, as Leonid Brezhnev sent them to save a communist regime in Afghanistan. This assault created a fear in the monarchies that no obstacles stood between Moscow and the Gulf, and made them more doubtful of Soviet intentions.[2] The American reaction – helping the Afghan mujahidin defeat the Soviets – further inflamed anxieties in the region about the Gulf becoming an arena of struggle between the two superpowers, quite to its own detriment.

Immediately after the invasion, President Jimmy Carter declared Gulf security critical to American national interests and promised to defend the region:

Let our position be absolutely clear: an attempt by any outside force to gain control of the Persian Gulf region will be regarded as an assault on the vital interests of the United States. It will be repelled by use of any means necessary, including military force.[3]

Any attempted Soviet penetration, in other words, would bring with it a direct great-power confrontation. The US government then created the Rapid Deployment Force (later called the Central Command). Britain's Prime Minister Margaret Thatcher soon thereafter declared a readiness to participate in the force. But the Gulf states collectively refused to participate in Carter's project: instead, they asserted self-responsibility by forming the GCC.[4]

### Iran–Iraq War

The Iran–Iraq War that began in September 1980 worried the Gulf monarchies and the West as it appeared to be even more of a threat to the region than the Soviet invasion. The West saw both parties to the war as enemies, for – different as they were – Islamic Iran and Ba'thist Iraq shared an intense antagonism to the West, and had either clearly won the war it would no doubt have sought to establish hegemony over the Gulf, thereby threatening vital Western interests. The West's best strategy was to have the two parties exhaust each other. In contrast, the GCC states considered revolutionary Iran a greater potential threat, due to its radical Islamic ideology and its special appeal to Shiites, and so backed Iraq. They did not favor a prolongation of the war, seeing this – correctly – as a spur to Iraq to build a huge military arsenal.

## FORMING THE GULF CO-OPERATION COUNCIL

The above five events came fast and hard within a single decade, both moving the region from the periphery of world affairs to its very heart and including it as a theater of the Cold War. To take at least some control of their own fate, Arab states of the Gulf found they had to react collectively. Sensitivities and mistrust among the six still existed but the perceived external threats, plus the internal repercussions, exceeded all other concerns. With the security and stability of the region at stake – and so the very legitimacy of the regimes – the GCC had to be formed.

On 4 February 1981, the foreign ministers of Bahrain, Kuwait, Oman, Qatar, Saudi Arabia and the United Arab Emirates signed a declaration bringing the Gulf Co-operation Council into existence. A few months later, on 25 May 1981, the leaders of the six states signed its constitution, The Basic Law of the Co-operation Council for the Arab States of the Gulf, which calls on the members to co-operate in all fields, with the eventual goal of political unification.

This grand talk notwithstanding, security concerns were the main catalyst for forming the organization. As a result, the GCC's efficacy depends on the fear of threats. In times of tranquility, tensions among the GCC states grow; in times of turmoil, these disappear. As the well-known Arabic proverb puts it: 'I and my brother against my cousin, and I and my cousin against the stranger.' The two-year period between the Iraq–Iran War and the invasion of Kuwait (August 1988–August 1990) when threats receded, saw the council lose importance. In sum, the GCC is purely a security institution; the rest is window-dressing.

## SENSITIVITIES AND MISTRUSTS

Most GCC countries became sovereign states only after the British withdrawal of 1971, following which they enjoyed an economic boom that permitted them to attain affluence without passing through the throes of economic development. The combination of recent independence and financial power created a range of tensions within and among the GCC states. Ideally, the Council should encourage concession and counter-concession among members within a framework of common objectives and interests. But this has not been the case: tense national feelings and delicate sensitivities obstruct GCC coherence. Collective efforts have accomplished very little; virtually all the GCC's achievements have been attained through bilateral agreements.

25

In particular, bilateral agreements have solved several border disputes, the most threatening problem within the GCC – such as those between Saudi Arabia and both Oman and the UAE.

Drawing on a phrase of Alexis de Tocqueville, what is missing from the GCC is the art of 'working together.' Its requirement that political decisions are unanimous is a sure way to stymie a collective organization. That the élites mistrust each other adds a second level to the problem; indeed, almost every GCC state sees the other states as a potential threat. Small states fear larger ones. The members of one dynasty belong to this tribe and that one to that tribe – and in the desert, tribal relationships are based not on recognizable territories with fixed border lines but on pure, rapidly shifting, power relationships. The mix of this historical background with the modern state gives the Arabian Peninsula much of its singularity. The oil boom, by allowing states to disburse oil wealth instead of taking the usual paths to modernization, exacerbated this overlap of tradition and modernity. For example, it created interest groups that fear any sort of co-operation among the six; this phenomenon is most observable in Oman and in some components of the United Arab Emirates (UAE).

The concept of a nation-state remains utterly alien to the region though Saudi Arabia, which came into existence through military campaigns, and so depended more on direct participation of its citizens, is more of a nation than the other GCC states, which came into existence as a consequence of the British withdrawal in 1971. Kuwait has the most highly developed political institutions. Oman has an acute sense of history.

Border disputes have become the most threatening factor within the GCC. Borders have special importance in the Gulf region, where huge pools of oil might lie below any piece of land or water, no matter how remote. Thus, any slight reduction in size could significantly harm a state's finances. Should the border follow colonial lines, historic dynastic domains, tribal areas controlled by a certain dynasty, bilateral agreements between leaders prior to independence, or *de facto* circumstances at a particular time? In contrast to the Organization of African Unity, which requires members to accept the colonial borders –

no matter how implausible – to pre-empt potential disagreements, the GCC has no such rule.

## EXTERNAL THREAT PERCEPTIONS

Westerners – and Americans in particular – see Iran and Iraq as the major state actors threatening the Gulf region. Internal instability is also seen as a very real potential threat.[5] In the GCC states, quite different views of the external threat exist; as usual, there is no view common to the GCC as a whole, but individual ones in each state. Overall, the GCC states suffer from few immediate or direct external threats. As Gregory Gause observed in 1995: 'By a conventional definition of security, that is to say protection from foreign military attack, the states of the Gulf Co-operation Council are more secure than any time in their independent existence.'[6]

### Saudi Arabia

With 70 percent of the GCC nationals and 88 percent of its total land area, Saudi Arabia is the great power of the GCC. The well-being of the whole region depends on its security and stability. Threats to Saudi Arabia are thereby synonymous with threats to the GCC itself.

Saudi Arabia has no urgent potential external threats, particularly since the waning of the Iranian Revolution and the defeat of Saddam Hussein. Iran had been a threat through the 1980s as it attempted to export a revolutionary ideology that had some appeal to Saudis, especially the 8–10 percent of the Saudi population that is Shiite. A settlement in 1993 between the regime and Shiite dissidents largely halted the potential Iranian interference, though Tehran can still intervene in Saudi affairs through indirect means – for example, by meddling in the domestic affairs of other GCC states. Iraq and Yemen had been considered the major external threats, but are less so after the defeat of Iraq in Operation Desert Storm and the Saudi resolution of border disputes with Yemen.

With these threats dissipated, the Saudi political élite sees American pressure to carry out political and economic reform as the major external threat to their country. Unlike other GCC states, Saudi Arabia was established on the basis of a puritanical religious political movement. Religion and politics are intertwined, and Western pressure is looked upon as potentially devastating to society and polity alike. The Saudi élite approaches very cautiously any development, external or internal, that would drastically change its own traditional role.[7]

If the relationship between society and polity in Saudi Arabia were expressed in the form of an equation, it would go as follows: the state's political hegemony + the élite's traditional role = the society's welfare. Diminish the left side and the right goes down too, and vice versa.

### Kuwait

Prior to the Iraqi invasion of 1990, Kuwaitis had doubts about the intentions of some GCC states, particularly Saudi Arabia, but the GCC solidarity with Kuwait during the occupation eliminated almost all mistrust. Today, Iraq is the only major external threat, and it endangers not just the regime but the very existence of the state. Iraq has become an obsession to Kuwaitis, élites and average inhabitants alike. Iran, on the other hand, no longer seems to be treated as a potential external threat. Kuwaitis – and especially the 25 percent of them who are Shiite – find the Iranian revolution less appealing after the Iraqi invasion, an event that unified Kuwaitis and created a national consensus on the legitimacy of the regime.

### Qatar

Qatar was long considered an echo of Saudi Arabia in foreign policy, oil policy and domestic conditions, owing to the two countries' many social and ideological similarities. However, the accession of a younger generation in the palace coup of June 1995 brought with it policies which expressed resentment toward – for example – Saudi Arabia for taking Qatar for granted and siding with Bahrain in a territorial dispute. All the other

GCC states consider Qatar's new foreign policy provocative. The real problem, it seems, lies in a Qatari resentment of the Saudi role as the big brother; a new generation, replete with enthusiasm and 'modern' national feelings, is asserting its place. The older generation usually dealt with tensions by the traditional means, such as personal visits or asking for generosity. Such ways worked beautifully to solve even the most disruptive problems, far away from 'modern' political negotiations. By contrast, while the new generation may have some modern skills, it lacks both a modern mentality and familiarity with traditional experiences, so it flounders between the two.

## Oman

Oman appears not to be perceived as an external threat. Sultan Qabus Bin Sa'id follows a 'balanced policy' that aims not to provoke anyone. He attempts to resolve fully border problems with neighbors and normalize relations with all parties, including Iran, Iraq and Israel. Although this appears similar to Qatar's foreign policy, there is a major difference: Omani policies are predictable and balanced, and so do not antagonize the other council states.

## Bahrain

Iran is Bahrain's major external threat, primarily through its interference in Bahraini domestic affairs. With some 70 percent of Bahraini citizens being Shiite, the mullahs in Tehran have a particularly strong appeal in this small island country. Bahrain's Shiites are more affected by harsh economic conditions than other segments of society, increasing their openness to the revolutionary rhetoric coming from Iran. The disturbances of recent months were but one example of the effects of deprivation combined with outside ideological agitation. According to the Bahraini authorities, Tehran sought not only to mobilize the Shiite population against the status quo but to gain power on the island through violence. Further, although Iran formally renounced its territorial claims in Bahrain in 1970, political indicators suggest that it will never truly renounce such a claim.

Bahrain has a tense relationship with Qatar, to the point that the two countries have almost come to blows on several occasions. Their territorial disagreement reflects historic differences between the countries' governing dynasties. Bahrainis also fear that Qatar is becoming Iran's stalking horse in the GCC, adopting positions that could one day harm Bahrain in a crisis.

## The United Arab Emirates

Iranian expansionism is the most worrying external threat. While Tehran has no apparent ambitions in the Emirates itself, and its revolutionary agitation has no appeal in Emirati society, it seeks a hegemonic role in the Gulf. This led it to occupy the islands of Abu Musa and the Tunbs, previously part of Al-Sharjah, a component emirate of the UAE. This dispute will likely be resolved through negotiation; military confrontation is a remote possibility. In contrast, India and Pakistan could pose a profound threat to the Emirates, for citizens of those two countries make up more than 50 percent of the UAE population. New Delhi or Islamabad might interfere in the domestic affairs of the Emirates by calling on their nationals to claim their full rights, as expressed by the UN Human Rights Declaration, or to go on strike if state-to-state relations deteriorate. Such steps would paralyze the whole state, which would be forced to do what these outside powers demand.

### INTERNAL THREATS

If the GCC states face no major external threats, they do have significant internal problems. All of them have serious economic difficulties due to a combination of decreased oil prices, lavish and irrational governmental spending (on defense and security in particular), unsound economic arrangements and growing indebtedness. As a result, standards of living are in decline.

Combined with the high rate of foreign employment, these economic conditions create social problems: growing unemployment; escalating crime; and emerging terrorism. These may have political consequences: more discontent; an incapacity by the state to assimilate new social elements; an expanding ideological diversity; more claims for political participation; and growing pressure for drastic reforms.

Individual GCC states have their own problems as well. Saudi Arabia has difficulties accepting modern political institutions, with economic rationalization and social integration. Kuwait has the problem of the biduns – literally, 'withouts' – individuals whose families have long lived in Kuwait and who serve in every sector of the society and state, but who do not enjoy Kuwaiti, or any other, citizenship. Bahrain has an aggravated level of unemployment among nationals, difficult economic conditions, and growing sectarian problems. The UAE has problems with too many foreigners and a weak state structure.

## IMPROVING THE GULF CO-OPERATION COUNCIL

The best policy for deterring external threats is to eliminate internal problems. Building huge armies with massive arsenals is not enough to safeguard against external dangers, nor does it construct a long-lasting stability if the country itself is not stable. Russian military strength prior to the First World War did not prevent the Bolshevik Revolution; nor did a huge arsenal prevent the collapse of the Soviet Union. The Shah of Iran could not fend off revolution with a sophisticated and modern defense system or security apparatus. In the long term, coercion alone does not ensure regime stability.

This applies to the GCC as well, where stability and security cannot be achieved through the mere accumulation of weapons or the ascendance of the security apparatus. Saudi Arabia must develop political institutions and legal structures, and rationalize its economy. Kuwait must define and implement a flexible concept of citizenship. Bahrain cannot have a stable future if its economic and sectarian problems become endemic. The UAE must find plausible solutions to the population imbalance, and strengthen federal institutions.

The most important step toward solving the GCC's internal troubles – and also toward deterring its external threats – lies in transforming it into a politically unified federal state. This federal state could construct a wide framework for free labor and capital movements, which would go far toward reducing the influx of foreign labor and balance the population in countries like UAE by allowing the national surplus labor in countries like Bahrain to seek jobs held by foreign labor.

Second, Yemen should have a place in the GCC, either by becoming a member or associating in some other arrangement; for, as a major state in the vicinity, it should not be left isolated. Such isolation encourages Yemen to seek arrangements outside the Gulf region, and these could threaten GCC security. Yemen's membership in the Iraqi-sponsored 'Arab Co-operation Council' prior to the Kuwait War shows what mischief this can cause. Integration would also bring the Yemeni labor force to the GCC states, where it is most needed.

Third, the GCC states should work out a collective agreement that accepts the current boundaries. Without such an agreement, the GCC could implode from internal differences.

## NOTES

1. Abdallah al-Ashal, *Al-Itar al-Qanuni wa's-Siyasi li'l-Majlis at-Ta'awun al-Khaliji* (Riyadh: n.p., 1983), p. 77.
2. Gulf Center for Arab Studies, *The Political Report*, March 1981, p. 22.
3. State of the Union address, 23 January 1980.
4. Ibid., pp. 16–17.
5. This is the outlook, for example, in Robert E. Hunter (ed.), *The United States and the New Middle East: Strategic Perspective after the Persian Gulf War* (Washington, DC: Center for Strategic and International Studies, 1992); and in Shahram Chubin and Charles Tripp, *Domestic Politics and Territorial Disputes in the Gulf* (Abu Dhabi: International Institute for Strategic Studies, the IISS Regional Security Conference, 13–16 June 1993).
6. F. Gregory Gause III, 'The Political Economy of National Security in the GCC States,' paper presented at the Gulf-2000 conference, Emirates Center for Strategic Studies and Research, Abu Dhabi, 27–29 March 1995, p. 1.
7. See Turki al-Hamad, 'Political Order in Changing Societies, Saudi Arabia: Modernization in a Traditional Context,' an unpublished dissertation presented to the University of Southern California, January 1985. See also Peter W. Wilson and Douglas F. Graham, *Saudi Arabia: The Coming Storm* (Armonk, NY: M.E. Sharpe, 1994), chaps 2, 5, 6.

# 3

# What Wealth Cannot Buy: UAE Security at the Turn of the Twenty-first Century

## SEAN FOLEY

At the beginning of the twenty-first century, the United Arab Emirates (UAE) enjoys a particularly favorable strategic position, especially when compared to the rest of the southern Gulf states. The federation faces no immediate threat of invasion, nor is it threatened by debt, organized domestic opposition, or economic collapse. The Emirates' rivalries have largely abated, and a civil society on the federal level is beginning to appear. Abu Dhabi maintains relations with all regional and world powers. In addition, the United States insures the federation's security.

Yet the UAE must grapple with the same challenges that have afflicted its neighbors: rapid population growth, lack of economic diversification, volatile oil prices, low water supplies, privatization and dependence on foreign labor. Moreover, the UAE's only president – the charismatic Abu Dhabi Ruler Shaykh Zayid – is in poor health and lacks a strong successor. Indeed, many analysts question how long Shaykh Zayid's heir apparent, Shaykh Khalifa, will be able to govern after Shaykh Zayid's death.

In addition, the UAE's military forces – either on their own or in combination with those of the Gulf Co-operation Council (GCC) – cannot deter the federation's principal security threat, Iran. The federation claims that Iran illegally occupies Abu Musa and the Greater and Lesser Tunbs, but Tehran has refused to relinquish control over these three islands. UAE officials believe that the best way to restrain Iranian expansion in the southern Gulf is to integrate a unified and militarily strong Iraq into the Gulf's balance of power. There are, however, two problems with this strategy.

First, the United States, which currently dominates the Gulf's military balance, believes that the current regime in Baghdad threatens regional security, and is opposed to any plan that would reintegrate Iraq into an international security structure. Second, Riyadh, the UAE's most important regional ally, has sought to improve the relationship of Saudi Arabia and the other states of the GCC with Iran since the election of Iranian President Muhammad Khatami in 1997. In Riyadh's eyes, Iran is critical to the security and stability of the GCC as well as to the ability of the Organization of Petroleum Exporting Countries (OPEC) to control world oil markets.

Although the UAE is not currently threatened by an invasion or economic collapse, the federation will have to reform its society and develop collective and integrated security arrangements with its allies to maintain its security in the future. If the federation does not address its domestic and security challenges soon, its problems will become as critical as those of its neighbors.

## THE UNITED ARAB EMIRATES AND ITS STRATEGIC IMPORTANCE

Unlike the rest of the southern Gulf states, the UAE is a federation of seven tribally-based emirates that control the southeastern portion of the Arabian peninsula south of Bahrain and Qatar. The seven states or 'Emirates' are: Abu Dhabi; Dubai; Sharjah; Ras al Khaimah; Fujairah; Umm al Qawain; and Ajman.

The federation covers 90,599 square kilometers and is bordered on the north by the Persian Gulf and Iran, on the east by Oman, and on the south and west by Saudi Arabia. The UAE also separates Oman from the Musandam peninsula and extends 90 kilometers along the Gulf of Oman, an area known as the al Batinah coast. Most of the federation is arid desert and salt flats, but there are mountains in the north-east that rise to 1,527 m. Rainfall is very low and there are few fertile areas except in the north and among the oases.[1]

The UAE is strategically important because it produces ten percent of the world's oil supply; it also possesses the third largest oil and the fourth largest natural gas reserves in the world.[2] Over the past 30 years, the UAE has used these resources and strategic position to become one of the wealthiest states in the world. It was a founding member of the GCC and has supported Western security policies in the Persian Gulf. The UAE provided $6.572 billion in assistance to the United States during the Gulf War, and permits the United States to use the federation's air bases and ports, which are the only harbors in the Persian Gulf deep enough to berth an aircraft carrier. In the long run, the stability of the UAE is critical to the free flow of shipping through the Strait of Hormuz and to the defense of the GCC from Iran and Iraq.

## History

Despite its now critical role in regional stability, the UAE was formed in 1971 and only adopted a permanent constitution in 1996. For much of the nineteenth and twentieth centuries, Britain administered the territories that would become the UAE (the so-called 'Trucial Coast' states) as protectorates. When Britain announced that it would withdraw from the Persian Gulf, Whitehall assumed that the UAE would include the Trucial Coast as well as Qatar and Bahrain. These latter two territories, however, refused to join the UAE and became independent states when Britain left in 1971. Ras al Khaimah also sought independence, but it lacked the resources and the international support to survive on its own. It joined the federation in 1972.

## The Seven Emirates and their Residents

The largest and wealthiest of these Emirates, Abu Dhabi, covers 88.3 percent of the UAE's total area and accounts for 90 percent of the federation's oil and gas production and 60 percent of the UAE's gross domestic product (GDP). Because its oil and gas reserves are much smaller than Abu Dhabi's, Dubai has worked to become a regional commercial and transportation center. It now accounts for 70 percent of the UAE's non-oil trade.[3] Sharjah also has oil and gas deposits, but it has focused on light manufacturing and port facilities.[4] The rest of the Emirates – Ajman, Fujairah, Ras al Khaimah and Umm al Qawain (collectively known as the northern Emirates) – are considerably poorer than the other UAE Emirates; together they accounted for less than ten percent of the UAE's GDP in 1998.[5]

Most of the seven Emirates' 2.94 million inhabitants are Muslim and live in communities that hug its 650-km Persian Gulf coastline. Abu Dhabi, Dubai and Sharjah collectively govern 66 percent of the population. Close to 80 percent of the population of the federation is comprised of expatriate nationals and nearly 60 percent of the population is male. South Asian guest workers, mainly Indians and Pakistanis, make up 45 percent of the population. The next three largest expatriate ethnic groups are Iranians (17 percent), Arabs from other parts of the Middle East (13 percent), and Westerners (five percent). UAE cities tend to be ethnically heterogeneous and to house a large amount of male residents, while there are more women and UAE nationals in rural areas. Virtually all of the federation's Iranians and the Shiites (16 percent) live in Dubai.[6]

## Military Strength

The UAE maintains armed forces of 65,000 men and women, nearly a third of whom are expatriates. There are 425,248 males fit for the military within the federation's borders; 23,538 males reach military age annually.[7] Only a few of these men are UAE citizens, however, and, hence, eligible for military service. As a percentage of the federation's population, UAE armed forces are high compared to those of other Arab countries.[8] This is largely due to the fact that the federation's military forces coexist with individual Emirate defense provisions. In addition, Abu Dhabi provides at least 80 percent of the UAE's military manpower and defense budget.[9]

## GOVERNMENT AND POLITICS

The UAE's armed forces' organization reflects the political structure of the federation itself, in which there is a central government in Abu Dhabi and each Emirate retains broad autonomy. There are rivalries among the Emirates and within the ruling families. Dubai does not acknowledge that it falls under the UAE's OPEC quota and annually forces Abu Dhabi to underproduce in order to stay within OPEC limits. Abu Dhabi and Ajman backed Iraq during the Iran–Iraq War, while Dubai, Sharjah and Umm al Qawain maintained close ties with Iran. In contrast, Ras al Khaimah allies with no other party and wants to create a state that would include Sharjah. Ras al Khaimah even won the Soviet Union's support for its failed attempt to seize part of Oman in 1978.[10]

There are also few legally-defined boundaries, so that every Emirate has an ongoing border dispute either with one of the other Emirates or Oman. The only time these rivalries became violent was in 1987 when Abu Dhabi and Dubai backed different candidates for the ruler of Sharjah, and Abd al-Aziz Mohammed al Qasimi attempted to overthrow his brother's government there.[11]

### Shaykh Zayid's Role

Throughout the UAE's 29 years of existence, the ruler of Abu Dhabi, Shaykh Zayid al Nahyan, has served as the federation's president and has helped to mediate its various disputes. Gulf analysts praise Shaykh Zayid for keeping the federation together through times of crisis, which have strained the sometimes tenuous ties of the seven Emirates. Shaykh Zayid has used Abu Dhabi's wealth and his political skills to bridge the gap between 'tribal' and 'modern' forces within the federation. In spite of the fact that both the UAE's provisional and permanent constitutions stipulate that each Emirate should provide half of its revenues to the federal government, Abu Dhabi annually provides about 75–90 percent of the UAE's federal budget. Dubai has generally covered the remainder.[12]

## Dubai's Rivalry with Abu Dhabi

Shaykh Zayid has been most successful in addressing Dubai's desire for autonomy. Dubai had a long history of autonomy before the UAE was formed, and its leadership remained suspicious of Abu Dhabi's power after the establishment of the federation. Initially, Dubai maintained its own military command and refused to integrate its armed forces into the UAE's military. Shaykh Zayid has been able to convince Dubai's ruling family to hold key UAE cabinet positions, such as those of defense and finance. He has also allowed Dubai to have veto power over all federal legislation. Through informal agreement, the ruler of Abu Dhabi serves as president, and the ruler of Dubai serves as vice president and prime minister. Until quite recently, many Gulf analysts warned that Dubai's conflict with Abu Dhabi was very serious and could threaten the stability of the federation.

The threat from this rivalry, however, may be abating rapidly. Since 1997, Dubai has slashed defense spending and integrated its armed forces into the UAE military command. Dubai officials reportedly believe that: 'there is no obvious need to maintain an independent force in Dubai' because 'the UAE Armed Forces General Headquarters (GHQ) provides a fully-fledged defense capability.'[13] This type of comment would have been unthinkable as recently as 1996. Moreover, it is widely expected that Dubai will soon transfer authority over its police force to Abu Dhabi, which will then shoulder the costs of maintaining police in Dubai.[14]

Although the primary reasons Dubai cut its defense spending were to compensate for the 35 percent decline in its oil production since 1993 and to forestall the need to privatize state industries,[15] the decision suggests that Dubai realizes that it no longer has the resources to compete against Abu Dhabi. The decision suggests that, after 20 years of co-operation with Abu Dhabi, Dubai no longer fears the power of the UAE's largest Emirate. Equally importantly, Dubai has not challenged Abu Dhabi's right to retain the UAE presidency after Shaykh Zayid's death. Taken together, these events suggest that Dubai's disputes with Abu Dhabi will now be fought out within the federal structures of the UAE.[16]

## The Federation's Political Structures

The political structure in which Abu Dhabi and Dubai's rivalry will most likely take place is the Supreme Council of Ministers, the federation's highest constitutional authority. Composed of the seven Emirate rulers, this body establishes federal policies and sanctions legislation. It also elects the UAE's president. Most council decisions are reached through a consensus of the Emirate's rulers and leading families. Since the council meets four times a year, the UAE cabinet runs the day-to-day affairs of the federation. The president chooses the cabinet and members of the federal judiciary.

## The Technocrats and the Emergent Civil Society

It is generally assumed that, apart from the Supreme Council of Ministers, the UAE lacks a political culture and strong federal institutions. Events since 1996, however, have called this assumption into question and suggest that the UAE may be developing a civil society and political élites outside of the Supreme Council of Ministers. The driving force behind these changes is young Western-educated technocrats whom Shaykh Zayid has appointed to the UAE cabinet in recent years; among them, Information Minister Shaykh Abdallah bin Zayid, one of the youngest of Shaykh Zayid's sons.

Shaykh Abdallah and his colleagues are the first generation of Western-trained technocrats to come of age well after the creation of the federation. Unlike their predecessors, these officials are not familiar with the time period before the UAE was founded, and define themselves and the UAE's problems in national terms. Their ascendancy marks an important first step in the development of a truly 'national' citizenry in the UAE, a citizenry that devotes its primary political loyalty to the federation's government as opposed to a region or tribe. In addition, these officials are prepared to criticize government policy much more openly than their predecessors and believe that open and fair public dialogue is central to good governance. In fact, Shaykh Abdallah himself told the UAE's media in November of 1999 to 'criticize freely.'[17]

The technocrats' influence within the UAE government was greatly enhanced by Muhammad Khalifa al Habtur's election as the Federal National Council's speaker in January of 1998. Al Habtur is a US-educated petroleum engineer from Dubai who, along with his opponent, actively sought the support of individual delegates before the election. Elections deciding the speaker of the Federal National Council have never been previously contested. The council, which reviews and suggests amendments to laws proposed by the Council of Ministers, has 40 members who are appointed by their respective Emirates: eight each from Abu Dhabi and Dubai; six each from Sharjah and Ras Al Khaimah; and four from each of the other three Emirates.

The London-based Arabic language daily *Al Wasat* noted that al Habtur's margin of victory, 24 to 15, was important because it 'underscores the existence of blocks in the UAE parliament, despite the lack of political currents or parties in the UAE.' In other words, the election shows that the UAE is beginning to develop a civil society in which different constituencies negotiate with the government for power. If this is the case, it would be an important factor in a society in which a small group of family 'leaders' had previously held all the power. The newspaper added that the election also suggested that the National Council will have a greater influence in the UAE government in the future.[18]

Al Habtur's election is also indicative of a trend towards consultative bodies within the UAE and the rest of the GCC. In 1995, Abu Dhabi appointed a 45-member council to review the Emirates' laws. Similar institutions have been proposed in the other southern Gulf states and Saudi Arabia. Thus, it is not unlikely that the Federal National Council could evolve into an institution that resembles Kuwait's parliament. It could become an important national symbol for UAE nationals in much the same way that the Kuwait parliament functions as a significant element in the identity of Kuwait's citizens.[19] This will be especially true if Shaykh Zayid keeps his promise to allow women to join the Federal National Council: 'with the full right to participate in politics and the decision making.'[20]

Nonetheless, tribal history and loyalties to individual rulers remain important factors in the UAE's politics.[21] Individual rulers still hold the most power in UAE society and will probably do so for many years to come. As William Rugh pointed out in September 1997 (*Middle East Policy*), many of the institutions commonly associated with civil societies, such as a large and fully independent middle class, do not exist in the UAE. Clearly the new technocrats – the core of the UAE middle class – are only beginning a process of change that may take many decades to unfold.[22]

## Succession and the Future of United Arab Emirates' Policies

The absence of strong national structures in large part explains why many in the region have worried that the UAE will not survive Shaykh Zayid's death. The heir apparent to the UAE presidency and the leadership of Abu Dhabi is Shaykh Zayid's eldest son, the crown prince of Abu Dhabi, Shaykh Khalifa. Although Shaykh Khalifa, like his father, has been in poor health for many years,[23] he has run the day-to-day operations of the Abu Dhabi government for much of the 1990s.

Shaykh Khalifa's position is far from certain, however. Two of Shaykh Zayid's eldest sons, Shaykh Khalifa's half brothers – UAE Army Chief of Staff, Mohammed bin Zayid, and the head of the UAE's secret police, Shaykh Hazaa bin Zayid – may challenge Shaykh Khalifa's position. Both men have leadership skills, are bright, and retain important individual power bases. They are also Western-educated and have recently cultivated personal relationships with US State Department officials. In October 1999, Martin Indyk noted in a speech that the 'preparations for succession [were] already underway in the UAE.' His statement was widely perceived in the federation and in the region as proof that the United States was actively involved in the UAE succession issue. Shaykh Zayid's frequent visits to US and UAE medical clinics in 1999 and 2000 as well as his absence from important GCC conferences have also intensified the uncertainty over the succession issue in Abu Dhabi.[24]

In spite of the uncertainties about leadership and the rivalries between Emirates, long-term political trends indicate that the federation will remain unified after Shaykh Zayid dies. No one disputes Abu Dhabi's right to govern; the only question is which Abu Dhabi prince will become leader and for how long after Shaykh Zayid's death. Here too the picture is much clearer than it appeared to be just two years ago: today, most analysts believe that Shaykh Khalifa will succeed his father, although they are uncertain how long Shaykh Khalifa will be able to govern on his own. Some analysts believe that Shaykh Khalifa's half brothers are already fighting to become his successor. Dubai's decision to integrate its armed forces into the UAE military is important because it suggests that the Emirate has firmly tied its future to the success of the federation. Furthermore, there is no organized opposition to speak of, and Islamic fundamentalism is unlikely to appear.[25] The appointments of both open-minded and Western-educated technocrats to key positions within the government bodes well for the federation's stability. Finally, all of the Emirates benefit greatly from the current federation, so it is unlikely that any Emirate would contemplate leaving the federation in the near future.

## UNITED ARAB EMIRATES' FOREIGN POLICY

Whoever leads the UAE after Shaykh Zayid's death will contend with a regional political system that is simultaneously favorable and unfavorable to the UAE's strategic position. The UAE currently enjoys commercial and diplomatic relations with all of the Gulf powers, including Iraq and Iran, and faces no imminent threat of invasion. Iran, the only power that might conceivably invade the UAE in the future, lacks the resources to carry out anything but small-scale attacks. Indeed, the Emirates' Center for Strategic Studies and Research noted in a recent report that with the US naval presence in the Persian Gulf, there is no short-term danger of an Iranian invasion because any such 'invasion by sea will require enormous amphibious capabilities and air bridges, which Iran lacks.'[26]

At the same time, the UAE cannot guarantee its security on its own. It is a small state surrounded by very large states and it has weak military forces. Abu Dhabi therefore must balance the federation's position against the often-differing outlook of larger regional and international powers. The UAE's most important political and security relationships are with the southern Gulf states, Saudi Arabia and the United States. In addition, Abu Dhabi hopes that its relations with Russia, Europe, Asia and, to a lesser extent, Iran, will counter the United States' military and political dominance in the Gulf as well as Saudi Arabia's pre-eminent position within the GCC.

Relations with Washington are now strained because Abu Dhabi does not share the US view of the northern Gulf states or of Persian Gulf security. Nor does Abu Dhabi support Washington's policy for the 'dual containment' of Iran and Iraq. The UAE holds that a strong Iraq will be the most enduring check to Tehran's ambitions in the Gulf. The federation also believes that Iran is critical to Persian Gulf security. Equally importantly, US officials suspect that the UAE may have supported Osama bin Laden and the Pakistani nuclear program. In addition, the UAE's ties with Saudi Arabia are strained because the kingdom attempted to improve bilateral ties and the GCC's relations with Iran before Abu Dhabi had reached a settlement with Iran over the Abu Musa and Tunbs islands dispute. The disagreements between the UAE and Saudi Arabia over Iran have intensified the two countries' diverging perceptions of the economic structures of the GCC, regional security arrangements and the delineation of the common borders between Saudi Arabia and the UAE.

### Border Disputes

The UAE's foreign policy, much like its domestic politics, has been defined largely by border disputes and the politics of the individual Emirates. Currently the UAE has territorial disputes with three of its immediate neighbors: Iran; Oman; and Saudi Arabia. The most serious such conflict, however, is the long-standing dispute with Iran over three Gulf islands: Abu Musa and the Greater and Lesser Tunbs. Since 1992, this dispute has come to define the UAE's entire relationship with Iran.

*Iran and the Dispute over Abu Musa and the Tunbs*
Before discussing the strategic importance of the islands dispute, it is important to review a few facts about the islands themselves. Abu Musa has a population of around 600 people and is situated at the mouth of the narrows of the Strait of Hormuz. The other islands are closer to the Persian Gulf's sea lane, but only one of these, the Greater Tunbs, is inhabited, with a population of about 350 people. There are few significant resources on the islands apart from red oxide and oil, and only Abu Musa can accommodate large ships. Tehran claims that Britain took the islands from Iran and gave them to the Arabs in the nineteenth century. The UAE counters that Arabs from the eastern Gulf littoral have always controlled the islands, and that Iran has no claim to either Abu Musa or the Tunbs.[27]

While it is true that the Iranians currently deployed on Abu Musa and the Tunbs could harass Gulf shipping or attack UAE cities, the fact remains that the United States maintains a strong enough military presence in the Persian Gulf to drive Iran off the islands. Moreover, Tehran has bases in Bandar Abbas, Qishim Island, and several other areas near the Strait of Hormuz, that are much better situated for attacks on Gulf shipping than either Abu Musa or the Greater or the Lesser Tunbs. Because of the short distances separating Iran and the UAE, neither state today could take military action against the other's positions on the islands without jeopardizing its own security. The vulnerability in large part explains why the dispute over Abu Musa and the Tunbs has been, and likely will remain, largely a war of words.[28]

The islands dispute became a significant international issue only when Britain withdrew from the Persian Gulf in 1971 and Iran claimed sovereignty over Bahrain. Reportedly, Iran suspended its claims to Bahrain in exchange for Britain's acceptance of Iranian occupation of the islands. Although the Shah claimed full sovereignty over the islands, he promised to permit the islands' civilian population to remain under Arab administration and to share proceeds from nearby oil fields. He also promised to subsidize the Emirates Sharjah and Ras al Khaimah, which had previously governed the islands. Sharjah accepted, but the ruler of Ras Al Khaimah refused. He died resisting the Iranian troops that were sent to occupy the Tunbs.[29]

The islands dispute has also caused serious friction within the UAE. Ras al Khaimah and Sharjah advocate tough measures against Iran. Dubai, on the other hand, believes that the conflict is unnecessary and does not want anything to threaten its profitable trade and close cultural links with Tehran. Iran is currently Dubai's largest re-export market, accounting for 20–30 percent of Dubai's trade and providing access to markets in Afghanistan and Central Asia.[30] Indeed, the Crown Prince of Dubai, Shaykh Muhammad, has stated publicly that he believes the tensions over the islands have been fabricated by the United States.[31]

Shaykh Zayid, the UAE president, has reconciled these opposing interests by using his personal authority to forge a consensus in support of a policy that uses peaceful means to pressure Iran to relinquish control of the islands. He has also exploited his reputation for piety and rectitude to heighten the moral urgency of the UAE's claim to the islands – an urgency impossible for the region's governments, including Iran's ally Syria, to ignore. Every Arab state is on record as supporting the immediate 'restoration' of the UAE's sovereignty over Abu Musa and the Tunbs. Other countries, such as the United States, have signed similar documents.

Between 1971 and 1992, Iran and Sharjah jointly administered Abu Musa under a Memorandum of Understanding and shared the revenues from the off-shore oil fields equally with few problems.[32] But several incidents on Abu Musa in 1992, when Iran allegedly violated the Memorandum, rekindled the dispute and sparked a diplomatic clash between Iran and the UAE. Negotiations since that time have gone nowhere. Iran has now built an airstrip, substantially increased its military presence – from 700 to 4,000 troops – and has opened a university on Abu Musa. It is also possible that Tehran has deployed chemical weapons and five 'Hudong' class Chinese-built fast-attack patrol boats. US officials warn that these deployments threaten Gulf shipping and indicate that Iran should be contained.[33]

Might there be a way out of the quagmire for the UAE? Since the election of the reformist Iranian president Muhammad Khatami in 1997, senior Iranian officials, including the foreign minister, Kamal Kharazi, have stressed that improving Iran's relations with the GCC and fostering regional 'stability and security' are Tehran's top foreign policy goals. Few believe that it would be possible for Iran to achieve these goals without meaningful progress on the islands issue. Kharazi has stated on numerous occasions that he would be very happy to go to Abu Dhabi to negotiate a solution to the dispute in an atmosphere of 'mutual confidence and understanding.'[34]

At the same time, Kharazi has been wary of entering into negotiations that do not assume Iranian sovereignty over the islands, or that involve third party mediation. According to Arab press accounts, United Nations (UN) Secretary General Kofi Annan attempted to resolve the islands dispute in the winter of 1998 and won preliminary approval from President Khatami for minister-level negotiations under the auspices of the UN. But when Abu Dhabi suggested a timetable for the UN-sponsored talks and suggested as well that both states should accept international arbitration if the talks failed, Kharazi informed Annan that Iran would not participate. Nonetheless, Kharazi welcomed the formation of a committee composed of the Saudi, Qatari and Omani foreign ministers to discuss the islands dispute. He told reporters in Tehran that Iran always: 'stressed (the importance of) bilateral talks for settling the dispute' and was 'confident that the problems will be solved in due time.'[35]

For its part, the UAE remains skeptical of Kharazi and fearful that Tehran will use improved relations with Washington or the GCC states in order to avoid the islands issue. This would be a defeat in Abu Dhabi's eyes because it would remove most of the international pressures on Iran to evacuate Abu Musa and the Tunbs. The editorial in the Al Khaleej, 1 December 1999, was typical of UAE views. It warned that: 'these last few months,

Iran has taken steps ... to have the question of the islands forgotten, thanks to the interests it shares with certain GCC members.' The paper added that any measure that improved GCC–Iranian relations without addressing the UAE's concerns about the islands: 'could be wrongly interpreted by Iran and used to raise new obstacles.' When the Iranian press attacked the editorial as false, *Al Khaleej* responded that these accusations were: 'shameless lies' meant to hide a campaign designed 'to win favor with the United States for hardliners in Iran.'[36]

*Saudi Arabia*

Chief among those GCC members to whom *Al Khaleej* alluded was Saudi Arabia, the federation's largest and most important neighbor. For much of the last 30 years, Shaykh Zayid supported the Kingdom's pro-Western policies and leading position in the GCC. Saudi–UAE territorial disputes were thought to have been largely put to rest when Shaykh Zayid ceded the Zarrarah oil field to Riyadh in exchange for Saudi recognition of UAE sovereignty over the Burami Oasis in 1992 – the two states, along with Britain and Oman, had fought a brief war over the territory in the 1950s.

Relations declined rapidly in 1999, however, in large part due to differences over how to approach Iran. UAE officials were incensed by the warm welcome received by President Khatami throughout his trip to Saudi Arabia in May 1999, as well as by Saudi Crown Prince Abdallah's public sympathy for Iran's right to self-defense. In an unusually blunt television interview, UAE foreign minister Rashid Al Nuami labeled Riyadh's efforts to improve Saudi relations with Iran – before the islands issue had been resolved – as a betrayal of Riyadh's commitments to the GCC: 'which Tehran has interpreted ... as an abandonment of the UAE.' The UAE was also angered by Saudi Arabia's development of the Shaybah oil field – part of whose reservoir lies under UAE territory – and the Kingdom's unwillingness to help the Palestinians or Iraq. Indeed, Shaykh Zayid threatened to withdraw the UAE from the GCC and renege on the terms of the 1992 UAE–Saudi border agreement to register his ire at Saudi Arabia's *rapprochement* with Tehran.[37]

Saudi Arabia, by contrast, rejected the UAE's criticisms as groundless. Saudi officials emphasized that the islands dispute was a top priority for them but that Abu Dhabi could not expect Tehran to return the islands until relations were normalized between the GCC and Iran. At the same time, Riyadh noted that the UAE would not dictate its policies and that Abu Dhabi had failed to uphold its own commitments to the GCC by becoming reconciled with Baghdad, which still threatened the security of several GCC states. Riyadh also argued that Abu Dhabi's complaints about Iranian–Saudi relations were hypocritical given that the UAE had the closest economic and cultural relations among the GCC states with Iran. In July 1999, the Saudi defense minister, Prince Sultan, even went so far as to note that the UAE was practically 'half Iranian.'[38]

In reality, the UAE's economic relations with Iran are an especially important issue because of Saudi resentment at the UAE's insistence in July 1999 that the GCC states adopt a low unified tariff to protect Dubai's trans-shipment trade,[39] much of which is composed of Iranian goods that enter the kingdom at the GCC's low internal rates and undermine the competitive position of Saudi Arabia's non-oil industries[40] – Saudi Arabia heavily subsidized these industries and has spent billions developing them. Consequently, UAE–Saudi tensions remain high and show few signs of abating soon.[41]

*Oman*

In contrast to the federation's dispute with Iran over the islands, the UAE has been able to address its territorial problems with Oman by direct negotiation and by skillful use of Abu Dhabi's oil wealth. Here, Shaykh Zayid built a close rapport with Sultan Qabus, to whom the UAE president has given substantial subsidies as well as political and military assistance. This relationship helped Shaykh Zayid resolve two serious border clashes in 1978 and 1992. Today, Oman and the UAE conduct joint military exercises, and their citizens travel between the two countries without visas or passports. Nevertheless, the border is not delineated and is a potential source of future conflict.[42]

## Relations with Qatar and the Rest of the GCC

Although the UAE does not maintain close relations with Kuwait, the federation works closely with Bahrain as well as Qatar, whose current emir, Hamad bin Khalifa Al Thani, was once highly objectionable to Abu Dhabi and Bahrain. He came to power in a coup in 1995 in which he ousted the previous emir, to whom Abu Dhabi subsequently granted asylum. The UAE, along with Bahrain, then worked to contain Qatar's influence in the GCC. After the previous and the current emirs of Qatar normalized ties in January of 1998, however, Shaykh Khalifa traveled to Qatar and solved most of the 'misunderstandings between Abu Dhabi and Doha.'[43] Since that time, the UAE and Qatar have agreed to develop Qatar's gas reserves and to permit their nationals to travel between the two states without passports.[44] Doha has also proven to be Abu Dhabi's closest ally in the GCC. Few were surprised when Qatari Emir Shaykh Hamad bin Khalifa Al Thani mediated the initial tensions between Abu Dhabi and Riyadh over Iran and proposed the GCC tripartite commission to resolve the Abu Musa–Tunbs islands dispute.[45]

## The United States and the Balance of Power in the Persian Gulf and South Asia

The UAE's relations with Iran and the GCC states are part of the federation's larger relationship with the United States, the only country that possesses the projection capabilities necessary to defend the federation.[46] The relationship of the two states blossomed in the late 1980s and early 1990s, when Abu Dhabi supported the 'Tanker War' and provided important financial – $6.455 billion – and logistical assistance to Operation Desert Storm. In 1991, Abu Dhabi and the United States signed a loose defense pact, which permits Washington to base equipment within federation boundaries. The UAE has also emerged as one of the world's largest markets for US arms manufacturers. Abu Dhabi spent $360 million on US arms between 1992 and 1994; in 1998, it agreed to buy 80 fighter-jets valued at $8 billion.[47]

Since the Gulf War, Jebel Ali, a port in Dubai, has become

crucial to US naval operations in the Persian Gulf because it is the most important liberty port in the region and the only harbor in the Gulf deep enough to berth an aircraft carrier. Were the Strait of Hormuz closed off, Fujairah, which faces the Indian Ocean and is connected to the Gulf coast by a modern road, would be critical to American operations. In addition, the United States flies warplanes out of UAE air bases on support missions for Operation Southern Watch over Iraq and has pre-positioned material on UAE soil.[48]

In recent years, however, US–UAE relations have deteriorated because the UAE objects to Washington's policy of containing Iraq and supporting Israel. Senior UAE officials, such as Vice President Maktum, argue that Iraq has: 'fulfilled most of its obligations to the international community' and that a 'militarily strong and united Iraq' is needed to balance Iranian power.[49] Shaykh Zayid himself lobbied the GCC in 1997: 'for a full rupture with the US over Iraq.'[50] The UAE media, which usually reflects the government's positions on foreign policy, has asserted that the UN weapons inspectors in Iraq were American 'stooges' and that the United States and Britain intentionally kill civilians by bombing targets in the northern and southern 'no-fly' zones in Iraq.[51]

The UAE now provides millions of dollars of food and medicine to Baghdad. Iraqi government officials also frequently meet with UAE journalists and senior military and political officials. The UAE also permits merchants to violate UN sanctions against Iraq, as a spate of oil spills of Iraqi oil on the federation's coastline in 1997 made all too clear to the rest of the world.[52] In addition, there have been allegations that Abu Dhabi permits Baghdad to use UAE front companies to purchase weapons that Iraq is prohibited from acquiring by UN sanctions.[53]

Equally importantly, the UAE has tried to balance Washington's power in the Gulf and to reintegrate Iraq into the regional balance of power by cultivating commercial and military ties with the United States' regional and international rivals. While UAE–Iranian relations remain tense, Abu Dhabi does not support US sanctions against Iran and allows Dubai merchants to sell millions of dollars in American products to Iranians. The UAE also maintains close commercial and political ties with all of the permanent members of the UN Security Council and Japan.[54] Shaykh Zayid has used large civilian and military contracts to further the UAE's political objectives; this has been a boon to French and Russian firms, which have seen their shares of the UAE market increase substantially since 1994 – in 1998, nearly 60 percent of all exports of French arms ($5 billion out of a total of $8.3 billion) went to the UAE.[55] In addition, the UAE has tried to lessen its military dependence on the United States by signing 'mutual defense pacts' with France, the United Kingdom and Turkey.[56]

The strategy of attempting to offset US influence, however, has done little to enhance the UAE's security or lessen its reliance on the United States. Britain, France and Turkey cannot safeguard the UAE's territory on their own because they lack the capability to project power into the Gulf without US assistance. All three states have made significant reductions in their military forces since the Gulf War and cannot be counted on to match the deployments they made in 1991. France's promise to deploy 85,000 troops, 130 combat aircraft, and an aircraft carrier battle group if the UAE is ever invaded is ludicrous. This is the same country that struggled to deploy 15,000 soldiers in Desert Storm.[57] Indeed, the chief of staff of the French army, Jean-Pierre Kelche, told the Dubai daily *Al Bayan* that: 'the United States is the number one guarantor of the stability of the Arab part of the Gulf region.'[58]

At the same time, the UAE has sought to check US power in South Asia, where Washington seeks to contain the nuclear weapons programs of India and Pakistan. When India tested a nuclear device in 1998, Islamabad reportedly decided to conduct the nuclear tests only after the UAE, along with Saudi Arabia, promised not to cut oil shipments. Subsequently, senior Pakistani officials frequently visited Abu Dhabi and Riyadh, which are thought to have compensated Islamabad for the loss of foreign loans and credits due to the US-led international sanctions imposed after the tests. There have even been reports that Abu Dhabi provided substantial financial assistance to Pakistan's nuclear program.[59] It should come as no surprise that

General Pervez Musharraf's first trip abroad – after over-throwing the government of Nawaz Sharif in October 1999 – was to the UAE.[60] In addition, there have been several allegations that Osama bin Laden funneled money through the government-controlled Dubai Islamic Bank.[61]

Overall, Abu Dhabi's strategy in the Persian Gulf and in South Asia has had mixed results. While Pakistan may soon have full nuclear capability, Abu Dhabi has failed to achieve its chief political goal: lifting the UN sanctions against Iraq and reintegrating Baghdad into the Persian Gulf's balance of power. UN sanctions are still in place because Washington remains vehemently opposed to Baghdad. Moreover, American hostility towards Iraq's current regime all but guarantees that Iraq won't be integrated into the Gulf's military balance of power in the near future, even if the UN sanctions are lifted. Nor does it appear likely that the United States will cease bombing targets in Iraq or that Iran will withdraw from the islands in the near future. The islands dispute appears especially hopeless for the UAE as Riyadh improves ties with Tehran.

### The United Arab Emirates' Security Dilemma over the Next Decade

The challenges facing the UAE as it tries to balance the Great Powers and insure its security in the future will be ones of geo-graphical scale and military capability. Put simply, the US and Iran are much larger and more powerful than the UAE; they will pursue whatever policies they feel are in their interests despite what Abu Dhabi thinks or how many advanced weapons it purchases. Although some states and international organiza-tions may be able to check American, Saudi or Iranian power, none can realistically guarantee the UAE's security or prevent unilateral military action by Riyadh, Tehran or Washington. The United States is, and will most likely remain, the only country with the capability to meet the federation's security needs in the foreseeable future.

The UAE's leaders are aware of this geopolitical reality. Although Shaykh Zayid has attacked US and British air strikes against Iraq as 'loathsome' and 'unjust,' Abu Dhabi reportedly assured Washington that the US could use the prepositioned matériel if it was needed in an action against Saddam Hussein.[62] The UAE also publicly supported Operation Desert Fox and works closely with the US to combat international terrorists, including Osama bin Laden.[63] Similarly, Shaykh Zayid never carried out his threats to leave the GCC or to review the 1992 UAE–Saudi border agreement. Equally importantly, in November 1999, the UAE accepted the first GCC communiqué since 1992 that did not openly support the UAE's claims to the islands or demand that Tehran submit the island dispute to the International Court of Justice at the Hague or criticize Iran's occupation of the islands. Reportedly Bahrain, Kuwait, Oman and Qatar were originally inclined to support Abu Dhabi's claim to the islands in the communiqué, but Saudi Arabia convinced them that supporting the UAE was less important than Saudi–Iranian relations, which, Riyadh argued, would suffer a serious setback if the communiqué criticized Iran.[64]

## MILITARY POLICY

The UAE military's principal challenges are identical to the federation's chief dilemma in foreign affairs: geographical scale and military capability. No matter how much money the UAE spends, its armed forces will never surpass, or even achieve parity with, the federation's most likely adversary, Iran. Nor will the UAE ever be able to achieve parity in numbers, or in the quality of its soldiers, with any of its neighbors. Thus, the UAE military's primary mission is to serve as a trip wire that can hamper an invading army and hold its ground until reinforcements arrive. Unfortunately, the UAE's armed forces cannot meet either of these objectives effectively.

### Arms Procurement

Though UAE defense spending has held relatively steady since 1992, the UAE traditionally devotes a great deal of its resources to defense: as much as $4.9 billion – or 13.6 percent of its GDP – and 66.9 percent of its yearly budget. Between 1991 and 1998 alone, the UAE acquired $6.8 billion worth of new military aircraft.[65] If the UAE approves pending contracts for F-16s and Hawk aircraft, that figure will increase by $11 billion.[66] Unfortunately, the politicization of arms purchases has undermined the investment in modern weapons. The UAE has switched primary suppliers four times since 1980 and maintains weapon systems from a dozen countries. Abu Dhabi's insistence on unique and high-tech weapons impedes procurement as well and pointlessly increases costs by creating diseconomies of scale.

Possibly the best recent example of the politicization of arms acquisition is the negotiations regarding the UAE's purchase of 80 F-16 fighter aircraft from US aerospace firm Lockheed–Martin. First announced in May 1998, the purchase marked the culmination of a decade-long search by the UAE for new jets. From the start, the negotiations were rocky since Abu Dhabi demanded that the planes include source codes for an array of radar and electronic weapons which Washington had previously released only to Britain and Germany. The UAE also wanted to spend $3 billion to develop radar systems, radar-jamming devices and computerized flight controls for the aircraft – systems that are far more sophisticated than similar equipment aboard the United States' F-16s. In addition, Abu Dhabi demanded that the United States permit the federation to contract up to 200 Pakistani pilots to fly the planes.[67]

Although US officials acceded long ago to virtually all of Abu Dhabi's demands regarding the new aircraft, the federation continues to postpone signing the contract. Shortly before the Dubai air show in December 1999, Lockheed–Martin negotiators worked for days to bring all final issues to closure, yet the company reported no movement in the UAE's position. With no resolution of the negotiations in sight, Lockheed–Martin officials are reportedly worried that European aerospace firms are still competing to win the UAE order. One official told the *Dallas Morning News*: 'Even though the French were eliminated as a competitor for this deal in May of [19]98 they'd like to get back in the fray.' Similarly, US officials are reportedly beginning to question the sincerity of negotiations involving the UAE. The UAE has yet to receive any combat aircraft out of these negotiations and has earned the mistrust of many aerospace companies and the federation's chief ally, the United States.[68]

An equally telling example of the UAE's politicized procurement process is the so-called 'offset' program, which requires arms manufacturers to invest 60 percent of the value of their sales to the UAE in non-oil industries. Offset is designed to take advantage of the world arms market and escape the dilemma of 'guns *versus* butter.' By law, an Emirate must retain 51 percent of the capital in the partnership. Virtually all offset projects must be completed within seven years. If the obligations are not met by the target dates, the company is penalized 8.5 percent of the unfulfilled portion of the obligation.[69]

No one, however, can realistically develop the civilian investments envisioned by the 'offset' program within seven years. The UAE is actually fully aware of this fact, and the program's stringent requirements are currently being relaxed. When French arms manufacturer Giat missed its target dates in 1997, Abu Dhabi quietly extended Giat's target dates well past 2000.[70] Although the program has netted more than $800 million in investment so far, it has done little to improve the federation's security, strategic position, or non-oil economy.[71]

Even if procurement were not so heavily politicized, the UAE military would not be standardized because individual Emirates buy weapons systems without consulting the federal government. Dubai's Lion tanks, for instance, are not compatible with Abu Dhabi's Declerck tanks; nor does Abu Dhabi's air defense system protect Dubai. The army alone has three types of tanks: the Lion; the Declerck; and the BMP. None of these tanks is standardized or interoperable in terms of supply or sustainability. Though this problem will subside as Dubai cuts its defense spending, it will take years to reverse.[72]

### Fighting Capabilities

The most important consequence of the UAE's decentralized and politicized procurement process is that the federation's armed forces are not compatible with those of its allies. Saudi Arabia and Oman, for instance, operate the Bradley and the Chieftan tank respectively, which have completely different configurations from those of the UAE's tanks. The proposed acquisition of the Russian S-300V2 anti-tactical ballistic missile system is another example of the UAE's refusal to integrate its armed forces with those of its allies. While the Russians are offering substantial discounts, the S-300V2 lacks an identification and a friend-or-foe system compatible with Western systems. Washington reportedly worries that the S-300V2 increases the likelihood of fratricide – shooting down one of your own jets – and has threatened to bar US aircraft from the UAE if Abu Dhabi buys the system. There is thus a real danger that the UAE could actually impede its allies' military operations.[73]

The above-mentioned problems are compounded by poor organization and the low quality of the personnel under UAE command. As noted above, many of the UAE's military assets are controlled by the seven Emirate rulers. The chain of command remains ambiguous and subject to abuse or rivalries. Technical training is poor as well, and the UAE has difficulty finding qualified personnel to maintain its high-tech weapons – new recruits reportedly receive only five weeks of basic training.[74] Logistical support, usually provided by Third World contractors, is of low quality, even by Gulf standards. In addition, it is generally assumed that the UAE's forces could not function effectively far from their bases.[75]

## The United Arab Emirates' Air Force

The élite of the UAE's military forces is the 4,000-strong Air Force. It is, however, highly dependent on foreign technical assistance and has a very high ratio of personnel to aircraft. The UAE has 101 combat aircraft, 49 armed helicopters, and 22 transport aircraft; this includes nine Mirage 2000Es, 17 Hawk 102s, 17 Hawk Mk/63s, and 22 Mirage 2000 EADs. The Air Force also has an air defense brigade, five batteries of Hawk missiles, 12 Rapiers, nine Croatles, 13 RBS-70s and 100 Mistral Sams. The Air Force has three missions: to control the UAE's airspace; to protect the federation's economic and military facilities; and to destroy Iran's strategic assets, notably around Tehran. The last mission is important because it is the only way the UAE can check Iranian power.[76]

These are unrealistic missions, however, and they would be difficult even for a genuinely élite air force to achieve. The UAE's most advanced aircraft, the Mirage 2000E, for example, has a maximum range – on a single fueling with a fuel tank – of 1,261 nautical miles, barely half the distance of the round-trip between Abu Dhabi and Tehran.[77] In addition, the Mirage 2000Es are only now being converted to multi-role status; they were originally intended solely for air defense.

The UAE also does not currently have the technology to use in-flight refueling or airborne battlefield management. It must train its pilots to fly missions deep into enemy airspace and to support allied ground and naval forces, instead of concentrating on intercept missions and air-to-air combat. New long-range jets and AWACS-type aircraft may improve the UAE's capabilities, but it is unclear when or if those sales will happen. The UAE has yet to integrate its new aircraft into its military forces, and it is unknown where new jets will be deployed since the UAE currently only has one modern air base.[78] Equally as important, the UAE lacks qualified pilots. The UAE contracted Pakistanis to fly the new F-16s, and hoped they would also pilot the new Mirage 2000E jets. Reportedly, it also is negotiating similar contracts for Dutch Air Force pilots.[79]

## The United Arab Emirates' Army

The federation's Army has only 59,000 soldiers. It would have great difficulty fulfilling its primary missions: protecting federal borders and assisting in the defense of the GCC. Its order of battle is: a royal guard brigade; two armed brigades; three mechanized infantry brigades; two infantry brigades; one artillery brigade; and, now, Dubai's two infantry brigades.[80] There are three divisions: the Western Command; the Central Military District; and the Northern Military Region.[81] The Emirates also have their own forces. Reliability is now questionable in light of the refusal on the part of Omani citizens in the UAE Army to attack Oman in 1978.[82]

Finally, the UAE cannot transport or maintain its military assets over great distances, so it is doubtful that the UAE Army could render much assistance if one of its allies came under attack.[83]

## The United Arab Emirates' Navy

The UAE's Navy could not aid the GCC or the United States in a crisis. The federation's Navy has 2,000 personnel, most of whom are expatriates. The UAE has two frigates, two Corvettes, eight Missile Craft, nine in-shore patrol boats, three amphibious boats and three support craft. The Navy defends the federation's islands and off-shore oil facilities, and provides early warning in the event of an Iranian attack. Here the paucity of technologically-trained personnel is acute, though offset partnerships with Newport News, Mechanic of Normandy and the Netherlands Maritime Consortium should help. The proposed purchase of anti-submarine weapons, marine surveillance aircraft and even submarines is absurd because the UAE is unlikely to be able to use them properly, and such purchases will do little to check Iran's growing naval strength. UAE naval power remains weak, and many experts agree that it will stay that way for a long time.[84]

## Internal Security

Finally, each Emirate funds paramilitary and security forces that monitor the expatriate community, the military and foreign soldiers. The federal government administers the UAE's border police and coast guard. The US State Department's *Human Rights Report* notes that these forces are not excessively oppressive and that they respect many basic liberties[85] – the UAE government claims to have investigated and proven all allegations of torture and abuse against these forces as baseless.[86] Reportedly, Abu Dhabi is worried about infiltration by Iranians and South Asians, whom the UAE believes may be trying to undermine the UAE by promoting their own governments' interests within the federation. UAE officials also worry about illegal immigrants, most of whom cannot be traced or monitored easily because they lack fixed addresses.

## The Lack of a Credible Deterrent

Altogether, the UAE has gained little from its investment in arms. It cannot operate its weapons, organize its military forces rationally, co-operate with its allies, or devise realistic missions. Still, in August 1999, the UAE's semi-official daily in Abu Dhabi, *Al Ittihad*, noted that: 'The most senior military commanders in the advanced countries voiced their extreme admiration for [the UAE's] forces' superb capability and quick comprehension of the latest sophisticated military technologies.'[87] In reality, the UAE's adversaries know that its badly managed procurement program and force structure will not improve the UAE's combat capabilities. Indeed, the UAE's poor planning and obliviousness to the weaknesses of its own armed forces may turn out to be its greatest military drawback, rendering it far more vulnerable than it could otherwise be.

## ECONOMIC AND SOCIAL CHALLENGES

While the federation's foreign policy and military structure are crucial to its strategic position, the UAE's internal strengths and weaknesses are important as well. This is true because the UAE will not be able to buy weapons, improve its strategic assets, or fund Western military operations without a prosperous and rationally organized society. Currently per capita income is $16,070 – the highest in the Middle East – and the UAE maintains high trade and capital accounts surpluses.[88] Its overseas investment fund is worth at least $350 billion.[89] While the UAE government annually runs a budget deficit, it does not have external debt. As noted above, the federation is blessed with large oil and gas supplies.[90]

The UAE also has a modern infrastructure that has made it a regional transportation center. According to published Central Intelligence Agency (CIA) statistics, as of 1999 the UAE has 6,500 km of roads, virtually all of which are paved.[91] The Abu Dhabi–Dubai highway has been upgraded several times, and the links from Dubai to the northern Emirates are of a good standard as well. Rashid and Jebel Ali in Dubai are the largest of the UAE's 15 ports; together they handled 2.6 billion TEUs[92] of cargo in 1998, the 13th largest volume in the world.[93] Dubai's airport is the largest of the UAE's six airports. A federation-wide electrical network is also being planned.[94]

Still, behind the facade of wealth and stability there are significant social and economic problems. Wealth is not divided evenly among the populace or within the federation. While Abu Dhabi and Dubai are wealthy modern cities, many outlying villages lack running water, reliable electricity and simple health care. There is little transparency in UAE budgets, and it is estimated that 29 percent of the UAE's oil revenues between 1990 and 1994 did not appear on national accounts.[95] Per capita income is half of what it was in 1980, and it declined by nearly ten percent between 1998 and 1999.[96] While non-oil sectors of the economy are thriving, oil still accounts for 35 percent of GDP as well as approximately 78 percent of the UAE's total exports.[97] The scarcity of water supplies remains an acute problem, and the total population is growing rapidly: the UAE estimates its population grew by 6.5 percent in 1998 and will reach 3.48 million by 2005.[98] With as much as 40 percent of the population under the age of ten, these population growth numbers represent an important demographic shift.[99]

*Oil Revenues and Economic Growth*

The UAE's most vexing problem, however, is the extreme volatility of oil prices. The crash in oil prices in 1998 caused the UAE's economy to contract by 5.83 percent in nominal terms and the federation's deficit to balloon to $7.87 billion – this figure is estimated to be 41 percent above the 1997 level and 17 percent of gross domestic product. The trade and current account surpluses tumbled in 1998 to $5 billion and $1.78 billion respectively – a 66 percent decrease from 1997 – their lowest levels since 1993. Even before the most recent drop in oil prices, sagging oil sales had already cut into the UAE's economic growth; between 1991 and 1997, its annual average growth rate did not exceed 1.3 percent.[100] This rate illustrates the principal problem facing the UAE as it tries to diversify its economy: the driving force in the federation's economy remains large capital and infrastructure projects, which are paid for by government oil revenues or by drawing on the UAE's large overseas investments.[101]

Since Japan accounts for 60 percent of the UAE's oil exports and 29.8 percent of all exports, another factor limiting the UAE's oil income is Japan's weak economy.[102] Even when Japan's economy fully recovers, the UAE's oil exports to Japan are unlikely to grow substantially because Tokyo is diversifying its oil sources and building a strategic oil partnership with Saudi Arabia. Riyadh also wants a partnership with Tokyo but has tied any agreement to the renewal of the upstream concession that the Japanese-based Arabian Oil Company currently maintains in the kingdom's neutral zone. Reportedly, the Saudi government has refused to renew the Arabian Oil Company's concession unless Japan invests $6 billion in Saudi Arabia. The agreement would include a 1,500-km-long railway linking the northern and eastern region of the Kingdom. As of January 2000, Riyadh and Tokyo had not signed an agreement, and senior Japanese officials had expressed doubts about the profitability of the proposed Saudi railroad.[103]

Even if the Saudi–Japanese agreement is successful, the UAE should be able to find alternative markets because oil is a fungible resource and a world commodity. The UAE will most likely invest in Asia, which has large populations, minimal oil reserves and low per capita consumption of oil. The transition to other Asian markets, however, may impact UAE security. As the UAE increases exports to Asian nations other than Japan, US officials will find it difficult to convince the American public that the United States should defend a state that provides oil to countries perceived as competitors or enemies. Indeed, Washington faced severe internal criticism for protecting the oil of its closest allies, Europe and Japan, during the Gulf War.

What alternative does the UAE have to oil? Gas presents a natural alternative since the UAE has 204.9 trillion cubic feet (Tcf) reserves of gas – the world's fourth largest.[104] Abu Dhabi alone has 189 Tcf of gas, and the Emirate's non-associated Khuff gas reservoir is among the largest in the world. At the same time, exporting gas raises new problems: gas competes directly with oil in world markets; much of Abu Dhabi's gas reserves are difficult to access and have a high sulfur content; and there is growing demand for gas in the UAE itself, where gas is the primary source of energy. This final point is crucial. According to the US Energy Information Agency, Abu Dhabi's demand for gas doubled in the 1990s and is expected to double again by 2005. Dubai's demand for lighting and air conditioning alone has risen by 20 percent annually since 1995. Similar problems plague the other seven Emirates.[105]

One proposed solution to the UAE energy and gas shortages is the $8–10 billion 'Dolphin' gas trans-shipment project proposed by the UAE offset group. The backers of Dolphin argue that Abu Dhabi should purchase gas from Qatar – which has 100 Tcf more gas than the UAE – and distribute that gas to the UAE, the Arab Gulf states and the wider region. If this plan is fully implemented, Abu Dhabi would use its financial resources to become the hub for a Gulf regional gas network and also for a massive investment in South Asia. So far, however, there has been no agreement on pricing and it is not clear if there will be sufficient demand for the gas in Pakistan or Oman to justify the project. In addition, not a single member of UAE's élite has committed himself publicly to supporting the project.[106]

Other alternatives to hydrocarbon production include high technology, manufacturing, downstream oil development and petrochemicals. It is unlikely, however, that these industries could generate the revenues needed to offset a decline in oil sales. The UAE could also promote its already highly successful service industry, which is currently dominated by expatriates. One project is Dubai's Internet City, which has attracted multinationals such as Microsoft, Hewlett–Packard, Oracle and Cisco through strict enforcement of intellectual property laws and liberal rules on foreign direct investment, including renewable land leases.[107] Another project already in the planning stages is the Saadiyat free zone, which aims to create a global financial center on the scale of London, New York, or Tokyo on an island next to the coast of the Abu Dhabi Emirate. Even if successful – many financial analysts think that Saadiyat and other projects like it are sheer madness – these approaches would surely undermine the UAE's attempt to give preference to nationals, most of whom lack the skills to fulfill jobs in modern industry or finance. Furthermore, unemployment of nationals has been a rallying point for the Islamic opposition in Saudi Arabia.[108]

### The Problem of Expatriate Labor

This last dilemma illustrates one of the UAE's greatest challenges: weaning itself from its long-term dependence on foreign labor. Expatriates create expensive long-term structural problems,[109] and, as noted above, are a potential threat to the UAE's security. Some expatriates in recent years have even absconded abroad; for instance, in May 1999, Indian businessman Madhav Patel fled Sharjah with $245 million in unpaid loans from UAE and Western banks.[110] However, many nationals have little incentive to pursue work outside of the already bloated government bureaucracy or cannot fill the jobs currently held by expatriates; and the labor market already favors the latter – Emirate citizens must receive higher salaries and better benefits than foreigners. These problems are illustrated by the fact that only 254 of the 43,218 workers in Abu Dhabi's industrial sector were nationals in 1999.[111] Equally as important, 2,000 new citizens join the job market annually and the number of jobless citizens swelled to an estimated 20,000 by the end of 1999.[112]

Recent government measures to address these problems and 're-balance' the federation's demographics – refusing to issue visas to unskilled South Asian laborers or unmarried Russian women, raising utility bills to expatriates, and encouraging medium and large UAE companies to hire UAE nationals – have only succeeded in increasing domestic employment in the banking sector.[113] Given recent history, these measures offer little hope of success in the long run. The expulsion of 300,000 expatriates in 1996 caused high inflation and labor shortages, and reduced economic growth. Moreover, most of the expatriates expelled had returned to the UAE by the middle of 1997. Dubai businesses are already complaining about the drop in Russian tourism, which is partly due to the restrictions on Russian immigration into the UAE. Unfortunately, there is no easy or painless answer to the labor imbalance, so the UAE will have to cope with it for many years to come.[114]

## Water Resources and Desalination

There is no simple solution to the federation's dearth of water supplies, which may become a chronic economic and political problem in future years. Average annual rainfall is 42 mm, except in Ras al Khaimah where it is 150 mm per year. The World Bank estimates that renewable water resources per capita are 189 cubic meters, and that there has been a 15 percent annual increase in water demand in Abu Dhabi alone.[115] The UAE has addressed this problem through the development of underground wells – which have rapidly depleted the water table – and desalination.[116] Today, 82 desalination plants, many of which are also power plants, supply about 420 million gallons per day to the federation, and meet 82 percent of its total water needs. Due to the depletion of renewable resources through farming and excessive urbanization, there is no alternative within the UAE to desalination. Economies of scale dictate that the plants be large and near the coast.[117]

The UAE's reliance upon desalination may cause tensions within the federation and could conceivably become a strategic liability. While the wealthy Emirates can afford desalination, the situation in the northern Emirates, where supply interruptions are common, is critical. Decreased federal budgets have forced the poorer Emirates to privatize, and it is not clear whether these plans will work; a serious water shortage in the north, for example, would be crippling. Moreover, the desalination plants are something of a strategic liability: they are difficult to defend, easy to sabotage, and the UAE is wholly dependent upon them for the bulk of its water and electricity. Iran could easily blackmail the federation by threatening to destroy one of the UAE's desalination plants.[118]

Finally, the UAE could import water via pipeline from Iran,

which currently has 17.5 billion cubic meters of excess water. According to the Dubai-based *Gulf News*, the cost of importing Iranian water into the UAE is about 70 percent of the cost of desalination, and Tehran is eagerly pursuing plans to supply water to Kuwait, Qatar and Saudi Arabia. Although Iranian officials submitted a proposal to the government of Dubai in 1994, there has been no response from Emirate officials. This is, of course, not surprising given that water pipelines from Iran would give Tehran even greater opportunities to pressure Abu Dhabi during a crisis than it already has.[119]

### Long-term Demographic and Economic Trends

It is important to keep a proper perspective when evaluating the trends in the UAE's economy and their impact on the federation's strategic position. Although the UAE's economic and budgetary problems are serious, they are not nearly as bad as those of its neighbors. The UAE has large reserves of natural resources and the most developed non-oil private sector in the Gulf. According to the US Arms Control and Disarmament Agency, the relative burden of military expenditure is low, particularly in comparison to Oman and Saudi Arabia.[120] The UAE can now pay all its military bills, although such comparative financial health will not last forever.

### CONCLUSION: THE UNITED ARAB EMIRATES' FUTURE SECURITY NEEDS

There are many important favorable aspects to the UAE's strategic position at the beginning of the twenty-first century. The federation does not face an immediate threat of invasion, organized domestic opposition, or economic collapse. Nor does the UAE have any foreign debts. It has considerable wealth, which will give it several years to address the economic, environmental and social imbalances of the federation before they become overwhelming. The next president will undoubtedly be one of Shaykh Zayid's most prominent sons, all of whom have shown that they can govern well. The rivalry between Dubai and Abu Dhabi has abated, and there seem to be the beginnings of a genuine civil society. Although there are vast policy differences between Abu Dhabi and Washington, the United States will likely guarantee the federation's security in the near term.

At the same time, the UAE's strategic position is undermined by Abu Dhabi's inability to achieve progress in reaching its goals through its economic, military or political policies. Despite an enormous investment in arms, for instance, the UAE's armed services – either on their own or in combination with the GCC – cannot provide an effective deterrent against the federation's most likely enemy, Iran. Nor have the defense treaties with Britain and France decreased the federation's dependence on US force projection capabilities. Iraq remains outside of the balance of power, and it is unlikely that the UAE will be able to construct a regional security order that includes Baghdad soon. Similarly, the islands dispute appears years away from resolution. In addition, the UAE has also not found permanent solutions to its principal internal challenges: demographics; the dominance of oil in the state; and the paucity of water supplies. Sadly, all of these problems worsened during the 1990s.

The UAE's favorable strategic position is thus more tenuous than it might first appear. A small state, the federation cannot possibly impact the politics of the region without the assistance of a large power, such as the United States or Saudi Arabia, and it has been lucky not to have been undermined by its own policy mistakes. Thus, things could be very different if the UAE faced a military crisis: after all, the UAE's economic and social problems are very real, and will merely intensify if they are not addressed soon.

The UAE is aware of these problems, however, and has already begun to address the federation's challenges. Abu Dhabi is privatizing large state-owned firms and investing millions in non-oil sectors of the economy. Abu Dhabi National Oil Company (ADNOC), Abu Dhabi's state-owned oil and gas company, is now in the process of modernizing the federation's gas and oil facilities. For all its problems, the offset program does offer a way of developing the UAE's economy and ensuring its future security. In addition, the Western-educated technocrats are displaying a degree of frankness about the UAE's problems rarely shown by their predecessors. Finally, the higher oil prices from OPEC's production cuts in March 1999 should bring significant increases in Abu Dhabi's economy and government revenues in the near term.

Unfortunately, most of these policies exacerbate the federation's security problems. On the domestic front, the gap in wealth between the poorer and richer Emirates could aggravate tensions in the future. Abu Dhabi has combined its privatization programs with deep cuts in subsidies to the northern Emirates, a move that has only enlarged this gap. Privatization also favors the UAE's service sector, which expatriates dominate. This, too, could cause very serious social tensions. In addition, the offset program is contingent upon the UAE spending billions on arms for years, an expenditure that is likely to become a great burden. Thus, the UAE's principal security challenge in the next century will be to build a viable society whose economic success does not undermine its political stability.

Still, the UAE's challenges must be understood within their historical context. In reality, the UAE's government has dealt with the issues discussed above for many years; the paucity of water supplies, for instance, actually predates the federation itself. The fact that the UAE's comparative strategic position remains strong – despite Abu Dhabi's inability to solve the country's long-term challenges – bodes well for the federation's future. Indeed, it is reasonable to assume that the Emirates' strategic position will remain sound in the near term, even if the UAE government cannot devise workable solutions to the federation's structural problems over the next ten years.

## NOTES

1. 'Special Report: UAE', *Middle Eastern Economic Digest*, 10 December (1999) (hereafter cited as *Special Report*); EIU *Country Report, United Arab Emirates, 1997–1998* (London: The Unit, 1998), pp. 2, 23 (hereafter cited as *Country Report*); United States Library of Congress, *Country Guide to the United Arab Emirates*, http://lcweb2.loc.gov/frd/cs/aetoc.html, 30 January (1998).
2. The UAE's 1998 barrels of proven oil reserves are greater than those of

Kuwait and Iran, and are five times those of the United States. Only Saudi Arabia and Iraq, with 261.6 and 112 billion reserves, respectively, have more. The federation also has the fourth largest gas reserves in the world behind those of Russia, Iran and Qatar. US Energy Information Agency, '1999 Country Report: UAE', http://www.eia.doe.gov/emeu/cabs/uae.html, 2 January (2000).

3. Ibid.

4. It has been estimated that Sharjah now accounts for at least one-third of the UAE's annual industrial production. Barclay's Bank, *Barclay's Bank Country Report. United Arab Emirates: Structural Features*, 22 December (1999).

5. Ibid.; and EIU, *Country Report*, pp. 2, 13, 21, 38.

6. CIA, 'United Arab Emirates', *World Fact Book*, http://www.odci.gov/cia/publications/factbook/tc.html, 20 December (1999) (hereafter cited as *World Fact*); EIU, *Country Report*, pp. 2, 20–1.

7. CIA, *World Fact*.

8. EIU, *Country Report*, p. 11.

9. Jane's Sentinel, *Country Report: United Arab Emirates 1996*, p. 42.

10. Joseph Keichichan, *Oman and The World: The Emergence of An Independent Foreign Policy* (Santa Monica, CA: RAND Corporation, 1995), pp. 76–82. (Hereafter cited as *Oman and the World*.)

11. Richard Schofield, 'Borders and Territoriality in the Gulf and the Arabian Peninsula during the Twentieth Century', in R. Schofield (ed.), *Territorial Foundations of the Gulf States* (New York: St Martin's Press, 1994).

12. Janet Matthews Information Service, Quest Economic Database, *Barclay's Bank, Country Report: UAE*, 16 October (2000), p. 1. EIU, *Country Report: United Arab Emirates* (London: The Unit, 2000), p. 28.

13. Peter Kemp, 'Confident that the Growth will Continue', *Middle Eastern Economic Digest*, 5 December (1997). (Hereafter cited as *Confident*.)

14. Robin Allen, 'UAE survey: Abu Dhabi's Assets Keep UAE Afloat in Gulf', *Financial Times*, 2 December (1999) (hereafter cited as *Assets*).

15. Ibid.

16. Kemp, *Confident*; William A. Rugh, 'What are the Sources of UAE Stability?', *Middle East Policy*, 4, 3 (1997), pp. 14–24. (Hereafter cited as *Stability*.)

17. Robin Allen, 'United Arab Emirates: New Forces Bring Changes', *Financial Times*, 21 December (1999).

18. 'United Arab Emirates: "Youthful Trend" in UAE Parliament', *Al Wasat*, 22 December (1997).

19. This argument was made by Jill Crystal in *Oil and Politics in the Gulf: Rulers and Merchants in Kuwait and Qatar* (Cambridge: Cambridge University Press, 1993).

20. 'By Women, For Women', *Al Shindagah-Dubai*, 20 January (1998).

21. The UAE has six principal tribes spread throughout the federation: the Bani Yas, the Manasir, the Qasimi, the Al Ali, the Sharqiyin and the Nu'aim. David E. Long and Bernard Reich, *The Government and Politics of the Middle East and North Africa* (New York: Westview Press, 1995), p. 136.

22. Rugh, *Stability*.

23. There have been rumors for years that Shaykh Khalifa is an alcoholic. But most US officials I have talked to about the issue have questioned the validity of these rumors.

24. Robin Allen, 'United Arab Emirates: Shifting Sands: Foreign and Defense Politics', *Financial Times*, 21 December (1999); 'Emirates' President leaves clinic in good health', *Deutsche Presse-Agentur*, 20 December (1999).

25. F. Gregory Gause III, 'Political Opposition in the Gulf Monarchies', paper presented at the conference on the 'Changing Security Agenda in the Gulf', Doha, Qatar, 24–26 October (1997).

26. Richard Scott, 'Gulf Navies Look Further Offshore', *Jane's Navy International*, 1 March (1997).

27. Richard Schofield, 'Border Disputes: Past, Present and Future', in Sick G. and Potter L. (eds), *The Persian Gulf at the Millennium: Essays on Politics, Economy, Security and Religion* (New York: St Martin's Press, 1997), pp. 127–66.

28. Ibid.

29. J.B. Kelly, *Arabia, the Gulf and the West* (New York: Basic Books, 1980), p. 82. For a more pro-Iranian view of these events, please see Hooshang Amirahmadi, *Small Islands, Big Politics: the Tonbs and Abu Musa in the Persian Gulf* (New York: St Martin's Press, 1996).

30. According to Dubai government statistics, the Emirate re-exported $782 million worth of goods to Iran in 1996, which accounted for 65% of all of Dubai's re-exports that year.

31. 'Abu Musa: Island Dispute Between Iran and the UAE', http://www. ColumbiaUniversityLibrary/Mideast/UAE.edu, 20 February (1998). Shaykh Muhammad reportedly made this statement at Ohio State University in 1995.

32. Iran, however, did not share any of the proceeds from the oil revenues with Sharjah and the UAE between 1971 and 1978. William Rugh, 'Foreign Policy of the United Arab Emirates', *Middle East Journal*, 50, 1 (1996), pp. 61–2 (hereafter cited as *Foreign Policy of UAE*).

33. Dan Caldewell, 'Flashpoints in the Gulf", *Middle East Policy*, 3, 1 (1996), pp. 50–57.

34. EIU Country Report, *United Arab Emirates*, 4th Quarter (1997), p. 14.

35. 'Iran welcomes latest proposal on disputed islands', *Deutsche Presse-Agentur*, 1 December (1999); 'Secrets', *Al Watan Al Arabi*, 25 December (1998), *Foreign Broadcasting Information Service: FBIS-LAT-99-008* (8 January 1999), pp. 14–16.

36. 'Gulf summit sent wrong message to Iran, says Emirati daily', *Agence France Presse*, 1 December (1999); and 'UAE Paper Slams Iran's "Shameless Lies"', *Agence France Presse*, 27 December (1999).

37. Ed Blanche, 'Saudi Efforts at Reconciliation with Iran Make Waves in the Gulf', *Jane's Intelligence Review*, 1 July (1999); and 'UAE Head Not to Attend Summit in Protest over Islands Dispute with Iran', *BBC Summary of World Broadcasts*, 29 November (1999). The Al Shaybah oilfield is thought to contain 14 billion barrels of oil and 26 million cubic meters of gas.

38. Ibid; 'Qatari mediation bid appears to yield progress', *Deutsche Presse-Agentur*, 19 June (1999).

39. Trade represented 25 percent of Dubai's GDP in 1998. Mark Hubbard, 'United Arab Emirates: Desert Pearls to Desert Flights', *Financial Times*, 21 December (1999).

40. The re-export sector is actually important to the entire UAE economy.

According to *Info-Prod Research*, the re-export sector has an annual turnover of close to $6.54 billion. 'Importance of Re-Exports to Economy', *Info-Prod Research*, 1 July (1999).

41. 'Saudi Arabia, UAE at Odds over Gulf Customs Union,' *Agence France Presse*, 28 November (1999). Saudi Arabia charges tariff rates up to 20 percent, while the UAE charges as low as 4 percent.

42. Keichichan, *Oman and The World*, pp. 76–82.

43. 'UAE/Qatar Reconciliation', *Al-Wasat*, 22 December (1997).

44. 'Identification Card May Replace Passport Under Qatar-UAE Travel Agreement', *Info-Prod Research*, 25 November (1999).

45. 'Qatari Mediation Bid Appears to Yield Progress', *Deutsche Press-Agentur*, 19 June (1999).

46. Geoffrey Kemp and Robert Harkavy noted this reality: 'None of the countries outside the greater Middle East, with the exception of the United States, seems capable, much less inclined, to project power into the region for the foreseeable future.' *The Strategic Geography and the Changing Middle East* (Washington, DC: Carnegie Endowment/Brookings, 1997), p. 252 (hereafter cited as *Strategic Geography and the Changing*).

47. 'Value of Arms Transfer Deliveries, Cumulative 1992–1994', http://www.acda.gov, 1 February (1998).

48. Anthony Cordesman, *US Forces in the Middle East* (Boulder, CO: Westview Press, 1997), pp. 76–7; 'Manama No Longer', *New York Times*, 4 May (1997). Various conversations with US military personnel in the UAE in 1996.

49. Abdallah Al-Shayeji, 'Dangerous Perceptions: Gulf Views of the US Role in the Region', *Middle Eastern Policy* 4, 3 (1997), pp. 3–4.

50. Jeffrey Gardner, 'Kofi Annan Clinches UN Peace Deal with Saddam', *Financial Times*, 23 February (1998); Aziz Abu-Hamad, 'Gulf State No-Shows', *Washington Post*, 20 March (1998).

51. 'UAE Newspaper: "US, Britain Intentionally Kill Civilians"', *Xinhua News Agency*, 20 August (1999); 'Editorial: Albright's Statement Went Too Far', *Al Bayan*, 30 January (1999).

52. 'UAE and UN Sanctions', *Financial Times*, 6 December (1996); 'Sanctions Busting: An Oily Tale', *Economist*, 17 January (1998).

53. Muhammad Ahmedullah, 'Iraq's Military Restocking in the United Arab Emirates', *Defense Week*, 3 January (2000). Reportedly, Iraqi officers were seen at the 1999 Dubai air show talking to representatives of Russian aerospace firms, which are now taking orders from UAE companies that have not previously had any requirement for Russian-made material. Ahmedullah argues that it is not likely that other Middle Eastern states with Russian or Soviet weapon systems would ship through the UAE.

54. Rugh, *Foreign Policy of UAE*.

55. Anthony Cordesman, 'New Balance of Gulf Suppliers', *Middle East Policy*, 6, 4 (1999), p. 88.

56. The UAE signed a defense pact with France in 1995, Britain in 1996 and Turkey in 1997.

57. 'The Gulf Protection Racket', *Foreign Report*, 18 December (1997). Reportedly, French officials signed the treaty even though they didn't believe that Iran would ever invade the UAE.

58. 'Interview with Jean-Pierre Kelche', *Al Bayan*, 1 March (1999); *Foreign*

*Broadcasting Information Service: FBIS-NES-1999-0302*: pp. 2–6.

59. 'Pakistan Again Explodes Bomb: Spiraling Nuclear Rivalry Feared', *Washington Post*, 31 May (1998); 'Pakistani Says A-Strike Was Planned on India', *New York Times*, 2 July (1998); 'Pakistan May Stop Debt Payments', *Financial Times*, 7 July (1998).

60. 'Musharraf to visit Saudi Arabia, UAE', *The Hindu*, 25 October (1999).

61. James Risen and Benjamin Weiser, 'US Officials Say Aid for Terrorists Came Through Two Persian Nations', *New York Times*, 8 July (1999).

62. Paul Richter, 'Anti-Hussein Coalition Firming Up', *Los Angeles Times*, 11 February (1998).

63. Barry Schweid, 'Senior Officials Quietly Join Probe of Terrorism Suspect', *Associated Press*, 8 July (1999).

64. 'Differences Between Saudi Arabia and UAE Resurface at GCC Summit', *Mideast Mirror*, 30 November (1999).

65. John D. Morrocco, 'Military Sales Level Off Following Oil Price Drop', *Aviation Week & Space Technology*, 8 November (1999), pp. 86–7.

66. Jim Lobe, 'Arms: Arms Sales to Developing Nations Decline', *Interpress Service*, 6 August (1999).

67. Andy Chuter, 'Pakistani Pilot Deal Linked to US Block on UAE Technology Release', *Flight International*, 24 March (1999), p. 8; Vince Crawley, 'Pentagon: UAE May Sign Fighter Deal This Month', *Defense Week*, 13 September (1999); and Katie Fairbank, 'UAE Negotiates for Technologically Superior Jets', *Dallas Morning News*, 4 December (1999), pp. A1 and A23.

68. Reuben F. Johnson, 'Aviation Firms See Major Gulf Deals As Mirage', *St Petersburg Times*, 21 December (1999) (hereafter cited as *Mirage*).

69. Amin Badr El-Din, 'The Offsets Program in the United Arab Emirates', *Middle East Policy*, 4, 3 (1997), pp. 120–123.

70. 'Gulf States Told to Get Tough Over Offsets', *Jane's Defense Weekly*, 10 December (1997); Peter Kemp, 'Special Report France', *Middle Eastern Economic Digest*, 24 October (1998).

71. Ed Blanche, 'Offset Industry to Gain from UAE programs', *Jane's Defense Weekly*, 29 January (1997). There are many proponents of this program, but virtually everyone I have talked to about offset, as well as my own analysis, has led me to believe that it has not truly benefited the UAE's security or economy very much.

72. International Institute for Strategic Studies, *The Military Balance for 1998–1999* (London: ISS, 2000), p. 156 (hereafter cited as *Military Balance*); Anthony Cordesman, *Bahrain, Oman, Qatar and the UAE: Challenges of Security* (Boulder, CO: Westview Press, 1997), pp. 353–61 (hereafter cited as *Challenges of Security*); 'Special Report UAE', *Middle Eastern Economic Digest*, 5 December (1997).

73. Bernard Grey, 'Trends Towards Innovation', *Financial Times*, 10 June (1996); Andy Chuter, 'Russian/US Tussle over UAE Air Defense System Intensifies', *Flight International*, 24 March (1999).

74. Jane's Sentinel, *Country Report: United Arab Emirates 1996*, p. 45.

75. Cordesman, *Challenges of Security*, pp. 353–61.

76. Nick Cook, 'GCC Air Forces', *Jane's Defense Weekly*, 24 April (1996); Jacques de Lestapis, 'Jacques de Lestapis Looks at the UAE's Weapon

Purchasing Priorities', *Jane's Defense Weekly*, 18 March (1995) (Hereafter cited as *UAE's Weapons Purchasing Priorities*); International Institute for Strategic Studies, *Military Balance*, p. 156; Ed Blanche, 'The Old and the New: Changing the Face of Middle East Airpower', *Jane's Defense Weekly*, 10 November (1999).

77. Australian Aerospace Publications, *International Director of Military Aircraft* (Canberra: Aerospace Publications, 1996), p. 89.

78. International Institute for Strategic Studies, *Military Balance*, p. 156; 'UAE Buy Raises Doubts', *Jane's Defense Weekly*, 25 November (1995). The UAE reportedly plans to build two new air bases.

79. Paul Beaver, 'UAE Examines Dutch F-16 Buy', *Jane's Defense Weekly*, 8 December (1999).

80. International Institute for Strategic Studies, *Military Balance*, p. 144.

81. Cordesman, *Challenges of Security*, p. 368.

82. Keichichan, *Oman and The World*, pp. 76–82.

83. de Lestapis, *UAE's Weapon Purchasing Priorities*; Ed Blanche, 'GCC Nations Continue to Need Allied Shield', *Jane's Information Group Limited*, 12 November (1997); International Institute for Strategic Studies, *The Military Balance for 1997–1998* (London: ISS, 1998), p. 143; Cordesman, *Challenges of Security*, pp. 353–61.

84. Ed Blanche, 'UAE Considers Underwater Warfare Capability', *Jane's Defense Weekly*, 12 March (1997); Richard Scott, 'Gulf Navies Look Further Offshore', *Jane's Navy International*, 1 March (1997); de Lestapis, *UAE's Weapon Purchasing Priorities*; *Military Balance*, p. 144; 'UAE Naval Programmes – Getting Closer?', *Naval Forces*, January (1997); *Middle East Economic Digest*, July (1999), p. 34.

85. US State Department, *1998 Country Reports on Human Rights Practices: United Arab Emirates*, http://www.state.gov/www/global/human_rights/1998_hrp_report/uae.html, 27 December (1999).

86. Ibid.

87. 'Editorial: Strength for Peace', *Al Ittihad*, 24 August (1999). *Foreign Broadcasting Information Service: FBIS-NES-1999-0826*: p. 24.

88. Barclay's Bank, *Barclay's Bank Country Report: UAE: Structural Features*, 22 December (1999).

89. Allen, *Afloat*. It is widely thought that $120 billion of that amount is invested in US securities. The US, however, buys very little oil from the UAE and currently enjoys a favorable balance of trade with the federation. Access to US markets was a point of friction between the United States and all the GCC states, including the UAE. 'Trade Issue Dominates GCC, US Economic Talks', *Xinhua General News Service*, 17 October (1999).

90. Angus Hindley, 'MEED Abu Dhabi Special Report', *Middle Eastern Economic Digest*, 20 February (1998).

91. CIA, *World Factbook*.

92. TEU is a shipping term used to determine the size of ships and ports. It is an abbreviation for 'Twenty foot Equivalent Unit'. http://www.marad.dot.gov/glossary.html.

93. Janet Matthews Information Services, *World of Information Country Report. United Arab Emirates: Economy*, August (1999).

94. EIU *Country Report*, pp. 25-7.

95. Gary Sick, 'The Coming Crisis', *The Persian Gulf at the Millennium: Essays on Politics, Economy, Security and Religion* (New York: St Martin's Press, 1997). p. 21. Sick also notes that a percentage of these 'off-book' expenditures most likely funded secret defense projects.

96. World Bank, *World Development Indicators 1997* (Baltimore: Johns Hopkins University Press, 1997), pp. 9, 17. Overall UAE GNP per capita declined by 4 percent between 1970 to 1995.

97. Barclay's Bank, *Barclay's Bank Country Report. United Arab Emirates: Summary*, 22 December (1999).

98. 'Local population growth rate hits 6.5 percent', *Al Ittihad*, 15 July (1999). http://www.alittihad.co.ae, 15 July (1999).

99. 'Symposium: Shaykh Zayid and the UAE', *Middle East Policy*, 6, 4 (1999), p. 7.

100. Barclay's Bank, *Barclay's Bank Country Report. United Arab Emirates: Recent Trends and Outlooks*, 22 December (1999).

101. 'Finalising the figures for 1998', *Middle East Monitor* 9, 8 (1999); 'UAE', *Middle Eastern Economic Digest*, 29 October (1999); and EIU *Country Report*, p. 30. It is estimated that the UAE earned $24 billion from its overseas investments in 1998.

102. Barclay's Bank, *Country Profile. United Arab Emirates: Foreign Trade*, 22 December (1999).

103. 'Yosano Said Ends Visit With No Progress on Oil Issue', *Tokyo Kyodo*, 29 May (1999); and 'Japanese Official to Visit Riyadh to Negotiate Oil Rights', *Kyodo News Service*, 21 December (1999).

104. US Energy Information Administration, '1998 Country Analysis Briefs: United Arab Emirates', http://www.eia.doe.gov/emeu/cabs/uae.html, 19 November (1999).

105. Ibid. Robin Allen, 'Survey: United Arab Emirates: Palace Politics Intrudes into Oil', *Financial Times*, 21 December (1999) (hereafter cited as *Palace Politics*).

106. Allen, *Palace Politics*; 'Gas: Dolphin Project Leaps Ahead', *Middle East Monitor* 9, 4 (1999); and 'Dubai to Get Qatari Gas', *Power Economics*, 15 July (1999).

107. EIU Country Report, *February 2001* (London: the Unit, 2001), p. 30.

108. 'Sandcastles in the Air', *Economist*, 24 July (1999); and 'Too Big to Fail?' *Middle East Monitor* 9, 9 (1999).

109. These problems include high payments for social services to expatriates and capital outflow.

110. 'The House that Patel Built', *Middle Eastern Economic Digest*, 29 October (1999).

111. '43,218 Industrial Employees in Abu Dhabi', *Al Ittihad*, 26 July (1999). http://www.alittihad.co.ae, 26 July (1999).

112. 'Special Report: UAE', *Middle Eastern Economic Digest*, 10 December (1999).

113. 'Emirati President Aims to "Rebalance" the State's Demographics', *Agence France Presse*, 1 December (1999). 'Abu Dhabi Ups Expat Utility Charges', *Agence France Presse*, 29 December (1999). Johnson, *Mirage*.

114. Kasra Naji, 'UAE Exodus Hits Projects', *Financial Times*, 28 September (1996); Alan George, 'Labor Exodus Hits UAE's Growth', *Jane's Intelligence Review*, 1 February (1997).

115. Peter Kemp, 'Special Report: Water', *Middle Eastern Economic Digest*, 26 January (1996).
116. In 1987, then-Turkish prime minister Turgut Özal proposed a third solution; a pipeline that would channel water from Turkey to the Arabian peninsula. This proposal has been ignored because Iraq, Syria and Saudi Arabia are wary of allowing Turkey to control their access to fresh water.
117. EIU, *Country Report*, p. 23.
118. Angus Hindley, 'UAE: Focusing on rapid rise in desalination', *Middle Eastern Economic Digest*, 26 January (1996); Geoffrey Kemp and Robert E. Harkavy, *Strategic Geography and the Changing*, p. 337. The two authors note: 'Yet as was realized during the Gulf War, water desalinization plants are at risk of being destroyed or damaged during an armed confrontation. The reality is that as more and more fresh water production plants are built, they become more vulnerable in the event of conflict.'
119. 'Iran Eager to Provide Water to the UAE', *Xinhua General News Service*, 5 December (1999).
120. '95burden', http://www.acda.gov, 1 March (1998).

# 4

# The Enigma of Political Stability in the Persian Gulf Monarchies

## DANIEL L. BYMAN
## AND JERROLD D. GREEN

This chapter explores strategies that governments use to keep societies at peace. Stability is more difficult to understand than conflict. Scholars have offered many conceptual explanations of why and how people rebel, the causes of war and the dynamics of revolution.[1] The sources of societies at peace, however, have received far less scrutiny.

Often, stability is explained as merely the absence of conflict. Yet this explanation is valid only for wealthy, ethnically-homogenous democracies that face few challenges from neighbors. More perceptive scholars have gone one step further, explaining peace by delving into the nature of the societies in question and exploring how their culture or popular expectations defuse conflict. These explanations, while encouraging, have proven themselves insufficient. Stability does not simply occur, it is often fostered, imposed, encouraged, bolstered, or maintained. Governments of all sorts have actively and successfully prevented conflict through adroit management of potential disputes.

Explaining societal peace remains an important question. Since the fall of the Berlin Wall, civil conflict has supplanted war as the most common form of violence. Although the spread of democracy promises greater social harmony, democratization can lead to strife, both civil and international.[2] Modernization, nation-building, and economic growth – all solutions to conflict proposed by social scientists in the past – have proven to bring mixed blessings to many countries. Thus, it is important to understand the measures that governments can take to keep the peace under difficult circumstances.

Herewith is an examination of several countries that suffer from economic dislocations, hard-to-control social change, corruption, political exclusion, and meddlesome foreign powers, yet remain stable: the Arab monarchies of the Persian Gulf. The ruling families in Bahrain, Kuwait, Oman, Qatar, Saudi Arabia and the United Arab Emirates (UAE)[3] have held power, largely unchallenged, for decades if not centuries. The Al Saud family consolidated its power from 1902 to 1934; the Al Khalifa took power of Bahrain in 1783; the Al Thani consolidated power in Qatar in 1878; the Al Said took power in Oman in the mid-eighteenth century; the Al Sabah became hereditary rulers of Kuwait in the eighteenth century; and the emirate members of the UAE consolidated power at various times in the mid-nineteenth century.[4] The stability of these countries is hardly perfect. Terrorism, often directed at the United States, has at times led to dozens of deaths in the 1980s and 1990s. Coup attempts occurred in Saudi Arabia in the 1960s and in Bahrain in 1981. During 1994–96, Bahrain suffered a series of protests and riots that led to dozens of deaths and hundreds of arrests. Nevertheless, the governments in these countries have held firmly onto power and, in general, maintained social peace.

The stability of this region is baffling. The Gulf states have modernized at a breathtaking pace since the Second World War. At the same time, their progress has been uneven as their wealth rose and fell with the price of oil, soaring in the 1970s and plummeting in the 1980s and 1990s.[5] Education levels have risen steadily, and expectations of and demands on national government have grown. Discrimination against Shiites has been rampant in several countries, and anti-government religious militancy has grown. Even more mysteriously, the Gulf political systems appear an anachronism. All the Gulf states have traditional monarchies, the last hold out of this system in a modern world.

The region itself is in turmoil, with revolution and war threatening to swallow the Gulf states. Commentators in the

1950s and 1960s wondered how long the Gulf states could survive the assault of Arab nationalism, which toppled monarchs in Egypt, Libya and Iraq, and brought new governments to Syria and Algeria. After the late 1970s, this concern switched to a fear of Islamic extremism: Iran and Sudan succumbed, and Islamic radicalism helped fuel civil wars in Algeria, Afghanistan and Lebanon, and instability in countless other states ranging from Turkey to Afghanistan. After the fall of the Soviet Union and the *annus mirabilis* of 1989, analysts began to question whether the next wave of democratization might sweep the region. Yet despite these pressures, the monarchies remain strong. Although Egypt, Iran and sub-state actors such as Lebanese Hizballah have tried to promote revolution and unrest in the Gulf, their efforts have failed.

This chapter argues that social peace in the Gulf, and perhaps more generally, is maintained by the clever and consistent use of a variety of government strategies to promote social order. Gulf governments use a combination of six strategies: strong security services; the co-optation of potential dissidents; divide-and-rule measures; ideological flexibility; token participation; and accommodative diplomacy. Taken together, these strategies preserve islands of social peace in an area of turbulence.

These strategies keep the peace through a variety of means. First, they defuse potentially explosive social issues, preventing them from leading to violence. Second, they broadly inhibit social organization. Even when individuals or groups seek to mobilize and use violence, the Gulf governments prevent them from organizing. Third, government strategies reduce, though hardly eliminate, incentives for foreign powers to meddle. The remainder of this chapter tries to answer four related questions. Why does conflict appear likely in Gulf societies? What strategies do Gulf regimes use to keep the peace? How do these strategies work in practice? What are the limits of these strategies? Although definitive answers to these questions are impossible, this chapter attempts to assess the likelihood of continued stability for the countries in question in the coming decade.

## POTENTIAL SOURCES OF CONFLICT

The Gulf states are best defined by what they lack. In an era when democracy is the world's dominant political system, the Gulf regimes are traditional autocracies. Gulf governments are not accountable to their citizens, and political alienation and corruption are widespread. Contrary to popular stereotypes of wealthy Gulf sheikhs, economic progress has been mixed and uneven. Demographic pressures squeeze the Gulf states. Traditional ways of life are under siege, as nomadic, largely illiterate societies have rapidly become sedentary, urbanized and educated. The region's *zeitgeist* also favors violence, where guerrillas are lauded and peacemakers ridiculed.

Discrimination is rampant against Shiites, who form a large segment of several Gulf states' populations, and religious militancy is widespread, threatening to undermine the area regimes' legitimacy. As if these problems were not enough, the neighbors of the Gulf states have regularly tried to foment war and revolution. Alone, any one of these problems could lead to unrest. Together, they seem to signal disaster.[6]

## POLITICAL EXCLUSION AND A LACK
## OF ACCOUNTABILITY

One of the most potent grievances Gulf citizens make against their government is the lack of accountability, which in turn promotes abuse of power and rampant corruption. Decision-making is dominated by a few individuals privileged by birth, not by merit. The Gulf states, with the partial exception of Kuwait, lack the means to mediate citizen grievances or to ensure accountability. Institutions for organizing political opposition are limited or non-existent. All important positions – those that control spending, internal security, and the military – are dominated by family members or those close to them. Traditional checks on government authority – a free press, an independent judiciary and a strong 'civil society' – are either lacking or kept intentionally weak in the Gulf states.[7] Although several states have advisory bodies appointed by the regime, these at best reflect only élite opinion, and they seldom have an impact on decision-making or satisfy popular desires for a true voice in government.

Because the ruling families dominate politics, many Gulf citizens correctly perceive their political systems as exclusive. Bahraini opposition groups have called their country a 'tribal dictatorship', directly attacking the Al Khalifa family's domination of the states.[8] Even in comparatively democratic Kuwait, opposition newspapers criticize the preferential treatment accorded the ruling family. The Saudi Shiites, a relatively small minority, also suffer extreme political exclusion. Not surprisingly, interviews indicate that many Gulf citizens believe that peaceful political activity cannot influence their country's leadership. This opposition could have dangerous repercussions: throughout the world, rather moderate political groups have often become violent after years of repeated failures in proposing compromise.[9]

The alienation of social and economic élites is particularly dangerous. As oil wealth has empowered the ruling families that control the state, traditional tribal and family élites have lost influence.[10] Newly-educated technocrats often are angered by the rampant corruption and inefficiency in the Gulf and question why their countries are controlled by poorly-educated family members who have few qualifications for office. Similarly, religious scholars resent the state-sponsored, and often intellectually inferior, religious leaders who dominate their countries' religious establishments.[11]

Corruption and unaccounted-for government spending levels are quite high. Money derived from the sale of oil noted in balance of payment statements often fails to appear in oil revenues reported in the state budget. In recent years, from 18 to 30 per cent of the revenue from petroleum exports was not reported in budgets in the northern Gulf states.[12] This missing money – billions of dollars a year – enriches the royal families. Opposition groups frequently criticize the regime for allowing ruling family members to mismanage the country and charge that the traditional monarchies are simply kleptocracies with scepters. A Bahraini opposition group, for example, accused the ruling family of: 'squandering the wealth of the nation.'[13] Similarly, in a 14 July communiqué, the Movement for Islamic Reform in Saudi Arabia blamed Al Saud family members for corruption and contributing to the country's economic woes.[14]

## ECONOMIC AND DEMOGRAPHIC PROBLEMS

The Gulf states, Bahrain and Saudi Arabia in particular, suffer from a combination of high expectations, rapid population growth and falling oil revenues: a potentially-explosive combination. In the 1970s, the rapid inflow of oil wealth led all the Gulf states to create extensive welfare systems. Governments provided health-care, education, and other services for free to all citizens, and any citizen with an advanced degree was entitled to a lucrative government job. Since the early 1980s, however, the price of oil has fallen dramatically – with disastrous results for the budgets of regional governments.[15]

The Gulf states today lack the wherewithal to satisfy their burgeoning populations. The per capita incomes of many Gulf residents have plummeted since the 1970s after the price of oil began falling in the early 1980s. From 1984 to 1994, real per capita gross domestic product (GDP) fell from $12,740 to $7,140 in Bahrain; $22,480 to $16,600 in Kuwait; $6,892 to $4,915 in Oman; $31,100 to $15,070 in Qatar; $11,450 to $6,725 in Saudi Arabia; and $27,620 to $14,100 in the UAE.[16] Although all figures are skewed by poor census-taking procedures and the large numbers of expatriates often included in Gulf population figures, in a general sense this figure reflects the decline of individual wealth in the Gulf states. As the price of oil fell in the 1980s, Gulf citizens saw government subsidies decline and high-paying jobs evaporate. In 1994, for example, only a third of the graduates from Saudi universities could find jobs in the public sector.[17]

At the same time, rapid population growth – some Gulf states have averaged almost four percent annual growth in the last two decades – has created a large and restive youth population.[18] Rapid population growth is destabilizing for several reasons. First, such growth generates tremendous economic pressure. Simply to retain the same levels of wealth on an individual basis, Gulf economies must grow at rates in excess of 10 percent a year. Second, rapid growth exerts pressure on governments to expand education, medical care and social services at breakneck speed. Even when governments have considerable wealth, this rapid pace can lead to bottlenecks and inefficiencies. When government revenues are stagnant or declining – as they are in the Gulf today – rapid population growth creates pressures that regimes are not able to satisfy.

TABLE 1
THE GULF STATES: A PROFILE

| Country | Total population (July 1997) | Non-nationals (July 1997) | Percent of population aged 14 or under (July 1997) | GDP ($ billion 1996) |
|---|---|---|---|---|
| Bahrain | 603,318 | 221,182 | 31 | 7.7 |
| Kuwait | 1,834,269 | 1,381,063 | 33 | 32.5 |
| Oman | 2,264,590 | 400,000 | 46 | 20.8 |
| Qatar | 670,274 | 516,508 | 28 | 11.7 |
| Saudi Arabia | 20,087,965 | 5,164,790 | 43 | 205.6 |
| UAE | 2,262,309 | 1,546,547 | 32 | 72.9 |

Source: CIA *Factbook 1997*, <http://www.odci.gov/cia/publications/factbook>; accessed 30 October 1998. The non-national figure for Oman is drawn from Gause, *Oil Monarchies*, p. 6. Gause's figures are from 1992; however, the number of expatriates in Oman has stayed roughly constant in the period between 1992 and 1997.

A rise in expectations accompanied this decline in wealth. Gulf youths today expect more from government than did their parents, even though they are receiving less. Most Gulf residents under the age of 30 – easily more than two-thirds of the population – have grown up accustomed to a high standard of living. They continue to expect high-quality health care, housing and other services that their parents never knew as children. Furthermore, many received higher degrees, increasing their ostensible qualifications for high-status, high-paying jobs. As a result, many Gulf residents consider jobs involving physical labor unacceptable and believe it is their right to have an undemanding, high-paying, government job.

The profligate royal spending found in the Gulf compounds the resentment created by disappointed expectations. In Bahrain and Saudi Arabia, residents resent the conspicious consumption of many royal family members. Saudi Arabia has perhaps 20,000 princes and princesses, all of whom receive stipends from the Saudi state that range from thousands to millions of dollars a month.[19] Although they may be exaggerated, these income figures are widely accepted by Saudis throughout the Kingdom. Even more troubling, Saudi royal family members encroach increasingly on the private sector. In the 1970s, when skyrocketing oil prices seemed to promise enough wealth for everyone, royal interference was lower and more tolerable. Today, there is less money but there are more princes. Thus, the royal family interferes with business more and more to maintain its standard of living, while businessmen complain there is less money to go round. The Saudi government has shown little inclination to cut down on stipends for princes or building lavish palaces, or to curtail the size of the welfare state.[20] Bahrain's Al Khalifa, while fewer in number, also maintain an extravagant lifestyle and are perceived to interfere regularly in business for their own enrichment.[21]

Economic stagnation has made resentment over corruption and wealth disparities more acute. Although the Gulf states are hardly poor – and some (such as the UAE, Qatar and Kuwait) remain extremely wealthy – the prospects for an ever-rising standard of living are dim. In Saudi Arabia, Oman and Bahrain, the numbers of well-paying, high-status jobs has fallen as the populations have grown. Kuwait, Qatar and the UAE have large enough reserves to satisfy the wants of their populations for decades to come, but only the UAE – and in fact only the Emirate of Dubai – has a significant non-oil economy. Although the decline in the price of oil is largely to blame, opposition groups rightly note that the regimes squander the available resources.[22]

The economic situation in Bahrain is particularly grim. Unlike its oil-rich neighbors, Bahrain has almost no appreciable gas and oil reserves. In recent years, sporadic violence and government corruption have led it to lose its role as the financial center of the Gulf to Dubai, which is seen by many investors as more stable and less corrupt. The result is a steadily declining economy, with younger Bahrainis becoming increasingly disenchanted with the regime. Bahrain's large Shiite community, which is at least 70 percent of the overall population, bears the heaviest load.[23] Unfortunately, the economic outlook for Bahrain is bleak, and resentment is likely to grow. Bahrain has done little to address the core of its problems: corruption; untrained workers; and an over-regulated economy. Violence in Bahrain is worsening an already tenuous economic situation.

## TRADITIONS UNDER ASSAULT

The traditional way of life in the Gulf is under assault from modernization and Westernization. In recent decades, the Gulf has gone from a poor, nomadic society to a wealthy, settled one. Thirty years ago, many citizens of the UAE, Oman, Qatar and Saudi Arabia lived in the desert and had little contact with the outside world. Beginning in the 1970s, these populations settled, began living in modern homes, and came to depend on the state for their livelihoods.

Similarly, technology and international trade have connected the Gulf states to the world at large. Foreign television shows and movies exposed Gulf citizens to jarring new ideas and ways of life, particularly with regard to gender roles, sexuality and family relationships. The spread of new ideas, new forms of communication, urbanization, literacy and other sources of change, disrupted the rhythms of daily life and social hierarchies. Inevitably, some traditional leaders lost their influence and almost all individuals faced the need to change their lifestyles.[24] Not surprisingly, resentment is common. Many establishment voices decry the transformation of their societies. In addition, members of traditional merchant and tribal élite families are often shunted aside and resent the upstart royals who were equals, or at times even inferiors, several generations ago. Even in relatively calm Kuwait, Islamist youths have pressed the government to remove satellite dishes and VCRs to fight spiritual pollution.[25]

## GLORIFYING FIGHTERS AND WRITERS

The presence and glorification of individuals who use violence, particularly Islamic radicals, also has the potential to lead to unrest in the Gulf. For years, stories of brave Palestinian fedayeen, willing to risk their lives to recover Arab and Muslim lands from the Zionist invaders, were nurtured by much of the Arab and Muslim world. The successes of anti-Soviet Mujahidin, the Lebanese Hizballah, and Bosnian Muslim fighters also became the stuff of legend, and the Arab media lionized many fighters.

The intellectual environment of the Gulf is favorable to radical causes. The Arab nationalism of the 1960s and 1970s at times called for the masses to turn against their regimes and the Western powers. Seizing power through violence – that is, a military coup or a bloody revolution – was the model proffered. While Arab nationalism has faded in recent years, radical Islamic sentiments have grown stronger; and, political Islam also endorses violence in politics. Although the particular doctrines of many radicals vary, some influential theologians have in essence declared certain regimes heretical, implying that the faithful should overthrow them by any means possible. Often theologians play a direct role in the formation and direction of radical groups.[26]

## DISCRIMINATION AGAINST SHIITES

In Saudi Arabia and Bahrain, discrimination against Shiite citizens abounds. The Saudis are particularly brutal, restricting the religious practice of the Shiite minority – approximately ten percent of the total population – and banning the import of Shiite religious literature.[27] Moreover, Shiite are taught the ultra-conservative Saudi religious doctrine, which brands their school of Islam heretical. Shiites face rampant employment discrimination and lack political power. Saudi Shiites are regularly arrested and harassed by the security services. Perhaps most importantly, Shiites are stigmatized socially; both the government and much of the Sunni majority sees them as tantamount to apostates.[28]

In Bahrain, Shiites face less encompassing discrimination, but because they are a majority community their exclusion from political power rankles more. Bahraini Shiites are poor while the Al Khalifa, and many leading Sunni families, consume conspicuously. Unemployment exceeds 30 percent among the Shiites, and is possibly significantly higher for young Shiite males.[29]

## RELIGIOUS MILITANCY

Religious militancy is growing in several Gulf states. Perhaps the most dangerous threat to stability in Saudi Arabia comes from Sunni religious militants.[30] Sunni radicals have also threatened the peace in Oman.[31] Although information about these groups is difficult to obtain, some include veterans of the war in Afghanistan. On 13 November 1995, Sunni radicals bombed the US Army Matériel Command's Office of the Program Manager for the Saudi National Guard, killing seven people. Militants may also have been involved in the 1996 attack on Khobar Towers. These radicals are presumed to have a significant following at a local level.[32]

Sunni radicals regularly criticize the Saudi regime as un-Islamic.[33] These radicals oppose the very concept of secular authority and are zealous in their condemnation of any deviation from their view of the true faith. Charges that the regime is corrupt, that it is a puppet of the United States, and that the royal family is not providing for its citizens are common.[34]

The Sunni radical challenge is not new, and the regime is well aware of its serious dimensions. Even before the founding of the Saudi state, ultra-conservative Saudis found fault with the Al Saud. Periodic criticism occurred as the Al Saud consolidated power. Clashes at times turned violent, with the regime using the army against radicals. In November 1979, Sunni radicals seized the Grand Mosque in Mecca during the hajj, claiming that the Al Saud was illegitimate because it transgressed against the puritanical Wahhabi credo of Islam. Saudi security forces stormed the facility, leaving dozens dead.[35]

Past attempts at divide-and-rule have sown the seeds for the latest challenge. In the 1960s and 1970s, the regime encouraged religious radicals to organize, correctly anticipating that this would reduce the influence of the then-dominant school of Arab nationalism, which was often anti-monarchist. In so doing, however, the regime strengthened groups that would later challenge it. The mosques and organizations supported by the regime in the 1960s and 1970s created a network among Sunni radicals, the most radical of whom have additional contacts due to their support for, or participation in, fighting in Afghanistan.

## FOREIGN MEDDLING

In addition to instability generated at home, the Gulf states have faced active meddling by a number of foreign powers and movements. Iran has repeatedly supported militants in the Gulf, and radical groups such as the Lebanese Hizballah also have ties to Gulf militants.

Iran tried to create and organize a Bahraini Hizballah organization before and during the recent spate of violence in the mid-1990s. To this end, the Revolutionary Guard's Al Qods Force trained several Bahrainis studying in Iran as a local leadership cadre and provided the group with limited financial support. Bahraini Hizballah actively spread propoganda against the Al Khalifa, but it was not linked to any actual acts of violence or to the larger demonstrations that occurred.[36] In 1996, Bahrain arrested 44 citizens accused of acting on Iran's behest. Today, Bahraini Hizballah probably retains limited organizational capabilities in Bahrain itself, and it almost certainly has some organizational capacity in Iran.[37]

Iran's efforts to foment unrest was particularly strong in the 1980s. Iranian-backed radicals tried to initiate a coup in Bahrain in 1981. The Iranian-supported Da'wa group, which originated in Iraq but became affiliated with what later became Lebanese Hizballah, carried out six bombing attacks in Kuwait in 1983 with personnel, weapons and explosives smuggled from Iran. Throughout the mid-1980s, Iranian-backed groups attacked US, French, Kuwaiti, Jordanian and other targets associated with perceived backers of Iraq in order to dissuade these govern-ments from supporting Baghdad.[38] Iran has also used political violence to discredit the Saudi regime. Throughout the 1980s, Iran orchestrated demonstrations at the hajj that spilled over into violence; in 1987, hundreds of Iranian pilgrims died in riots in Mecca. In 1989, a bomb planted by a Hizballah offshoot killed one person in Mecca.[39] During this time, the Iranian government repeatedly called for Gulf residents to overthrow their governments.[40]

Egyptian-inspired Arab nationalism posed a similar threat to the Gulf regimes in the 1950s and 1960s. Egyptian President Nasser, lionized throughout the Arab world, made powerful radio broadcasts promoting Arab unity and at times attacking the Gulf regimes, particularly Saudi Arabia. Nasser also spon-sored Saudi exiles, including members of the royal family, in their attempts to overthrow the monarchy. Arab nationalism helped topple regimes in Syria, Iraq and Libya – but the Gulf states weathered the storm.

Organizations calling themselves 'Hizballah' have appeared in Kuwait and Bahrain.[41] It is likely that thousands of loosely-organized Arabs, trained in Afghanistan, also are active in the Gulf seeking to eliminate the US presence from the region and to promote more Islamic political orders.[42]

## STRATEGIES OF CONTROL

Given this grim picture, why is the Gulf so stable? The answer lies in the strategies Gulf governments have used to maintain peace. Ruling families have proven skilled at anticipating, and preventing, political violence before it explodes. The regimes employ mixtures of carrots and sticks, using aggressive security services to monitor, and at times suppress, opposition, while co-opting potential opposition leaders with wealth, jobs and high-status positions. In addition, regime leaders are cunning political chameleons, changing their outside appearance to match the issues of the day, while maintaining their hold on power.

To control unrest, the Gulf states use a combination of six

tools, described below, to counter political violence. Together, these strategies hinder anti-government organization, lessen popular hostility toward the regime, satisfy would-be aggressors abroad and otherwise reduce the immediate potential for political violence.

## Strong Security Services

Gulf security forces, often staffed by foreigners, do not hesitate to suppress dissent.[43] This is particularly evident in the two countries where unrest has proven most common: Saudi Arabia and Bahrain. The Saudi services closely monitor all organizations, political and otherwise, in the Kingdom, including the activities of religious groups. Bahrain's police force and the Bahrain Security and Intelligence Service (BSIS) have arrested and jailed participants in anti-regime demonstrations, and they suppress any gathering of protesters almost immediately. Bahraini opposition members claim that more than 10,000 people have been detained since 1994 and that the security services have injured more than 500 citizens and ransacked mosques and other religious gathering places.[44] The security services in Kuwait, Qatar, Oman and the UAE are less active given the low level of domestic opposition the regimes there face, but they vigilantly monitor the large expatriate worker populations in their countries and guard against foreign-backed political violence.[45] Nor do they hesitate to crack down whenever they perceive a threat. The Omani security forces arrested more than 200 individuals in 1994, only later deciding that not all of them were involved in a suspected anti-government plot.[46] The security services both deter unrest by threatening to punish political activists, and deny groups the ability to function effectively even if they are willing to risk the threat of punishment.

Coercion also shapes the Gulf's intellectual environment and offsets the corrosive influence of outside powers. Security services in several Gulf states monitor intellectuals and spiritual leaders, leading both to avoid strong anti-government statements. Thus, these potential critics, through self-censorship, have become voices of restraint.

All Gulf regimes pay particular attention to foreign-inspired political activity in their countries. Individuals who study or travel abroad, particularly those who travel to Iran or Lebanon, often are monitored by security services. After the Khobar bombing, the Saudi government began scrutinizing the activities of Saudis who had fought in Afghanistan. Thus, foreign government agents – as well as many innocent citizens – are often quickly rounded up if they encourage political activity.[47]

In general, repression is limited to anti-regime political activities. If citizens play by the rules, the regimes do not restrict their activities – though this rule is often broken with regard to Saudi Arabia's Shiite population. Gulf governments carefully monitor potential dissidents, but they seldom beat or imprison them, preferring to bribe them or their families or otherwise press them to conform.[48]

So far, the Gulf states have avoided the indiscriminate use of security forces. The regimes arrest and harass dozens or hundreds, not tens of thousands. Indiscrimate use of security services can backfire and lead peaceful reformers to support violence. When peaceful tactics fail to move the government, and any sort of opposition is prohibited, reformers are apt to lose hope in the political system. As a result, political alienation increases. Indeed, when an opposition organization is destroyed, its members, particularly its leaders, are often forced underground to avoid arrest, imprisonment, or worse. Once underground, they become more dependent on clandestine techniques to survive and may have to seek foreign assistance. This dependence may lead them to turn violent, to extort money from hesitant supporters, to intimidate potential informers, or to keep the goodwill of a foreign sponsor.

## Co-opt Potential Dissidents

Gulf regimes are experts at using largesse to silence critical voices. Critics of all sorts, both secular and religious, are often given jobs or government contracts in exchange for their acquiescence. It is not uncommon for a once-hostile religious leader to receive a lucrative position in exchange for his support, or for an academic critic to become the head of a government-sponsored institute.[49] Continued dissent, however, jeopardizes government patronage. For example, after opposition to the Al Khalifa grew in 1994 and 1995, the government dismissed several important professors and government employees from their jobs.[50]

All Gulf governments are remarkably skilled at using economic control to ensure their hold on power. Oil wealth allows the state to dominate the economy. In Kuwait and Saudi Arabia, perhaps 90 percent of citizens work for the government. In Bahrain, Oman, Qatar and the UAE, large numbers of people hold government positions, often also working in family businesses simultaneously. The Al Sabah work closely with wealthy Shiite families, using their largesse to gain their support, or at least avoid their opposition. Even Saudi Shiites are not completely excluded. Despite rampant discrimination, the Al Saud provided the Shiite community with additional funding after demonstrations in 1979. The ruling families also exercise more subtle forms of financial control. Housing, health care and other important benefits are often provided by the state, giving the regimes even more leverage over their citizens.[51]

To control the media, Gulf governments rely more on subsidies and the threat of suspending publication than on formal censorship. Governments often pay editors and reporters directly and provide funding for publication – all conditional on laudatory coverage of government activities and little coverage of opposition. As a result, papers censor themselves. Moreover, most journalists in the Gulf are expatriates from other Arab countries. Thus, they have little status and are completely dependent on the goodwill of the state to remain in the country.[52]

By co-opting critics, Gulf governments alleviate much of the immediate social tension. Potential critics' aspirations, for example, often are fulfilled on an individual level, with many disaffected leaders receiving a subsidy, official position, or other tokens of wealth and esteem. The regimes build religious centers, medical facilities, and other services to placate disaffected areas, using the promise of assistance to buy off anger.[53]

## Divide-and-Rule

Gulf governments also are adept at creating divisions within communities and fragmenting any political opposition. Saudi Arabia and Kuwait have long worked with Islamic forces against leftist Kuwaitis. In the 1970s, for example, the Al Sabah supported the Social Reform Society, then a non-political Islamic group, against Arab nationalist groups.[54] The Al Khalifa in Bahrain are proven masters at exploiting Sunni suspicion of Shiites. Even many Sunnis who are appalled by the Al Khalifa and favor a return of the National Assembly have gradually withdrawn their support from the reform movement, fearing that Shiites will dominate it. The Al Khalifa play up this division. For example, in 1995 they arrested Shiite activists but let Sunni activists remain free. The Al Khalifa also successfully divided the Shiite community, co-opting wealthier Shiites while cracking down on poorer ones. Thus, Bahrain's opposition is rent by both sectarian and class divisions.[55]


## Ideological Flexibility

Despite their traditional nature, Gulf ruling families are cunning politicians. During the 1950s and 1960s, they often claimed to champion Arab nationalism, sending token support in the fight against Israel and funding revolutionary Palestinian groups. After the 1979 Iranian revolution, Gulf leaders portrayed themselves as pious Muslims, fervent in their support for traditional religion. In the 1990s, the Gulf states have played the civil society game, pretending to increase popular input into decision-making.

Such ideological and practical measures offset a tremendous amount of immediate hostility on the part of Gulf residents. On a practical level, government measures in the name of the cause of the moment exceed any incentives offered by opposition groups. A government-run 'Islamic' clinic, after all, will be more lavish than a private Islamic clinic.

Ideological flexibility offsets outside meddling. After the Iranian revolution, for example, Khomeini and other Iranian clerics lambasted the Gulf monarchs as un-Islamic and corrupt. In response, the Gulf royal families made public shows of piety. The Al Saud, for example, emphasized the title 'Custodian of the Two Holy Places' – the sacred sites of Mecca and Medina, both of which are in Saudi territory – to bolster its credentials.

## Pseudo-Participation

To varying degrees, the Gulf states also use appointed and representative institutions to provide for discussion and input into decision-making. Where these institutions are relatively strong, such as in Kuwait, they demonstrate the accessibility of the regime to the people and reduce the sense of political alienation created by the ruling family's domination of politics. Even where they are weak, they suggest that the ruling families are willing to go outside their own ranks when weighing decisions.[56]

Kuwaitis have more political freedom and a more accountable government than do the citizens of other Gulf states. In recent years, Kuwait's National Assembly has served as a safety valve for social pressure. Parliamentarians investigate corruption and oversee some government spending, thus reducing charges of a lack of accountability so common elsewhere in the Gulf. When individuals seek to change society or to oppose a government policy, they now have a legitimate forum in which to express themselves. This has undercut popular support for both Shiite and Sunni radicals by providing groups with a voice in and some influence over decision making.[57]

Unlike the other Gulf states, Kuwait is home to legal political associations and a vibrant civil society.[58] Informally, there are large numbers of gathering places (*diwaniyyas*) where Kuwaitis regularly come together to discuss politics. Kuwait also retains associations and organizations that play a role in the political debate, and Kuwaiti labor unions claim thousands of members and are an important base for secular forces in Kuwait.[59] Evidence of this comparative vibrancy can be seen in the somewhat tumultuous recent elections in which the government was not always able to have its own way.

In Bahrain, Amir Isa gradually extended the role of an appointed council in response to continued unrest on the island. In the fall of 1992, the Amir appointed a 30-member Consultative Council in response to post-Desert Storm calls for a greater popular voice in decision-making. Initially, the Council was evenly split between Shiites and Sunnis. It had no legislative power, and its initial meetings were not reported in the media. In 1996, after two years of anti-regime protests, the Amir expanded the size of the Council, appointing more Shiite members. He also increased media coverage of Council events.[60]

In Oman, the Sultan created a popular assembly in 1991, and expanded the assembly in 1994. Although the assembly is a forum for debate and can question government ministers, it has no formal powers. All security and foreign policy decisions remain in the Sultan's hands.[61]

Pseudo-legislative forums are particularly weak in Saudi Arabia, Qatar and the UAE. After calls for reform became increasingly loud following the Gulf War, Saudi King Fahd announced in March 1992 that he would appoint a consultative council and, in August 1993, he chose 60 members to serve on it. Council members represent a cross-section of the Saudi élite, including religious officials, merchants, university professors and technocrats. The UAE has a Federal National Council, whose members are appointed by the regime. The Council engages in some debate over government policy, such as over the division of services to various emirates.[62] Shaykh Hamad al-Thani of Qatar has announced that he will hold municipal elections and eventually create an elected national assembly – promises that, even if implemented, will probably allow at best token input into decision-making.[63]

The small size of Kuwait, Bahrain, Qatar and the UAE offsets these weak institutions. To varying degrees, all the Gulf ruling families and élites provide some access to their citizens by holding regular, but informal, meetings where citizens can air complaints, petition for redress of grievances, or otherwise try to influence decision-making. As one Bahraini interlocutor noted: 'I don't worry too much about whether I have a vote or not – after all, I can talk to someone who talks to the ruling family simply by picking up the phone.'[64]

This inclusion undermines violence generated by political alienation. The local gatherings, informal talks and weak legislatures bolster the regimes' claims that they respect, and listen to, the voices of the citizenry. Indeed, the one-to-one contact with the ruling families generates a sense of common identity between the rulers and the ruled. Élites in general have more access to the ruling families and are often chosen to sit on local or national councils. Thus, their resentment of the upstart ruling families is lessened somewhat by the higher status accorded to them.

## Accommodative Diplomacy

The Gulf states try to placate potential foreign adversaries with non-controversial foreign policies and generous aid. In the 1960s and 1970s, the Gulf states lavishly funded radical Palestinian groups and 'front-line' states – Syria, Egypt and Jordan – in their fight against Israel in order to insulate themselves from criticisms that they did little to advance the Arab nation's cause. Indeed, they initiated the oil embargoes of 1967 and 1973 to offset criticism that they were not on the side of Arab nationalism. Similarly, Kuwait in the 1970s bought Soviet arms in an effort to appease Iraq,[65] and all the Gulf leaders have at times made token gestures related to Iran's importance in regional security, even as they have carefully avoided any substantial Iranian role.[66]

Similarly, when political Islam rose, the Gulf states aided some radical Islamist groups and burnished their international credentials to pre-empt any criticism. Saudi Arabia founded the Islamic Conference in the mid-1960s and has kept it strong as a way of demonstrating its commitment to international Islamic causes. In response to the seizure of the Grand Mosque in Mecca by Islamic radicals in 1979, Riyadh tried to become the champion of Islamic opposition to the Soviet Union, which had just invaded Afghanistan.[67] In the 1990s, the Gulf regimes have publicly pressed the West on the peace process and on Bosnia to demonstrate their Islamic solidarity.

## IMPACT ON STABILITY

Although the above six strategies are short-term palliatives, they have helped keep the peace for many years. In and of themselves, the strategies do not stop social modernization, revive stagnant Gulf economies, ease demographic pressure, or reduce corruption. They have, however, raised the popularity of governments and diluted anger about foreign aggression. Perhaps most importantly, regime tools hinder an organized opposition and mitigate the politicizing events that often lead disaffected individuals to become violent.

## CLOUDS ON THE HORIZON

Despite the considerable stability of the Gulf, several problems may arise in the future. Gulf regimes have at best a limited recognition of the need for political and economic reform. Some Gulf leaders often deliberately conflate anti-regime complaints with support for violent radicals. The Al Khalifa, for example, tried to cast all their opponents as Iranian-backed terrorists, even though many of those involved in anti-regime protests had quite modest agendas. Although the ruling families of other states are often more politically astute, Gulf rulers still see their countries as personal fiefdoms rather than a land for all their citizens.

Unrest may increase as government resources shrink in the future. Gulf leaders may become less able to buy off dissent. Already in Bahrain, the Al Khalifa are torn between sating family greed or buying off other Bahraini élites. Oman, while having a less rapacious ruling family, is also running low on revenues and has a large population to satisfy. Such problems will increase over the years as the Gulf populations grow and oil wealth stays constant.

Even if they were willing, Gulf governments face severe constraints in their efforts to implement reform. Barring an unexpected upswing in the oil market, regime revenues are not likely to increase dramatically in the coming years even as local populations grow. Most regime officials are cautious and act only with a large degree of élite consensus, making it hard to respond rapidly to new developments. Sweeping reforms are particularly difficult, as Gulf ruling families depend heavily on tradition to legitimate their rule. Furthermore, most political and economic reforms will directly affect the ruling family's own power and wealth, making it hard for rulers to gain support for such reforms among key decision makers even when they recognize the need for change.[68]

In the short term, reform would also exacerbate the 'expectations gap'. The expectations of the good life remain high. Any belt-tightening or even continued stagnation will only highlight that the government is not fulfilling its expected role. The regimes' lukewarm efforts to cut the social safety net and increase prices closer to market levels have already engendered criticism.[69]

The Gulf regimes' co-optation can contribute to the overall level of discontent. There is often little relationship between acumen and financial success in the Gulf. Individuals who receive poor educations in economically unproductive subjects such as religious studies receive lucrative government positions and have little incentive to train for a modern economy. Similarly, the safety net in general decreases incentives for individuals to take entry-level jobs that require considerable labor.

Gulf groups also are increasingly able to organize overseas. Saudi and Bahraini opposition groups are active in London, spreading anti-regime messages in press releases and via the internet.[70] So far, these organizations have not threatened the security of the Gulf regimes, but they represent a possible chink in their armor.

The Gulf states will find it difficult to control the intellectual environment. Images of brave Palestinian fedayeen or zealous Afghan Mujahidin serve as role models for Gulf youths, leading them to see violence as an acceptable form of political action. Similarly, the intellectual environment in the Gulf is influenced by radical thinkers in Egypt and elsewhere. These intellectuals and theologians often provide an ideological foundation that justifies violent action even when local intellectuals support the regime. Thus anti-Saudi activists make a point of declaring the Al Saud un-Islamic, an attack that compels the faithful to resist the ruling family.

Completely stopping direct foreign intervention will also be difficult if not impossible. For strategic, domestic and ideological reasons, both Iran and Iraq might seek to incite unrest in the Gulf, particularly if they see it as a tool to weaken the US presence on the peninsula. Such support might consist of infiltrating provocateurs into the Gulf, training local radicals, or providing funds to recruit members and buy weapons.

On their own, the Gulf states lack the military means to defend against foreign governments directly. Calling in the United States, however, runs the risk of discrediting the regimes even further with their own peoples. Instead, the Gulf states have used an accommodative foreign policy to try to gain their neighbors' and other radicals' goodwill, a policy which has generally led to peace. However, foreign meddling could increase according to the caprices of foreign powers.

Two countries particularly likely to face trouble are Bahrain and Saudi Arabia. Of all the Gulf states, the Al Khalifa confront the most instability with the fewest resources. Iran has regularly meddled in Bahraini politics, and rampant discrimination, economic woes and political exclusion keep the Shiite community simmering. Riyadh faces a different set of challenges. Although its economic problems are not as extreme as Bahrain's, the coming decades will probably see continued stagnation and declining living standards. Moreover, many Saudis see the Al Saud as too close to Washington. For both these countries, the opposition appears to have too few resources to directly challenge the ruling families. The Al Saud and the Al Khalifa have weathered similar storms in the past, and they will not hesitate to clamp down on any organized dissent.

## FINAL WORDS

The above clouds should not obscure the high level of stability in the Gulf. Regardless of their merits, the Gulf governments must be lauded for their skill in staving off unrest. Despite a host of potentially destabilizing factors, these governments have kept the peace with remarkably few problems. These monarchies may seem bastions of a traditional order, but they are also tremendously innovative, with leaders who know how to foster, as well as accommodate, political change.[71]

The Gulf states' experience suggests lessons for both scholars and policymakers. Some of the lessons, such as the ability to keep the peace by co-opting and repressing activists, might be applied to other turbulent regions. Indeed, when asking why violence breaks out around the globe, we should examine the capacity of states to repress, bribe and pursue other policies to limit internal conflict.

Yet other elements of the Gulf environment are distinct: few governments in the world control wealth as completely as do the Gulf regimes. The region's unusually porous intellectual environment, and the monarchical political systems, also limit comparisons that can be drawn to the Gulf experience. Despite these limits, scholars can learn more about keeping the peace in turbulent environments from regions like the Gulf.

## NOTES

1. For a survey on the causes of conflict, see Stephen R. David, 'Internal War: Causes and Cures', *World Politics* 49 (1997), pp. 552–76; Ted Robert Gurr, *Minorities at Risk: A Global View of Ethnopolitical Conflicts* (Washington, DC: US Institute of Peace Press, 1993); Stephen G. Brush, 'Dynamics of Theory Change in the Social Sciences: Relative Deprivation and Collective Violence', *Journal of Conflict Resolution*, 40, 4 (1996), pp. 523–45; Jeff Goodwin and Theda Skocpol, 'Explaining Revolutions in the Contemporary Third World', *Politics and Society*, 17, 4 (1989), pp. 489–509; Edward N. Muller, *Aggressive Political Participation* (Princeton: Princeton University Press, 1979); Theda Skocpol, *States and Social Revolutions* (Cambridge: Cambridge University Press 1979); Charles Tilly, *From Mobilization to Revolution* (Reading: Addison-Wesley, 1978); Donald Horowitz, *Ethnic Groups in Conflict* (Berkeley: University of California Press, 1985).
2. See Daniel Byman and Stephen Van Evera, 'Why Do They Fight? Hypotheses on the Causes of Contemporary Deadly Conflict', *Security Studies*, 7, 3 (1998), pp. 45–50, for a discussion of democratization and civil conflict. See Edward D. Mansfield and Jack Snyder, 'Democratization and the Danger of War', *International Security*, 20, 1 (1995), pp. 5–38.
3. This essay examines these six states as a similar class of cases, when in fact they differ in many important ways. To name only a few: Bahrain, in contrast

to the other five states, has a majority Shiite population. Saudi Arabia is much larger than its neighbors and, along with Qatar, champions a puritanical form of Sunni Islam. Kuwait has a nascent democracy, while Saudi Arabia remains a narrow autocracy. Bahrain and Oman have relatively little oil or gas; the other four states have enormous reserves. Such differences, of course, have a tremendous impact on the politics of these countries. However, we contend the similarities outweigh the differences and thus they can be analyzed – carefully – together. Further work distinguishing the characteristics of these states would be highly valuable.

4. For much of this time, all the Gulf states except Saudi Arabia were, in essence, British protectorates. Britain withdrew from the area in 1971.

5. For the United States and entire industrialized world, stability in this region is vital. The relative share of Gulf energy is likely to grow in coming decades, as reserves elsewhere decline. Anthony Cordesman, *Bahrain, Oman, Qatar, and the UAE: Challenges of Security* (Boulder, CO: Westview Press, 1997) (hereafter cited as *Challenges of Security*); and Gary G. Sick, 'The Coming Crisis in the Persian Gulf', in Gary Sick and Lawrence G. Potter (eds), *The Persian Gulf at the Millennium: Essays in Politics, Economy, Security, and Religion* (New York: St Martin's Press, 1997), p. 15. (Hereafter cited as 'The Coming Crisis'.)

6. This report does not examine the potential problems stemming from the large number of expatriate workers in the Gulf, which are often more than half the total population in the country.

7. For a review of civil society in the Gulf, see Jill Crystal, 'Civil Society in the Arabian Gulf', in Augustus Richard Norton (ed.), *Civil Society in the Middle East, Vol. II* (New York: E.J. Brill, 1996). (Hereafter cited as *Civil Society*.) Crystal argues that civil society in Kuwait is growing but that it remains limited elsewhere in the region, largely due to government restrictions.

8. 'Bahrain: Alleged Conspiracy used as a Cover for Consolidating Tribal Dictatorship', Bahrain Freedom Movement, 3 June (1996) communiqué.

9. For more on this phenomenon, see Donatella Della Porta, 'Left Wing Terrorism in Italy', in Martha Crenshaw (ed.), *Terrorism in Context* (University Park, PA: The Pennsylvania State University Press, 1995), pp. 105–59.

10. For a fascinating review of this process, see Jill Crystal, *Oil and Politics in the Gulf: Rulers and Merchants in Kuwait and Qatar,* (New York: Cambridge University Press, 1995).

11. Crystal, '*Civil Society*', p. 274; Gregory F. Gause, *Oil Monarchies: Domestic and Security Challenges in the Arab Gulf States* (New York: Council on Foreign Relations Press, 1994), pp. 88–101 (hereafter cited as *Oil Monarchies*); and authors' interviews with US government officials, January and May 1998.

12. Sick and Potter, *Persian Gulf at the Millennium*, p. 21.

13. See, 'Bahrain: Economy goes down as Al Khalifa imports more foreign troops', Bahrain Freedom Movement, 20 February (1997) communiqué.

14. The Movement for Islamic Reform in Arabia, 14 July (1998) communiqué, e-mail version.

15. In 1996, Bahrain depended on oil and gas for some 65 percent of its total revenues. The figures for the UAE, Saudi Arabia, Oman, Qatar and Kuwait are 84 percent, 73 percent, 76 percent, 68 percent and 73 percent, respectively. Sick in Sick and Potter, *Persian Gulf at the Millennium*, p. 17.

16. Cordesman, *Challenges of Security*, p. 7, Table 4.
17. Sick and Potter, *Persian Gulf at the Millennium*, p. 17.
18. In Oman and Saudi Arabia in particular, the youth population is large. In these two countries, over 40 percent of the population was under 14 in 1997. *CIA Factbook 1997*; <http://www.odci.gov/cia/publications/factbook/country-frame.html> Accessed on 19 October (1998).
19. This figure includes all princes and princesses, even those from minor branches of the family, who receive some state money. Simon Henderson provides a similar figure in *After King Fahd: Succession in Saudi Arabia*, Policy Paper 37 (Washington, DC: The Washington Institute, 1994), p. 7, note 1.
20. Authors' interviews with US government officials, February 1998.
21. Authors' interviews with Bahraini government officials and journalists, January 1998.
22. See, for example, 'Your Right to Know, the End of the Deference Era', *CDLR Bulletin*, 30, 13 January 1995, FBIS-NES-95-027, internet version (hereafter cited as *Your Right to Know*). Saudi opposition groups blame the Al Saud for the 'destruction' of the Saudi economy.
23. Historically, in the Gulf states the Sunni sect of Islam has dominated the Shiite sect. The split between the two sects occurred shortly after the Prophet Mohammed's death and concerned the issue of who would lead the Muslim community. Over time, the Shiites have developed their own communal identity that is distinct from that of the mainstream Sunni community. In the Middle East, Shiism is dominant only in Iran. Iraq, Bahrain and Lebanon also have Shiite majorities, but in all three countries the Sunni community dominates political power.
24. The literature on the effects of modernization is vast. A survey would include Samuel Huntington, *Political Order in Changing Societies* (New Haven: Yale University Press, 1968); Karl Deutsch, *Nationalism and Social Communication: An Inquiry into the Foundations of Nationality* (Cambridge, MA: MIT Press, 1966 (1953)); and Walker Connor, 'Nation-Building or Nation-Destroying', *World Politics*, 24 (1972), pp. 319–55.
25. 'Kuwait: Youths Said to be Seizing Satellite Dishes, VCRs', *Cairo Al Akhbar*, 30 January 1997, p. 2. FBIS-NES-97-024.
26. For reviews of Arab nationalism, political Islam and their ability to mobilize, see Fouad Ajami, *The Arab Predicament* (New York: Cambridge University Press, 1991 (1982)); Hamid Dabashi, *Theology of Discontent: The Ideological Foundations of the Islamic Revolution in Iran* (New York: New York University Press, 1993); Jerrold D. Green, *Revolution in Iran: The Politics of Counter-mobilization* (Westport, CT: Praeger, 1982); Emmanual Sivan, *Radical Islam* (New Haven: Yale University Press, 1985); and Jacob M. Landau, *The Politics of Pan-Islam* (Oxford: Clarendon Press, 1994).
27. Michael Collins Dunn, 'Is the Sky Falling? Saudi Arabia's Economic Problems and Political Stability', *Middle East Policy*, 3, 4 (1995), p. 38. (Hereafter cited as *Is the Sky Falling?*)
28. For an overview, see Mamoun Fandy, 'From Confrontation to Creative Resistance: The Shia's Oppositional Discourse in Saudi Arabia', *Critique* (1996), pp. 1–27.
29. Louay Bahry, 'The Opposition in Bahrain: A Bellwether for the Gulf?', *Middle East Policy*, 5, 2 (1997), p. 50 (hereafter cited as *Opposition in Bahrain*); authors'

interviews with US government officials, February 1998. Unemployment information for the Gulf states is difficult to gather, as individuals have no incentive to register as unemployed because they receive no financial benefits for doing so. The 30 percent figure for Bahraini Shiites may be conservative. Munira A. Fakhro, 'The Uprising in Bahrain: An Assessment', in Sick and Potter, *Persian Gulf at the Millenium*, p.177.

30. The Islamic opposition in Saudi Arabia can be divided into four groups, although the boundaries blur in practice. Perhaps the most important, and the least known, groups are the followers of the religious leaders such as Safar al-Hawali and Salma al-Auda, who gained widespread support after the Gulf war. Many of the thousands of Saudis who fought in Afghanistan may support these religious figures or others with a similar agenda. A second group consists of The Committee for the Defense of Legitimate Rights (CDLR), the Movement for Islamic Reform (MIRA), and other groups that operate from overseas but have little following in the Kingdom itself. Saudi Shiites represent a third group, but they are carefully monitored by the Kingdom's security services and appear to have a moderate agenda. The fourth group, which is probably quite small, involves the Committee for Advice and Reform, which is headed by Osama bin Laden, one of the world's most important sponsors of political violence. See Mottahedeh and Fandy, 'The Islamic Movement: The Case for Democratic Inclusion', in Sick and Potter, *Persian Gulf at the Millennium*, pp. 307–8.

31. In 1994, the Omani government arrested over 200 people in connection with a radical Sunni plot to destabilize the country. The government charged 131 of these suspects and tried them in secret; all prisoners were released in November 1995 as part of a general amnesty. Cordesman, *Challenges of Security*, pp. 136–7.

32. In 1994, in Burayda, the regime arrested 157 people who were protesting the arrest of a religious leader. Dunn, *Is the Sky Falling?*, p. 35. Opposition groups claim thousands were arrested – authors' interviews.

33. Even non-violent religious leaders often oppose the regime. In 1992, 107 Saudi religious leaders signed a petition that, among other things, called on the government to implement Islamic law more strictly, reduce corruption and sever relations with non-Islamic countries and the West. It also called for a formal role in government for religious leaders. Anthony Cordesman, *Saudi Arabia: Guarding the Desert Kingdom* (Boulder, CO: Westview Press, 1997), p. 38. (Hereafter cited as *Saudi Arabia*.)

34. Cordesman, *Saudi Arabia*, pp. 35–41; Gause, *Oil Monarchies*, pp. 94–8, 156–60.

35. Nadav Safran, *Saudi Arabia: The Ceaseless Quest for Security* (Ithaca, NY: Cornell University Press, 1988), p. 357. (Hereafter cited as *Saudi Arabia: Security*.)

36. See, 'Bahrain: Defendants' Confessions Reported', Manama WAKH, FBIS-NES-96-110, 5 June (1996); and 'Bahrain: Interior Ministry on Arrest of "Hizballah of Bahrain" Group', Manama WAKH, FBIS-NES-96-107, 3 June (1996).

37. Authors' interviews, conducted in October 1997.

38. John W. Amos II, 'Terrorism in the Middle East: The Diffusion of Violence', in Yonah Alexander (ed.), *Middle East Terrorism: Current Threats and Future*

*Prospects* (New York: G.K. Hall & Co., 1994), p. 154. Later, freeing the terrorists captured in Kuwait became a major goal of terrorists in Lebanon and in Kuwait.

39. Edgar O'Ballance, *Islamic Fundamentalist Terrorism, 1979–1995* (New York: New York University Press, 1997), p. 152.

40. See Phebe Marr, *The Modern History of Iraq* (Boulder, CO: Westview Press, 1985); and Patrick Seale, *The Struggle for Syria* (New Haven: Yale University Press, 1987).

41. Kuwait's Hizballah's true membership size, while unknown, is probably quite small. The term, however, is used indiscriminately to include Shiite ideologues, those with pro-Iran sympathies, and Islamists who oppose a US military presence in the region.

42. Cordesman, *Saudi Arabia*, p. 42; authors' interviews with US government officials, March 1998.

43. For the best theoretical work on the use of security services and other forms of political control to keep the peace – albeit in very different circumstances – see Ian Lustick, 'Stability in Deeply Divided Societies: Consociationalism *versus* Control', *World Politics*, 31, 3 (1979), pp. 325–44.

44. 'Bahrain Uprising: 3 Years Old', Bahrain Freedom Movement e-mail. 4 December (1997).

45. Bahry, *Opposition in Bahrain*, pp. 44–53; Cordesman, *Challenges of Security*, pp. 107–14, 282, 196–201, and 374–6; authors' interviews.

46. Cordesman, *Challenges of Security*, p. 137.

47. Cordesman, *Saudi Arabia*, p. 42; Cordesman, *Challenges of Security*, p. 137.

48. Authors' interviews with US government officials and Gulf citizens, January and February 1998.

49. For examples of co-optation, see *Your Right to Know*.

50. Cordesman, *Challenges of Security*, p. 53; authors' interviews.

51. Shafeeq Ghabra, 'The Islamic Movement in Kuwait', *Middle East Policy*, 5, 2 (1997), pp. 58–72 (hereafter cited as *Islamic Movement in Kuwait*); authors' interviews with US government officials.

52. Cordesman, *Challenges of Security*, pp. 114–15, 198–9, 283, 375.

53. The definitive account of co-optation remains Martin Zonis, *The Political Élite of Iran* (Princeton: Princeton University Press, 1971).

54. Ghabra, *Islamic Movement in Kuwait*, p. 59; authors' interviews with US government officials.

55. Bahry, *Opposition in Bahrain*, pp. 52–4; authors' interviews with Bahraini academics and government officials, January 1998.

56. Authors' interviews with Gulf state officials, October 1997 and January 1998.

57. Authors' interviews with US government officials, September 1998.

58. Article 44 of the Kuwait Constitution only allows the formation of associations, not political parties. After 1991, however, many associations have become in essence political parties. Kuwait has three Islamist associations: The Islamic Constitutional Movement (ICM), the Islamic Popular Alliance (IPA), and the Islamic National Alliance. In the 1996 elections, these forces won (by some counts) 15 seats. All three groups elected several deputies directly affiliated with them. However, six Sunni Islamists who were nominally independent but have ties to both the ICM and the IPA were also elected. Kuwait's secular leaders are grouped together in the Democratic Forum.

59. Shafeeq Ghabra, 'Voluntary Associations in Kuwait: The Foundation of a New System?' *Middle East Journal*, 45, 2 (1991), pp. 199–215.
60. Cordesman, *Challenges of Security*, pp. 52–3; authors' interviews of US government officials, September 1998.
61. Cordesman, *Challenges of Security*, pp. 134–5.
62. Gause, *Oil Monarchies*, p. 116; William A. Rugh, 'What are the Sources of UAE Stability?' *Middle East Policy*, 5, 3 (1997), p. 19.
63. Cordesman, *Challenges of Security*, p. 231.
64. Authors' interviews of Bahraini businessmen, January 1998.
65. Safran, *Saudi Arabia: Security*, p. 269.
66. For example, the Gulf Co-operation Council Secretary General declared: 'Iran is an essential participant with the GCC states in the security of the waters of the Gulf.' As quoted in Gause, *Oil Monarchies*, p. 135.
67. See Safran, *Saudi Arabia: Security*, pp.116–19, 235.
68. An excellent description of these tensions can be found in Gregory F. Gause, 'The Political Economy of National Security in the GCC States', Sick, *Persian Gulf at the Millennium*, pp. 61–84.
69. See, 'On Saudi Events', CDLR Bulletin No. 31.
70. See, for example, the CDLR's website at <http://www.ummah.org.uk/cdlr> or the Bahrain Freedom movement at <http://ourworld.compuserve.com/homepages/Bahrain>.
71. This observation was made about Middle East monarchies in general by Lisa Anderson, 'Absolutism and the Resilience of Monarchy in the Middle East', *Political Science Quarterly*, 106, 1 (1991), p. 3.

# 5

# Kuwait and the Dynamics of Socio-Economic Change*

## SHAFEEQ GHABRA

In transitional societies such as Kuwait, where socio-economic changes are rapid, socio-economic groupings are very important. The nature of tension and coexistence, of power and powerlessness, revolves around the identities of those socio-economic groups. While the groupings are distinct in certain ways, some of their characteristics overlap with those of other groupings, making some individuals members of more than one group. Students, merchants, Shiites, bedouins, women and naturalized Kuwaitis are examples of such overlapping groupings, which have emerged since the 1950s, and have played a role in shaping the policies of the Kuwaiti government.

These various societal groups are relevant to the political process because political organizations and parties in Kuwait have traditionally built their power bases on religious, ethnic and tribal identification and social position. For example, Islamist forces in Kuwait today are trying to take advantage of the bedouins' conservative values and attitudes as well as their feelings of marginalization *vis-à-vis* more established segments of urban society, in order to co-opt them. The situation is similar for the Shiite Community, whose status as a minority makes them the target of Shiite religious groups.

In transitional societies in particular, the relations between the state and society are complex. On the one hand, the state seeks to remain independent from internal social forces; on the

* An earlier version of this study appeared in *Middle East Policy*, 5, 2 (1997).

other, those forces – which include tribe, family, sect, region and class – compete for control over state resources and power. This competition at times becomes intense, and affects the government bureaucracy and the society at large. There is also the possibility that the government may fall under the control of one particular group, the objectives of which may not reflect the needs of a society that is changing so rapidly. If that happens, the policies of the state may no longer contribute to the betterment of society but focus on maintaining the position of the group already in power. Such a scenario could lead to repression and absolutism, or to anarchy and instability. In societies shifting from absolute state to democratic forms of government, or from fragmented societies to more cohesive ones, the act of transition is a major factor affecting the relations between state and society.

## TRANSITION IN THE MIDST OF WEALTH

Since oil began to be exported from the Burqan oil field in Kuwait in 1946, Kuwait's socio-economic and political developments have been intricately linked to its oil industry. By means of its oil wealth, Kuwait developed from a tribal entity into a state, moving from subsistence to state-sponsored welfare, and from a nation of little importance to one of significant power in regional and international affairs. Oil lifted Kuwaiti society out of its traditional economic environment of hunting, pearl-diving and limited trade. The entire way of life of Kuwaitis changed in a very brief period of time. While in 1946 Kuwait's income from oil did not exceed $760,000, by 1971 it had risen to $963 million, and by 1977 $8.9 billion.[1] It is within this context of rapid economic development that new social forces emerged in Kuwait.[2]

With the rapid growth of the oil industry, old societal arrangements began to give way to new ones, with the demise of traditional networks and the vast improvements in living conditions. Through a large-scale redistribution of its oil revenues, Kuwait sponsored a massive education program, created jobs for all its citizens, and provided free health care and modern housing on newly-developed plots of desert. The government offered generous subsidies to replace with new buildings the old mud brick houses in the neighborhoods located in the center of Kuwait City. Many Kuwaitis moved outside the historical walls surrounding Kuwait City, which had symbolized their isolation and fear of the outside world, leaving their traditional neigh-borhoods behind for surrounding desert areas sprouting with modern houses and new quarters. By the late 1960s, the city was surrounded by a belt of developed and inhabited areas that extended many miles from the old walled city.

Under the new welfare state, the number of Kuwaiti citizens tripled between 1957 and 1975, from 113,622 to 470,123.[3] By 1999, the total number of Kuwaiti citizens had reached 786,000, while the number of non-Kuwaiti residents was 1.5 million (total 2.3 million).[4] This last figure included the *biduns*, individuals with no travel documents, of whom there were an estimated 100,000–150,000.[5]

## STUDENTS: SOCIAL PROGRESS AND A CRISIS IN THE MAKING

Education as a force of change, social mobilization and strati-fication has also been a contributing factor to political conflict in Kuwait. While in 1936 there were only 600 boys studying in Kuwait's two schools, by 1945 there were 3,600 boys and girls.[6] In 1990–91, female high school students numbered 26,000, while male students numbered 24,000.[7] By 1993–94, there was a total of 230,000 Kuwaiti students enrolled from kindergarten to high school, or one-third of all Kuwaiti citizens.[8] The numbers of Kuwaiti students had risen to 320,000 by 1999–2000.[9]

The pattern is similar in regard to institutions of higher learning. Kuwait University, established in 1946, opened with 400 male and female students; but by 1995, there were over 16,000 students, and it reached 18,000 in 1998.[10] Today, Kuwait University students are motivated to study in order to forestall the mounting unemployment crisis caused by the graduation of 5,000 high school students each year.[11] The number of students graduating annually from Kuwait University is now approximately 2,000.[12] The total number of those graduating annually from scientific institutions, colleges of higher education and high school – that is, people potentially looking for work – is about 10,000 per year. This figure represents approximately seven percent of the total national labor force in Kuwait.[13]

The 1980 and 1985 censuses showed that more than 60 percent of Kuwaitis were below the age of 19, while one-third was below the age of nine.[14] These numbers foreshadowed the growing demands on the government to create more jobs.[15] Unfortunately, the economy in the 1990s did not grow in proportion to Kuwait's employment needs.[16]

With the end of the oil boom in the late 1980s, new graduates began facing employment difficulties, which were exacerbated by the 1990–91 Gulf War. The expense of liberating Kuwait from Iraqi forces and assisting other Gulf economies led to cuts in social spending and subsequent drops in employment. Kuwait's international investment savings today are slightly under $50 billion.[17] Just prior to 1990, the Kuwaiti government had at its disposal more than $100 billion.[18] In 1996–97, total state income was $9 billion, with a $3 billion budget deficit.[19] One factor behind this shortfall is the government's overspending on welfare programs, and on the employment of more than 90 percent of all working Kuwaitis in the government sector. Salaries and retirement plans alone cost the state $6 billion in 1997, that is, 70 percent of all government income and 50 percent of its budget.[19] While the government is looking toward privatization to help solve some of its economic problems, the question of employment for the coming generation remains a major problem. It is expected that by the early years in the 21st century unemployment will be a source of tension in society.

## MERCHANTS: CONCEPTS OF THE MIDDLE CLASS

Prior to the growth of the oil industry, Kuwait City was composed of three main social groupings. The first was the ruling family, whose role was political and who protected the city from attacks emanating from the desert. It also sought to widen its influence in the desert areas surrounding the city. The second was the merchant group, dominated by a few well-known and influential families who were the core of traditional Kuwaiti society. Revenue from their trade was the basis of the city's income, as the merchants paid taxes to the rulers. The third group consisted of laborers, including many who worked as divers and seamen on ships owned by the merchants.[20]

Any discussion of the socio-economic structure of Kuwait cannot ignore the important role of merchants and their families in the state's development. They were the basis of civil society in Kuwait City prior to the discovery of oil. They traveled during the nineteenth century and first half of the twentieth century to India, Iraq, Persia, Syria and Yemen, and brought back to Kuwait a variety of goods, including wheat, dates, sugar, spices, tea, textiles and other products.[21] They also opened the first school in 1911 and the second in 1920, started the first library in 1920, and produced the first magazine in 1928. The merchants established networks of relations beyond Kuwait, and observed other systems of government, which led them to seek change in their own society. It is they who became the driving force of the reform movement in 1938, which resulted in an elected assembly that sat for six months.[22]

The thriving economic environment that emerged after the discovery of oil enhanced the role of the established merchant families, perpetuating their dominant role in society. Their members became car dealers and contractors, and the younger generations, with modern education, expanded their family businesses internationally. The Kuwaiti Chamber of Commerce, established in 1958, was dominated by the major commercial families.

Also during the 1960s and 1970s, a new group of small business entrepreneurs took advantage of the available opportunities and made fortunes. Thus, to the traditional merchant sector was added this new commercial élite that had become successful after having started essentially from nothing. From this new group emerged government ministers, administrators, members of parliament, and board members of banks and major companies.[23]

After independence in 1961, an urban intellectual élite emerged from among the members of this new commercial élite as well as from the older established families. It was education that united these two groups. The intellectual élite included university professors, teachers, writers, lawyers, doctors and journalists who had been influenced during the 1950s and 1960s by modernist ideas as well as by Arab nationalism. This segment of the middle class was critical of the traditional Kuwaiti political and social systems. Some of its better known political critics were Ahmed Khatib and Jasim al-Qattami of the Arab Nationalism Movement,[24] a movement that has played a crucial role in Kuwait's parliamentary system since independence.

The old and new commercial groups, though not intellectually cohesive, possessed certain distinct urban values that reflected their way of life. After all, Kuwait City was and continues to be, a center of commerce. Kuwaitis began educating women in the 1930s. They provided scholarships for girls and sent them to universities in the West and the Middle East. They were also the first people in the Gulf to employ women in the public and private sectors. Kuwait's urban families saw no contradiction between Islam and economic and social progress. Their forward-looking mentality was the basis for progress in Kuwait until the early 1980s.

In the 1980s, however, a new set of rather rigid values was presented by Islamist groups as the 'true' Islamic values. This narrowed down the intellectual discourse, and much of the positive cultural impact of the commercial group was pushed aside.[25] Although the state's power had increased with the oil boom of the 1970s, it still lived in fear of the criticism and power of the commercial élite and its intellectual supporters. In order to counter its critics, the state looked for new allies and found some beyond the city wall and its environs; namely, the bedouins. The state also felt that the Islamists could become a counter-balance to the commercial élite. This policy caused stagnation and many crises between government and parliament, diminishing the commercial élite and the liberal-oriented culture that represent its breathing space.

## BEDOUINS: THE URBANIZATION MOVEMENT

As modern state structures emerged in Iraq, Kuwait and Saudi Arabia, desert tribes moved across state borders in search of employment. Slowly but surely, these tribes moved from the desert to urban centers and began to settle there. Tribal migration to the urban centers of Kuwait began in the 1950s as a result of that country's rapid educational and economic development. Most migrants settled in Kuwait City, and a few went to other developing urban centers such as Abu-Hulayfa, Ahmadi, Fahahil, Jahra, and Salmiyya. As urbanization increased, Kuwait City expanded beyond its walls, urbanizing the desert as it did so and redefining Kuwaiti citizens to include many of the desert's tribes.

With the availability of employment in Kuwait, hundreds of shanty huts built by newly–settled bedouins rose on the landscape, usually built around oil facilities. According to Hind al-Naqib, whose book covers much of the details of those settlements, the number of inhabitants who settled in those huts in the early 1960s rose to 17,000 annually. Many of the bedouin settlers later found employment in the Kuwaiti military.[26] By 1970, the number of inhabitants in shanties reached 131,000, of which Kuwaitis comprised only 20 percent, the rest being new immigrants coming from Iraq, Saudi Arabia and Syria.[27] During the period 1965–70, approximately 36,000 benefited from limited-income housing built by the government. During this period, 80 percent – or 29,529 – of those naturalized by the government of Kuwait were among this group of recent immigrants.[28]

Of the various tribes that came to Kuwait in the 1950s and early 1960s, 66 percent came from the deserts of Saudi Arabia, while 21 percent came from the desert of Iraq; additionally, some three percent were from the desert of Syria. Not surprisingly, the closer the original tribal area was to Kuwait, the more relatives and acquaintances a tribe had in the capital. There were tribal groupings that had lived in Kuwait prior to 1921 and that had helped build the wall around Kuwait City. Some had even participated in the famous Jahrah battle of 1920 against militants of

the Wahhabi movement in Saudi Arabia. Those historical affiliations were the basis upon which some tribes were later able to
claim Kuwaiti citizenship.[29]

In the 1950s, Kuwait was still a protectorate of Britain and had
no laws governing nationality. People moved freely from other
settlements in the Gulf to Kuwait and vice versa. After independence in 1961, when the Kuwaiti government announced it had
issued a new law on citizenship, chaos ensued as everyone who
could prove a link to the country applied for citizenship. The
percentage of people, most bedouin immigrants, who came
illegally to the country and became Kuwaiti citizens immediately
after arriving was 35 percent.[30] After the discovery of oil,
Kuwaitis felt they had to distinguish themselves from those who
came to the state later. This was done through the granting of
nationality rights, based on having had ancestors in Kuwait
before 1920, that is, when Kuwait was poor and not an attractive
place. Thus, those who could prove that members of their
families had resided in Kuwait before 1920 could claim a first
category citizenship, and only these individuals had the right to
vote and the opportunity to reach high government posts.
Members of the tribes who lived within the present boundaries
of the state of Kuwait, or in the deserts surrounding it, and
became citizens came from the tribes of the 'Adawin, 'Ajman,
'Atayba, 'Awazim, Dawasir, Fudul, Hawajir, Inizah, Khawalid,
Mutayr, Qahtan, Rashayda, Shammar, Subay', Suhul, and
Thufayr.[31] From 1965 to 1981, approximately 220,000 people
became naturalized citizens, the overwhelming majority of them
bedouins.[32] Only a small proportion was given the right to vote
at the time.

The government encouraged naturalized bedouins to work
and settle in Kuwait not simply because they were needed
as manual laborers, but also because the authorities feared
that large numbers of workers from other Arab countries,
seeking job opportunities in Kuwait, would overwhelm the
economy. Policymakers also believed that the traditional
bedouins would be more loyal to the Emirate than the more
radical and urban-oriented Lebanese, Palestinians and Syrians.
They also hoped that government-provided services and

employment opportunities made available to bedouins would lead to electoral support at the polls[33] and, in part, counter the rising opposition from the urban commercial establishment. In order to change the electoral balance of power to the dis-advantage of the urban commercial élite, the Kuwaiti govern-ment gave, in the 1960s and 1970s, a percentage of newly-naturalized bedouins the right to vote. To provide such rights, the documents of several thousand naturalized Kuwaitis had to cover up the fact that they were new immigrants.

Not all tribal groups were naturalized, however. In the 1970s, the issue of the *biduns* began to evolve into a serious problem. The *biduns*, mostly bedouins, migrated to Kuwait from the Gulf area, Iraq and Syria, following their relatives who had previously migrated to Kuwait. Unlike their relatives, however, they arrived too late. Many of them claimed to be from parts of the Kuwaiti desert, but did not have identification papers, or did not renew their original passports or national identity cards – usually Iraqi, Jordanian, Saudi, or Syrian. Instead, they applied for Kuwaiti citizenship, but were denied it. Among the *biduns* was a group of bedouins who were offered naturalized citizenship, but rejected it because it came without voting rights. Over the decades, this group with no documents or citizenship increased to 200,000. Today they number approximately 150,000 in Kuwait, the others having left the country after the 1990 invasion.[34] In 2000, the Kuwaiti government made a concentrated effort to solve the problem by naturalizing segments of the *biduns* and also granting ten years' residency rights to those who show their original papers. The cutting-off point for citizenship for the *biduns* is now arrival in Kuwait before 1965.

With the enormous increase in oil revenues and the con-sequent employment opportunities, Kuwaiti bedouins moved to the neighborhoods and cities newly built by the state to accom-modate them. The urbanization initiated by the state became an attempt at integrating the tribes into the fabric of Kuwaiti society. The bedouins became the backbone of the army, police and security forces.[35]

Despite the fact that the bedouins became integrated into Kuwaiti society, they retained many of their customs and traditions. Patriarchal family values, marriage to more than one wife (for some), tribal cohesion and solidarity, and competition with outsiders and other tribes continued to characterize bedouin life. This did not help social cohesion in Kuwait, as these cultural differences continued to separate bedouins from long-term urbanites. As a result of those differences, urbanites looked down at the bedouins, making them feel politically and socially marginalized, and pushing them to cling more tenaciously to each other and to their tribal values and relations. Furthermore, as migrants continued to settle next to their fellow tribesmen, the areas they inhabited became overpopulated. Over time they also began to suffer from inadequate services.

The tribes that once barely scratched out a living in Kuwait City have become a new center of power. Because of their high birth rates, bedouins today account for an estimated 65 percent of the total population.[36] Although they have become the numerical majority, the former urban majority – in particular, the leading merchant families – have remained the dominant political and economic group, retaining control of the private sector. This new and evolving reality has created social tensions and political contradictions that have contributed to the rise of opposition politics and populism among the bedouin majority.

Despite its rapid development, Kuwait was not able to cope with the large number of bedouins who settled in its cities and towns, or absorb them into its social, legal and political structures. The government's policy vis-à-vis the bedouins focused primarily on short-term gains. Its primary objective was to keep in check the urban commercial opposition. The government's aim was to garner the bedouin vote for its own candidates, particularly in the 1967 elections, in order to counter that of the urban merchants who, according to the government, sought to undermine the position of the Al-Sabah family and supported radical Arab nationalist causes. This tactic further exacerbated the relations between the newly-naturalized bedouins and the old urban power structure.

Furthermore, the government responded positively to tribal loyalties and tribal traditions and values and encouraged them, and in so doing, promoted the conservative social practices of the bedouins. It also closed its eyes to tribal elections that contributed to tribal competition in electoral districts. These elections were unofficial primaries held in tribal areas to determine which two candidates would run in the name of that tribe in the district. Once the two candidates were selected, it was expected that all tribal members would vote for them. The state hoped that this primary process would expand its alliances in society and create a role for it as arbitrator among the tribes. Ideally, the state's new allies were to help it deal with its critics at the polls. As a result of this policy, some segments of the bedouin population came to view their relationship with the state as one based on a quid pro quo: services and employment in return for political and electoral loyalty. It is worth noting that parliament initiated a law preventing tribal election in 1998. In the 1999 elections, tribes that conducted tribal elections were prosecuted and fined. This means that in future elections this phenomenon will take tacit forms.

In other large segments of the bedouin community, national loyalty remained secondary to tribal loyalty. This was demonstrated during the 1990 Iraqi invasion and occupation of Kuwait, when bedouins' priority to protect their tribe meant leaving Kuwait for safer areas. This does not mean that bedouin participation in the Kuwaiti resistance was any less than others, but it indicates that such participation would probably have been higher had the state attempted to incorporate the tribes, over the decades, into an urban nationalist framework that did not separate or create social distance between them and other Kuwaitis. The bedouins, as a whole, still feel quite separate from the rest of Kuwait's urban society. The degree of their feeling of alienation depends on the tribe, its origins, background, number and relationship to the state.

## DESERTIZATION

Ironically, the government became a victim of its own strategy regarding the bedouins. In its attempts to isolate the leftist, nationalist, pan-Arab opposition, it undermined its own legitimacy. It recruited and accepted new groups into its ranks, without adequately acculturating them through education and institution-building. The bedouins were only partially urbanized. Furthermore, 'desertization' of the city took place along a bedouin–urban divide.[37] Desertization here means the transfer of the desert's customs, traditions, beliefs, dress codes and mentality into the city. This process was accelerated when the leadership role of the commercial class and the major urban families was weakened in the 1980s. The urban attitude of openness to the outside world and to modern values was undermined, as was the liberal outlook toward religion and nation-building.

Desertization brings into the urban milieu the ultra-conservative values of the desert, which are often mixed with Islamist populist beliefs. This process destroys those aspects of urban life that allow for the assimilation and acculturation of newcomers and new ideas. It puts the national, civil framework at risk and prevents it from maturing and coalescing. Religious fervor, in addition to creating divisiveness based on values, can also highlight sectarian (Shiite–Sunni) and societal (bedouin–urban) differences involving minutiae, such as style and time of prayer, dress codes, and so on.[38]

With the transformation of the bedouins into a relatively underprivileged sector of Kuwaiti society, lagging behind in services and education, and located – literally and figuratively – on the fringes of the capital, that sector became a base of popular anger and protest. The inability of the bedouins to attain influence, status, or positions compatible with their numbers, made them more susceptible to the call of Islamist groups in Kuwait. The ground was laid for the penetration of Islamic fundamentalism into the tribal areas. The outcome of this development was apparent in the 1992 and 1996 elections to parliament of an Islamist and fundamentalist majority.[39]

The societal divisions in Kuwait are not, however, clear-cut. Many of the barriers between Kuwaitis disappeared as a result of the Iraqi invasion. A renewed sense of Kuwaiti nationalism emerged as well as a belief in equality and justice for all Kuwaitis. The occupation led bedouin and urban families to interact at all levels, including the national level, in the line of duty and under stress. The chance for social, economic and political integration, in conjunction with the strengthening of a coalescing Kuwaiti identity, is still possible. National integration of all sectors of Kuwaiti society is important to everyone concerned with the future of Kuwait.

## THE SHIITES: A MINORITY AT A CROSSROADS

The spread of education among the Shiite community has contributed to the Shiite's positive role in modern Kuwait. Shiites make up 20–30 percent of the population. They are an urban group that migrated to Kuwait in stages from the Arabian Peninsula and from Iran.[40] They were attracted to Kuwait by its rapid development and by employment opportunities. Shiites have since distinguished themselves in both trade and finance. Some Shiite families play pivotal roles in the private sector and have a good deal of financial clout.

In general, Shiites are known for their work ethic, and many are highly educated. It can be argued that the Shiite community's search for an enhanced role in Kuwait's political and economic life has put it in competition with the rest of society. The Iran–Iraq War, that climaxed in the mid-1980s, added to that tension and created antagonism between the Sunni and Shiite components of society. The war also made many Shiites feel outside the pale of Kuwaiti politics because their loyalty to the state was questioned at the time. That some young members of the community became involved in terrorist activities against Kuwaiti installations did not help the situation.[41]

The revolutionary message of Iran's Ayatollah Khomeini had an impact on certain sectors of the Shiite community in Kuwait. The emergence of Iran as the first Shiite theocracy in modern times, appealed to many members of the faith. Iran's revolution created a wave of religious revivalism among them as well as among other sectors of Kuwaiti society. This, in turn, led to the formation of several small Shiite political groups in Kuwait, of which the Islamic National Alliance (INA),[42] formed in 1992, is the most important, with two representatives in the Kuwaiti national assembly. The INA has roots in al-Jam'iyya al-Thaqafiyya, a cultural organization that represented certain sectors of the Shiite community. That organization was closed down after several bombings that occurred in Saudi Arabia in 1979 were linked to some of its members. Differences within the INA over policy and ideology have led to further factionalism in the Shiite community.

Shiites have come a long way in Kuwait and, compared with their co-religionists in other Gulf countries, have attained a certain measure of equality with the Sunni majority, although they still face some discrimination. Unfortunately, though understandably, Sunni fanaticism contributes to Shiite fanaticism and vice versa. Sunni fundamentalists continue to see Shiites as second-class citizens, and Shiite fundamentalists view Sunnis with suspicion. Those negative perceptions are reflected in both personal and business relationships. They also permeate institutional thinking and practices. For example, in the teaching of religion in public schools, a Sunni teacher with a fundamentalist orientation may speak harshly of the Shiite sect and its traditions, rather than address the issue on the basis of the common denominator between different sects of Islam. Much more of the nation's attention needs to be focused on the necessity of teaching and practicing tolerance.

## THE ROLE OF WOMEN IN KUWAITI SOCIETY

Education and employment have transformed women's role in society. The majority of Kuwaiti graduates from institutions of higher education are women; about 70 percent of Kuwait University students, for instance, are female.[43] There are 10,500 female school teachers in contrast to 2,800 male teachers.[44] In 1988, almost 40 percent of the labor force was female – a total of 33,000 women were employed as compared to 84,000 men.[45] A similar ratio holds today. While there are 96,000 Kuwaiti men in government jobs, there are 48,000 Kuwaiti women.[46] Women also have been appointed Rector and Dean of Kuwait University and Assistant Secretary of State. They are an important presence in the professions of law and medicine. That women are moving out of their traditional role in the home and into the work force has brought about significant economic and socio-psychological changes on more than one level.

Many of the older traditions, however, continue to be obstacles to the advancement of women in Kuwait. The progress of women has not changed the views of large segments of society about women's independence and their evolving roles. For example, a sizable minority of men still marry more than one woman. There is also legal discrimination in divorce, and in the application to women of other laws and judicial decisions. In the more conservative sectors of society, the practice remains widespread of the family imposing marriage on their 16-year-old daughter, or obliging female members of their family to wear a veil or a *niqab* – clothing covering the body from head to toe. Many families also interfere in the educational choices of women by allowing them, for instance, to specialize only in education in order to become teachers in segregated women's schools. Furthermore, women are still denied the right to vote, although in many other Muslim countries they are allowed to cast ballots.

What makes the situation of women in Kuwait particularly difficult, despite their visible and largely independent role, is that they have become a target of the Islamist fundamentalist movement. Leaders of the movement tend to be critical of the appearance of women in public and the co-mingling of the sexes in education, sports, performing arts and travel. The fundamentalists hope to weaken the liberal forces of society, thus jeopardizing the civic gains made by women in the 1960s and 1970s.[47]

The state is aware of the pivotal role of women in society, but this awareness needs to be translated into open support for women. To maintain its central commercial position in the region, Kuwait needs the full participation of its women in the work force, and to ensure their participation it must limit the ability of the Islamists to put into place regressive measures affecting women's status and education. The process of privatization and the expansion of modern economic enterprises will not move forward in Kuwait unless women – in whom the state has heavily invested – are fully absorbed into the work force and treated as equals.

The recent emiri decree granting women in Kuwait the right to vote and be elected to office represents a major change. While parliament voted down the emiri decree 32 to 30 the chance of women's suffrage has been enhanced. Women are using new tactics and the debate on women's political rights is intensifying. The year 2000 and beyond will witness new attempts to address the issue.

## NATURALIZED KUWAITIS

As mentioned above, approximately 200,000 Kuwaiti citizens are naturalized, that is, about 30 percent of the current Kuwaiti population. The majority have bedouin backgrounds, and came to Kuwait during the 1950s and 1960s. Other naturalized Kuwaitis came from urban areas in the Gulf, including Iran and Iraq. A minority are of Palestinian or other Arab descent. Naturalized citizens include among their ranks professionals, business contractors, entrepreneurs and other members of the middle class. However, this group is at the bottom of the political ladder, because, until 1994, most naturalized Kuwaitis could not vote nor run for office. The appointment of a naturalized citizen to a senior-level government position required a special dispensation by the government. Not surprisingly, this group has felt marginalized psychologically and politically, yet has tended to overlook this marginalization because of the enormous privileges it has received from the state. In fact, since the 1950s and 1960s, this group has had all the rights the rest of the Kuwaiti population has enjoyed regarding the ownership of property, educational and business opportunities, social welfare, retirement pensions and other benefits.

The reason naturalized citizens were denied full political rights was because, after the infusion of oil money, the state feared the impact that a sudden increase in the number of political participants would have on the political system. This segmentation of society is currently changing, and moving toward greater equality. Time and education have changed the relations between the old guard and new societal forces, and between traditional outlook and the realities of modern Kuwait.

Again, it was the Iraqi invasion that brought to the forefront the issue of social divisions in Kuwait. During the occupation, differences between Kuwaitis were minimized. To the Iraqis, all Kuwaitis were subject to discrimination irrespective of their origins. Resistance groups consisted of Kuwaitis of different backgrounds, including bedouins and urban dwellers, Shiites and Sunnis, old and young, and those Kuwaitis of Iranian, Iraqi, Palestinian and Saudi origin. There were also many *biduns* who participated in the resistance cells. Many of those who survived the experience of occupation established lasting friendships with members of other social and religious groups. Invasion and occupation created a sense of solidarity and eroded social cleavages. The change in attitude was particularly apparent among younger Kuwaitis.

While the older generation of naturalized Kuwaitis did not demand their political rights, the younger generation, born in Kuwait, has begun to seek equality. This generation also feels more strongly that it belongs to Kuwait. The issue of national unity and of voting rights for naturalized citizens was raised during the election campaign of 1992. The government of Kuwait, acquiescing to popular demand, passed a political rights law that was approved by the parliament during the summer of 1994. The new law stated that every male born to a Kuwaiti father, whether that person was naturalized or not, was a Kuwaiti by origin. This meant that he would be granted the rights to vote and to run for office.[48] The same law gave those who were naturalized the right to vote after 20 years – instead of 30 – of having the Kuwaiti citizenship.

Despite this victory, the national identity certificates of the naturalized group continue to show that they are of non-Kuwaiti origin. This has contributed to the opening of new – and old – wounds. This group continues, however, to face discrimination in some areas, as for instance, in promotion to senior government positions. The right of the Ministry of the Interior to withdraw the citizenship of a naturalized Kuwaiti places limits on political rights and activities, and is a constant reminder of the lower and less-than-secure position in society of this group. It is no secret that Kuwait, in the past, has used these laws against certain individuals such as al-Mahri, a Shiite activitist who, during the Iran–Iraq War, was too critical of the government. Human rights reforms in this area, however, are taking place. Ignoring such issues will only create further divisions and tensions and undermine societal cohesion.

## PLURALISM OR CONFLICT?

Because of Kuwait's rapid development, new strata of society have emerged, and new demands and aspirations have been expressed in Kuwaiti society. The developments in education, the media, employment and financial opportunities, govern-ment subsidies and immigration policies have increased social mobility and transformed the society. At the same time, these changes have polarized certain sectors of Kuwaiti society, includ-ing the inevitable clash between the new and the old social forces: city *versus* desert; Shiite *versus* Sunni; old money *versus* new money; men *versus* women.

Over the course of several decades, in the midst of Kuwait's rapid social transformation and as a result of it, tensions developed between the state and various sectors of Kuwaiti society. Opposi-tion to the ruling family grew. Members of the merchant class who identified with Arab nationalism became critical of the Kuwaiti political system. That opposition, however, declined in the 1970s. There was also the Islamist movement, with its desert and conservative orientation, which grew in the 1980s and was also critical of the modernization taking place in Kuwait. The 1979 Iranian Revolution mobilized major sections of the Shiite community, and the Iraqi invasion of Kuwait shook that country's very foundations. Traversing these historical events, the bedouins moved from the desert to the city, from minority to majority, and their values began to overpower the urban values of Kuwaitis in the 1990s.

Despite these stresses and strains, an element of stability and continuity has characterized the relations between state and society in Kuwait. No major rebellion has threatened this stability, and a resiliency and an ability to coalesce in times of crisis has enabled the society to overcome the difficulties of nation-building.

This article has examined the relations between the various strata of Kuwaiti society, and analyzed the causes of division and cohesion in Kuwait. The ability of the government to be a neutral entity capable of providing justice and equal opportunity for all citizens is essential to the state's continuing evolution and maturity. Loyalty to the state and national integration are essential for its development, as a state based on just laws and on respected institutions can only emerge in the context of political equality and expansion of the democratic process.

The elections of July 1999 were unique. They expressed a direction Kuwait might take. The decrees by the Emir of Kuwait on women's electoral rights, protection of intellectual property rights and the right for foreign investors to invest freely in Kuwait without a Kuwaiti partner or guarantor created an intensive debate. Privatization and diversification in the midst of liberalizing the economy and the policy seem to be the future direction of the country. But the process is complex, and traditional beneficiaries of the welfare state oppose it. The present parliament puts pressure on the government to slow down its reform program. In all, the conflict over issues continues, and opposition to change is inherent in both the conservative/liberal divide and the social divisions. What will be hard for Kuwait is to figure out the balance between the long-term well-being of society (reform needs), and the correct political decisions needed for stability and legitimacy.

## NOTES

1. M.W. Khouja and P.G. Sadler, *The Economy of Kuwait: Development and Role in International Finance* (London: Macmillan Press, 1979), pp. 14–26. Today, Kuwait's oil revenues are in excess of $9 billion per year. See *Al-Qabas* (*Kuwaiti Daily*), 3 November (1999), p. 15.
2. See 'Abd al-'Aziz Husayn, *Muhadarat 'an al-Mujtama' al-'Arabi bi al-Kuwayt* [*Lectures on Arab Society in Kuwait*] (Kuwait: Dar Qurtas li al-Nashr wa al-Tawzi', 1994).
3. Ministry of Planning, Kuwait, *Al-Majmu'a al-Ihsa'iyya fi 25 'Aman. 'Adad Khas*

[*The Statistical Report for 25 Years: A Special Issue*] (Kuwait: Ministry of Planning, Central Statistical Administration, 1990), p. 21.

4. Statistics provided by al-Hay'ah al-Ammah Lilma'l Umat al-Madaniyyah. (The general authority for civil information government agency.)

5. *Al-Watan* (Kuwait City), 23 November 1994, p. 1, reported official statistics that stated that 126,000 *biduns* had applied for Kuwaiti citizenship.

6. Ministry of Planning, Kuwait, *Al-Majmu'a al-Ihsa'iyya al-Sanawiyya 1993* [*Annual Statistical Collection 1993, Issue 3*] (Kuwait: Ministry of Planning, Central Statistical Administration, 1994), pp. 259, 266; see also, 'Abd al-'Aziz al-Rushayd, *Tarikh al-Kuwayt* [*History of Kuwait*] (Beirut: Hayat Bookshop Press, n.d.), pp. 295–6 (hereafter cited as *Tarikh al-Kuwayt*).

7. Ministry of Planning, Kuwait, *Al-Ihsa'at al-Ijtima'iyya 1990–91* [*Sociological Statistics, 1990–91, Issue 20*] (Kuwait: Ministry of Planning, Central Statistical Administration, 1994), p. 11.

8. Ministry of Planning, Kuwait, *Al-Majmu'a al-Ihsa'iyya al-Sanawiyya, 1993*, pp. 259, 266; see also, Al-Rushayd, *Tarikh al-Kuwayt*, pp. 295–6.

9. Provided to the author by the Ministry of Education, *Ministry of Education Statistics, 1999–2000*.

10. Annual Statistical Collection, Ministry of Planning, 1999–2000.

11. Ministry of Planning, Kuwait, *Al-Ihsa'at al-Ijtima'iyya*, p. 11.

12. Ministry of Planning, Kuwait, *Al-Majmu'a al-ihsa'iyya al-Sanawiyya*, p. 287.

13. Higher Council of Planning, Kuwait, *Bada'il li-Siyasat al-Tawzif* [*Alternatives to the Employment Policy*] (Kuwait: Higher Council of Planning, Economic Department, 1996), p. 12.

14. Ministry of Planning, Kuwait, *Al-Majmu'a al-Ihsa'iyya al-Sanawiyya*, p. 277.

15. Ministry of Planning, Kuwait, *Al-Majmu'a al-ihsa'iyya al-Sanawiyya fi 25 'Aman*, pp. 11, 14.

16. 'Amir al-Tamimi, 'Al-'Ajz' [The Deficit], in *Al-Zaman* [Kuwait City], 5 March 1995, p. 6 (hereafter cited as *Al-'Ajz*).

17. There are no official figures to confirm this amount. However, this figure has been used by members of parliament and economic experts over the last three years.

18. The government did not publish these figures, but did present much of the economic outlook to the parliament in a closed session in January 1996.

19. Ministry of Finance statement, and 1996–97 balance of payment estimates in *Al-Qabas*, 24 July 1996, p. 19; see also al-Tamimi, *Al-'Ajz*, p. 7.

20. Hind Ahmad al-Naqib, *Al-Tanmiyya al-Ijtima'iyya wa Atharuha fi Tawtin al-Badu fi al-Kuwayt* [*Social Development and its Impact on the Settlement of Bedouins in Kuwait*] (Kuwait: That al-Salasil Press, 1981), p. 151 (hereafter cited as *Al-Tanmiyya al-Ijtima'iyya*).

21. Al-Rushayd, *Tarikh al-Kuwayt*, pp. 297, 315–33, 366–76.

22. Khalid Sulayman al-Adsani, *Nisf 'Am li al-Hukm al-Niyabi fi al-Kuwayt* [*Half a Year of Parliamentary Rule in Kuwait*] (Kuwait: n.p., 1947); Najat 'Abd al-Qadir al-Jasim, *Al-Tatawwur al-Siyasi wa al-Iqtisadi fi al-Kuwayt, 1914–1939* [*Political and Economic Development in Kuwait, 1914–1939*] (Kuwait: n.p., 1973), pp. 205–51.

23. Kamal al-Munifi, *Al-Hukumat al-Kuwaytiyya* [*Kuwaiti Governments*] (Kuwait: Sharikat al-Ruba'an li al-Nashr, 1985), pp. 25–33.

24. Ahmad Abdallah Saad Baz, 'Political Elite and Political Development in

Kuwait' (PhD dissertation, George Washington University, 1991), pp. 105–7. (Hereafter cited as *Political Elite*.)

25. See Muhammad Jabir al-Ansari, *Takwin al-'Arab al-Siyassi wa Maghza al-Dawla al-Qutriyya: Madkhal ila I'adat Fihm al-Waqi' al-'Arabi* [*The Political Making of the Arabs and the Significance of the State: An Understanding of the Arab Reality*] (Beirut: Center for Arab Unity Studies, 1994) (hereafter cited as *Takwin al-'Arab al-Siyassi*).

26. Al-Naqib, *Al-Tanmiyya al-Ijtima'iyya*, pp. 188–9.

27. Ibid., p. 188.

28. Khaldun al-Naqib, 'Al-Dimuqratiyya wa al-Intikhabat: Nahwa Ta'miq al-Tajruba al-Dimuqratiyya fi al-Kuwayt' [Democracy and Elections: The Deepening of the Democratic Experience in Kuwait], *Al-Qabas*, 15 February 1992, p. 17 (hereafter cited as 'Al-Dimuqratiyya wa al-Intikhabat').

29. Al-Naqib, *Al-Tanmiyya al-Ijtima'iyya*, p. 234.

30. Ibid., p. 235.

31. Ibid., p. 219.

32. Al-Naqib, 'Al-Dimuqratiyya wa al-Intikhabat', p. 17.

33. Baz, *Political Elite*, p. 104.

34. According to Kuwaiti government files, registered *biduns* number 120,000. An equal number moved from Kuwait with the Iraqi forces during Kuwait's liberation in 1991. Most of them were of Iraqi descent. See Human Rights Watch/Middle East, *The Buduns of Kuwait* (New York: Human Rights Watch, 1995).

35. One can make a case that the Sabahs and the 'Utubs, who originally migrated from Najd to Kuwait in the eighteenth century, were originally bedouins. It was the process of urbanization that made them, after several generations, a settled urban group that lost its bedouin characteristics in both style of living and worldview.

36. The electoral files confirm that those voters living in the densely populated districts known as the Outer Areas are a tribal constituency. It is the population of these areas that makes up the new majority. In addition to migration to the city, bedouins have much higher birth rates than urban families, and therefore, it is not surprising that their numbers have increased more rapidly than that of their urban counterparts. See Khaldun al-Naqib, 'Tahlil al-Mu'ashirat al-Siyasiyya wa al-Ihsa'iyya li Nata'ij Intikhabat October 1992' [Analysis of the Political and Statistical Results of the Elections of October 1992], *Al-Qabas*, 15 November 1992, p. 36.

37. 'Desertization' is a term used by Muhammad Jabir al-Ansari in *Takwin al-'Arab al-Siyassi*, pp. 56–7.

38. See *Al-Qabas*, 6 March 1993, for the story of a Shiite child denied by a teacher the right to pray in school with other children because of differences in the manner of prayer.

39. Shafeeq Ghabra, 'Democratization in Kuwait, 1993', *Middle East Policy*, III, 1 (1994), pp. 102–19. Two Sunni Islamist political groups have emerged in Kuwait since 1992, and slowly have gained important footholds in bedouin areas. The Islamic Constitutional Movement (ICM) has its roots in the Muslim Brothers in Kuwait and in al-Islah al-Ijtima'i (Social Reform), an influential Islamic group that has been gaining strength since the 1970s. The Islamic Popular Alliance, better known as al-Salaf (Ancestral), has roots in

the Jam'iyyat Ihya' al-Turath (Society for the Revival of Islamic Tradition). This group, which has been attracting followers since the 1980s, is more literal than the ICM in its interpretation of Islam.

40. James Bill, 'Resurgent Islam in the Persian Gulf', *Foreign Affairs* 63, 1 (1984), p. 120.

41. At the height of the Iran–Iraq War, and in particular between 1982 and 1986, numerous terrorists attacks occurred in Kuwait. Some were committed by external Shiite groups and others by Kuwaiti Shiite groups. The most famous of these attacks was an attempt to assassinate the Emir of Kuwait in 1985.

42. The INA, before it split into more than one grouping, was faithful to the Islamic ideology expressed by Iran. It has, however, committed itself to peaceful opposition and participated in elections in 1992. INA representatives usually hold two or three seats in the Kuwaiti parliament.

43. Kuwaiti University Student Data Base, Center of Computer Services, Kuwait University, 20 August 1996.

44. Ministry of Planning, Kuwait, *Al-Majmu'a al-Ihsa'iyya al-Sanawiyya, 1993*, p. 266.

45. Ibid., p. 81.

46. *Al-Watan*, 13 May 1997, p. 7.

47. For a unique and updated study on Kuwait women, see Haya Mughni, *Women in Kuwait: The Politics of Gender* (London: Saqi Books, 1993).

48. See Law 44 in *Al-Kuwayt al-Yawm* (Kuwait City), 17 July 1994.

# 6

# Saudi Arabia: Elements of Instability within Stability

## DARYL CHAMPION

To outsiders, Saudi Arabia appears calm and stable. Western governments friendly to the Saudi dynasty are keen to promote the image of a firmly entrenched and legitimate regime, as of course, is the Saudi royal family itself.[1] How accurate are these appearances?

It appears that all in the Kingdom is not as stable as the image-makers would have us believe. The dramatic social and economic developments of recent years are now visibly opening gaps between generations and enlarging those that already exist among economic classes. A poorly-performing economy and a rising – albeit hidden – level of youth unemployment also throws up serious challenges to the regime. Adding to these concerns is the fact that the political development permitted by the absolute monarchy lags far behind the unsteady social and economic changes that are already taking place.

An era of very difficult economic, social and political management has dawned for the Al Saud; however, a number of domestic reforms aiming to redress some of the problems have been initiated. For example, the regime is attempting to restructure the Saudi economy, the system of higher education, and workforce. It also maintains strict control over the country's determined – albeit fragmented and now greatly diminished – political opposition.

Although Saudi Arabia may face a rocky time in the coming years, it is unlikely that the world will witness another Iranian-style revolution in the Kingdom anytime soon.

## CHALLENGES TO THE AL SAUD DYNASTY'S SURVIVAL

For a time in the mid-1990s, Al Saud rule appeared headed for a period of acute instability. Financial crisis threatened the country in the 1993–94 period, and 1995 ushered in a cycle of violence. The August 1995 execution of an opposition activist in the Kingdom, for example, was followed in November by the bombing of a US-run Saudi National Guard installation in Riyadh. Less than a year later, the beheading of four Saudis on 31 May 1996 for the Riyadh bombing was again followed by an opposition attack. This time, a much more devastating bomb hit US military barracks in Khobar, near the eastern city of Dahran, on 25 June. Nineteen American servicemen were killed.

Meanwhile, the regime was increasingly repressing opposition movements that had surfaced since the 1990 Gulf crisis. A new focus of opposition shifted to the Committee for the Defense of Legitimate Rights (CDLR), established in London in 1994, adding another dimension and renewed vigor to political dissent both inside and outside the Kingdom.[2] As the CDLR endeavored to create some kind of structure for – non-violent – dissent, the organization became a two-way conduit for regime-damaging socio-political and economic information moving into and out of the Kingdom by way of fax, e-mail, and toll-free telephone numbers. CDLR propaganda activity was prolific, and became a source of agitation for both the Saudis and the British establishment.[3]

Responding to heavy pressure from the Saudi government, the British Home Office in November 1994 formally denied political asylum to the high-profile CDLR dissident, Muhammad al-Mas'ari, signaling that he would be deported to the country of his escape route: Yemen. In March 1995, the tides turned in Mas'ari's favor when the British Immigration Appeals Tribunal upheld Mas'ari's appeal. However, continued pressure from the Saudi government and British arms manufacturers led the Home Office to virtually circumvent British law by ignoring the Tribunal's decision and attempt once again to deport Mas'ari, this time to the Caribbean island-state of Dominica. The case received wide publicity from early January to April 1996 and developed into a near scandal in which: 'the symbiotic relation-ship between the [British] arms firms and various branches of [the British] government' was exposed.[4] This second depor-tation attempt also failed on appeal and resulted in severe embarrassment for the Saudi and British governments. Back in Saudi Arabia, CDLR-associated campaigners had become a target for repression in what appeared to be a tightening cycle of violence leading up to the November 1995 Riyadh bombing in which dissidents were arrested and even executed.[5]

By 1997, however, it was clear that the political opposition had been effectively silenced – domestically, through repression, and internationally, through various means of pressure in collu-sion with Western governments, agencies and multinational interests, as demonstrated by the two-year string of affairs surrounding the CDLR and Mas'ari in the UK. Saudi Arabia had regained some financial composure and there were no more headline-grabbing acts of sabotage.

Various factors contributed to the dynasty's recovery, which are likely to remain important lynchpins of the regime into the fore-seeable future. First of all, time has played its part in establishing the Al Saud as traditional rulers in a land where tradition is revered. The religious aspect of Al Saud legitimacy is also a well-entrenched tradition that has been bolstered over the last 75 years through custodianship of the holy sites of Mecca and Madina, and through the co-optation of the state's conservative religious establishment. The Al Saud's religious status is taken seriously by the regime; it is an important pillar of their rule, although not as central as it once was to regime survivability.[6] Second, oil wealth has enabled the Al Saud to be patriarchs and patrons to their subjects – a respected role in Arabian tradition – basically purchasing a great deal of domestic socio-political stability. Third, the government employs an active internal security service, *al-Mabahith al-'Amma* – 'General Investigations' – together with a policy of harsh punishment for dissenters and reconciliation with repentants that keeps opponents in check. Fourth, the regime skillfully tracks and responds to the nuances of public opinion. Last, political opposition in the Kingdom is fragmented, meaning that there is no concrete alternative to the Al Saud.[7]

Thus a relative calm descended over the Kingdom during the course of 1997, although the emphasis should be on 'relative'. The dynasty that molded the modern state and gave it its name has entered a period of troubled change. But whatever challenges the regime faces – and it will face inter-related socio-economic problems of increasing seriousness, especially, in the years ahead – the ultimate viability of the monarchy should not be threatened.

## INSTABILITY AND CHANGE IN THE
## SOCIO-ECONOMIC SPHERE

The Saudi economy is not as healthy today as it once was. The heady oil boom of the 1970s and early 1980s is truly a phenomenon of the past. Yet, despite attempts at diversification, the Kingdom's economy is still dependent on oil. As a clear consequence, Saudi revenues are prone to extreme fluctuations, and fiscal planning remains vulnerable to forces largely outside the government's control. The result has been that, since the oil price crash of 1986 which more than halved oil revenues from around $42.6 billion in 1985 to around $20 billion in 1987, the Saudi economy has been struggling.[8]

The era of high budget deficits actually began in 1983 with the onset of recession, and continued into the 1990s. In addition to weak oil prices, the direct and indirect expenses of ten years of war – Iran–Iraq and Gulf – both financially costly to Saudi Arabia, and of military and security expenditures in general, took their toll on the Saudi economy.[9] It is no secret that world financial institutions, at least during the early 1990s, have been concerned and have: 'raised questions about how deep the Saudi official (as opposed to royal) pockets really are.'[10]

Gloomy budget forecasts were eclipsed by actual deficits totaling 19 percent of gross domestic product (GDP) in 1991, nearly 15 percent in 1992, and still more than 14 percent in 1993. Only in 1994 did the deficit shrink below 10 percent – to 8 percent – taking on the dimension of a relatively positive achievement.[11] In describing Saudi economic affairs at the

time, many commentators and scholars have routinely employed phrases such as 'economically enfeebled', 'fragility of the
economy', and 'economic crisis of the 1980s and 1990s'.[12]

The situation improved from 1994, and the 1995–97 period
saw deficits of five percent of GDP or less.[13] In fact, in 1995, many
commentators were implying that the Kingdom's economic
woes were over. Former Saudi American Bank (SAMBA) chief
economist Kevin Taecker, for example, regards the Saudi financial scare of the early 1990s as: 'silliness' and 'uninformed'. His
view is shared by the director of the Oxford Institute for Energy
Studies, Robert Mabro, who believes the scare: 'was exaggerated
from outside.'[14] In a public effort to allay fears, King Fahd said
to his newly-appointed cabinet in August 1995: 'We have succeeded in dealing with the (financial) crisis',[15] in effect acknow-
ledging that there was, at least, a widespread perception of
turmoil.

Strong oil prices contributed to the country's economic
improvement in 1996 and 1997, but 1998 saw a return to the
precipice of economic disaster. Oil prices dropped and the budget deficit once again climbed to 8.2 percent of GDP.[16] In a now-
familiar fiscal pattern, 1999–2000 extended the promise of
financial poise with dramatically rising prices, but the Kingdom
delivered its 17th consecutive budget deficit in 1999.[17] The goal
of the sixth Saudi Five-Year Development Plan was to eliminate
the government deficit by the year 2000: this was always an
unlikely objective. In fact, Riyadh is projected to run deficits of
more than three percent of GDP well into the next century.[18]

This pendulum-like vulnerability is obviously not conducive
to sound national management in any sphere of the economy
or society, and it is precisely what many influential economists
and organizations, including the International Monetary Fund
(IMF), would like to see reduced through the acceleration of
long-delayed strategic economic reforms.

Officially, the oil sector accounts for about one-third of total
Saudi GDP, but the extent of its importance to the Saudi
economy is understated by the GDP figures: oil still accounts for
approximately 90 percent of export earnings and 75 percent of
budget revenues.[19] The inherent vulnerability of heavily relying

on one financial resource is accentuated by poor planning practices, mismanagement and waste. Saudi Arabia suffers from a
bloated, inefficient and undeveloped bureaucracy where favoritism is common. It also features opaque government–business
links. In addition, dubious business practices are widespread.
Consider the existence of commission farming, whereby Saudi
nationals acting as agents and brokers for large, foreign-sourced
contracts – typically for construction and infrastructure projects
and armaments purchases – charge commissions as a percentage
of total contract value, thus adding significantly to the cost of
such contracts for the Saudi state. This state of affairs is eroding
the regime's political and religious legitimacy both domestically
and throughout the Muslim world and the global economic
community.[20]

The country's limping economy features prominently in
stories told by Arab and non-Arab expatriate workers in Saudi
Arabia. Some expatriates were even preparing to return to their
homes in Pakistan and Bangladesh because they were no longer
earning enough to make their sacrifices worthwhile. Others
mentioned that friends working on construction sites had not
been paid for up to six months, and most spoke of a noticeable,
conservative change in the attitudes and spending habits of
Saudi nationals.[21]

Although the outlook improved during 1999 and 2000, a
cloud remains over the future of the Saudi economy. If public
spending continues to be reined in, socio-economic sore points
such as unemployment – especially youth unemployment –
falling standards of living and increasing poverty will only be
exacerbated, threatening the government's role as patron. In
conjunction with the post-Gulf War's restless political climate,
a reduction in government largesse may have further unpalatable political ramifications. It is a scenario that is not unlikely
and would inevitably re-focus attention on the ability of the Al
Saud to maintain stability.[22]

It should be noted that despite serious difficulties, the Saudi
economy is hardly on the verge of collapse. But, the social implications of a weakened economy will accentuate problems.
Although some believe that: 'Gulf youths today expect more

from government than did their parents,'[23] the evidence now coming from Saudi Arabia suggests otherwise. More realistic socio-economic expectations appear to be gradually gaining prevalence, alongside a growing recognition that the government cannot, and perhaps even should not, present a career and a comfortable lifestyle on a platter.[24]

The volatility of the link between high socio-economic expectations and the government's declining ability to deliver is decreasing. Inflated expectations in and of themselves are unlikely to contribute to future socio-political instability, unlike the more tangible, if longer-term, consequences of economic decline such as falling living standards and rising unemployment. Paradoxically, socio-economic and political expectations may enjoy an inverse relationship: accepting lower socio-economic expectations may prompt demands for political development and greater political participation, reversing the social contract which has been in place since the 1973–74 oil boom whereby the Al Saud support a generous welfare state in return for political quiescence.[25]

One area of potential social, and perhaps political, liability is the combination of a high rate of population growth – estimated to average around 4.3 percent annually for the period 1980–97[26] – and high unemployment. Such rapid population growth is destabilizing because of the tremendous economic pressure it generates: it automatically decreases per capita wealth in the absence of extraordinarily high economic growth, and strains infrastructure and social services.[27]

Regarding unemployment, a senior figure in the Saudi Chamber of Commerce and Industry has stated that: 'nobody has accurate figures,'[28] although figures ranging from 10 to 25 percent have been widely floated.[29] In fact, the Sixth Development Plan (1995–2000) states that the: 'participation rate [of Saudi nationals in the domestic labor market in the mid-1990s] ... is at the internationally low level of only 30.2 percent.'[30]

This situation is not helped by the fact that expatriates comprise approximately 27.3 percent of the Kingdom's population – 4.62 million people of a total of 16.92 million, according to the 1992 census.[31] An optimistic view of the employment situation interprets the 'Saudiization' of the workforce as equivalent to 'de-expatriatization'. According to this view, employment for approximately 2.5 million young Saudi nationals already exists, excluding unpalatable menial jobs.[32] The government has indeed initiated a Saudiization plan that necessitates radically revamping education and training programs – along with some social engineering – to ensure that young Saudi nationals are technically qualified, and willing, to take jobs currently filled by foreign workers.[33] The plan, originating in the early 1980s, has encountered enormous problems, including a 'hierarchical' view of jobs – that is, the *mudir* syndrome,[34] which dictates that nothing less than a position of authority, status and respect is honorable – and an uneven application of the policy among Saudi and non-Saudi companies.[35] Saudiization faces an additional obstacle: '... [e]stimates indicate that 27.9 percent of new labor market entrants during the Sixth Plan period will be dropouts from elementary level and adult vocational training programs.'[36]

Saudi efforts to counter these problems are not expected to reap the desired economic and social benefits for at least another ten years.[37] Ultimately, according to Saud al-Shubaily of the Saudi Chamber of Commerce and Industry: 'the demand for jobs is high, the key is qualifications,' and this is why the Saudi education system is now attempting to channel young nationals away from universities toward technical training.[38] Restructuring the workforce is related to the broader economic strategy of decreasing reliance on the petroleum sector by diversifying the economy. The Saudi industrialization process is currently oriented to replacing imports and has enjoyed some degree of success. The longer-term aim is to gear Saudi industry to export, a necessity due to a 'shortage of local markets, which are limited, and excess capacity.' Saudi products are now being made to international standards.[39]

Slowly, cautiously, if not even half-heartedly, the Saudis have also initiated a privatization policy.[40] At stake are monolithic and massively profitable concerns such as the Saudi Basic Industries Corporation (SABIC), the holding company for Saudi Arabia's principal petrochemical concerns. Privatization could be a mixed bag for the Saudis, as noted in one specialist publication:

> Privatization could throw up ... unexpected problems. Such a project entails the creation of a new legal frame-work, transparency of ownership and public accountability. Such habits may prove hard to acquire for the family which not only rules Saudi Arabia but owns it as well. Loosening financial control without loosening its absolute political authority could prove a delicate exercise.[41]

Although these adjustments may prove delicate, the Saudis appear determined to embrace them – at least to a minimal extent – with the aim of joining the World Trade Organization (WTO) by the year 2002. Senior Saudi industrial and commercial officials admit that WTO membership will require changes to the Kingdom's economy and trade practices and regulations, a process that is by no means guaranteed to go smoothly.[42] For example, in May 1997, after the third round of negotiations on Saudi Arabia's application to join the WTO, trade diplomats said the Kingdom: 'must do more to present detailed offers on market access.'[43] Other predictions are proving prophetic:

> Implementation of wide-ranging reforms is still expected to be a long process ... as many of the reforms required for WTO membership, including measures such as easing restrictive practices in the banking sector, are likely to be strongly resisted by vested interests in the Kingdom.[44]

Privatization, WTO membership, and opening the Saudi economy to free trade and unhindered foreign investment and capital flows, are all aspects of economic globalization, the benefits of which the Saudis do not want to be deprived. Indeed, the Gulf Co-operation Council (GCC) countries are looking to form a common market, a process that is receiving vigorous encouragement from the United States.[45] Such economic reforms necessitate greater transparency, and issues of transparency, corruption, 'good governance,' and even social and political reform, are now priorities on the agendas of the IMF, WTO, World Bank and the Organization for Economic Co-operation and Development (OECD).[46] Saudi policymakers appear quite prepared to discuss the Kingdom's economic challenges, but other hurdles exist. According to the emerging trends of globalization, the necessary and quite substantial economic reforms that are required in many developing countries cannot be sustained without accompanying political and social reforms. The Saudis are trying to pick and choose what aspects of globalization they accept and reject in order to enjoy economic benefits without having to implement any major reforms.

## INTERNAL SECURITY AND THE IMPORTANCE OF PUBLIC OPINION

In the absence of scientific mechanisms for gauging public opinion, such as surveys and polls, the royal family utilizes informal networks of informers: 'with links to academics, businessmen, tribesmen and other sections of the community' to keep on top of grassroots sentiments.[47] The state security apparatus is also involved in monitoring public opinion, with a special branch of the professional intelligence service dedicated to gathering information on any societal item that may have political connotations, including: 'whatever is said in general discourse including ... jokes about the king and [senior] princes.'[48]

Keeping a finger on the pulse of the Saudi population has strengthened the regime. Consider the Saudi response to the February 1998 Iraq crisis over UN weapons inspections, a forerunner to the standoff that provoked Operation Desert Fox on 17 December 1998, the heaviest military assault against Iraq since the 1991 Gulf War. During the February crisis, the Saudi government – aware that most Saudis and Arabs from other countries opposed US military strikes – refused to permit the United States to launch strikes from Saudi bases.

However, within these broad mechanisms designed to bolster stability exist the seeds of potential instability. In a society where privacy, patron–client relations and the tradition of informal, personal links are so highly valued, the reliability of informants can be compromised. For example, by wishing to curry favor with their masters, many informants make sure to deliver only good news. Additionally, many informants are denied access to certain circles of Saudi society, both because they are known to be linked to the regime and because their status – sometimes even official to the point of being on the government payroll – as a companion/friend/dependent of a prince (*khawi*), is shunned as being lowly and of dubious personal honor. Perceptions of honor and shame, the deference paid to senior royals, and the patron–client relations that exist even between royalty and professional agents of the state tend to result in intelligence of widely varying accuracy and utility. The combination of informal networks of informers and professional intelligence services, however, creates another efficient mechanism of regime security in society: that of an insidious intimidation and fear.[49]

The Saudi regime is also not known for its light treatment of those who challenge its social or political norms. Amnesty International (AI) has noted a steady rise in the number of executions since the 1991 Gulf War.[50] Although the number of executions in the Kingdom can vary considerably from year to year, 1995 saw more than 140 people executed – the highest number in recent years.[51] Apart from public executions, detention and arrest are common, particularly in socio-political cases. For example, 1994 saw unprecedented public displays of support for young, dissenting *ulama* (religious scholars) and dissatisfaction with the regime – events that precipitated a series of massive security crackdowns and resulted in thousands of arrests.[52]

Alleged criminals are the victims of most executions carried out in the Kingdom. However, a significant milestone in the history of Saudi dissent and punishment was passed on 12 August 1995 with the execution of Abdallah al-Hudhaif, a political prisoner. Hudhaif was accused of attacking a security officer with acid and sentenced to 20 years imprisonment. AI reports that it: 'does not know how his prison sentence was increased to the death penalty as the trial has been, and remains, shrouded in secrecy.' The same bulletin reports that four others were sentenced for assisting to plan the attack on the security officer, three of whom received prison terms of 15 years; the fourth, Abd al-Rahman al-Hudhaif, was given 18 years and 300 lashes.[53] Five others were sentenced to between three and eight years of imprisonment for providing refuge to the executed man and assisting in his abortive attempt to secretly flee the country, and for holding dissident (CDLR) meetings and receiving dissident (CDLR) leaflets.

## FRAGMENTED OPPOSITION

Opposition to the Al Saud began to find greater voice from the time of the Iraqi invasion of Kuwait in August 1990, when the Kingdom hosted hundreds of thousands of Western troops.[54] This opposition, however, was not violent. Aside from the public sermons of a relatively small number of very vocal young religious scholars, such as Safar al-Hawali and Salman al-'Auda, the upsurge took the form of letters, petitions and 'advice' to King Fahd. Participants ranged from: 'moderate liberal business-men and intellectuals,' to 'a broad-based coalition between the different streams in the ranks of the *ulama*.'[55] But the alignment of these various groupings, which was indeed a worry to the regime, was always tenuous and co-operation between them soon began to break down.[56]

The opposition in Saudi Arabia has always been fragmented and this situation is unlikely to change in the foreseeable future. The splitting of the CDLR in March 1996 is a classic case: the two principal figures in the CDLR, Muhammad al-Mas'ari and Saad al-Fagih, fell out over what the CDLR stood for and how its campaign should operate and be focused. Until its split, the CDLR had been the most organized and professional Saudi political opposition group.

Mas'ari was allowed to keep the CDLR name but, cut off from

Fagih, who was the principal organizer and networker, he was officially declared bankrupt: after the split, the CDLR existed virtually in name only, and Mas'ari as an individual campaigner has been relatively ineffective. Fagih, on the other hand, formed a new organization in London, the Movement for Islamic Reform in Arabia (MIRA), which is much more low-key than the old CDLR, but still very active.

The Riyadh and Khobar bombings also prove there are maverick loose groups of individuals unconnected with the more 'moderate' fronts such as the CDLR and MIRA, and who may be associated with the now high-profile Saudi dissident in exile in Afghanistan, Osama bin Laden.[57] The fragmented nature of Saudi opposition was confirmed by Fagih himself, who wants to use MIRA to create a 'vertical structure' among Islamists working for reform in the Kingdom.[58] Before the split, Mas'ari also agreed with the notion that the CDLR was attempting to position itself as the opposition's middle ground by providing a focus, and was therefore appealing to, and developing policies that would appeal to, the spectrum of opposition.[59] He still feels that it remains a major task, saying that: 'the underground is fragmented,' that 'there is no leading figure,' and that it takes time to develop a serious and credible opposition movement that can achieve results – 'four years is not long.' On the political opposition within Saudi Arabia, Mas'ari believes that: 'without day-to-day guidance, they are headless,' and that 'the main handicap ... is lack of organization.'[60]

Other expert observers can testify to the absence of organized political opposition: in a government-promoted 'fractured' society, individual Saudi citizens are prepared to criticize, but do little.[61] Opposition within the Kingdom is limited and it comes 'from different directions.'[62] Also testifying to the ethereal nature of Saudi dissent, a Middle Eastern analyst for the BBC believes there are no opposition movements as such, and that 'vague words' are required to describe the Saudi opposition.[63]

While it may be encouraged by the regime for political purposes, the fractured nature of Saudi society also testifies to the country's pluralism, as well as to the dramatic effects of rapid modernization and development. This pluralism is often overlooked. Differences exist between the *Hanbali muwahhidun* ('Wahhabis') and other Sunni *madhabs* as well as Saudi Shiites; between Hijazis and Najdis and those from the south; between urban dwellers and rural and nomadic lifestyles; and between the traditional and the modern. Thus, Saudi society is not as homogenous as generally believed. This diversity, in turn, is reflected in the disunity of the political opposition.

Saudi Arabia's Shiite minority, concentrated in the Kingdom's eastern province – formerly al-Hasa – and traditionally discriminated against, has in turn been a source of agitation. Violent riots by Shiites in 1979 touched off nearly a decade of disturbances, principally at the time of the annual hajj. The disturbances of the 1980s occurred against the backdrop of the eight-year Iran–Iraq War, but acute Saudi suspicion and intolerance of Shiites ran through and even beyond the 1990–91 Gulf crisis.[64] Latter Saudi concern over its Shiite population has been linked to severe civil disturbances involving the Shiite majority in Bahrain.

Saudi behavior in relation to the Shiite community demonstrates the regime's astute divide-and-rule policy that exploits already-present social divisions. In a program amounting to a campaign of coercion through largesse, the regime has, since 1979, steadily worked at defusing the Shiite threat.[65] The Gulf War provided further impetus to reconcile with the community and in 1993, a low-key deal was struck between the regime and prominent Shiite dissidents abroad, which resulted in an amnesty and 'political concessions' in return for the cessation of anti-Saudi propaganda.[66] The settlement with the Shiite community was, according to Mas'ari, a 'masterly stroke' by King Fahd to ease pressure on the regime at a time of increasing calls for reform from the Sunni mainstream.[67] In this context, it was important for the regime to cut off any possibility, however unlikely, of this widest fissure in the political opposition being bridged. In 1995, it is interesting to note, Mas'ari paralleled this turnaround in Saudi policy by affirming that the CDLR advocated freedom of speech and expression for all citizens, including Shiites – and non-Muslims – effectively ending their alienation from mainstream society.[68] The policy of divide-and-rule, however, is one that demands constant attention and updating.[69]


## AN ABSOLUTE MONARCHY: LAGGING POLITICAL DEVELOPMENT

The Saudi royal family exercises absolute power. Political participation has been very restricted in the past – mainly limited
to traditional practices of tribal and élite representation and
petition which has often been labeled as 'desert democracy.'[70]
In practice, the opportunity to raise and discuss issues with the
king was not the same as participation in the decision-making
process: the historical *majlis* ('sitting/gathering session') system
may be interpreted as a traditional public relations exercise – but
a generally accepted one in the Arabian context – on behalf
of the king and, by extension, of the royal family. The exercise
bolstered specific decisions, the general royal decision-making
process, and overall Al Saud legitimacy, by promoting the image
of consultation, discussion and consensus, and for providing the
king and senior royals with the opportunity to be benevolent
patrons and patriarchs.[71]

This is the socio-political legacy the Al Saud are expected to
uphold today. Historically informal and non-institutional – if
compared with any Western system of rule – the process of discussion and consensus-building remains an important point of
legitimacy and stability for the regime, and is a precursor to any
significant policy changes. The system provides a forum for the
exchange of views, but one in which the ruler will always rule,
and which the ruler will use to explain decisions and persuade
élite representatives – and through them the general population
– of the need for any changes. This process is necessary in order
to minimize political risk, but at the same time it is still the
major factor in the very slow rate of policy development and
implementation in the Kingdom. Senior royalty must be perceived as acting in the best interests of the people, and the
people must feel as if they have had some input, however
minimal and indirect, into the decision-making process.

By and large, according to one former British ambassador to Saudi Arabia, the Saudi political system has not altered significantly since the time of the modern Kingdom's founder and first king, Abd al-Aziz bin Abd al-Rahman al-Saud ('Ibn Saud,' d. 1953).[72] In the late 1980s, the ambassador described two methods by which decisions in the Kingdom are reached. The first is through the Council of Ministers, which may be equated with the cabinet of a Western-style government: 'In theory policies and measures are discussed by the Council and approved or disapproved. In practice, such is the authority of the King and the deference paid to him that frank debate is hardly possible.' The second method: '... is the King's personal fiat, usually after discussion within a small circle of advisers, in private and informal session.'[73]

However, evoking the image of desert democracy: '[i]t is not true to say that there is no democracy at all, for the King and Government take much account of public opinion'. This, together with an 'attach[ment] to the idea of social democracy' despite having 'no belief in institutional democracy,'[74] provides the traditional, attitudinal context for the establishment of the Consultative Council (*majlis al-shura*) in 1993. It is noteworthy that promises of greater political participation have been made since the reign of King Faisal (1964–75). The immediate political context for the final inauguration of such a Council, of course, was the Gulf crisis-associated rise in calls for reform in the Kingdom and the influence of intense popular pressure on Kuwait's Al Sabah ruling dynasty for the reinstitution of the Kuwaiti parliament, dissolved in 1986, and reconvened in 1992 after elections.[75]

The following points illustrate the circumstances of the (eventual) establishment, and nature, of the Saudi Consultative Council:

- The intention to establish a Consultative Council within six months was announced to the Council of Ministers at the end of February 1992. The Council's chairman was appointed in late 1992, but it was not until 20 August 1993 that the Council was inaugurated.

- The Council's members – increased in July 1997 from the original 60 to 90 members, and increased again in May 2001 to 120 members – serve for four years in an advisory capacity only, and are appointed and dismissed by royal decree.

- The King has the right to dissolve the Council and to restructure it – the same power granted to the King with respect to the Council of Ministers.

Basically, the contemporary Consultative Council represents the formalization and institutionalization of the traditional *majlis* system of tribal consultation. It is a concession to, or a gesture toward, the modernization of governmental processes. Where such a gesture may ultimately lead remains in the realm of speculation; some optimistic interpretations of the Council's establishment have been posited, although they come from predictable, sympathetic sources. A US diplomat, for example, said that the new *majlis al-shura*, along with the Basic Law of Government, was a genuine step toward greater participation in decision-making – significant in a Saudi context – which represents progress in the institutionalization of government. The diplomat admitted, however, that progress is so slow that it is 'almost imperceptible' from an outsider's point of view.[76]

Even close allies of the Saudis recognize that in dealing with problems, a favored policy of the regime is: 'not to do anything and hope it goes away – sometimes it works, sometimes it doesn't.'[77] However, one issue which the regime will have to address is the dichotomy between economic and social changes and lagging political development. This problem is accentuated by the young age of the Saudi population: around 60 percent of Saudis are under 21 years of age.[78] A new generation of educated and unemployed Saudis, influenced by the West, may demand greater political development. In fact, Mas'ari – although probably deliberately exaggerating – maintains it is only the state's 'social net' that supports highly-educated unemployed young graduates, that is preventing a revolution in the Kingdom.[79] Greater political expectations, in fact, may be encouraged by economic – and social – restructuring. Saudis in general may gradually be accepting that the good times of the oil boom era are over, but the resultant lower – not higher – socio-economic expectations may yet result in increased pressure on the government to provide some form of compensation in greater political participation. Another significant agent of social change is the creeping influence of Western culture, which is increasingly being felt in Saudi Arabia as it is in other parts of the world. Satellite dishes, which have occasionally incited the wrath of *mutawwa'in* ('religious police') and were officially banned in mid-1994 (but unofficially ignored), have become ubiquitous. Satellite television is now a major medium of Western culture as, to a lesser extent, is the English-language Saudi Channel 2.

Western influence has most visibly influenced young males below the age of 20, creating the basis of a generation gap that may lead to social dislocation in the future.[80] The cumulative effect of this culture creep is augmented by travel and studies in Western countries. Many of these young people will probably come to occupy positions of influence in Saudi society, threatening to challenge the traditional perspectives upon which much of the current social system is based, and therefore contributing to change from within the society. An opening to Western culture has also introduced new elements to Saudi society, which the regime has no experience addressing. Drug use, for example, is on the rise. An anti-drugs campaign already runs on Saudi television, and drug traffickers are well represented in the annual tally of executions in the Kingdom. On the other hand, a certain proportion of educated and under-employed youth exposed to Western culture is bound to oppose the regime on religious and traditionally conservative grounds and would probably work to change the regime from within.

The battleground is a cultural one as much as a political one. The regime is now advocating globalization, although attempting to take only what it wants from the whole globalization bag. The overall result is that Saudi conservatives are much more likely to increasingly oppose the regime. Some of this latter group of disaffected youth might resort to violence to pressure the regime to repel the accelerating (Western) forces of modernization and globalization. Violence is by no means unprecedented in the Kingdom. However, the radically differing makeup of young, potential malcontents only serves to illustrate further the fractured nature of opposition to the Al Saud – a socio-political trend that favors the regime and is likely to continue well into the future.

Another weak link in the monarchy's political development is the question of succession.[81] There is no institutional process for the succession. Most recently, the internet intelligence/news agency, Stratfor.com, provided a speculation-oriented update on Saudi succession, with the conclusion that: 'Abdallah's all but certain ascent to the throne will mark only a brief period of stability in one of the world's most important nations; what follows will most certainly be a period of distinct instability.'[82] At some stage power will pass to the second, or even the third, generation of princes, and the potential for chaos exists during the period after Prince Sultan – if he comes to the throne after Abdallah, as is generally expected – if not in the twilight of Abdallah's coming reign. Saudi history is steeped in the devastating consequences of family feuding, most notably leading to the fall of the second Saudi realm in the late-nineteenth century. The current number of princes is estimated at between 6,000 and 10,000 – some of them, no doubt, ambitious. However, the grimmest speculation – that the royal family will tear itself apart from within and that the regime will subsequently collapse – is probably overstated. It would be surprising if the wisdom of presenting a united front in the best interests of the dynasty, despite any bitter differences, were lost on the senior royals.

CONCLUSION

The Saudi government is attempting to come to terms with the restructuring of the economy, and with extensive reforms in higher education and the workforce – the former to comply with globalization, the latter to serve economic restructuring as well as to address uniquely Saudi Arabian socio-economic problems. Although the Saudi economy largely bolsters the Al Saud's position, the question remains whether limited social and economic reforms will work before instability in these spheres combines with the forces of instability in other spheres. The next decade with bring social and economic changes that will eventually rise to the political level, and this eventuality may well coincide with a crisis of political development.

Considering the rapid and unsteady pace of socio-economic development, a Consultative Council which is more an exercise in public relations – albeit an astute one – rather than a genuine step toward greater political participation only serves the regime's short-term interests. Unless the regime redresses the gap between social change and political development, it may find itself having to take more repressive steps against its own – increasingly young, unemployed and restless – population.

The US–Saudi relationship – once described as 'special' and now, at times, stressful – has become a liability for Saudi legitimacy domestically. The relationship has suffered during successive crises over Iraq. However, a US withdrawal to an over-the-horizon Gulf presence, if implemented, will relieve some of the pressure on the Al Saud, who suffer from an image of being too closely associated with 'infidel' America. Yet, the Al Saud are unlikely to be critically tested by the relations with the United States unless other, domestic crises happen to coincide, or unless a serious regional development once again pits US interests directly against those of popular Arab perception.

It is possible that the crisis over the 11 September 2001 airliner hijacking-suicide attacks in New York and Washington may eventually engulf the Middle East. The longer-term effects of the anti-Taliban/anti-Osama bin Laden campaign, even if confined geographically to Afghanistan, will certainly affect the wider region indefinitely. Saudi support for the US 'war against terrorism' has not been without ambiguity: Riyadh has once again refused permission for the USA to use its bases for their offense, and has linked the fight against terrorism with a satisfactory outcome for Palestinian aspirations for a viable, independent state. With one eye on domestic sociopolitics, where underground support for bin Laden and bin-Ladenesque groups has become uncomfortably apparent, and one eye on its strategic relationships, the Al Saud will continue to tread a fine line where domestic and international interests intersect. The Middle East peace process, the 'war against terror,' and the relationship with the United States are likely to be just some of the major issues facing the Al Saud during an upcoming difficult period at home surrounding succession to the throne.

Saudi Arabia is indeed entering a period of turbulence which will, nevertheless, see the Saudi dynasty come through intact. The dual problems of reform and development in the socio-economic sphere should not be underestimated. It is reasonable to predict that these challenges will be met with varying degrees of success, and that the Saudi economy and society will be different, and in some areas quite different, ten years from now. Some of these reforms will have unpredictable consequences, but some will bring further political concessions from the regime, if not more significant political change.

## NOTES

* A general note on confidential sources: Saudi Arabia is a notoriously closed society, which is hypersensitive about privacy and image. Access to information is severely restricted, and those dealing in information face the prospect of retaliation in one form or another. During field research, I found that current and former diplomatic service personnel, journalists, and even some academics, routinely spoke with a request that the meeting be 'off the record.' In other cases, common sense – as with diplomats currently serving in Saudi Arabia and in other Middle Eastern countries – and a responsible attitude toward the welfare or even the safety of other sources more directly exposed to retaliation, such as Saudi nationals and expatriate workers, dictate that specific identity, and sometimes the specific locations and dates of interviews or conversations, be reserved. Thus, 'confidential' preceding citation details indicates the interviewee specifically requested anonymity. Where I have not provided the identity of the interviewee but have also not specified the interview was confidential, I have deliberately omitted the identity of the interviewee out of consideration for the individual's personal and professional interests.

1. The choice of any particular year to mark the beginning of Al Saud power this century is an arbitrary exercise. The Saudis prefer 1902, when Ibn Saud re-captured Riyadh from the Rashidis and, indeed, official centenary celebrations – according to the Islamic calendar – were held in 1999 to mark 100 years of 'Saudi Arabia.' Another auspicious year is 1932, when the modern Kingdom of Saudi Arabia was formally proclaimed. Another is 1925, which brought the conquest of the Hijaz, with its religious centers of Mecca and Madina and the commercial–diplomatic center of Jedda. Yet another could be 1930, when Ibn Saud prevailed – albeit with at least indirect British assistance – over the Ikhwan revolt, which may be described as the first serious act of internal dissent since the completion of the conquest of the territories

which would be consolidated as a single realm in 1932.

2. The CDLR's origins lay with the loosely-knit political reform groups that began expressing themselves after the 1991 Gulf War. The organization was founded in Riyadh on 3 May 1993; on 11 May it was banned and, within days thereafter, many of its members were arrested. The CDLR was re-founded in London by exiled members and sympathizers in April 1994. The highest-profile CDLR member was its Secretary-General, Muhammad al-Mas'ari, around whom several controversies raged in the UK from 1994 to 1996.

3. For example, the *Economist* reported that the CDLR faxed 800 copies of its newsletter into the Kingdom on a weekly basis, there to be further copied and distributed (*Economist*, 'Challenge to the House of Saud', 8 October (1994), p. 71. Commencing on the effect of up to 1,000 faxes per week transmitted to the Kingdom, Mas'ari has said: 'Perhaps 150,000 people see what we write and perhaps 80 percent of people oppose the government ... 10,000 of them are activists ...' (quoted in Christopher Lockwood, 'Dissident tries to topple rulers by fax', *Electronic Telegraph*, 22 February (1996); <http://www.telegraph.co.uk:80/et?ac=000148889415120&rtmo=aTa5u5aJ&atmo=99 999999&pg=/et/96/2/22/nsaudi22.html>. See also Mamoun Fandy, *Saudi Arabia and the Politics of Dissent* (New York: St Martin's Press, 1999), pp. 10–12, 126–35. (Hereafter cited as *Saudi Arabia: Dissent*).

4. Seumas Milne and Ian Black, 'Arms Bosses' Secret Plot', *Guardian Weekly*, 14 January (1996), p. 10 (international edn, after *Guardian* daily, 6 January 1996). The article revealed the following: that the chief executive of the armaments firm Vickers, Sir Colin Chandler, was a former head of arms exports at the Ministry of Defence (MoD); that Vickers' director of international relations was also a former MoD official; and that the new British ambassador-designate to Saudi Arabia, Andrew Green, was a non-executive director of Vickers Defence Systems. The *Guardian* exposed communication between these three men and senior executives of two other British arms manufacturers, British Aerospace and GKN, and between all of them and the British government, over Mas'ari's activities. The arms firms executives reportedly had discussed CIA and MI6 concern over Mas'ari's activities, and had referred to: 'direct Saudi intervention ... to stifle [Mas'ari] personally.' Revelations also abounded over the dramatic 300 percent increase in British aid to Dominica at the time. The British Foreign Office defended the government's stance and role in the Mas'ari affair and government–arms firms links. See also: Russell Hotten and Colin Brown, 'Vickers Director Our Man in Saudi', *Independent*, 6 January (1996), p. 1; David Rose, 'Labour MP Lashes Captains of Industry over "Stifling" of Saudi Dissident Cleric', *Observer*, 7 January (1996), p. 1; Colin Brown, Patrick Cockburn, Steve Crawshaw and Phil Davison, 'Secret Deals in Arms and Bananas that Condemned a Man to Exile', *Independent*, 7 January (1996), p. 1; Peter Beaumont, 'Twenty Billion Reasons for Greed', *Observer*, 7 January (1996), p. 11; Louise Jury, 'Tories Charged with Appeasing Saudi Rulers', *Independent*, 7 January (1996), p. 1; Colin Brown and Michael Sheridan, 'Saudi Threats Forced Britain's Hand', *Independent*, 5 January (1996), p. 2; Russell Hotten, 'Riyadh Pressured Defence Firm', *Independent*, 5 January (1996), p. 2; Seumas Milne and Ian Black, 'UK Bows to Pressure over Dissident', *Guardian Weekly*, 14 January (1996), p. 1.

5. See Nick Cohen and Robert Fisk, 'Saudis Plotted to Kill Me, Says Dissident', *Independent on Sunday*, 7 January (1996), p. 1. The persecution of Mas'ari's relatives and personal supporters began in 1994 immediately after his flight from the Kingdom; see Anthony H. Cordesman, *Saudi Arabia: Guarding the Desert Kingdom* (Boulder, CO: Westview Press, 1997), p. 40 (hereafter cited as *Saudi Arabia*); Leslie Cockburn and Andrew Cockburn, 'Royal Mess', *The New Yorker*, 70, 39, 1994), pp. 54–72. See also note 53 below and associated main text.

6. My research on Saudi Arabia has led me to concur with an important conclusion outlined by Cordesman, *Saudi Arabia*, p. 76: '... Saudi Arabia's key security challenge is not external threats, or internal extremism, but the need to come firmly to grips with its economy.' A brief note on the role of Islam in the Kingdom is, however, warranted at this point. Al Saud religious stature dates back to the mid-seventeenth century when a Saudi *amir* from central Arabia formed a 'religio-political' alliance with a religious reformer, Muhammad bin Abd al-Wahhab (1703–92). Thus was the austere 'Wahhabi' interpretation of Islam born – within the Hanbali school of Sunni juris-prudence and on the back of early Saudi conquests – and Saudi rulers have enjoyed religious as well as political authority ever since. This religio-political authority was strengthened in 1925 with the Saudi conquest of the Hijaz and subsequent management of the annual pilgrimage to Mecca (hajj) – then an important source of revenue as well as of religious prestige, and now the basis of continuing Saudi claims to 'custodianship of the two holy mosques.' The regime has for long sought sanction in all-important matters from the state's official religious establishment. Saudi religious legitimacy is not specifically dealt with in this paper, but this is not meant to imply that it is not important: the topic has been treated extensively by other scholars of the Kingdom, and these works should be consulted – see for example: George Renz, 'Wahhabism and Saudi Arabia', in Derek Hopwood (ed.), *The Arabian Peninsula: Society and Politics* (London: Allen & Unwin, 1972); Christine Moss Helms, *The Cohesion of Saudi Arabia: Evolution of Political Identity* (London: Croom Helm, 1981), pp. 76–126 (hereafter cited as *Cohesion of Saudi Arabia*); Derek Hopwood, 'The Ideological Basis: Ibn Abd al-Wahhab's Muslim Revivalism', in Tim Niblock (ed.), *State, Society and Economy in Saudi Arabia* (New York: St Martin's Press, 1982) (hereafter cited as *State, Society and Economy*); James P. Piscatori, 'Ideological Politics in Sa'udi Arabia', in J.P. Piscatori (ed.), *Islam in the Political Process* (Cambridge: Cambridge University Press, 1983); Alexander Bligh, 'The Saudi Religious Elite (*Ulama*) as Participant in the Political System of the Kingdom', *International Journal of Middle East Studies*, 17 (1985), pp. 37–50; Joseph K. Kechichian, 'The Role of the *Ulama* in the Politics of an Islamic State: The Case of Saudi Arabia', *International Journal of Middle East Studies*, 18 (1986), pp. 53–71; John Esposito, *Islam and Politics*, 3rd edn (Syracuse, NY: Syracuse University Press, 1991), pp. 102–12; Fandy, *Saudi Arabia: Dissent*, pp. 36–8.

7. One recent analysis which groups Saudi Arabia, Kuwait, Bahrain, Qatar, the UAE and Oman as a monarchical collective presents the following reasons for their overall stability:

> ... [S]ocial peace in the Gulf ... is maintained by the clever, and

consistent, use of a variety of government strategies to promote social order. Gulf governments use a combination of six strategies: strong security services; the co-optation of potential dissidents; divide-and-rule measures; ideological flexibility; token participation; and accommodative diplomacy. Taken together, these strategies preserve islands of social peace in an area of turbulence ...

... Although the above six strategies are short-term palliatives, they have helped keep the peace for many years. In and of themselves, the strategies do not stop social modernization, revive stagnant Gulf economies, ease demographic pressure, or reduce corruption. They have, however, raised the popularity of governments and diluted anger about foreign aggression. Perhaps most importantly, regime tools hinder an organized opposition and mitigate the politicizing events that often lead disaffected individuals to become violent.

(Daniel L. Byman and Jerrold D. Green, 'The Enigma of Political Stability in the Persian Gulf Monarchies', *Middle East Review of International Affairs*, 3, 3 (1999). e-mail edn (hereafter cited as *Enigma of Political Stability*.)

8. The combination of oil producers' price discounting and ignored production quotas led to the collapse of oil prices in 1986 when they fell to an average of $13–14 per barrel – and reached lows of $8–10 per barrel in mid-1986 – from an average price of more than $27 per barrel in 1985. Despite implementing a slowdown in spending and drawing severely on foreign reserves, the Saudi budget deficit went from 6.4 percent of GDP in 1983 to 25.3 percent of GDP in 1987. See Saudi Arabian Monetary Agency, *Thirty-Fourth Annual Report, 1419H (1998G)*, (Riyadh: SAMA Research and Statistics Department, 1998), pp. 125–306; Eliyahu Kanovsky, *The Economy of Saudi Arabia: Troubled Present, Grim Future*, WINEP Policy Paper, No. 38 (Washington DC: The Washington Institute for Near East Policy, 1994), pp. 19–21; 73–4 (hereafter cited as *Economy of Saudi Arabia*); Peter W. Wilson and Douglas F. Graham, *Saudi Arabia: The Coming Storm* (New York: M.E. Sharpe, 1994), pp. 181–2 (hereafter cited as *Saudi Arabia: The Coming Storm*).

9. Considering costs of between $50 billion and $70 billion for the 1991 Gulf War, arms purchases since the war of around $50 billion, and approximately $26 billion lost in aid to Iraq during the 1980–88 Iran–Iraq War, the Saudi economic position can be pictured as one that was not enjoying good health for the decade 1985–95. See, for example, Kanovsky, *Economy of Saudi Arabia*, pp. 57–71; Rayed Krimly, 'The Political Economy of Adjusted Priorities: Declining Oil Revenues and Saudi Fiscal Policies', *Middle East Journal*, 53, 2 (1999), pp. 257–8 (hereafter cited as *Political Economy of Adjusted Priorities*); Joseph A. Kechichian, 'Trends in Saudi National Security', *Middle East Journal*, 53, 2 (1999), pp. 242, 249; Richard H. Curtiss, 'Four Years after Massive War Expenses Saudi Arabia Gets its Second Wind', *The Washinton Report on Middle East Affairs* (September 1995), p. 51; Wilson and Graham, *Saudi Arabia: The Coming Storm*, p. 189; David Pike, 'Reforms Begin as Business Bounces Back', *Middle East Economic Digest* (MEED Special Report, Saudi Arabia), 20 March 1992, p. 9.

10. Fareed Mohamedi, 'The Saudi Economy: A Few Years Yet Till Doomsday', *Middle East Report* (November–December 1993), p. 14 (hereafter cited as

*Saudi Economy*). See also Wilson and Graham, *Saudi Arabia: The Coming Storm*, pp. 195–6; Committee for the Defense of Legitimate Rights, *Saudi Arabia: A Country Report. The Political and Economic Situation* (London: CDLR, 1995), pp. 47–8, note 2.

11. See Mohamedi, *Saudi Economy*, p. 16; Kevin Taecker, *Outlook for the Saudi Economy: Fall 1997* (Saudi American Bank Publication, Riyahd 1997), p. 2 (Hereafter cited as *Outlook for Saudi Economy*); Saudi Arabian Monetary Agency, *Economy of Saudi Arabia*, p. 125.

12. *Economist*, 'Saudi Arabia's Future: The Cracks in the Kingdom' (18 March 1995), p. 21; Kathy Evans, 'Shifting Sands at the House of Saud', *The Middle East*, 253 (1996), p. 9; Kiren Aziz Chaudhry, *The Price of Wealth: Economies and Institutions in the Middle East* (Ithaca: Cornell University Press, 1997), p. 269 (hereafter cited as *Price of Wealth*).

13. See Taecker, *Outlook for Saudi Economy*, 1997, p. 2. Taecker pointed to a better-than-expected 1997 performance, with a deficit of 1.1 percent of GDP: see Kevin Taecker, 'Update on the Saudi Economy: January 1998', Saudi American Bank economic paper, 15 January 1998, p. 2.

14. Taecker, personal interview, Riyadh, 9 March 1998; Mabro, personal interview, Oxford, 14 May 1998. Taecker resigned from SAMBA mid-1999 to launch his own economic consultancy on Saudi Arabia. He is generally known to be 'a Saudi optimist' (Australian diplomat no. 3, personal communication, Riyadh, 23 February 1998), although his analysis of the Saudi economic position for this period is supported in principal by Mabro, who is a detached and independent academic.

15. King Fahd, 7 August 1995: quoted in John Cooper, 'Better times ahead', *Middle East Economic Digest*, 18 August 1995.

16. See Kevin Taecker, 'Saudi Arabia 1999 Budget: Analysis of the Press Reports', Saudi American Bank economic paper, 25 January 1999; Economist Intelligence Unit, 'Saudi Arabia: Country Outlook', *Country View*, 20 August 1999. Wilson and Graham, *Saudi Arabia: The Coming Storm*, pp. 191–2, are skeptical about the level of Saudi deficit spending: The real figure may be substantially higher since Saudi budget figures are notoriously inaccurate and often serve as rough guidelines for spending. There are also large discrepancies between projected and actual figures; the latter are usually released the following year and purport to show real revenues and expenditures. However, many expenditures such as defense spending and payments to the royal family occur off-budget.

17. In mid-March 1999, Saudi Arabia led the effort to ensure agreement among the world's most significant oil producers to reduce production output. Saudi Arabia made the greatest sacrifice, with a pledge to cut production by 585,000 bpd, to 7.438 million bpd. A total of 2.1 million bpd – three percent of the daily worldwide supply – was pledged to be cut from collective production, beginning 1 April 1999 for one year to the end of March 2000. The strategy proved to be effective almost immediately. A benchmark crude, West Texas Intermediate (WTI), which was languishing at around $12.40 per barrel in early March 1999, had risen to around $18.40 per barrel by the end of April, and by mid-November had breached the $27 mark. Oil prices continued to soar, with WTI breaching $37 per barrel in September 2000.

18. Economist Intelligence Unit, 'Saudi Arabia: Country Forecast Summary',

*Country View*, 14 July 1999. Whether citing the aims of the Five-Year Plans offer any comfort at all, though, should be considered in the light that at least one professional involved with Saudi Arabia is of the opinion that the Plans: 'are not worth the paper they're written on' and that they, 'at best ... are an expression of hope' (Australian diplomat no. 1, personal interview, Canberra, 14 July 1995). Further undermining confidence in the Plans, and in the ability of the Saudis to manage their economy efficiently – especially in the face of increasingly serious adversity – are such practices as outlined by Chaudhry, *Price of Wealth*, p. 167: Government statistics were literally manufactured in the Ministries of Finance and Planning. All but the first of the various Five-Year Plans begin with fictitious parameters based on unsupported assumptions and proceed to build even more fantastic projections. In 1981, the budget format was 'reformed' to make already opaque figures even more impossible to interpret.

19. Kevin Taecker, 'Gulf Capital Markets and Family Businesses', Saudi American Bank economic seminar paper (Riyadh), 8 March 1998, p. 4; US Central Intelligence Agency, 'Saudi Arabia', in *CIA World Factbook* (internet edn, 1999).

20. Notes 16 and 18 gave notice of, and provide clues to, these areas of Saudi economic and, ultimately, socio-political vulnerability. This aspect of Saudi vulnerability is a study in its own right; although it is relevant to this particular paper, the scope of the topic is such that it cannot be indulged much beyond mention. Chaudhry, *Price of Wealth*, pp. 61–192, in her work on the Saudi political economy, provides a detailed exposition of the ascent of the Najdi bureaucratic–business élite, with the associated nepotism and favoritism due to family and regional ties; she also makes mention of Saudi 'commission entrepreneurs' (p. 154). See Fandy, *Saudi Arabia: Dissent*, pp. 10, 23–9 on 'the dominant ethos of familialism (*a'iliyya*) within the larger context of *qaraba* (closeness both in space and social relations) society' (p. 23). Such close personal ties weave the socio-economic fabric of the informal Saudi system of "*asabiyya* capitalism': see Daryl Champion, 'Saudi Arabia on the Edge of Globalisation: *Asabiyya* Capitalism and Socioeconomic Change at the End of the Boom Era', *Journal of Arabic, Islamic and Middle Eastern Studies*, 5, 2 (1999). See also Abdul Rahman Osama, *The Dilemma of Development in the Arabian Peninsula* (London: Croom Helm, 1987), pp. 17–119 (hereafter cited as *Dilemma of Development*); Abdelrahman al-Hegelan and Monte Palmer, 'Bureaucracy and Development in Saudi Arabia', *Middle East Journal*, 39, 1 (1985), pp. 48–68; A. Reza S. Islami and Rostam Mehraban Kavoussi, *The Political Economy of Saudi Arabia* (Seattle: Department of Near Eastern Languages and Civilization, Univeristy of Washington, 1984), pp. 75–81. For the more popular and rhetorical accounts of regime and royal excess, see Geoff Simons, *Saudi Arabia: The Shape of a Client Feudalism* (New York: St Martin's Press, 1998), pp. 26–31; Saïd K. Aburish, *The Rise, Corruption and Coming Fall of the House of Saud* (London: Bloomsbury, 1995), *passim*. For an example of newspaper reports and other articles which form a link between the more scholarly works and the writings of authors such as Simons and Aburish, see Philip Taubman, 'US Aides Say Corruption is Threat to Saudi Stability', *New York Times*, 16 April 1980, p. 1; Dilip Hiro, 'Saudi Dissenters Go Public', *The Nation*, 28 June 1993. For several years to mid-1999, a well-presented example

of the case against royal malpractice could be studied on the Internet site (last accessed 6 July 1999) of the US-based dissident organization, the Committee Against Corruption in Saudi Arabia. By October 1999, however, the site appeared to be no longer accessible <http://www.saudhouse.com/>.

21. Various informal conversations, Riyadh, January–March 1998. The Saudi government's practice of delaying contractual payments dates back to the recession of the 1980s – a policy of *de facto* default which caused much hardship and many bankruptcies: see Chaudhry, *Price of Wealth*, pp. 273 note 6, 279, 297, 297 note 80; Kanovsky, *Economy of Saudi Arabia*, p. 75. Delaying payments, although not expected to reach the severity of earlier years, was a policy revisited with the financial problems of the 1990s: see Sarah Abuljadayel, 'Workers Still Await Salaries', *Arab News*, 14 July 1999 (distributed electronically by Reuters Business Briefing Select, 28 July 1999); Reuters, 'Saudi Issues Some $1.1 bln in Bonds for Contractors,' 1 August 1999. Taecker (personal interview, Riyadh, 26 January 1999) noted that government contract payments, although recently 'slowed' from three months to around six months, do not breach contractual agreements.

22. The reader should be reminded at this point that issues of corruption, as a link between economic and political stability, are relevant. See note 20 above.

23. Byman and Green, *Enigma of Political Stability*.

24. Various sources agree in pointing to falling standards of living and lower expectations: Taecker (personal interview, Riyadh, 26 January 1999) believes the expectations of young Saudis 'are greatly diminished' – an adjustment from the boom days encouraged by the fact that it is 'in current living memory' of what life was like in the pre-boom days. Mabro (personal interview, Oxford, 14 May 1998) maintains there is 'no doubt' that young Saudis today have 'lower expectations [of living standards and lifestyle.]' Krimly, *Political Economy of Adjusted Priorities*, pp. 260–1, implies that 'almost surreal expectations' are gradually coming down to earth. Likewise, a confidential business contact is adamant that living standards are definitely falling in Saudi Arabia (confidential personal communication, 1 May 1996). A US diplomat has observed the twin signs of a greater incidence of poverty and a decline in conspicuous consumption (personal interview, Riyadh, 9 March 1998). A veteran Australian diplomat who has served in Riyadh has revealed his conclusion that some Saudi citizens are 'sliding into poverty' (Australian diplomat no. 2, personal communication, Canberra, 18 June 1997). A former British ambassador to Saudi Arabia with firm connections with the Kingdom has confessed that he is 'beginning to hear of poor Saudis' (confidential personal interview, London, 26 May 1998).

25. On 'The Saudi social contract', see Cordesman, *Saudi Arabia*, pp. 47, 73–6. This 'social contract', in combination with the 'Saudi welfare state', incorporates the 'legitimacy of largesse' [my term] which, basically, has allowed the regime to consistently 'buy off any potential hostility long before it has time to develop into anything like a serious threat'. Helen Lackner, *A House Built on Sand: A Political Economy of Saudi Arabia* (London: Ithaca Press, 1978), p. 216; see also Wilson and Graham, *Saudi Arabia: The Coming Storm*, pp. 81, 185. The term 'Saudi welfare state' is not uncommon and has even been employed and emphasized by the Saudis themselves: Royal Embassy of Saudi Arabia, London, *The Kingdom of Saudi Arabia: A Welfare State* (London: Royal

Embassy of Saudi Arabia, 1997); Wilson and Graham, *Saudi Arabia: The Coming Storm*, p. 54; Cordesman, *Saudi Arabia*, p. 74. The negative effects of unemployment in a poorer economic environment are multiplied – in the view of a serving diplomat – by the fact that Saudi Arabia is a family-based society: despite the 'welfare state', the concept of a greater society doesn't exist, therefore the poor and disadvantaged who, as noted, are likely to be increasing in numbers, are left to fend for themselves (Australian diplomat no. 1, personal interview, Canberra, 14 July 1995).

26. See World Bank, *World Development Report 1998/99: Knowledge for Development* (New York: Oxford University Press, 1999), p. 195.

27. Byman and Green, *Enigma of Political Stability*.

28. Saud al-Shubaily, personal interview, Riyadh, 7 March 1998. Al-Shubaily is the Director of the Contractors' Department and Executive Director of the Contractors' National Committee at the Saudi Chamber of Commerce and Industry.

29. US diplomat, personal interview, Riyadh, 9 March 1998. It has also been suggested that the real rate of unemployment is 40 percent (business consultant, confidential personal communications, 1 May 1996). Using Saudi figures from the Fifth Plan, Wilson and Graham, *Saudi Arabia: The Coming Storm*, pp. 254–5, reveal unemployment rates of 45.6 percent for men and 94.7 percent for women. See also Chaudry, *Price of Wealth*, pp. 275, 297.

30. Ministry of Planning, *Sixth Development Plan: 1414–1420 A.H./1995–2000 A.D.* (Riyadh: Ministry of Planning Press, 1994), p. 170. (Hereafter cited as *Sixth Development Plan*).

31. Wilson and Graham, *Saudi Arabia: The Coming Storm*, p. 12 and notes, point out that these statistics, like most when it comes to Saudi Arabia, are 'suspect'. Some estimates have put the number of foreign workers in the Kingdom at around nine million by 1997 (Saudi official, confidential personal communication, December 1999). At times during the post-1973 development boom, expatriate workers have been estimated at up to 80 percent of the total civilian workforce. See Kanovsky, *The Economy of Saudi Arabia*, p. 49. On 'suspect' figures and the difficulty of obtaining information in general, see also Fred Halliday, review of: *Saudi Arabia: Government, Society and the Gulf Crisis* by Mordechai Abir (1993), in *Middle Eastern Studies*, 30, 3 (1994), pp. 691–2; CDLR, *Saudi Arabia: A Country Report*, pp. 7, 31–2. Even Saudi academics who might be expected to enjoy a relatively privileged position regarding research on their own country, complain that 'reliable information was sometimes scarce, inaccessible or unavailable' – a systemic affliction which also affects the performance of the Saudi bureaucracy (see Osama, *Dilemma of Development*, pp. 3, 31–4).

32. Taecker, personal interview, Riyadh, 26 January 1999.

33. For example, the Saudi government is promoting technical jobs and trades in a subtle and well-produced television recruiting campaign (personal viewing, Riyadh, January–March 1998). Of about 15 minutes duration, a program – a fusion of documentary and advertisement – will typically feature young Saudi men speaking about their work in manufacturing industry. Cleverly, whilst actually aiming to ease young Saudis out of the *mudir* syndrome (see note 34 below), the television programs tend to emphasize the supervisory roles in factories.

34. [See note 33] '*Mudir* syndrome' is my term: *mudir* is the Arabic word for 'director.' Muhammad al-Mas'ari claims matter-of-factly that this 'syndrome' is due to a bedouin background (personal interview, London, 20 May 1998). One former professional with a great deal of experience with Saudi Arabia independently agreed with Mas'ari, explaining that this attitude stems from a bedouin legacy where a man's role is seen to be that of a warrior and desert survivalist, and in which manual work is not honorable. He also reported that senior Saudis are worried about the 'moral' effects of this attitude (former British ambassador to Saudi Arabia, confidential personal interview, London, 26 May 1998). The trait is widely acknowledged and is recognized as an obstacle to progress in reducing unemployment and improving the Kingdom's long-term economic prospects (al-Shubaily, personal interview, Riyadh, 7 March 1998; various informal conversations with Saudi nationals and Arab expatriates, Riyadh, January–March 1998). Palmer, Alghofaily and Alnimir write that 'manual labor tends to be disdained [and is] generally regarded as '*aib* or shameful by traditional norms': see Monte Palmer, Ibrahim Fahad Alghofaily and Saud Mohammed Alnimir, 'The Behavioral Correlates of Rentier Economies: A Case Study of Saudi Arabia', in Robert W. Stookey (ed.), *The Arabian Peninsula: Zone of Ferment* (Stanford, CA: Hoover Institution Press, Stanford University, 1984), p. 20. See also: J.S. Birks and Clive A. Sinclair, 'The Domestic Political Economy of Development in Saudi Arabia', in Tim Niblock (ed.), *State, Society and Economy in Saudi Arabia*, (New York: St Martin's Press, 1982), pp. 202–3. This predisposition has clearly been reinforced by the 'new rentier pattern of behavior' which has dealt 'a serious blow to the ethics of work', a product of 'the oil disease' which has 'contaminated' Saudi Arabia along with the other Arab oil states: see Hazem Beblawi, 'The Rentier State in the Arab world,' *Arab Studies Quarterly*, 9, 4 (1987), p. 393. See also Wilson and Graham, *Saudi Arabia: The Coming Storm*, p. 256, for treatment of this issue: the legacy of slavery is cited as another factor in the persistence of the syndrome.

35. Former British ambassador to Saudi Arabia, confidential personal interview, London, 26 May 1998.

36. Ministry of Planning, *Sixth Development Plan*, p. 171.

37. Abdallah al-Shidadi, personal interview, Riyadh, 7 March 1998; T. al-Nashwan, personal interview, Riyadh, 7 March 1998. Shidadi is the General Director of Research Training and Information, Saudi Chamber of Commerce and Industry; Nashwan is the Sales Manager, Chemical and Plastic Products Division, Saudi Industrial Export Co. Shidadi has since re-affirmed the ten-year time frame for Saudiization, although he said it would be a good result if Saudiization were, in fact, achieved in ten years (personal interview, Riyadh, 26 January 1999).

38. Shubaily, personal interview, Riyadh, 7 March 1998. Shidadi (personal interview, Riyadh, 26 January 1999) also emphasized the problematic nature of the qualifications of Saudi nationals. As indicated above, the task of re-directing the interest of young Saudis to technical and trade occupations is a difficult one. It is, in fact, a fight that is being lost, according to one well-informed observer, who gave the example that much has been made by Saudi authorities of large numbers in technical training intakes, but that a large drop-out rate is not mentioned: former British ambassador to Saudi Arabia, confidential

personal interview, London, 26 May 1998.

39. Fahd M. Aslimy, personal interview, Riyadh, 7 March 1998. Aslimy is the Assistant Secretary General for Export, Saudi Export Development Center.

40. See, for example: 'Sabic Eyes the Future', *The Middle East*, 238 (1994), pp. 22–3; 'Privatizing the Business', *The Middle East*, 244 (1995), p. 24; 'Gulf push towards privatization', *The Middle East*, 246 (1995), pp. 30–1.

41. Kathy Evans, 'Shifting Sands at the House of Saud', *The Middle East*, 253 (1996), p. 9; see also 'Privatizing the Business', *The Middle East*.

42. Reuters, 'Saudi to Start Bilateral WTO Talks next Year', 5 August 1997; 'Kingdom to be Full Member of WTO in 2002', *Saudi Gazette*, 4 August 1997 (distributed electronically by Reuters Business Briefing Select, 8 August 1997).

43. Reuters, 'Saudi to Start Bilateral WTO Talks next Year'.

44. Economist Intelligence Unit (EIU Electronic), 'Saudi Arabia Investment – New Impetus in Privatizations', *Country Alert* (distributed electronically by Reuters Business Briefing Select, 14 August 1997); see also Clement M. Henry, 'Guest Editor's Introduction', *Thunderbird International Business Review*, 41, 4 (1999), pp. 3–4.

45. See, for example, the address given to the Gulf 1999 Conference in Abu Dhabi in March 1999 by Jan Kalicki, Counsellor to the US Department of Commerce: Jan H. Kalicki, 'The US and the Gulf: Trade, Investment and Economy', transcript of address to Gulf 1999 Conference, Abu Dhabi, 10 March 1999 (USIA Washington File, 15 March 1999. US Information Agency Internet website: <http://www.usia.gov/regional/nea/mena/kala315.htm>. An overview, from a security perspective of the socio-economic issues discussed here is presented by Cordesman, *Saudi Arabia*, pp. 47–76, which also helps demonstrate US interests in the successful economic and social restructuring of Saudi Arabia. The GCC was formed in 1981; its members are Saudi Arabia, Kuwait, Bahrain, Qatar, the United Arab Emirates and Oman.

46. IMF publications are a rich source of information on the drive for global economic–political reform. See, for example, Michel Camdessus, 'Toward a New Financial Architecture for a Globalized World', transcript of address at the Royal Institute of International Affairs, London, 8 May 1998 (IMF Internet website: <http://www.imf.org/external/np/speeches/1998/050898.htm>; Shailendra Anjaria, 'The IMF: Working for a More Transparent World. How New Technology and the IMF are Beginning a New Openness to New Financial Markets', *Journal of Information Policy*, 11 January 1999 (reproduced with permission by the IMF External Relations Department, IMF Internet website: <http://www.imf.org/external/np/vc/1999/011299.htm>; Alassane Ouattara, 'The Political Dimensions of Economic Reforms: Conditions for Successful Adjustment', transcript of keynote address, Berlin, 9 June 1999 (IMF Internet website: <http://www.imf.org/external/np/speeches/1999/061099.htm>. *IMF Survey*, 'Improvements in Global Financial System Hinge on Transparency and Management of Risk', 5 September 1999, p. 110. Camdessus was IMF Managing Director from January 1987 to February 2000, Ouattara is Deputy Managing Director of the IMF, Anjaria is Director of the IMF's External Relations Department.

47. Saad al-Fagih, personal communication, 7 September 1998. Fagih was the second prominent figure in the CDLR after Mas'ari, and is the founder and

head of the Movement for Islamic Reform in Arabia (MIRA), based in London.
48. Fagih, personal communication, 7 September 1998.
49. Saad al-Fagih, personal communication, 12 September 1998, 22 October and 24 October 1999; Former British ambassador to Saudi Arabia, confidential paper on Saudi Arabia, authored 1987/88.
50. Amnesty International, 'Alarming Increase in Number of Executions', Urgent Action Bulletin, 20 April 1995 (AI Index: MDE 23/01/95) (Hereafter cited as *Increase in Executions*). Fifteen executions were recorded by AI for 1990, 29 for 1991, 66 for 1992, 88 for 1993, and 'at least' 53 for 1994, and the trend appears to be continuing. See also: 'Saudi Arabia: An Upsurge in Public Executions': Report, 15 May 1993 (AI Index: 23/04/93) (Hereafter cited as *Upsurge in Public Executions*); 'Amnesty International Report 1995' (London: Amnesty International Publications, 1995), p. 253. AI's general conclusion is that Saudi Arabia's criminal justice system 'is designed to cater primarily for the might of the state', and therefore displays a 'complete disregard for international standards regulating arrest and trial': AI, *Saudi Arabia. Behind Closed Doors: Unfair Trials in Saudi Arabia* (report compiled by the AI International Secretariat. London, November 1997. AI Index: MDE 23/08/97), pp. iii, 29.
51. See AI, *Upsurge in Public Executions*, p. 10; AI, *Increase in Executions*. As of early November 1997, 'at least' 118 people had been executed in that year: AI, 'Fear of Increase in Executions', Urgent Action Bulletin, 7 November 1997 (AI Index: MDE 23/16/97).
52. Two notable detainees were Safar al-Hawali and Salman al-'Auda. The arrest of the latter sparked a large protest demonstration in the shaikh's home town of Buraida, about 350 km north-west of Riyadh, on 13 September 1994. The event was secretly captured on video and sent to the CDLR in London. Footage of an anti-Saudi demonstration in London on 30 September 1994 – as well as what is apparently a professionally produced narration – were subsequently added, with the result that a VHS video tape, 'Buraidah Uprising', was released by the CDLR to publicize the reality of dissent in Saudi Arabia.
53. AI, 'Execution/Flogging/Legal Concern', Urgent Action Bulletin, 15 August 1995 (AI Index: MDE 23/05/95). The CDLR claimed that three of the accused had, in fact, been in prison 'for between two and three months at the time of the alleged offence'. CDLR, 'Saudi Judicial Murder Marks Beginning of New Stage in the Confrontation between Regime and its Opposition' (press release), 13 August 1995. The Riyadh bombing took place on 13 November 1995. A CDLR spokesman (personal communication, 20 September 1995) emphasized the importance of the Hudhaif execution as a political landmark, claiming its significance is due to Hudhaif being the first Islamic activist to be publicly executed for purely political reasons, without him having committed any act of violence or armed opposition against the regime: 'the first [totally] unjustifiable execution'. The spokesman said the regime had initiated bloodshed with this execution, and that this had a great effect with many young dissidents, with a 'psychological barrier' having been broken. The spokesman also predicted, quite accurately as it turned out, violent retaliation against the regime 'within the next two months'.
54. Since even peaceful opposition is not tolerated, opposition inside the Kingdom has often been expressed violently. The bombings of 1995 and 1996

157

should be seen in the context of periodical violent outbursts against the Al Saud, which include the Ikhwan revolt of 1927–30, the opposition to the introduction of television in the 1960s and, most dramatically, the siege of the Great Mosque of Mecca in 1979. Such eruptions testify to a subterranean world of discontent which runs beneath the usually calm surface of Saudi society, as do – even more so, in fact – reports that there have been a number of foiled bomb plots against US targets and Saudi royals since the June 1996 Khobar bombing (Saad al-Fagih, personal interview, London, 28 May 1998). Moreover, there has, apparently, been at least one successful attack against regime figures which was completely covered up, with no information what-soever being leaked to the Saudi public or to the foreign media: the attack reportedly killed 'at least' eight Ministry of Interior personnel in 1996 (Fagih, personal interview, London, 26 May 1998).

55. Mordechai Abir, *Saudi Arabia: Government, Society and the Gulf Crisis* (London: Routledge, 1993), pp. 188, 191 (hereafter cited as *Government, Society and Gulf Crisis*).

56. The 'coalition' of *ulama* ranged, in its own right, from the young and radical to the conservative, state-oriented religious establishment; it: 'also represented a departure from the traditional alliance between "state and church" within the framework established by Ibn Saud after 1930 and, therefore, [was] a threat to the regime's authority and legitimacy' (Abir, *Government, Society and Gulf Crisis*, p. 191) For a concise history of the early period in the development of this opposition after the Gulf War, see Abir, *Government, Society and Gulf Crisis*, pp. 180–203; also R. Hrair Dekmejian, 'The Rise of Political Islamism in Saudi Arabia', *Middle East Journal*, 48, 4 (1994), pp. 627–43. (Hereafter cited as *Political Islamism*). For the definitive insider's account, see Saad al-Fagih, *The Rise and Evolution of the Modern Islam Movement in Saudi Arabia* (rev. edn) (1998); posted on the MIRA Internet site: <http://www.miraserve. com/HistoryOfDissent.htm.>. First published as 'History of Dissent', serialized in 1996 in the MIRA monthly publication *Arabia Unveiled*. It was this rapid development of a relatively open and robust, but very loose, political opposition which led to the formation of the CDLR in 1993, mass arrests and the 'Buraida uprising' in 1994, the Hudhaif execution and the Riyadh bomb-ing of 1995, the Khobar bombing of 1996 and the emergence of Osama bin Laden as a notorious, international figure. An account of the Saudi indivi-duals and dissident movements driving these events is presented in Fandy, *Saudi Arabia: Dissent*.

57. Fagih informed me that only some of the above-mentioned foiled plots were planned by followers of Bin Laden (see Note 54 above). However, it is prob-able that Saudi veterans of the Afghan war were behind most if not all of these plots. Fagih also revealed that 60 Afghanistan veterans were arrested by Saudi authorities in March 1998, and that secret cells of 'Arab Afghans' are still being discovered in the Kingdom (Saad al-Fagih, personal interview, London, 28 May 1998). Additionally, according to Fagih, there are 'hundreds of thous-ands of people' in many, (totally) 'secret' underground movements which, for the most part, do not have any political agenda, but are instead devoted to the promotion of Islamic values. Even so, he maintains, the regime would crush these movements if it could (Fagih, personal interview, London, 20 May 1998).

58. Fagih, personal interview, London, 20 May 1998.
59. Muhammad al-Mas'ari, personal communication, 5 August 1995.
60. Mas'ari, personal interview, London, 20 May 1998. Mas'ari's comment that 'there is no leading figure' provides a clue to his falling out with Fagih. While Fagih and MIRA are working relatively quietly to build a 'vertical structure' – that is, concentrating on the institutionalization and co-ordination of the specifically Saudi Arabian opposition – Mas'ari is a believer in the strategy of a charismatic leader and the linking of Islamic struggles worldwide. Mas'ari was being positioned as such a figure during the time of the original CDLR, by both himself and by Fagih as a deliberate policy to appeal to the Arabian cultural tradition of personalized politics and the larger-than-life charismatic leader who is both patriarch and patron to his people. It was a strategy that Fagih thinks gained the CDLR much beneficial early publicity and popularity, but which ultimately proved to be a mistake (Saad al-Fagih, personal interview, London, 20 May 1998).
61. Australian diplomat no. 1, personal interview, Canberra, 14 July 1995.
62. Michael Austrian, personal interview, Canberra, 13 July 1995. Austrian illustrated his opinion with the example of traditional religious conservatives versus modernizers who are calling for more democratic reforms. Austrian is a former senior US Middle Eastern diplomat of extensive experience.
63. BBC analyst, confidential personal interview, London, 26 May 1998.
64. Saudi suspicion and intolerance is both religiously and politically motivated, and can be carried to an extreme. For example, in a 1990 fatwa, a member of the Council of Senior Ulama, Shaikh Abdallah bin Abd al-Rahman bin Jibrin, proclaimed that Shiites 'deserve to be killed'. AI, 'Saudi Arabia. Religious Intolerance: The Arrest, Detention and Torture of Christian Worshippers and Shia Muslims' (Report), 14 September 1993 (AI Index: MDE 23/06/93), p. 16; see also Dekmejian, *Political Islamism*, p. 639. When processing newly-arrived Iraqi refugees after the 1991 Gulf War, Saudi officials reportedly asked: 'Are you Sunni or *kafir* (infidel)?', Shiite Iraqi refugees, personal group interview, Sydney, 21 April 1996.
65. Joseph A. Kechichian, 'Islamic Revivalism and Change in Saudi Arabia: Juhayman al-Utaybi's "Letters" to the Saudi People', *The Muslim World*, 80, 1 (1990), p. 5.
66. Impact International, 'Shi'i Dissidents to Return Home', 12 November–9 December (1993), p. 14. See also Madawi al-Rasheed, 'The Shi'a of Saudi Arabia: A Minority in Search of Cultural Authenticity', *British Journal of Middle Eastern Studies*, 25, 1 (1998), pp. 135–8 (Hereafter cited as *Shi'a of Saudi Arabia*); Christopher Lockwood, 'Shi'a Backlash Puts Saudi Regime Under New Threat', *Electronic Telegraph*, 464, 30 August 1996 (hereafter cited as *Shi'a Backlash*); *Facts on File*, item on 'reconciliation accord' between the Saudi regime and the Shii Reform Movement, 18 November 1993, p. 859.
67. Muhammad al-Mas'ari, personal interview, London, 26 May 1998. See also Rasheed, *Shi'a of Saudi Arabia*, pp. 129–30, 134, 136–8. Detailed discussions with a Saudi national indicated that politically astute Saudis are well aware of their government's practice of cyclic divide and rule of the opposition according to which kind of ideology presents the most acute threat at any particular time (Saudi national, confidential personal communication, 1997).
68. Mas'ari, personal communication, 6 July 1995; A. Rahman N. Alohaly,

personal interview, Canberra, 13 July 1995 (Alohaly was then serving as Saudi Arabia's ambassador to Australia). To what extent Mas'ari's views actually represented the CDLR position is doubtful in light of the organization's split. For a fuller treatment of the Saudi Shiites in the contemporary politics of the Kingdom, including tension between Shiites and the more moderate main-stream of the Sunni political opposition as represented by – or, rather, through – MIRA, see Fandy, *Saudi Arabia: Dissent*, pp. 172–3, 195–228; also Rasheed, *Shi'a of Saudi Arabia*.

69. The 'truce' between the regime and the Shiite community was reported to have broken down by mid-1996. See Lockwood, *Shi'a Backlash, Facts on File*; Mas'ari, personal interview, London, 26 May 1998. Evidence of strained relations and continuing distrust was provided in the wake of the June 1996 Khobar bombing; although the work of the radical Sunni underground, many, possibly hundreds of, Saudi Shiites were arrested in the general round-up in the search for those responsible: Lockwood, *Shi'a Backlash*; BBC analyst, confidential personal interview, London, 26 May 1998. Although the effective re-emergence of the Shii Reform Movement may point to renewed trouble with the Shiite minority in the future, it is unlikely, by itself, to represent a serious threat to the regime. In the meantime, the Islah Islamic movement in the Arabian Peninsula is warning about the continuing discrimination against, and neglect of, Saudi Shiites, and one observer, whilst believing there is no Saudi Hizballah underground at present, thinks there may well be in a few years' time: BBC analyst, confidential personal interview, London, 26 May 1998. Mas'ari, however, maintains that a Saudi Hizballah has existed for many years, but is dormant; he also dismisses the alleged potential Shiite 'threat', saying that Shiism is exhausted as an effective political ideology: Mas'ari, personal interview, London, 26 May 1998.

70. Wilson and Graham, *Saudi Arabia: The Coming Storm*, p. 82; Abir, *Government, Society and Gulf Crisis*, pp. 7, 28; Tim Niblock, 'Social Structure and the Development of the Saudi Arabian Political System', in Niblock, *State, Society and Economy*, p. 89; Moss Helms, *Cohesion of Saudi Arabia*, p. 57.

71. See Niblock, *State, Society and Economy*, pp. 88–91; Wilson and Graham, *Saudi Arabia: The Coming Storm*, p. 86 note 131.

72. Former British ambassador to Saudi Arabia, confidential personal interview, London, 26 May 1998.

73. Former British ambassador to Saudi Arabia, confidential paper on Saudi Arabia, authored 1987/88.

74. Former British ambassador to Saudi Arabia, confidential paper on Saudi Arabia, authored 1987/88.

75. The Al Sabah finally relented and parliamentary elections were held in Kuwait in October 1992 – a development which disturbed the Al Saud: see Wilson and Graham, *Saudi Arabia: The Coming Storm*, pp. 73–4, 76–7.

76. US diplomat, personal interview, Riyadh, 9 March 1998. The Basic Law of Government refers to one of three royal decrees announced to the Council of Ministers by the King on 29 February 1992. The guidelines for the establishment of the Consultative Council were included in the first two of these decrees. The three original decrees were the 'Basic Statute of Govern-ment', the 'Statute of the Consultative Assembly' and the 'Statute of the Provinces'. See Wilson and Graham, *Saudi Arabia: The Coming Storm*, p. 71.

The King's absolute powers over the Consultative Council and the Council of Ministers are set forth most clearly in article 57, 58, 68 and article 3 of the first two of these decrees, respectively. Indirectly emphasizing the purely 'consultative' aspect of the Consultative Council, is article 70 of the Government decree, which states that: 'Systems, treaties, international agreements and privileges will be issued and modified by Royal Decrees'. An Australian diplomat quoted the belief the Council was established when it was so the royal family could 'spread the blame' when it came to institute unpopular financial reforms: Australian diplomat no. 1, personal interview, Canberra, 14 July 1995.

77. US diplomat, personal interview, Riyadh, 9 March 1998; see also Abir, *Government, Society and Gulf Crisis*, p. 191; Cordesman, *Saudi Arabia*, p. 44.

78. *Economist*, 1995, p. 22. According to the Sixth Plan, approximately 50 percent of the population is under 15 years of age: Ministry of Planning, *Sixth Development Plan*, p. 170.

79. Muhammad al-Mas'ari, personal interview, London, 26 May 1998.

80. I personally observed the occasional small band of young males in Riyadh wearing Nike baseball caps backwards and baggy Western-style trousers, and playing rap music on their ghetto-blaster. Saudis in their late-20s and 30s expressed to me their concern at such influence and developments and the effects they may have on cultural traditions and national heritage. I am not suggesting that a youth-culture revolution is about to sweep the Kingdom; rather, I am suggesting there are signs that certain social changes – or phenomena, or aberrations – are beginning to occur below the surface and around the fringes of Saudi society which are probably not going to be short-term, passing or transitional ones. It is difficult to imagine how the effect of these social – and, ultimately, psychological – breaks from the (traditional) past will not eventually filter into other aspects of the Kingdom, including politics.

81. See, for example, Simon Henderson, *After King Fahd: Succession in Saudi Arabia*, WINEP Policy Paper No. 37 (Washington, DC: The Washington Institute for Near East Policy, 1994); Alexander Bligh, *From Prince to King: Royal Succession in the House of Saud in the Twentieth Century* (New York: New York University Press, 1984); David E. Long, 'A Fight to Follow Fahd?', *Middle East Insight*, 12, 4–5 (1996), pp. 62–5.

82. Stratfor.com, 'The Saudi Succession' (Stratfor Special Report 0130 GMT, 990925), 25 Sept. 1999 (direct URL: <http://www.stratfor.com/MEAF/specialreports/special12.htm>).

# 7

## The Gulf States and the American Umbrella

### JON B. ALTERMAN

US policy in the Persian Gulf, which has changed so many times over the years, is again in the midst of debate and revision. The US strategy in the 1960s and 1970s was to side with Iran, partly to contain Iraq; in the 1980s to side with Iraq to contain Iran; and in the 1990s to try to contain both countries simultaneously in order to preserve Gulf stability and protect the Arab monarchies there.

Part of the difficulty in developing a policy for the early twenty-first century lies in the fact that past policies have helped keep the peace. Iraq has not threatened its neighbors since massing troops on the Kuwaiti border in 1994, and Iran is actively courting other Gulf powers, especially Saudi Arabia. As regional threats appear to be waning, the United States remains in a defensive crouch that may hamper its ability to take advantage of opportunities for a new regional security environment. A US view of the Gulf that so heavily concentrates on military threats may also miss the importance of internal political changes, which over the next decade may have a far greater impact on matters of interest to the United States than the military balance will.

For decades, US policy in the Middle East has been driven by three main principles: energy security; Israeli security; and a general desire for stability and the protection of friendly regimes. Over the last 20 years, developments in the Gulf have directly affected each of those principles.

The Iranian revolution of 1979 was a jolt to American strategy in the region. In a short few months at the beginning of that year, the United States lost an important ally, its designated police-man in the Gulf, and one of the two pillars of its Gulf strategy – the other being Saudi Arabia. As the new government of the Islamic Republic of Iran consolidated its power, it became increasingly vocal about its anti-Americanism, its anti-Zionism, and its desire to foster Islamic revolution throughout the Middle East. Words were followed by deeds. Iranian students, with the support of the government, overran the US embassy in Tehran in November 1979 and held US diplomats hostage for 444 days. There was also a series of internal purges, first of anyone loyal to the Shah, and then of those insufficiently committed to the goals of the Islamic revolution.

Saddam Hussein saw the Iranian revolution as a threat and an opportunity. He was the avowedly secular leader of a neigh-boring country, the majority of whose citizens shared the Shiite Muslim faith of Iran rather than the Sunni Islam of most Iraqi leaders. Saddam feared that a spillover of Shiite revolutionary fervor from Iran would not only threaten his grip on power but could also affect Iraq's character as a Sunni-led secular state. He elected to go on the offensive, taking advantage of perceived dis-array in Tehran to redress old territorial claims and perhaps topple the ayatollahs from power. Striking out across the border in September 1980, he rushed to portray his battle in ethnic terms, defending Arab honor from the encroachment of Persian invaders. In so doing, he sought – and gained – the financial support of the Sunni Arab kingdoms in the Gulf which felt just as threatened by revolutionary Shiite republicanism as he did.

Despite his proclivity for appearing in uniform, Saddam Hussein's background is in the security services of the Iraqi Baath Party and not the military. In the early years of the war, his limitations as a general showed. The Iraqi army appeared to have no concrete objectives and their maneuvering was plod-ding. By July 1982, once the Iranians had recovered from their initial shock and reconstituted their military, the Iranian army pushed the Iraqis back over the border and advanced deeper into Iraqi territory. Pressed against the wall, Saddam sought – and got – international support for his battle against the Iranians, both from his Arab neighbors and from the United States.

The total amount of Arab assistance to Iraq during the war can reasonably be estimated as at least $30 billion.[1] The United States contributed, too, offering grain credits in 1983 and satellite photographs of Iranian deployments. The American embrace of Saddam was never enthusiastic but American policymakers considered it necessary to counter the Iranian threat. As the battle evened out in the middle of the decade, American government officials took a more ambivalent role. They continued courting Iraq, but also made limited overtures to Iran. First hoping to free American hostages held by Iran's Shiite allies in Lebanon, and then seeking cash with which to support anti-Communist forces in Nicaragua. White House officials sold limited amounts of weapons – mostly HAWK missiles – to Iran in the middle of the decade. The American profile in the Gulf rose in the winter of 1986/87 when Kuwait sought protection for its tankers, and threatened to ask for Soviet protection if the Americans did not help. The United States agreed to Kuwait's appeals, and the US Navy increased its presence in the Gulf.

Had Iran ended the war in 1982 or 1983, it could have done so on its own terms. but Tehran perceived only a partial victory over the Iraqis as a defeat, and continued to press for the fall of the Baghdad regime. Partly due to foreign assistance, but also using chemical weapons, the Iraqi army notched victories in the mid-1980s. Finally, the two weary parties implemented a formal cease-fire in August 1989, two months after Ayatollah Khomeini's death.

To American policymakers, the war's end did not mean the end of the Iranian threat. American officials continued to favor Iraq as a balance to Iran, and hoped that the bloody conflict's end would induce Iraqi moderation. When Democratic congressional staffers set out in 1989 to investigate Iraq's use of chemical weapons against civilians in the Iraqi Kurdish village of Halabja – attacked as a suspected opposition stronghold – some Capitol Hill Republicans began a whispering campaign suggesting that the staffers were motivated by fealty to the pro-Israel lobby and not American interests. Money played a role as well. In Washington in the late 1980s, it seemed that everyone from oil companies and telecommunications executives to farmers sought export markets in Iraq.[2]

The policy of *rapprochement* with Iraq came to a screeching halt with its invasion of Kuwait on 2 August 1990. In crossing the border, Iraq sought to obtain additional oil wealth and to wipe out the huge Iraqi debt for Kuwait aid given during the Iran–Iraq War. Iraq also blamed Kuwait for allegedly exceeding its oil production quota, thereby dropping world prices and diminishing Iraqi oil income. By invading, the Iraqis threatened all three pillars of American policy in the Middle East. Saddam's saber-rattling and later his ineffective SCUD attacks on Israel were also intended to make him the Arab world's leader and to let him act further to change the region's power balance. In the end, though, he only obtained backing from those with little to give – the Palestinian Liberation Army (PLO) and Yemen, for example – all of whom paid dearly for their flirtation with Saddam.

Meanwhile, the invasion forces quickly succeeded in taking over Kuwait, though hundreds of thousands of Kuwaitis fled. In response, hundreds of thousands of troops from the United States, Europe and the Arab world flooded into the Gulf to roll back the invasion. The American ambassador to Iraq, April Glaspie, has taken much of the blame for allegedly giving the Iraqis a green light to invade Kuwait; in point of fact, she was delivering State Department guidance predicated on the idea that Saddam could be co-opted. Glaspie's statement to the Iraqi president before the invasion suggests that the State Department thought Iraq might seek to occupy a sliver of Kuwait but never contemplated that Iraq would completely overrun the country.[3]

The allied attack against Iraq began in January 1991, after a long series of warnings and threats. Although many feared that the Iraqi troops, and especially the vaunted Republican Guards, would prove worthy adversaries, the Iraqi army collapsed almost immediately. Under coalition pressure – especially from the Saudis and the Egyptians – to end the war quickly,[4] allied troops decided not to press on to Baghdad, and instead accept Iraqi promises to disarm.

In the subsequent decade, the US position in the Gulf remained consistent. The Iraqi invasion of Kuwait made clear to the oil-rich kingdoms that their wealth provided little protection from invading armies. Americans continue to perceive Iraq as a threat that must be contained, and express concern over Iranian designs on the Gulf. American troops have prepositioned billions of dollars worth of supplies in the region, although the US military seeks, to the greatest degree possible, to remain 'over the horizon' to minimize local opposition.

But the relative success of a Pax Americana in the Gulf creates a challenge for the American position as well. While American troop presence in the Gulf has brought stability, that stability has also served to erode the rationale for maintaining forces and containing potential threats. Nationalists from the Gulf countries and throughout the region have harped on the American presence as an example of imperialism, while at the same time benefiting from the presence of those troops. A Lebanese journalist often begins his discussions of the Gulf by relating a Saudi's description of the desired American role: 'We want you to be like the wind. We want to feel you, but we don't want to see you.'[5]

Since May 1993, official US policy in the Gulf has been one of 'dual containment'. This strategy departed from Washington's long-standing approach of siding with either Iran or Iraq to balance against whichever of the two appeared more threatening. The end of the Cold War provided Washington with the opening for a new kind of policy. As former national security adviser Anthony Lake explained in an article:

> We no longer have to fear Soviet efforts to gain a foothold in the Persian Gulf by taking advantage of our support for one of these states to build relations with the other. The strategic importance of both Iraq and Iran has therefore been reduced dramatically, and their ability to play the superpowers off each other has been eliminated.[6]

While dual containment does not necessarily suggest equivalence between Iran and Iraq, it still relies on rather blunt weapons such as sanctions, opposition to international loans, and a heavy troop presence to confront very different kinds of challenges. Moreover, the containment itself takes very different forms against Iran and Iraq. US containment of Iraq relies primarily on multilateral measures. The sanctions regime in place is primarily the one imposed by the UN Security Council following the invasion of Kuwait. While the United States can use its Security Council veto to prevent lifting the sanctions until all the requirements of the original UN resolutions are met, the sanctions are multilateral in terms of their effects and their implementation.

US containment of Iran, by contrast, is primarily unilateral. American laws passed during the 1980s prohibit various kinds of transactions with Iran by American individuals and corporations. While current law tries to extend some secondary sanctions to corporations and individuals that do business with Iran, the sanctions can only partly affect the behavior of corporations in other countries.

The extent to which US policy toward Iraq is multilateral in its conceptualization – if not always in its implementation – is almost unprecedented. Immediately following the Iraqi invasion of Kuwait, Washington led the call in the Security Council for tough sanctions to force an Iraqi withdrawal. Only four days after Iraqi troops crossed the border, the Security Council passed Resolution 661, placing an embargo on trade to or from Iraq or Iraqi-occupied Kuwait, in a move that was to work in tandem with the initial deployment of tens of thousands of American troops. Through the late summer and fall of 1990, the Security Council passed no fewer than 12 resolutions condemning Iraqi actions, insisting on their reversal, and imposing penalties for non-compliance.[7] Although the United States overwhelmingly took the lead in the fighting, Operation Desert Storm was conducted by an alliance of more than 29 countries, encompassing such unlikely allies as Afghanistan, Syria, Niger and Spain. The ceasefire ending the war was predicated on Iraq's acceptance of all relevant UN resolutions and was enshrined in Security Council Resolution 687. That resolution remains the cornerstone of US policy toward Iraq, as well as the authority under which most sanctions remain in place.

Resolution 687 formalized the cease-fire and affirmed the inviolability of the international border between Iraq and Kuwait. In addition, reacting to fear that Iraq would use chemical or biological weapons against allied troops during the Kuwait War – as it had done against Iranian troops during the Iran–Iraq War and against its own Kurdish citizens in a 1988 campaign – the resolution demanded that Iraq end its programs for building unconventional weapons, declare the full extent of those programs, and submit to the supervised destruction of all remaining such weapons. The UN created a special body called the United Nations Special Commission (UNSCOM), to monitor Iraqi compliance with the arms control provisions of the resolution.

What no one anticipated in 1991 was that Saddam Hussein would last another decade while so doggedly resisting compliance with the UN resolutions, despite the effect of continued sanctions on the Iraqi people's living standards. Indeed, what has been so striking about Iraqi policy is the apparent decision to avoid telling the truth at all costs. The Iraqi government has made a long series of 'full, final and complete disclosures' to the international community, each time admitting that, despite earlier protestations, the previous version was neither full, final nor complete.

Explanations for incongruities or inconsistencies were often fanciful. For example, Iraq imported tons of culture-growth media in amounts that far exceeded their medical needs. By one estimate, the amounts imported in 1988 alone would have lasted Iraq for two centuries.[8] Iraqi officials insisted that the medium had no nefarious purpose, such as biological weapons development. Instead, they said, the problem was simply that overzealous supply clerks kept upping the orders as they passed through the chain of command.[9]

Following up on information revealed by former weapons development chief – and son-in-law to Saddam Hussein – Hussein Kamal after his defection in 1995, UN weapons inspectors not only gained a deeper understanding of Iraq's weapons development systems, but also discovered how completely they had been deceived. The cache of more than a half million documents recovered from Hussein Kamal's chicken farm in Haidar shortly after he left Iraq was a revelation to the Western inspectors.[10] Reconnaissance photography also indicated that Iraqi officials had spent the previous two weeks purging the files of the most incriminating information.[11] Iraqi government officials kept a straight face as they tried to blame the whole program on Kamal, and professed complete ignorance of it.

In response to persistent Iraqi deception, UN inspectors – buttressed by the United States and other countries – engaged in an essentially legalistic effort to build a case against Saddam Hussein. They pieced together intelligence information, documentary evidence and seemingly contradictory Iraqi statements to build an understanding of what the Iraqis were trying to do and how they were doing it. Starting in 1997, UNSCOM devoted a good deal of its energy to trying to understand Iraqi concealment mechanisms. Not surprisingly, they found that much of the concealment effort came directly from Saddam Hussein's personal office and involved élite security forces especially loyal to the Iraqi president.

Reliance on a legalistic framework, however, may have been counterproductive. There is little question that the Iraqi leadership lied energetically, repeatedly and concertedly about their weapons development programs. In response, the international community – led by the United States and to a lesser extent Great Britain – has consistently declined to lift sanctions on Iraq, insisting that Iraq must fully comply with all the relevant UN resolutions as a precondition.

But the sanctions have turned into as much of a trap for the international community as for Iraq. Sanctions have not changed Iraq's behavior, while the suffering of ordinary Iraqis has undermined the international community's resolve to keep the sanctions in place. Pressure within the UN – especially from Russia, China and France – has steadily increased the amount of oil Iran can export. Further, Saddam's regime does not seem any weaker. To the contrary, the regime itself has profited from the sanctions, skimming off money for smugglers and black marketeers while ensuring élite loyalty through the resultant patronage. On the one hand Iraq is being contained politically and militarily, but on the other, the Iraqi regime is staying in power. There is little international appetite for an armed strike against Iraq, but there is little else the international community can do.

Since the Gulf War, the United States has fitfully worked for Saddam's removal. In 1995 and 1996, the campaign took the form of a covert action program working with Iraqi exiles in Jordan. According to published accounts, in late June 1996, Iraqi intelligence operatives broke up the operation and arrested more than 120 people involved in Iraq. The plotters were interrogated, tortured and executed.[12]

Subsequently, American policy has appeared to be more declaratory than active, since the Clinton administration doubted that any such covert program could succeed. Starting in November 1998, American officials have stated US policy toward Iraq is 'containment plus regime change,' thereby returning to a goal of the first Bush administration. Just how regime change will be implemented is unclear. Congress authorized spending $97 million pursuant to the Iraq Liberation Act, but the Clinton administration was loath to use the funds. Most of the spending appears to cover office supplies and travel for expatriate Iraqis, with little clear notion of how to change the situation on the ground in Iraq.

The dilemma of current policy was revealed starkly in the second half of 1998. Throughout the late summer and early fall, Saddam Hussein provoked a crisis with the UNSCOM inspectors, at various points restricting their movements and indicating that he would not co-operate unless sanctions were lifted. After several narrowly-averted crises, inspectors returned to Iraq in mid-November with a promise of full co-operation from the Iraqis. On 16 December UNSCOM chairman Richard Butler announced to the Security Council that, in fact, the Iraqis had not co-operated fully. Beginning the next day, American and British planes launched four days of punishing air attacks on Iraqi installations. The end result has been that sanctions remain in place, there are no inspectors in Iraq, and there appears to be no provision either for removing Saddam Hussein from power or lifting sanctions. The December 1999 decision to replace UNSCOM with a successor organization, the UN Monitoring, Verification and Inspection Commission (UNMOVIC) has not yet yielded any inspections, and the organization's ability to alter the stalemate between the United States and Iraq appears weak.

The US–Iraqi stalemate differs dramatically from the US–Iranian relationship. In the first place, as has been suggested above, American efforts to contain Iran are fundamentally bilateral – although some of the congressionally-imposed sanctions have an extraterritorial aspect. UN resolutions do not govern the US–Iranian relationship, and there are no international sanctions in place against Iran.

Second, the political situation in Iran is in a high state of flux. More than a decade after the death of the leader of the Iranian revolution, Ayatollah Ruhollah Khomeini, Iranians throughout the political spectrum are debating Khomeini's legacy, and in some extreme cases, whether Khomeini's legacy should govern Iran at all. Signs of political change are rife. In 1997, the moderate Mohammad Khatemi won a landslide victory in the presidential election over the clear regime favorite, Ali Akbar Nateq Nouri, and reformists supporting Khatemi trounced conservatives in parliamentary elections in the spring of 2000. Under Khatemi's leadership, there has been an efflorescence of newspapers and magazines, many of which criticize aspects of the regime. Iran has a collection of crusading journalists and courageous publishers, and even when conservatives move against them, they often set up shop under a new name or a new rubric. The current struggle in Iran is over how conservatives will be able to maintain influence despite their clear renunciation by so much of the public. The conservatives have allowed that criticism to take place and have permitted the election process, which has so discredited them, to go forward with relatively little meddling. It is difficult to predict the future, but the trends seem to indicate compromise between the factions rather than direct confrontation.

On the international scene, the scorecard is more mixed. For the last decade, Iran has been engaged in a broad-scale effort to 'reduce tensions' with the outside world. After ten years of supporting revolutionary Islamic movements in many countries, Iran has sought accommodation with its neighbors and other members of the Muslim *umma*. Some of this change may have been due to the 1989 death of Khomeini, whose ideas were so important in the Iranian revolution. Some may have been due to the fact that attempts to export the revolution had not been successful, resulting in Iran's own international and regional isolation. Another cause could be Tehran's calculation that Iran's real interest lies in building an anti-Iraq coalition rather than continuing to antagonize potential allies. Whatever the reason, reduced tensions with key regional partners such as Saudi Arabia and Kuwait have opened the door to trade, co-operation on oil pricing and a host of other benefits.

There has even been some reduction in tensions with the United States, especially with regard to the US troop presence in the Persian Gulf. Although Iranian officials continue to complain bitterly about US ships and sailors in Gulf waters, the Iranian Navy is careful to avoid confrontations with US ships.

Iran's relations with some neighboring states, however, are still tenuous, and it is still engaged in actions that the US government finds objectionable. In the regional framework, Iran continues to dispute ownership of three Persian Gulf islands which it occupied in 1971 and are claimed by the United Arab Emirates (UAE). The border with Afghanistan remains tense, partly due to rampant drug smuggling and partly because of animosity between Afghanistan's Sunni Taliban movement and Shiite Iran with its own Afghan clients. *Rapprochement* with Iraq seems quite far off, although from a US government perspective, the United States and Iran share a perspective on Iraq's role in the region.

Farther afield, Iran continues to provide support for groups that use violence to oppose resolution of the Arab–Israeli conflict including, but not limited to, Palestinian Islamic Jihad and Hamas. Tehran reportedly supplies these organizations with money, weapons and training. Americans view Iranian support for groups that attack civilians as reprehensible.

The Iranian government is also a source of some extraordinarily vitriolic attacks on Israel. In a widely noted speech on the occasion of Jerusalem Day in December 1999, Iran's powerful spiritual leader Ayatollah Ali Khamene'i stated: 'There is only one solution to the Middle East problem; namely, the annihilation and destruction of the Zionist state.'[13] On that and other occasions, Iranian leaders have accused the Palestinian leadership of treason for its efforts to make peace with Israel, and they have violently criticized other governments for similar gestures. While mere speech is just that, Iranian statements are accompanied by support for violent groups, as outlined above, as well as by bitter attacks on the United States. Such talk makes it difficult for Americans who wish to improve relations with Iran to do so, since Iranian officials themselves seem so antagonistic to the idea.

American sanctions against Iran concern two different aspects of Iranian behavior. Some target Iran as a 'state sponsor of terrorism,' both for its support for armed militant groups and its own alleged actions against Iranian dissidents abroad. A second set target Iranian weapons development programs, especially nuclear weapons. The restrictions are of three kinds: Executive Orders; government regulations; and laws. The first two can be lifted unilaterally by the president, while the last requires the consent of Congress, or the expiration of the laws themselves.[14]

Obstacles notwithstanding, the present question in US–Iranian relations seems to be less about whether relations will improve, but rather when and under what conditions. Washington has declared its willingness to engage in whatever sort of 'authoritative' dialogue the Iranians favor, without any preconditions. By stressing that the dialogue must be authoritative, the Americans are opening the door to exchanges involving non-government officials, but closing the door to dialogue with any official or intermediary who represents merely a faction of the Iranian government. For its own part, the government of Iran refuses to enter into a dialogue as long as punitive sanctions against Iran remain in place. Iran is hoping that business-to-business contacts will pave the way for government-to-government contacts; Americans take the opposite approach.

Both sides insist that the initiative lies with the other party. Secretary of State Madeleine Albright attempted to move things forward by announcing on 17 March 2000, that the US government would no longer bar imports of Iranian food products and carpets, and hinting at American contrition for its past relations with Iran. Iranian intermediaries had explicitly requested both gestures as confidence-building measures. The gestures, however, came at a time of political uncertainty in Iran. A month before, the first round of parliamentary elections had given a large majority to reformist candidates aligned with the president. Conservatives were planning their strategies for the second round in May 2000 – in which the reformists also captured a significant majority – and both sides were stepping gingerly around the domestic political scene. In addition, the Spring 2000 trial of 13 Iranian Jews in Shiraz accused of spying for Israel damaged relations between Iran and the outside world. In July 2000, the court convicted ten and sentenced them to prison terms ranging from four to 13 years. For many on the outside, the revolutionary tribunal was a stark reminder of the bad old Iran. The closed trial and the confessions of beleaguered defendants did little to build confidence that justice would be served.

It is important to note that it has been political constraints, rather than strategic ones, that have stymied US–Iranian *rapprochement*. The United States and Iran share broad interests in the region. Both are alarmed by the actions of the Taliban in Afghanistan and by the high levels of drug smuggling over the Afghan–Iranian border. Both strongly believe that Iraq must be contained – although both sides seek to check the other's influence in a post-Saddam Iraq, and to date Iran has taken a free ride on the US containment of Iraq, while at the same time criticizing the American role in the region. Both countries desire stable oil prices and freedom of navigation in the Persian Gulf. American oil companies have a deep interest in developing Iranian petroleum reserves, and Iranian Oil Company officials have a great desire to tap into American expertise.

But anti-Americanism and anti-Zionism are among the last standing pillars of the Iranian revolution, and they will not go away easily. In addition, many Iranians fear that American hegemony – both political and cultural – will sweep over Iran and destroy thousands of years of Persian – and more recently, Islamic – civilization. Finally, entrenched financial interests have a stake in the continuance of American sanctions, since they profit so handsomely from the resultant smuggling operations.

On the American side, few politicians see political benefits to be gained from an opening to Iran. As long as the image of Iran in American minds is of angry, fist-shaking mobs, fierce and hostile clerics and supporters of terrorism, it will be hard for American officials to move forward. Iranian statements on Israel have a doubly negative effect, on the one hand threatening America's premier ally in the Middle East, and on the other reminding Americans of an Iran that does not play by international rules. Continued Iranian support for groups that use violence against civilians deepens Americans' hesitancy, as does Iran's apparent interest in developing nuclear weapons and long-range ballistic missiles. Finally, Iran's working with Russia and China to develop its weapons of mass destruction raises concern in the US government, for both historic and future reasons.

Earlier attempts at dialogue also ran aground on the shoals of political opposition. In 1995, then-President Ali Akbar Hashemi Rafsanjani struck a billion-dollar deal with Conoco, an American petroleum company to develop the Sirri gas field in the Persian Gulf. On the Iranian side, the deal could be viewed as a courageous attempt by Rafsanjani to open the door to the United States, or a cynical one to take American capital while continuing to undermine American interests in the region. Although the deal was permissible under American law, it set off alarm bells for Americans who were trying to establish a tougher policy toward Iran. Deeply in pre-election mode, the Clinton White House quickly drafted two executive orders restricting business between Americans and Iran.[15] For its own part, Congress passed the Iran–Libya Sanctions Act, which barred investment in Iran's petroleum sector.[16]

Much of the impetus toward détente with Iran was said to be driven by President Clinton himself, who reportedly took a personal interest in this effort and who made remarks expressing understanding for Iranian grievances.[17] President Khatemi also appears to have a direct interest in improving his country's relationship with the United States, as witnessed by his January 1998 interview on CNN calling for an improved relationship between the two countries.[18] But despite the leaders' intentions – and especially given Clinton's departure from office in January

2001 – there will need to be political movement in both countries in order for satisfactory relations to resume, and progress will likely be incremental.

US policy in the Gulf has been driven by military threats. American diplomats have been low-key. Warriors like Generals Norman Schwartzkopf and Anthony Zinni, successive heads of the US Central Command (CENTCOM) have grabbed headlines. Washington has gently goaded the Gulf states toward opening up their political systems. But such efforts have been tentative and have been greeted coolly by most regional governments. Regimes such as Saudi Arabia have bitterly pro-tested when US officials met with opposition figures, and in at least one case in the late 1980s, requested the removal of the American ambassador for doing so. Because relations are primarily government-to-government, the tendency has been to accede to such official requests to downplay calls for democ-ratization and to shun extensive contacts with those working against the ruling governments.

In the intermediate term, however, the political and diplo-matic leg of American policy may turn out to be more important than the military aspect. Gulf countries – including Iran and Iraq – have young, rapidly growing populations. Despite the rises in oil prices of recent years, growth has slowed in these states. Unemployment or underemployment are widespread problems. At the same time, expectations in the region are high. Those currently coming on the job market grew up in times of relative plenty, yet they find their own options relatively limited. In addition, satellite television and the Internet provide them with a steady diet of images of prosperity and social openness that many find attractive. Some respond by closing themselves off to the West and its messages, and others by embracing it. In countries such as Kuwait, therefore, we can see a widening gulf within Kuwaiti society, as neo-traditionalists do battle with secular modernists. About the only things the two sides have in common are their language and cell phones.

The task of healing these divisions and putting Gulf societies on a sustainable track for the future lies primarily with the governments of the region, not Washington. However, US interests are clearly at stake. The difficult task that diplomats face is that the success of their efforts is far more difficult to measure than those of their military counterparts. They seem to receive much of the blame – as they did with the Iraqi invasion of Kuwait; but little of the credit – as they did for the re-opening of the Kuwaiti parliament.

Despite two decades of US efforts, the Gulf remains an area of significant instability. Iraq is unbowed. While it no longer threatens its neighbors, it is unclear how long the current US policy can be sustained. Even less clear is what happens when Saddam goes and how long he will be able to remain in power. There are encouraging signs from Iran, as the 1979 revolution begins a process of institutionalization and rationalization that may remove some of the excesses of the regime's first two decades. A period of violence and prolonged internal struggle is possible. The smaller Gulf states have remained relatively stable throughout this period, led by conservative elderly leaders with long experience in governance. How they or their successors will weather the coming demographic storms will be a primary determinant of the preservation of American interests in the Gulf in the coming decade.

## NOTES

1. Shahram Chubin and Charles Tripp, *Iran and Iraq at War* (Boulder, CO: Westview, 1988), p. 154.
2. In the words of one enthusiast of *rapprochement* in that period, 'Iraq and the United States Need Each Other'. See Laurie Mylroie, 'The Baghdad Alternative', *Orbis*, 32, 3 (1988), p. 351.
3. The account printed in Micah L. Sifry and Christopher Cerf (eds), *The Gulf War Reader* (New York: Times Books, 1991), pp. 122–33. has not been disputed by the State Department.
4. See, for example, US News and World Report's *Triumph without Victory: The Unreported History of the Persian Gulf War* (New York: Times Books, 1992), p. 395.
5. Hisham Melhem, conversation with author.
6. Anthony Lake, 'Confronting Backlash States', *Foreign Affairs*, 73, 2 (1994), p. 48.
7. Security Council Resolutions 660, 661, 662, 664, 665, 666, 667, 669, 670, 674, 677 and 678.
8. Tim Trevan, *Saddam's Secrets: The Hunt for Iraq's Hidden Weapons* (London: HarperCollins, 1999), p. 288 (hereafter cited as *Saddam's Secrets*).

9. Andrew Cockburn and Patrick Cockburn, *Out of the Ashes: The Resurrection of Saddam Hussein* (New York: HarperCollins, 1999), p. 199 (hereafter cited as *Out of the Ashes*).
10. According to Trevan, who was an UNSCOM inspector, the documents appeared to have been newly delivered to the site where they were disclosed, and Hussein Kamal denied having kept such a store of documents. Trevan, *Saddam's Secrets*, pp. 331–2.
11. See Cockburn and Cockburn, *Out of the Ashes*, p. 236.
12. Ibid., p. 228.
13. IRNA [in English], transcribed in FBIS Document ID FTS 19991231000386 (31 December 1999).
14. The relevant laws and regulations can be found in Kenneth Katzman (ed.), *US–Iranian Relations: An Analytic Compendium of US Policies, Laws and Regulations* (Washington, DC: The Atlantic Council of the United States, 1999).
15. Executive Order 12957 of 15 March 1995, and Executive Order 12959 of 6 May 1995. They can be found in ibid., pp. 40–1.
16. 50 USC 1701. The law expired on 5 August 2001.
17. For a copy of the President's comments at a White House Millennium Evening, see <http://www.whitehouse.gov/WH/EOP/First_Lady/html/generalspeeches/1999/19990412.html>.
18. An edited transcript is printed in Robert S. Litwak, *Rogue States and US Foreign Policy: Containment after the Cold War* (Washington, DC: Woodrow Wilson Center Press, 2000), pp. 265–70.

# 8

# Contradictions in US Policy on Iraq and its Consequences

## AMIN TARZI

*It should be the policy of the United States to seek to remove the regime headed by Saddam Hussein from power in Iraq and to promote the emergence of a democratic government to replace the regime.*[1]
(Iraq Liberation Act signed into law by the US President Clinton on 31 October 1998)

*Let me say, our position on Iraq is that we favor the proposal before the United Nations advanced by the British and the Dutch. It would provide for more money to Iraq to help the people there, with their human needs. But it would maintain a vigorous arms control regime, because we do not believe that Saddam Hussein should be permitted to develop again weapons of mass destruction.*[2]
(President Clinton, 1 July 1999)

On 16 December 1998, the United States, supported by only the United Kingdom, launched a massive aerial bombardment of Iraq. Although Operation Desert Fox officially lasted only three days, sporadic but continuous military strikes against Iraqi targets continue with no end in sight. However, the full consequences of this undeclared war may not be realized until the regime of President Saddam Hussein lashes out with fury against one of Iraq's neighbors or, in the most likely scenario, against Israel.

This article will analyze the United States' declared policy (or policies) on Iraq, immediately before and since Desert Fox and will highlight the contradictions in these policies. These contradictions, a result of US indecisiveness, may have dire consequences for several key states in the Middle East and the future of international arms control mechanisms.

## THE ROAD TO DESERT FOX

Operation Desert Fox (December 1998) and subsequent operations have been rooted in the behavior of the Iraqi regime of Saddam Hussein. The atrocities committed by Baghdad are well documented and need no elaboration. Herewith, is a recounting of the principal incidents that led to the US decision to open a military campaign against Iraq in December 1998.

On 5 August 1998, Iraq suspended co-operation with the United Nations (UN) Special Commission (UNSCOM) and the International Atomic Energy Agency (IAEA) regarding weapons inspections and ongoing monitoring and verification (OMV) activities at declared sites. Iraq indicated that it would resume co-operation with UNSCOM and the IAEA only if the UN Security Council lifted sanctions on Iraqi oil exports and reorganized the structure of UNSCOM, including moving its headquarters from New York to either Geneva or Vienna. This would, Iraq claimed, make the commission less susceptible to manipulation by the United States.[3]

As had been the case since the end of the Gulf War in 1991, the Iraqi regime balked at the Security Council's demands. This time, sensing the deep divisions among the five permanent members of the Security Council (P-5) and calculating that the true aim of the United States was the overthrow of Saddam Hussein, Baghdad effectively ceased co-operation with both UNSCOM and the IAEA on 31 October 1998. Nizar Hamdun, Iraq's permanent representative to the United Nations, announced that the UN inspectors were expected to leave Iraq,[4] a move condemned by the Security Council, which demanded that Iraq: 'rescind immediately and unconditionally' its decisions of 5 August and 31 October.[5]

In November, the Iraqis unsuccessfully tried to drive a wedge between the IAEA and UNSCOM by allowing the former agency access to the country, but not the latter. Meanwhile, the United States began to deploy more military equipment and personnel in the Persian Gulf region.[6] Washington, however, failed to create a broad coalition for a possible strike against Iraq to force it to readmit the UN weapons inspectors. Other than the United Kingdom, no other state – including close US allies such as Saudi Arabia – expressed its willingness to join in a military campaign against Iraq.

In an about-face, on 14 November, Iraq's deputy prime minister Tariq Aziz forwarded a letter to UN Secretary-General Kofi Annan announcing his government's intention to co-operate unconditionally with both UNSCOM and the IAEA. The Security Council, noting Aziz's letter, decided to resume weapons inspections in Iraq.[7] While P-5 members China and the Russian Federation welcomed Baghdad's pledge to co-operate fully and unconditionally with UN weapons inspectors, thus avoiding military conflict, the United States initially rejected the Iraqi offer. US national security adviser Sandy Berger referred to Aziz's letter as having 'more holes than Swiss cheese.'[8] However, following consultations between Washington and the United Nations, and after clarifications were presented by the Iraqis, the United States decided to postpone the impending air strikes against Iraq.

On 15 December, Kofi Annan forwarded to the President of the Security Council reports on the work of the IAEA and UNSCOM in Iraq covering the period from 17 November. The Director-General of the IAEA, Mohamed El Baradei, indicated in his report that Iraq: 'has provided the necessary level of co-operation' in order for the agency's work to be 'completed efficiently and effectively.'[9] However, UNSCOM Executive Chairman Richard Butler reported that his commission did not receive Iraq's full co-operation. Butler concluded that under the circumstances, UNSCOM would 'not [be] able to conduct the substantive disarmament work mandated to it by the Security Council.'[10]

On 16 December, US President Bill Clinton announced that

he had ordered strikes against military and security targets in Iraq. Operation Desert Fox began. Clinton presented Saddam Hussein's refusal to co-operate with the UN weapons inspectors, whom he called 'highly professional experts from dozens of countries,' as the principal reason behind his decision to order strikes.[11] Further elaborating on the need for American military action, Clinton said that while other states possessed weapons of mass destruction (WMD) and ballistic missiles, Iraq had repeatedly used these weapons. Clinton added that he had: 'no doubt today, that left unchecked, Saddam Hussein [sic] will use these terrible weapons again.'[12] Clinton noted that in the absence of a strong weapons inspection system, Iraq: 'would be free to retain and begin to rebuild its chemical, biological, and nuclear weapon program in months, not years.'[13]

Declaring the end to Operation Desert Fox three days later, Clinton announced his resolve not to allow Iraq to defy the international community by avoiding full co-operation with UNSCOM. He also praised the UN weapons inspectors for destroying weapons and missiles, which Saddam Hussein had insisted he did not possess. The US President also stated that as long as Hussein's regime remained in Baghdad, American policy on Iraq would consist of three main points:[14]

- First, the United States would maintain a strong military presence in the region which it would use should Iraq try to rebuild its WMD capabilities, attack its neighbors, challenge American or British aircraft patrolling the skies over northern or southern no-fly zones, or threaten the Kurdish population in northern Iraq.[15]

- Second, the United States would ensure that economic sanctions against Baghdad would remain in place and would support the oil-for-food program designed to allow Iraq to purchase food and medicine.[16]

However, only the last point in Clinton's stated policy touched on the return of the UN weapons inspectors to Iraq. Should Baghdad prevent UNSCOM from resuming its work, the United States would 'remain vigilant and prepared to use force' if Iraq attempts to reconstitute its WMD programs.[17]

Before moving into the domestic side of the American policy on Iraq, it is significant to review the fact that the main stated reason for launching Operation Desert Fox was to force Saddam Hussein to co-operate fully and unconditionally with UNSCOM. Moreover, in a letter to US congressional leaders on 3 March 1999, Clinton reiterated his reason to take military action against Iraq in December 1998 as being based on the report of Richard Butler to the UN secretary-general in which he stated that: 'Iraq was not co-operating fully with the Commission.'[18]

However, US policy post-Desert Fox focused on the removal of the Iraqi regime from power and, until then, containing Saddam – a policy that has come to be known as 'containment plus regime change.' In fact, the United States officially adopted the policy of attempting to oust Saddam Hussein when President Clinton signed the Iraq Liberation Act into law on 31 October 1998 – the same day Baghdad ceased co-operation with UNSCOM.

## THE IRAQ LIBERATION ACT (1988)

On 29 September 1998, a bipartisan group of eight US senators introduced a bill entitled the Iraq Liberation Act (ILA) to: 'establish a program to support a transition to democracy in Iraq.'[19] The bill, which passed the Senate unanimously without amendment, outlines Iraq's transgressions, from its invasion of neighboring Iran in 1980 to its unilateral suspension of co-operation with UNSCOM the previous August. The act stipulates that US policy should seek the removal of Saddam Hussein and assist in replacing his regime with a democratic form of government. The US is also to provide military assistance to the Iraqi opposition – the amount not to exceed $97 million – in addition to funding the United States Information Agency effort to publicize the opposition's struggle.

Concurrent with the signing of the ILA into law by President Clinton, Radio Free Iraq began broadcasting to Iraq. Then, in November 1998, US Assistant Secretary of State for Near Eastern Affairs, Martin Indyk, met with a delegation of 17 representatives from Iraqi opposition parties, urging them to work jointly towards the goal of forming a new government in Baghdad. The Iraqi group identified by the United States to spearhead opposition is the London-based Iraqi National Congress (INC). Early in 1999, the United States appointed Frank Ricciardone as Special Representative for Transition in Iraq (SRTI) and charged him with uniting the INC's political platform and facilitating Washington's contacts with the various Iraqi groups.[20]

On 11 August 1999, the eight senators and congressmen who were the principal proponents of the ILA sent a letter to President Clinton expressing their 'dismay over the continued drift in US policy toward Iraq.'[21] They pointed to four areas to which they believed the Clinton administration had not given proper attention. The first area addresses the absence of international weapons inspections in Iraq and argues that the 'whole point of Operation Desert Fox was' that the world could not afford to allow Saddam Hussein to reconstitute his WMD capabilities. However, following Desert Fox the administration is still unsure of what is taking place inside Iraq.[22] Other countries have also raised this criticism. In a commentary representative of his country's views, French journalist Alain Gresh wrote that the United States launched Operation Desert Fox to restore UNSCOM's right to conduct its weapons inspection and OMV in Iraq. However, many months have passed without UN inspectors in Iraq and the United States seems to be very relaxed about this state of affairs.[23]

The other three points in the letter to Clinton are all directed at the administration's lack of political and material support to the Iraqi opposition outside Iraq and its unwillingness to deliver assistance to opposition inside the country.

Perhaps in response to this letter, the Clinton administration was been more visibly active in pursuing Saddam's removal from late October 1999. Activities became centered on Washington's desire to forge a unified Iraqi opposition under the umbrella of the INC that would create a broad coalition of Iraq's main three population groups: Shiite Arabs, Sunni Arabs, and the Kurds.

In its official declarations, the INC claims to present 'a credible political alternative for all the Iraqi people without prejudice or differentiation and with full representation of all groups and communities' in the country.[24] The INC is known to Washington as a group with no anti-US sentiments – as is the case with most of the Shiite groups operating in Iraq – and its leaders do not hesitate to be identified with the United States.

To this end, with direct American support and encouragement, the INC opened its first session in seven years in New York on 29 October 1999. The meeting, in which 300 delegates participated, ended four days later with an elected 65-member Central Council and a leadership team comprising seven Iraqis.[25] Incidentally, in a letter from US Undersecretary of State for Political Affairs Thomas Pickering addressed to the seven leaders of the INC, only the names of three individuals match those of the group's elected leaders.[26] The four others named by Pickering who were not listed among the seven elected INC leaders include two Shiite Iraqi leaders. This indicates that perhaps Washington had a different INC leadership in mind – one that included Shiites – from the elected leadership. Or, it might point to confusion among US policymakers.

Hamid Bayat, a representative of the Supreme Council for Islamic Revolution in Iraq, the main Iran-based Iraqi opposition Shiite group, stated that his group's decision not to attend the New York meeting was based on the belief that the INC gathering was not a 'serious project for change in Iraq.'[27] Similar sentiments were echoed by the secular Awfaq movement, which deemed the INC's New York meeting ill-prepared to hold discussions on the future of an organized opposition against Saddam's regime.[28] Earlier this year, Shaykh 'Ali 'Abd al-'Aziz, leader of the United Islamic Movement, a Kurdish group based in Halabja, stated that while his party was ready to attend the meeting in New York, it challenged the United States to action rather than talk.[29]

According to the August 1999 congressional letter, the Kurds in northern Iraq asked for American protection to hold an opposition National Assembly inside Iraq in July, but US Deputy Secretary of State Strobe Talbott rejected their request.[30]

Regarding this point, Patrick Clawson, the director of research at the Washington Institute for Near East Policy, wrote that Iran would most likely provide the Kurds the protection promised but not delivered to them by the United States.[31]

Not only is the INC's leadership largely comprised of Kurds, but so is its fighting forces – hardly representative of Iraqi society. Since their 1996 defeat by forces loyal to the Iraqi regime, the Kurds have been engaged in internal conflicts and some of their groups are 'competing for Baghdad's favor.'[32] Even with a fighting force on the ground, the chances for an opposition military attack without Amercian ground support, are, in the words of one Iraqi opposition leader, like buying a lottery ticket.[33]

So far, no one in US policymaking circles has spoken about committing American troops to help the Iraqi opposition. Both the White House and the Pentagon have ruled out direct American military involvement in support of the internal Iraqi opposition. General Anthony Zinni, then commander of the US Central Command (CENTCOM), who would be responsible for any American military activity against Iraq, stated that not a single leader or person he has met in the region supports arming external opposition groups.[34] He has also ruled out American ground intervention to support the Iraqi opposition. The trainees reportedly include two former Iraqi military officers, but their training will be limited to non-combat subjects such as leadership and management of the post-Hussein military in Iraq.[35] The ILA does authorize military training for the Iraqi opposition and proponents of the move criticized the Clinton administration for not moving toward that end. In response, Clinton reportedly assured members of the US Congress that military training would become part of the package. However, a date has yet to be set for training and US Defense Department spokesman Kenneth Bacon has stated that organizational training is a necessary step towards the formation of a fighting force.[36] Also, the INC in its New York meeting failed to discuss the military matters on its agenda, postponing the matter for future discussions in a safe haven inside Iraq.[37]

Whereas the ILA represents the main vehicle for implementing the latter element in the 'containment plus regime change' policy, Saddam Hussein's moves are contained by US military aircraft patrolling the no-fly zones and by continued economic sanctions.

## 'OPERATION DESERT YAWN'

The termination of Operation Desert Fox signaled the beginning of what one observer has appropriately termed 'Operation Desert Yawn.'[38] The United States, supported only by the United Kingdom, conducted more than 150 air strikes in 1999, mostly targeting Iraqi military installations, especially radars and anti-aircraft batteries that menace American and British planes patrolling the no-fly zones. The air campaign has been so successful that recently an American official admitted that few military targets remain in the area covered by the no-fly zones and that the US Air Force has sought permission to bomb targets outside the no-fly zones.[39] The often unnoticed bombing represents the 'longest continuous US combat action since the Vietnam War.'[40] Yet American officials have admitted that they have no clear idea about activities inside Iraq so far as the reconstitution of WMD programs are concerned. Ironically, the bombings might have a negative effect on the OMV mechanisms installed in Iraq because many of the electronic systems installed by UNSCOM have either been damaged by the strikes or been wrecked by the Iraqis who then blame the American and British attacks.

On 15 July 1999, the *Washington Post* quoted an administration official who closely monitors intelligence on Iraq as saying that 'we have seen no evidence of reconstruction of weapons of mass destruction.'[41] US State Department spokesman James Rubin stated that:

> With respect to our ability to monitor outside inspections, let me say that is limited; that the only really effective way is to have inspections. Having said that, I think it's fair to say that we have no reason to believe there have been significant efforts [on the part of the Iraqi regime] to reconstitute their weapons of mass destruction program.[42]

The same uncertainty was echoed two weeks later by US Department of Defense spokesman Kenneth Bacon who, when asked whether Iraq was planning to reconstitute its WMD capabilities, replied: 'I don't have good information on that now.'[43]

On 25 August 1999, the White House reported to the US Congress that:

> We are concerned by activity at Iraqi sites known to be capable of producing (weapons of mass destruction) and long-range ballistic missiles, as well as Iraq's long-established covert procurement activity that could include dual-use items with (weapons) application.[44]

On 2 September, during a press briefing in the State Department, a reporter noted the inconsistency between the White House's alarmist view and the July statement by James Rubin in which he claimed that no information on such activity was available. A State Department spokesman, Philip Reeker, responding to this question, stated that the White House report outlines what is known about Iraq's WMD-related activities but:

> In the absence of UN inspectors on the ground carrying out the existing Security Council mandate, the uncertainties about the meaning of the Iraqi WMD activities will persist, and as time passes, the concerns of the US will increase.[45]

To that end, Reeker confirmed that the United States supports part of the ongoing political efforts at the United Nations to re-establish an inspection regime in Iraq.


### EFFORTS TO REVIVE INSPECTION SYSTEM OF IRAQI WEAPONS OF MASS DESTRUCTION PROGRAMS

Since the end of Operation Desert Fox, various UN Security Council member states have tried to re-establish dialogue and co-operation between the United Nations and Iraq. Several of these states have attempted to present draft proposals to reintroduce weapons inspections and OMV into Iraq – in other words, replace UNSCOM.

On 30 January 1999, the UN Security Council called for the establishment of three panels to examine the issues regarding the situation in Iraq and make recommendations to the Security Council. These panels were: disarmament and current and future ongoing monitoring and verification issues; humanitarian issues; and prisoners of war and Kuwaiti property.[46] In March 1999, the final reports of the three panels were submitted to the Security Council for consideration.[47]

The previous January, competing proposals circulated at the Security Council, aimed at reconstituting inspections.[48] One draft, proposed by France and supported by China and the Russian Federation, would abolish UNSCOM, create an even more intrusive verification program, and – most importantly – suspend the economic sanctions that have been in place since the 1990–91 Gulf War if Iraq allows UN inspections to function for a period of 60 days. The rival draft, sponsored by the Netherlands and the United Kingdom and supported by the United States, would also replace UNSCOM with a stricter United Nations Commission on Inspection and Monitoring (UNCIM)[49] but would offer only a limited suspension of sanctions after Iraq complies with the remaining conditions contained in relevant Security Council documents. However, the proposal fails to list those conditions, and without a timetable some sanctions could stay for an indefinite period of time. Malaysia is the only Security Council member that refuses to support either of the two resolutions.

The United States has stated that it will not entertain any discussion on removing sanctions until Iraq meets its obligations under Security Council resolutions 661 (1991) and 687 (1991), and other relevant resolutions. However, several officials representing the American administration have presented conflicting statements.

On 23 June 1999, Elizabeth Jones, Principal Deputy Assistant Secretary of State for Near Eastern Affairs, testified to the Senate Foreign Relations Committee: 'As long as the current

Baghdad regime is in defiance of the UNSC (United Nations Security Council) resolutions, we will never allow it to regain control of Iraq's oil revenue.' She added that the United States supports:

> the British–Dutch draft because it meets *our bottom line* [emphasis added] criteria: real arms control; expansion of the oil-for-food program on the basis of humanitarian need, insistence on a standard of full Iraqi compliance for action on sanctions.[50]

In her last point, Jones said that the United States would take action on sanctions after full Iraqi compliance. However, only a few days before Jones' testimony, the National Security Council's Senior Director of Near East and South Asian affairs, Bruce Riedel, stated that the United States will continue to ensure that Saddam Hussein never gets 'his hands on Iraq's oil wealth. That is our *bottom line* [emphasis added] on the UN sanctions regime. Simply put, this tyrant can never be again trusted.'[51] Riedel went on to say that Iraqi finances must be under United Nations control until 'we're all satisfied that there is a government [in Iraq that is] at peace with its neighbors and its own people.'[52]

The 'bottom line' in the current American policy on Iraq seemed to shift according to the domestic and international circumstances to which the Clinton administration wanted to respond. Dangerously, one element that ought to determine United States policy *vis-à-vis* Iraq remains unknown: that is, whether Saddam Hussein is planning or is actually reconstituting his WMD programs.

## DANGEROUS CONSEQUENCES

According to State Department spokesman James Rubin, the United States remains prepared to use military force if Saddam Hussein rebuilds his WMD programs. This, Rubin stated, is the best tool that the United States has to contain the Iraqi regime at this point.[53]

The only problem is that Washington is sending conflicting

messages about Iraq's WMD plans. Obviously, without on-site inspections and a very intrusive OMV program, it is close to impossible to ascertain what Saddam Hussein is trying to do. Based on his record, he can be extremely unpredictable. Should the United States discover that Saddam has indeed reconstituted one or more elements of his WMD programs, it may be too late for preventive action, perhaps not for the United States itself, but for Iran and Israel, the two most likely targets of an Iraqi attack.

Moreover, it is not certain whether American policy currently favors following UN Security Council resolutions that the United States has not only voted for, but also encouraged other states to endorse. Sanctions are not an end in and of themselves. They represent a means to an end, and that end is not the overthrow of Saddam Hussein's regime. Rather, it is compliance with the relevant Security Council resolutions. If the United States can gather sufficient international backing to indict Saddam Hussein and senior members of his regime for war crimes, then it would be legally acceptable to pursue the removal of the Iraqi leadership as part of the international discussions on Iraq.[54] Otherwise, 'the bottom line' referred to by Riedel becomes a non-starter in the Security Council. Also, as long as the United States insists that the removal of Saddam Hussein is a prerequisite for the easing of economic sanctions against Iraq, there is no incentive for Saddam to accept a new UN-inspection and monitoring system.

The removal of Saddam from power represents the best-case scenario not only for the United States but for most countries in the region. But to remove Saddam's regime, major efforts by a unified internal opposition backed by substantial military and economic assistance from abroad are needed. Currently, neither is forthcoming. There is no serious internal military threat nor is there a commitment from neighboring states to become the staging ground for military operations against Iraq. Comparing the situation in Iraq to that of Afghanistan in the 1980s, there is no country, not even Kuwait, which is willing to become what Pakistan became for the Afghan Mujahidin.

The Arab states, with the possible exception of Kuwait, are openly frustrated with the current stalemate over Iraq. Most

Arabs are displeased with the human effects of the economic sanctions on the Iraqi population. This sentiment was amplified by the Arab League in its January 1999 communiqué which calls for international efforts to lift the sanctions as soon as possible.[55] The concern of Arab states such as Saudi Arabia and Kuwait goes beyond their uneasiness about the suffering of the Iraqis. These regimes believe that there could be a backlash from their own populations which blame them for complicity in the suffering of the Iraqi people. Other Arab states such as Egypt link the issue of sanctions against Iraq to the larger problems in the Middle East. The decision by Egyptian President Hosni Mubarak to boycott the 1 November 1999 summit between the Israeli Prime Minister Ehud Barak, Palestinian Authority Chairman Yasser Arafat, and President Clinton in Oslo was partly related to Egypt's disapproval of US policy on Iraq.[56]

It is clear that Saddam Hussein is winning the propaganda war. Not only are the Arabs raising their voices about the suffering of the Iraqi people, but the UN secretary general has accused the United States of using its muscle to force the UN committee in charge of sanctions to withhold humanitarian aid to Iraq.[57] Talking to ABC News, Fabrice von Sponeck, the embattled UN humanitarian aid co-ordinator for Iraq, stated that while the Baghdad regime blames the death of Iraqi children on the sanctions and others blame the suffering on Saddam Hussein, the reality which has to be confronted is how to avoid the 'unnecessary death of children.'[58] Even staunch opponents of the Iraqi regime, such as former UNSCOM chief Richard Butler, have gone on record as being against sanctions. Butler has stated that sanctions 'seem to hurt the wrong people and don't necessarily bring about compliance.'[59]

The current stalemate over weapons inspection in Iraq has also damaged the prospects for any future international safeguard system against a belligerent state with WMD capabilities. The split among P-5 members of the Security Council can only encourage proliferation. Most importantly, the contradictions now apparent in US policy are themselves becoming a threat to the resolve of other states to abide by their commitment regarding Iraq.

194

There is no question that the best-case scenario for both the Iraqi people and Middle East states would be the end of Saddam Hussein's regime. However, to achieve this aim, the international community, and in particular the United States, must be prepared to absorb some of the damage. US congressman Benjamin Gilman, speaking before the INC assembly in New York, compared the ruthlessness of the current Iraqi regime to Hitler's Germany and Stalin's Russia. Then he stated that: 'America made great sacrifices to end those regimes, and we owe it to the people of Iraq to help you free your country as well.'[60] If the United States is serious about helping the Iraqis remove Saddam's brutal regime, then it must be ready to make sacrifices. By prolonging the agony of ordinary Iraqis who not only have to bear the burden of living under Hussein's rule, but are also bearing the brunt of the sanctions, the United States is neither achieving the policies stipulated under the ILA nor living up to its international obligations.

## NOTES

1. Iraq Liberation Act of 1998, United States Senate, document S.2525, 29 September 1998; <http://www.senate.gov/legislative/index.html>.
2. Remarks made by US President Bill Clinton, 'Press Conference by President Clinton and President Mubarak of Egypt', The White House, 1 July 1999; Office of the Press Secretary, <http://www.whitehouse.gov>.
3. The UN Security Council in its resolution 1194 of 9 September 1998 condemned this act by Iraq. For a chronology of main events leading to Operation Desert Fox and beyond, see <http://www.un.org/Depts/unscom/Chronology/chronologyframe.htm>. Also see Anthony H. Cordesman, *Iraq and the War of Sanctions* (Westport: Praeger, 1999), pp. 175–393.
4. Cordesman, *Iraq and the War of Sanctions*, p. 351.
5. See UN Security Council Resolution 1205 of 5 November 1998, adopted unanimously with no abstentions.
6. By 3 November 1998, United States forces in the Persian Gulf region included 21 warships and 174 aircraft, see Cordesman, *Iraq and the War of Sanctions*, p. 354.
7. See UN Security Council press release SC/6596 of 15 November 1998.
8. Quoted in Cordesman, *Iraq and the War of Sanctions*, p. 363.
9. UN Security Council document S/1998/1172 of 15 December 1998.
10. Ibid.
11. Statement by the President, The White House, 16 December 1998; Office of the Press Secretary, <http://www.whitehouse.gov>.

12. Ibid.
13. Ibid.
14. Remarks by the President on Iraq, The White House, 19 December 1998; Office of the Press Secretary, <http://www.whitehouse.gov>.
15. Ibid.
16. Ibid.
17. Ibid.
18. 'Letter to Congressional Leaders Reporting on Iraq's Compliance with United Nations Security Council Resolutions', Public Papers of the Presidents, 3 March 1999; <http://web.lexis-nexis>.
19. 'Iraq Liberation Act of 1998', United States Senate, document S.2525, 29 September 1998; <http://www.senate.gov/legislative/index.html>. The ILA was introduced by six Republican senators (Lott, McCain, Helms, Shelby, Brownback and Kyl) and two Democratic senators (Kerrey and Lieberman).
20. For an official US account of the steps taken towards the implementation of the ILA, see 'Letter to Congressional Leaders Reporting on Iraq's Compliance with United Nations Security Council Resolutions', Public Papers of the Presidents, 3 March 1999; <http://web.lexis-nexis>.
21. The letter is signed by US Senators Lott, Lieberman, Helms, Kerrey, Shelby and Brownback and the US House of Representative members Gilman and Berman. For a text of the letter, see <http://www.nci.org>.
22. Ibid.
23. Alain Gresh, 'Iraq's Silent Agony', Le Monde Diplomatique, July (1999). <http://www.monde-diplomatic.fr> (hereafter cited as Iraq's Silent Agony).
24. From the official webpage of the INC <http://www.inc.org.uk/english/inc/inc.htm>.
25. According to the official press statement of the INC, the leadership team of the congress elected on 1 November 1999, comprises of the following individuals: Dr Ayad Allawi (Iraqi National Accord); Mr Riyad al-Yawir (Independent); Sharif 'Ali bin al-Husayn (Constitutional Monarchy Movement); Dr Ahmad Chababi (Independent); Shaykh Muhammad Muhammad 'Ali (Independent, Islamic); Dr Latif Rashid (Patriotic Union of Kurdistan); and Mr Hoshyar Zibari (Kurdistan Democratic Party). <http://www.inc.org.uk/english/na/Finale.htm>.
26. Thomas Pickering's letter to the INC leadership, dated 1 November 1999 is addressed to the following individuals: Dr Ayad Allawi (Iraqi National Accord); Sayyid Dr Muhammad Bahr al-'Ulum (Ahl al-Bayt Center); Mr Mas'ud Barzani (Kurdistan Democratic Congress); Dr Ahmad al-Chalabi (Iraqi National Congress); Sayid Baqr al-Hakim (Supreme Council for the Islamic Revolution in Iraq); Sharif 'Ali ibn al-Husayn (Constitutional Monarchist Movement); and Mr Jalal al-Talabani (Patriotic Union of Kurdistan). <http://www.usia.gov/regional.nea/iraq/iraq.shtml>.
27. 'Iraqi Opposition Begins Strategy Debate in NY,' Jordan Times, 1 November (1999). <http://www.accessme.com/jordantimes>.
28. 'Iraqi Opposition Meeting in Danger,' Middle East Newsline, 24 October (1999). <www.menewsline.com>.
29. 'Nurid af' alan min al-Amirikiin la aqwalan,' Al-Hayat, 25 October (1999). p. 10.
30. For a text of this letter, see <http://www.nci.org>.

31. Patrick Clawson, 'Stealth Bombing: Our Silent War in Iraq,' 6 September 1999. <http://www.washingtoninstitute.org> (hereafter cited as *Stealth Bombing*).
32. Daniel L. Byman and Kenneth M. Pollack, 'Supporting the Iraqi Opposition', in P.L. Clawson (ed.), *Iraq Strategy Review: Options for US Policy* (Washington DC: Washington Institute for Near East Policy, 1998), p. 64.
33. Comments by Ghassan Atiyyah, quoted in Jon B. Alterman and Andrew Parasiliti, 'US Policy on Iraq: A Dangerous Drift,' *Middle East Economic Survey*, 18 October (1999). <http://www.mees.com>.
34. General Zinni is quoted in *Iraq's Silent Agony*.
35. BBC 'US military to train Iraqi opposition,' 29 October 1999. <http://www.news.bbc.com.uk>. (Hereafter cited as *Iraqi Opposition*).
36. Middle East Newsline, 'Iraqi Dissidents Will Begin US Training,' 29 October 1999. <www.menewsline.com>. Also, see *Iraqi Opposition*.
37. 'Iraqi Opposition Meeting Skips Military Discussions,' *Jordan Times*, 1 November (1999). <http://www.accessme.com/jordantimes>.
38. The term 'Desert Yawn' is quoted from *Stealth Bombing*.
39. Ronald G. Shafer, 'Iraq-Attack Dilemma', *Wall Street Journal*, 22 October (1999), p. 1.
40. David Wood, 'Our Un-War With Iraq Drags On, No End In Sight, *St Louis Post-Dispatch*, 23 September (1999). <http://ebird.dtic.mil>.
41. Karen De Young, 'Baghdad Weapons Program Dormant, *Washington Post*, 15 July (1999), p. A19.
42. US Department of State, Daily Press Briefing, 15 July 1999. <http://www.secretary.state.gov>.
43. US Department of Defense, Pentagon Regular Briefing, 3 August 1999. <us-iraqpolicy@info.usia.gov>.
44. Bill Gertz, 'Saddam Secretly Making Weapons', *Washington Times*, 2 September (1999), p. 1.
45. US Department of State, Daily Press Briefing, 2 September 1999. <http://www.secretary.state.gov>.
46. UN Security Council document S/1999/100, 30 January 1999.
47. UN Security Council document S/1999/356, 30 March 1999.
48. For an examination of the British–Dutch and the French draft resolutions on Iraq, see Douglas Scott, 'Iraq: Highlights of the Two Draft Resolutions Now Under Discussion in the Security Council' (to be published in *Arms Control Today*).
49. As this paper was being prepared for publication, reports from the UN indicated that a new version of the British–Dutch draft has been circulated among member states of the UN. This resolution calls for the establishment of the United Nations Monitoring, Verification and Inspection Commission (UNMOVIC) to replace UNSCOM. The new proposal was designed to secure the French vote in the Security Council; it has been assumed that Russia and perhaps China would abstain from voting on this draft resolution. However, in an unexpected turn of events, hours before the UN Security Council was to have began voting on the revised British–Dutch draft proposal on 14 December 1999, France asked for a delay. The French decision was likely based on the consideration that if Paris supported the draft resolution, Iraq would retaliate by keeping France out of future economic deals. On 17 December 1999, the UN Security Council adopted the Resolution 1284

which authorized the establishment of UNMOVIC as a replacement for UNSCOM. Three permanent members of the UN Security Council – China, France and the Russian Federation, along with Malaysia abstained from voting. For the text of Resolution 1284, see <http://www.un.org/Docs/scres/1999/99sc1284.htm>. (For more on UNMOVIC, see David Albright and Corey Hinderstein, 'Re-establishing UN Security Weapons Inspections in Iraq: Piecing Together a Coherent Picture of Progress', in *Institute for Science and International Security* Issue Brief, 24 November (1999). <http://www.isisonline.org>.)

50. State Department, Elizabeth Jones, On Iraq Policy at Senate Hearing, 23 June 1999. <us-iraqpolicy@info.usia.gov>.

51. NSC Director Outlines US Policy Toward Iraq, 18 June 1999. <us-iraqpolicy @info.usia.gov>.

52. Ibid.

53. US Department of State, Press Briefing by Spokesman James Rubin, 27 September 1999. <http://www.secretary.state.gov>.

54. For the transcript of Scheffer's speech laying out the US case for prosecuting Saddam Hussein for war crimes, see 'Scheffer Remarks at Iraqi National Assembly,' 29 October 1999. <us-iraqpolicy@info.usia.gov.>. Also, see 'Prosecution of Iraqi Regime,' 27 October 1999. <us-iraqpolicy@info.usia.gov>.

55. BBC, 'Arab League foreign ministers' final communiqué,' 25 January 1999. <http://news.bbc.com.uk>. The call for lifting of economic sanctions against Iraq was re-emphasized by most Arab states in their address before the UN General Assembly in September 1999.

56. Middle East Newsline, 'Egypt–US Tension Could Affect Strategic Talks,' 27 October 1999. <www.menewsline.com>.

57. Colum Lynch, 'Annan Confronts US on Iraq,' *Washington Post*, 25 October (1999), p. A22.

58. ABC News, 'Iraqis Confident That Sanctions Will Soon Weaken,' 27 October 1999. <http://abcnews.go.com>.

59. 'The Lessons and Legacy of UNSCOM: An Interview With Ambassador Richard Butler,' *Arms Control Today*, June 1999, p. 7.

60. Remarks of Congressman Benjamin A. Gilman, Chairman, Committee on International Relations, US House of Representatives,' 31 October 1999. <http://www.inc.org.uk>.

# 9

# Saddam's State, Iraq's Politics and Foreign Policy

## AMATZIA BARAM

By January 2000 the domestic and international position of Iraq's dictator, Saddam Hussein, was the most secure and promising since the 1991 Gulf War. Domestically, more than three years had passed since any meaningful *coup d'état* was exposed, and probably hatched, against him. Serious Shiite protests and a wave of guerilla operations against his forces in the Iraqi south, but also in Baghdad, reached their climax and started to recede. On the economic level, while the stagnation and even slow deterioration of Iraq's economy continued unabated, there were no serious food shortages nor signs of famine in Iraq, children's malnutrition had leveled off, and key elements of the country's infrastructure were slowly being reconstructed. There was widespread reluctance to oppose the regime and an unhappy acceptance of the status quo in which Saddam Hussein and his ruling élite continued to enjoy a luxurious lifestyle, while the vast majority of the nation settled for the harshest police state system in the Arab world, which produced a minimal degree of social stability, minimally sufficient food rations, social and economic stagnation and unemployment. However, a mass revolt would mean horrendous bloodshed, which few are ready to risk.

In the inter-Arab arena, Iraq has developed commercial ties with a number of Arab countries, including some Gulf Emirates, Syria, Jordan and Egypt; thus securing also a minimal level of diplomatic ties. In the international arena, contrary to the hope of US military planners, the mini-confrontations between the

Iraqi air defenses and the Anglo-American air sorties above the southern and northern no-fly zones are not deterring the Iraqi side from almost daily challenges, while costing their rivals a fortune. Furthermore, in late 1999 and early 2000, the United States and Britain came under the greatest international pressure to lift, or at least greatly relax, the international economic embargo against Baghdad. After almost ten years, humanitarians around the world, in co-operation with powerful international interests, hopeful of huge profits from Iraq's oil industry and reconstruction, have succeeded in putting the American and British policymakers on the defensive.

What is Saddam Hussein's secret? How has he survived a devastating defeat in the Gulf War and almost ten years of a crippling embargo? Why is the policy of containment that was so successful in the early and mid-1990s slowly collapsing in the new millennium? These are the questions this article will address. This article will also attempt to decipher Saddam Hussein's strategy and his aims for the next decade.

## SADDAM HUSSEIN'S POWER BASE AND ITS IMPLICATIONS

When the Ba'th party came to power in Iraq in July 1968 it was committed to a few ideological goals, first among which came Arab unity – the ideal of unifying the Arab states into one super state. Very soon, however, it became clear that the only candidates for immediate unification, Syria and Egypt, both governed by regimes not unlike the new regime in Baghdad, posed a grave danger to the fledgling Ba'th rule. Both Gamal Abd al-Nasir and Hafiz al-Asad – who was the *de facto* ruler of Damascus since March 1969 and *de jure* ruler since November 1970 – enjoyed much greater prestige in the Arab world, and even inside Iraq, than the inexperienced Baghdad leadership, which had already lost power once in 1963. Thus, rather than striving toward unification, the new regime turned against Syria and Egypt, accusing them of betraying the most cherished Arab values by failing to defeat Israel in 1967, and of sabotaging Arab unity in a variety of other ways. With very small fluctuations – mainly in 1978–79

– this has remained Saddam Hussein's policy since he became Vice President of Iraq in 1969 and President in 1979.

Eventually, under Saddam Hussein, Iraq developed a new brand of pan-Arabism, Iraqi-centered and imperial. Its main message was that, due to its heroic and rich history, starting with ancient Sumer and Babylon and ending with Saddam, Iraq is the natural leader of the Arabs. As a result, everything that benefits Iraq will eventually benefit all the Arabs. This message sought to legitimize political maneuvers that clearly contradicted Arab solidarity or seemed to detach Iraq from the struggle against Israel. The invasions of Iran and of Kuwait are two examples of such maneuvers.[1] It is quite possible that this ideological argumentation made it easier for Ba'th party members to stomach the regime's policies, which deviated from traditional pan-Arab values.

Another ideal professed by the new regime was secularism, or the separation of mosque and state.[2] Until the ascendancy of Ayatollah Ruhallah Khomeini in Tehran in February 1979, this ideal was essentially adhered to, even though the Ba'th regime introduced some important modifications by respecting Islam and involving it in politics more than one would expect from a secular nationalistic rule. Baghdad's policy went through a quantum leap when the Ba'th rulers were pushed by the Islamic regime across the border to demonstrate that they were not, as claimed, anti-Islamic atheists. After they 'Islamized' much of their rhetoric during the Iran–Iraq War, President Saddam Hussein left the Ba'th party in introducing some Islamic principles into the Iraqi legal system. This started a short while before the invasion of Kuwait, when Saddam made clear that whenever legislated laws clashed with the divine Sharia, the former must always give way. One day before the Allied bombing began the fighting in January, Saddam Hussein added the slogan: 'Allahu Akbar' [God is Great] to the Iraqi national flag.[3] During the war, Saddam's rhetoric was fully Islamized in a way unparalleled by any other Arab secular leader. By implication he presented himself as the carrier of the banner of the Prophet Muhammad in our days and a latter day revivalist of the Islamic faith (mujaddid al-din). He promised his warriors that, when the battle commenced, God would extend his hand and decide the battle for them as he had done in the battle of Badr, when a tiny Muslim army defeated a multitude of Meccan idol worshippers. The President also invoked the memory of a pre-Islamic battle between the Arabs and an Ethiopian invading army under a mythological hero, Abraha, that marched on Mecca with war elephants. The invaders, he promised, would be defeated in the same way that the army of Abraha was defeated through a miraculous, divine intervention.[4] It is not clear how useful these promises and analogies were in raising the troops' morale. From interviews with Iraqi soldiers who served in the war, it emerged that at least some believed that these mythological references were a symbolic way to refer to secret Iraqi electronic devices and weapons that could neutralize the American technological advantage. Of course, they were not.

Following the Iraqi defeat in the war there was no sign of a return to rational, secular rhetoric. Indeed, in 1994, when the economic embargo resulted in unprecedented suffering among the vast majority of Iraqis and run-away inflation, Saddam Hussein went one step further by introducing a combination of Islamic and non-Islamic punishments such as severing the right hand for theft and the death penalty for prostitution, defining all these punishments as Islamic. The Iraqi President also initiated laws forbidding the public comsumption of alcohol and introduced enhanced compulsory study of the Qur'an at all educational levels, including in party branches. The most amazing step in the same direction was the declaration, in 1989, that before his death the Christian Michel 'Aflaq, the founder and chief ideologue of the Ba'th party, in fact converted to Islam. None of the deceased founder's friends or family ever heard about such a momentous decision but this did not prevent the Ba'th secular regime from making this astounding post-mortem announcement.[5]

While there may be no doubt that the draconian punishments managed to further terrorize the already terrorized population, it is impossible to gauge the extent to which the 'Islamization' steps helped the Iraqi President and his ruling élite stay in power by more effectively legitimizing them. It would seem, however, that such a far-reaching turn-about had to be based on rational calculation. In addition to some indications leaking out of Iraq that there were growing Islamic sentiments in the Sunni Arab population – most Shiites have always been more traditional than their Sunni compatriots – one has to bear in mind that the most efficient and realistic information-gathering agencies in Iraq are the various internal security apparatus. This is one of the ways in which one could explain Saddam Hussein's survival. It may be assumed that as the socio-economic situation deteriorated, the President was told by his intelligence services that the public was turning to religion. Converting Ba'thi rhetoric into Islamic rhetoric, thus, may have been one of the strategies that helped the regime to stay afloat.

A similar mechanism, and a far more potent one, was the selective return to tribal values and, most importantly, to tribal affinities. While the process of Islamization started in earnest only after the Iran–Iraq War, the regime's neo-tribal policies were introduced a few months after it took over in 1968. Contrary to its ideological commitment to socialism, modernity, and anti-tribalism as part of its European-style integrated nationalism – whether Iraqi or pan-Arab – almost from day one the new regime adopted clear-cut tribal policies.

The first public sign that this was the case was difficult to identify. In November 1969 a little-known, young Saddam Hussein was chosen as Vice President of Iraq, Deputy Chairman of the Revolutionary Command Council (RCC) – the supreme, executive, judicial and legislative body in the state – and the Deputy Secretary-General of the all-Iraqi leadership of the Ba'th party. Saddam was by then already the czar of internal security, a duty all other and better known senior party leaders refused to take upon themselves. Other than that, however, his name was known only to very few. As reported by a senior Ba'th official who was himself at that time a member of the small Iraqi Regional Leadership of the Ba'th party (RL), the choice was not coincidental, nor was it influenced by Saddam's special duties. It was the result of a conversation between President Ahmad Hasan al-Bakr and his childhood friend and distant relative, Khayr Allah Talfah, who was also Saddam Hussein's maternal uncle, and in whose home Saddam was raised. Talfah pointed out to Bakr that the party had once lost power – in November 1963 – because it relied too heavily on party loyalty, rather than on family and tribal ties. For a socialist, revolutionary nationalist this was shocking heresy, but Bakr agreed. Talfah suggested his young nephew as Iraq's number two and assured Bakr that with Saddam Hussein behind him he would never need to look over his shoulder with concern for his life and position – in reality, in 1979, Saddam Hussein deposed his elderly relative and, according to unconfirmed reports, poisoned him in 1982.

From the early 1970s, Saddam Hussein fortified his position by recruiting young men from his hometown, Tikrit, as his body-guards. Within the Tikriti population, the innermost circle from which recruits were picked, was Al Bu Nasir, the tribe to which both Saddam Hussein and President Bakr belonged. The next phase was to introduce some of these young men into key positions in most of Iraq's internal security bodies. The most important amongst them was Jihaz Hanin (the Apparatus of Yearnings), later to become al-Mukhabarat al-'Amma (General Intelligence), the Ba'th party's intelligence organ that terrorized all of its opponents, as well as most party members. Later on, members of Saddam's tribe were also injected into al-Amn al-'Amm (General Security), the old and powerful internal security body established by the Iraqi state under the monarchy. When new security bodies were created by the Ba'th regime it was made sure that they would be effectively penetrated and controlled by key officers hailing from Saddam Hussein's tribe. This has been particularly the case with al-Amn al-Khass (Special Security) and al-Haras al-Jumhuri al-Khass (the Special Republican Guard).

During the Iraq–Iran War, far more diluted doses of al-Bu Nasir men were injected into the army and the Republican Guard. Indeed, following the defeat in al-Faw in February 1986, the President decided to 'tribalize' many élite units and the mid-level command of much of the army. He did so in the belief that tribal men, being purely Arab, unmixed with Iranian elements, were braver in battle and thus more reliable in a war against Iran. When he realized that his own tribe was far too small for such a massive assignment, he started recruiting young men from neighboring and friendly tribes, mostly Sunni-Arab ones but also some from southern Shiite tribes – as different from Shiite city dwellers. He recruited tens of thousands of young men from tribes like al-Hadithiyyun, al-Shaya'isha, al-Bu Khishman and al-Bu Bazun, all residing in and around Tikrit, but also from al-Jubbur, and other tribes who live mostly north and west of Baghdad. For these young men, coming from a very modest rural background and with relatively little education, a military career was an excellent avenue for upward social mobility[6] and there is little wonder that most of them remain loyal to the President and regime.

Even though there were a few cases when Republican Guard troops and even Special Republican Guard officers were involved in coup attempts, they were clearly the exception. Tribal loyalty is far from 100 percent, but when combined with meaningful social and economic benefits, it creates a strong bond. It is very likely that even this bond would melt away once these officers were certain or near certain of Saddam's impending demise, but fortunately for him, this has never happened. In the army, as opposed to the Republican Guard, support for the President is far less staunch, but the Republican Guard is placed between all army units and the capital city, and the Special Republican Guard is stationed inside of Baghdad, and thus between the Republican Guard and the inner rings guarding the President. As long as the regime looks reasonably stable, the Republican Guard, the Special Republican Guard, Special Security and the Palace Guard (or Presidential Guard, Himayat al-Ra'is) will remain loyal to Saddam Hussein. If he is removed they have much to lose: power and prestige; higher salaries than those of their army counter-parts; and other privileges that increase in direct relation to a soldier's proximity to the President.

Surprisingly, the weakest link in this tribal military chain is the President's extended family. Family troubles started for Saddam Hussein in 1988, when his elder son, 'Udayy, murdered his beloved bodyguard and valet, Hanna Jojo. It is possible that this was the result of Saddam's 1986 decision to marry his mistress, Samira Shahbandar, when she was about to give birth to his baby. Apparently, Saddam's first wife, Sajidah, and 'Udayy were incensed. Hanna Jojo served as the messenger between the President and Samira, and this is believed by many to have been at least part of the reason for 'Udday's hostility. As a result of the murder, 'Udday was briefly imprisoned and then released and sent to Geneva to stay with his uncle, Barzan Ibrahim Hasan al-Tikriti. He later returned to Baghdad and was reinstated in all his duties. 'Udayy also developed a deep hatred for Saddam Hussein's second cousin once removed, General Husayn Kamil. Finally, 'Udayy also came into conflict with his uncle, Watban Ibrahim Hasan, the Minister of the Interior.

In August 1995, 'Udayy threatened to expose Husayn Kamil's corruption, and as a result, Kamil, with his brother Saddam Kamil, and their wives – Saddam's two daughters – and other family members defected to Jordan, dealing a tremendous blow to the regime's efforts to conceal the remainder of their non-conventional weapons, as General Kamil was one of the most central figures in these efforts. In the same month 'Udayy also attempted to kill and seriously wounded his uncle Watban. The President again demoted his flamboyant son and the regime entered into a deep crisis. A few months later, the Kamil brothers and their wives returned. They were forced to divorce the President's daughters and were later murdered along with their father and a few other family members. Their children – Saddam's grandchildren – were spared.[7]

This was the beginning of Saddam Hussein's recovery. Since then no meaningful family confrontations have been reported. While 'Udayy was eventually reinstated as the czar of the Iraqi media and youth, and given back the command of a militia force, Fida'iyyi Saddam, his younger brother, Qusayy, has been put in charge of internal security. Today he is the chief supervisor of the Republican Guard, Special Republican Guard and Special Security and no army unit can move without his personal authorization. He is greatly aided by his older colleague, Saddam Hussein's chief bodyguard, 'Abd Ihmid Hmud, a Tikriti from Saddam Hussein's tribe. There is little doubt that there is deep suspicion and resentment between 'Udday and Qusayy, but the system seems to be stable all the same. The President's half-brothers were effectively neutralized after they were ousted from all their state positions, including Barazan's position as Iraq's ambassador to the UN in Geneva – Barazan returned to Baghdad in 1999. Even though there may be much resentment within Saddam's paternal cousins' family, the Majids, following the brutal murder of the Kamil branch, there has been no sign that any of them is trying to avenge their relatives.

In summation, it would seem that at the outset of the new millennium, the President of Iraq managed to put his house back in order in a reasonable fashion and thus is free to dedicate his undivided attention to other affairs of state. The opposition abroad is divided and the United States and Britain are extending it only very limited help. The Shiite opposition at home is capable of unpleasant pinpricks, but unable to jeopardize the regime's stability, and the Kurds are unwilling to engage once again in meaningful anti-regime activities. As a result, the main domestic danger to leader and regime lies now in the unknown: a palace coup d'état. All the indications are that this is where the Iraqi President is now looking for trouble.

## IRAQ'S REGIONAL POLICY

By 1999, Iraq's relations with a number of neighboring states showed clear signs of improvement. By far the most important change occurred in Iraqi–Syrian relations. Traditional mutual suspicion notwithstanding, since Iraq was allowed to sell its oil-for-food under UN supervision – see below – it finally possessed something that Syria wanted. With a portion of its oil revenues, since 1996 Iraq has been purchasing Syrian agricultural products and other goods. Even before any deals were signed, but more so afterwards, Syria reversed its policy and began to call for an end to the international sanctions.[8] On the diplomatic level, Baghdad and Damascus agreed to exchange interest offices – though by January 2000, the offices had not yet been established. Iraq even went so far as to announce that even if Syria signed a peace agreement with Israel, mutual relations would proceed apace, even though Baghdad would never follow suit.[9] Also, trade centers were opened in the two capitals. In June 1997, two border crossings were opened for the first time since 1982. State officials and also a few tourists have been allowed to cross in both directions, and businessmen are encouraged to conduct mutual visits. Advanced negotiations have been conducted on reopening the Iraqi–Syrian oil pipeline from Kirkuk and Haditha to Banias on the Mediterranean. The full capacity of the pipeline is 1.4 million barrels per day (bpd), but at present, it can deliver no more than 300,000 bpd.[10] All this is short of full diplomatic relations and truly open borders. But for Iraq, which is still besieged in many ways, it is a major breakthrough.

Relations with Egypt are the smoothest they have been since 1990. Egyptian businessmen and officials show up regularly in Baghdad, and Iraq buys various goods in Egypt as part of the oil-for-food program. Much like Damascus, Cairo is careful not to upgrade diplomatic relations to their full potential,[11] and occasionally Egyptian spokesmen and newspapers are critical of the Iraqi regime.[12] But on occasions, one can hear much more agreeable rumblings coming from Cairo either by spokesman or by the press. By the end of 1999, the demand to end the embargo was sounded both by Damascus and Cairo.[13] Maybe they can afford to make such a demand because they know that the United States and Britain are certain to prevent such a development, and in the process, both regimes can take up a cause that they believe is popular with many Arabs.

Jordan, whose economy has been heavily dependent on trade with Iraq, cannot afford to criticize Baghdad, even in the limited fashion that the Egyptian press does. Between 1995 and 1998, King Husayn was occasionally critical of the Iraqi regime's meddling in Jordanian domestic affairs and Iraq's general policy of confronting the UN. The King even offered support to the Kamil brothers upon their defection. However, in the last year of his life, the Jordanian monarch refrained from confronting Iraq and settled to a practical co-existence. His son, King Abdallah, has continued this policy, but has also introduced two innovations. In the first place, he greatly improved Jordan's relations with Kuwait and Saudi Arabia. Upon his visit to Kuwait, he announced Jordan's support for Kuwait's efforts 'to bring a positive end' to the issue of its war prisoners in Iraq.[14] The other innovation was to strengthen Jordan's ties with Damascus through personal and government-to-government contacts.

In January 2000, Jordan and Iraq signed a new trade agreement which, while far less beneficial to Jordan than expected by Jordanian authorities, was still extremely important for Jordan's economic well-being. As in previous years, Iraq would provide for half of its oil consumption, at a value of $300 million, free of charge. This was defined as Saddam Hussein's personal gift to the Jordanian people. The other half was to be sold to Jordan at a price lower than the international rate. Jordan demanded that it pay only $14 per barrel. Eventually the price agreed upon, to Jordan's chagrin, was $19 per barrel. This is still three or four dollars below the market price of this brand of oil, but for Jordan this is a high rate all the same. To compensate, the two countries decided to increase their trade volumes from $200 million in 1999 to $300 million. The total value of the contracts signed between Jordanian companies and the Iraqi government since the beginning of the oil-for-food program in 1996 is $842 million.[15]

Since 1991, relations with Iran have undergone fairly extreme fluctuations. Even though, theoretically, the main bone of contention should have been the permanent border issue on the Shatt-al-Arab and in a few small border zones further north – mainly Qasr Shirin and Sayf Sa'd – it seems that both Iraq and Iran are interested in far more pressing issues. The most painful one is that of prisoners of war. Even though on a few occasions, the two countries have exchanged POWs,[16] Iraq claims that Iran still holds around 14,000 Iraqi prisoners. It is not clear whether these people are alive or dead, and if they are alive, whether or not they would like to go back to Iraq. Certainly some prisoners joined the Iraqi anti-government forces fighting alongside the Iranian troops under the command of Ayat Allah Muhammad Baqir al-Hakim and the Da'wa Party.

The second problem poisoning relations is that of the 148 Iraqi cargo airplanes and jet fighters that crossed into Iran just before and during the Gulf War to escape the allied bombings. When Iraq demanded them back, Iran reported that it had sought the UN's advice and was told – very conveniently – that, as a result of the embargo, it was not allowed to return them. Naturally, Iraq was furious and denied that Iran had even approached the UN. Whatever the case, the airplanes are still in Iran. Last but not least, Iraq is accusing Iran of providing support to Shiite revolutionaries in the south. While the degree of Iranian support for such operations is not clear, there is no doubt that armed revolutionaries are attacking Iraqi units in the south, mainly from makeshift bases in the marshes. Iraq also regards Iran as responsible for occasional bombing operations in Baghdad.[17] Iran, for its part, points to official Iraqi support of the Mujahidin Khalq anti-Tehran movement, which has military bases on the border east of Baghdad. The last Mujahidin operation to date was a mortar attack on government buildings in downtown Tehran in February 2000.[18] At the same time, however, both Iranian and Iraqi spokesmen express the wish that bilateral relations be improved. In practice, too, trade relations are slowly being cemented, and Iranian pilgrims are allowed to visit Karbala.[19] Likewise, it is inconceivable that barges smuggling illegal oil products and heading for the United Arab Emirates could be hugging the Iranian shore, navigating all the time within Iranian territorial waters, without Iranian permission. This ambivalent pattern of bilateral relations, baffling as it is, is still a very incremental, if uneven, improvement. It would seem that in Iran the absence of a central decision-making authority is making it impossible for the Iranian leadership to act decisively one way or another. Stopping all support for the Shiite revolutionaries in the south is very difficult for ideological reasons, as well as because of the accumulated influence of some half a million Iraqi exiles in Iran. Recently the Iranian government took some steps to encourage these Iraqi expatriates to leave, but the results of this campaign are far from clear.[20] Seen from the Iraqi side, giving up the Mujahidin Khalq is such a major concession that Iraq may want to settle all unresolved issues first. Iran, it seems, is satisfied with a weakened regime in Baghdad: it can do business with it and, at the same time, has no immediate reason to worry about its military machine. While providing limited support to the Shiite opposition in the south, Tehran shows no interest in Iraq's disintegration: such a development may plunge Iran into conflict with the Arab world. A weak Saddam prevents disintegration, guarantees a large degree of

Iraqi isolation, and prevents pro-American forces from taking over in Baghdad.

While Iraq's relations with the United Arab Emirates (UAE) have improved since the mid-1990s,[21] those with Kuwait and Saudi Arabia remain extremely tense. While rejecting all American requests to use their territory as a base for launching bombing attacks against Iraq, the Saudis did agree to allow their air space to be used by American forces. American AWACS were also allowed to take off from Saudi territory.[22] In addition, American jet fighters patrolling the southern no-fly zone are using bases in Saudi Arabia. Iraq accuses Saudi Arabia of collaborating with US military attacks, including the December 1998 air raids,[23] and even though Iraqi spokesmen occasionally express a readiness to reconcile both with Saudi Arabia and with Kuwait, vicious media attacks against the Saudi and Kuwaiti regimes are frequent.[24] Saudi Arabia and Kuwait retaliate in kind, provoking further Iraqi diatribes.[25] It is clear then that, while most Arab countries – including North Africa, the Sudan and a united Yemen – are gradually inching toward more normal relations with Iraq, Kuwait (the victim of the 1990 occupation) and Saudi Arabia (its main supporter, which also felt immediately threatened by the invasion) are both still adamant in demanding Iraqi compliance with the most important UN resolutions: total relinquishment of its weapons of mass destruction (WMD) and the return of the Kuwaiti prisoners and property. However, due to Saudi Arabia and Kuwait's combined importance in the Gulf Co-operation Council (GCC), the organization has been towing a tough line against Iraq. The Gulf States have been demanding repeatedly that Iraq must prove its peaceful intentions towards its neighbors and admit that its invasion of Kuwait was a violation of Arab and international legitimacy, and of the charter of the Arab league. The Gulf states also distinguished between the Iraqi people and its rulers, saying they: 'sincerely shared the suffering of the fraternal country of Iraq the consequence of the policies and obstinacy of its government.' The fact that they stressed the need to: 'safeguard Iraq's indepatence and territorial integrity' did not make the pill less bitter to the Iraqi regime.[26]

Although relations with Turkey have been characterized by extreme contradictions, they have been remarkably stable all the same. Since 1991, Turkey has allowed an Anglo-American – at first also French – air force to use its Incerlik airbase to monitor the northern no-fly zone, and occasionally even to attack Iraqi targets outside the no-fly zone. Also, Turkish forces have invaded autonomous Iraqi Kurdish regions in mop-up operations against anti-Turkish Kurdish rebels. The Iraqi regime strongly protested both activities. Turkey also refused repeated Iraqi appeals to break the embargo by opening its pipelines to the free flow of Iraqi crude oil. Yet Turkey has allowed the flow of oil products in trucks through the common border and – like Iraq – greatly benefited from its cheap price. Those benefiting most were the Kurds of south-eastern Turkey, which helped soothe the ethnic discontent there. Since the beginning of the oil-for-food program, Turkey also enjoys a regular fee from Iraqi oil transit through the Iraqi–Turkish pipelines going from Kirkuk to Dortyol. Finally, in exchange for oil, Turkey sells Iraq a variety of products. Not surprisingly, the positions of Turkish politicians *vis-à-vis* the Iraqi regime are full of contradictions. Most of them no longer regard Saddam as dangerous. Because they fear the emergence of a Kurdish state, they prefer to see him back in the autonomous Kurdish zone, and because they need Iraqi business, they prefer that the embargo be lifted. However, the need for close military and political co-operation with the United States dictates caution, and thus most Turkish policitians prefer not to rock the boat. Also, because they do not fully trust the Anglo-American commitment that a fully-fledged Kurdish state will not emerge in northern Iraq, their best option is to carefully watch all parties concerned, and do what they can to prevent such an eventuality from materializing.[27]

## IRAQ AND THE UNITED NATIONS

With the end of Mikhail Gorbachev's government the Soviet Union, and later Russia, started to distance itself from American policies over Iraq – it will be recalled that even during the Gulf

War, the USSR was careful not to send any troops to join the coalition. By the mid-1990s, France also started to differ with the Anglo-American position, and China never supported the military action against Iraq to start with. In the second half of the 1990s, these three permanent Security Council members opposed any military action against Iraq, even when it meant abandoning UNSCOM. In terms of its rhetoric, France has always been closer to Anglo-American policies and far more committed than Russia and China to Iraq's disarmament, but in practice the differences between France and its two partners in the Security Council were small. While since 1998 the Russians supported the immediate lifting of the embargo,[28] claiming that Iraq has fulfilled all its obligations under UNSC Resolution 687 to disarm, France suggested an early end to the embargo once UNSCOM affirmed that Iraq had relinquished most of its WMD. The French formula held that the UN should not expect Iraq to comply with its resolutions to the letter. The Anglo-American approach was very different: Iraq had to satisfy 100 percent of UNSCOM's demands. Likewise, while the United States and Britain sought UN approval for military operations whenever Iraq seriously interrupted UNSCOM's military activities, Russia, France and China always objected. This led to the Anglo-American decision to bomb Iraq in December 1998 without asking for Security Council approval.

Saddam Hussein's strategy of driving a wedge between the two camps in the Security Council proved highly successful. By promising French and Russian companies lucrative oil deals and other contracts in Iraq after the embargo was lifted, he managed to secure their support. The result was that, in effect, Iraq acquired a virtual veto right in the Security Council over important aspects of weapons inspections. Between December 1998 and December 1999 UNSCOM stayed out of Iraq, and there were no military operations, save almost daily small-scale confrontations over the no-fly zones, which the Iraqi regime decided to challenge. At the same time, however, there was no way Saddam's supporters in the Security Council could legally lift the embargo because such a decision could always be vetoed by the United States and Britain. To end this draw, the five permanent members eventually agreed to UNSC Resolution 1284, which established a new and somewhat less independent inspection body, the UN Monitoring Verification and Inspection Commission (UNMOVIC).[29] A few weeks later, after Iraq vetoed one candidate, Dr Hans Blix, another Swedish diplomat, who had been for many years the Chairman of the International Atomic Energy Agency, was nominated as the new body's director. Iraq rejected the new resolution because it demanded full co-operation with the new inspection body for around one year before the embargo would be suspended and because suspension meant that it could be easily re-imposed – the suspension was to last for six months only, and to renew there needed to be a consensus in the Security Council.[30] No military measures were taken against Iraq for rejecting the resolution. Blix was more acceptable to Iraq, but, unless major changes were introduced, Iraq still could not accept the resolution as a whole. This created a new stalemate in the Security Council.


## CONCLUSION: WHAT NEXT?

What is Saddam Hussein's strategy for the next phase of his confrontation with the West? In a number of speeches, the Iraqi President has made it very clear that he does not expect the embargo to be lifted in one go. Between 1991 and 1999, he managed to get rid of the weapons inspections and – save four nights of aerial attacks in December 1999 – he was not punished for it. If he is successful in hiding his WMD production the United States will not bomb his installations in the future either. This is no small achievement. At present the unresolved issue is that of the economic embargo. Regaining full control of his oil revenues is crucial for Saddam Hussein if he wants to rebuild his armed forces, resuscitate Iraq's economy and turn Iraq into a regional superpower once again. There is no easy way to reach that goal. Judging by numerous expositions of Iraqi spokesmen, Iraq's intention is to convince, first of all, the Arab and Islamic states – foremost among them, Jordan and Turkey – but also Russia, France, China and other powers, to break the embargo by conducting normal dealings with Iraq. When Russian and French oil companies refused to move in, the Iraqi authorities threatened to cancel the contracts that they had signed with them.[31] To date, all these overtures were of no avail, except for relatively small-scale oil smuggling through Iranian territorial waters to the UAE, into Syria and into south-eastern Turkey. The Iraqi hope is clearly that in the new century, these breaches of the embargo will become a flood. To encourage its neighbors and some powers to move along this trajectory, Iraq has been offering lucrative deals. It seems that Russia is the first power ready to risk a confrontation with the United States over Iraqi oil smuggling: in February 2000 a few Russian vessels smuggling Iraqi heavy fuel were intercepted by the US Navy, and the Russian foreign minister admonished the United States in belli-cose tones, arguing that the oil was, in fact, loaded in Iran. The Iraqis poured oil on the diplomatic fire when they defined the incident as: 'sheer [US] piracy and [Russian] humiliation.'[32]

What are Saddam Hussein's options and strategic choices? Theoretically, Saddam can stop the oil-for-food program, and thus create such suffering in Iraq that the US-based humani-tarian community will apply more pressure on Washington to lift the embargo. The dangers are, however, that the humanitarian community will blame him, and not the US administration, for the suffering. More realistically, when people in Iraq feel that their daily sustenance is in immediate danger, they might get desperate and revolt despite the fear of fierce repression, and this time the United States may come through with strategic help. The regime has become the prisoner of its own policy in this respect: the oil-for-food program has become its opium. Alter-natively, the Iraqi President may declare that, if the embargo is not lifted, he would use his remaining WMD against Israel, or Kuwait, or Saudi Arabia, or all.

In practice, however, such a scenario is not likely unless his political survival is clearly threatened. But this is far from being the case. In early 2000, Iraq's international relations developed in a promising fashion as more and more countries were keen to establish some presence in Baghdad; the United States and Britain were on the defensive in the UN; and the domestic

American arena seemed to be changing. Since 1991, a very central component of Saddam Hussein's strategy has been exploiting the suffering of the Iraqi people to influence public opinion in the West to end the embargo. At first the American public paid little attention to humanitarian arguments. Since the late 1990s, however, the Iraqi claim – though largely inflated[33] – that 5,000 children were dying every month as a result of the embargo started to change the public mood. Saddam Hussein, Tariq 'Aziz and other Ba'thi luminaries cynically but successfully used the suffering of the children of Iraq, and mainly of Iraq's Shiite children whose parents revolted against them in 1991. Humanitarian delegations reported regularly of the very real plight of the children in 'Saddam's City' – a 2,000,000-person Shiite quarter of Baghdad – and in Shiite towns such as 'Amara and Karbala. That the Ba'th regime was responsible for the suffering did not detract from the tragedy. By late 1999, the oil-for-food program, introduced in 1996, greatly ameliorated the malnutrition problem: on average every person in Iraq was receiving by then the equivalent of 2200 kilo-calories for free – 2,500 KCal are usually regarded as sufficient for an adult. The program also provided Iraq with very large quantities of medicines and medical equipment, but malnutrition has been slow to disappear, and distributing the medical supplies takes time. Generally speaking, the Iraqi public health system suffered so heavily during the Iraq–Iran War (1980–88), the Gulf War and the mass revolts against the regime (1991), and the embargo, that to resuscitate it would require a few years. In the meantime the Iraqi regime can convincingly show that in certain parts of the country the suffering is still great. To date, the humanitarian reports from Saddam's City and the Shiite south are Saddam Hussein's most potent weapon against the embargo. The result was UNSC Resolution 1284 of 7 December 1999.

The resolution retained financial control over most of Iraq's oil revenues, but relaxed the embargo in some important areas. Most significantly, Iraq was given permission to sell unlimited quantities of oil – before it was limited to selling at the value of around $5.2 billion every 180 days. In February 2000, Iraq was producing only a little more than 2,000,000 bpd, and even though prices were high – more than $25 per barrel – it could not take advantage of the new regulation. Iraq will very likely exceed its quota as set by the Organization of Petroleum Exporting Countries, and the permission to sell unlimited quantities will become extremely important.

The resolution also allowed for the first time Iraqi producers to sell their products to their government through the oil-for-food program. This should have been allowed from the very outset, because it has a potential of greatly encouraging local farmers and other producers, as they would be receiving world market prices. Also, the resolution accepted the Iraqi request to substantially increase the amount of money allocated to the purchase of spare parts and technology for the oil sector. This will enable Iraq to overcome some very serious problems and to significantly expand its oil production. Finally, all contracts relating to food and medicines were to be automatically approved by the sanctions committee, so as to expedite the processes.

None of the aforementioned concessions seriously jeopardizes the embargo, because its main tool – namely UN control of Iraq's oil revenues and supervision over Iraq's contracts – remains in place. However, humanitarian concerns among the American public opinion are growing substantially and becoming a major threat to the US administration's strategy of hemming in Saddam by denying him control of Iraq's oil revenues. In mid-February 2000, 70 congressmen signed a petition addressed to President Clinton demanding an end to the embargo. At the same time two leading UN officials concerned with the humanitarian operations in Iraq resigned in protest against the embargo.[34] Before he resigned, Hans Von Sponeck, the UN humanitarian representative, demanded the 'de-link' of the military–political aspects of the embargo from the economic–humanitarian ones. This call was anything but clear, but other humanitarian activists simply demanded an end to the embargo, and this is probably what Von Sponeck meant. What the proponents of lifting the embargo demand is that Iraq be free to order and distribute any goods without any limits, but that border controls designed to prevent Saddam from importing weapons be substantially strengthened. This approach is fully supported by the Iraqi

217

government. Baghdad knows that the weapons embargo will continue for a long time, and that it will not be lifted as long as the present regime is in power. At the same time, Iraq's leaders also seem to believe that once they have all of Iraq's oil revenues again under their control, they can buy weapons' technology – from machine tools and know-how to fissionable material – that will enable them to turn Iraq into a regional superpower, not by rebuilding a one million-man army but, rather, by developing WMD. According to UNSCOM reports, Iraq still has a seed stock of such weapons and much of the know-how necessary to develop them.

It is anybody's guess what Saddam Hussein's grand design might be once he is again in possession of such weapons. The Iraqi President has proved that he understands well the most fundamental principles of Cold War-style mutual assured destruction (MAD). During the Gulf War, some threats notwithstanding, he carefully refrained from any use of such weapons, be it against the Saudis, the Allied forces, or Israel. However, he also demonstrated an unacceptable degree of risk-taking. For a non-nuclear power to threaten Israel, whom Iraq believes to be a medium-size nuclear power, is taking a huge risk. Saddam Hussein is also prone to doomsday thinking. According to interviews with three senior UNSCOM officials, during the Gulf War he delegated authorities to the commanders of his non-conventional missile force that should worry any Iraqi. The most dangerous order was to attack Israel with non-conventional missiles if communications between the missile force and Baghdad was severed and if the commanders believed that Baghdad was about to be conquered by the Allied forces. By giving his missile officers the instructions he did, the Iraqi President had to take into account the possibility of an Israeli nuclear response. The logic behind it was that Baghdad was better annihilated than conquered by the Allied forces. All the existing evidence points to one direction, namely that the Iraqi President is a high-risk gambler not only when it comes to his conventional army, but, also in terms of his non-conventional arsenal. Judging by his speeches and actions in the 1989–91 period, his first goal is to dictate oil prices to the Arab Gulf States and to neutralize the

Iranian influence in the Gulf. His next goal is to become the generally recognized leader of the Arab world, mainly through assuming a confrontational posture towards Israel and making far reaching promises to the Palestinians – in April 1990, for example, he promised Arafat to liberate Jerusalem with Iraqi missiles and air power alone. In 1990–91, Saddam Hussein also indicated that he saw himself as the potential leader of the whole Islamic world and, more dubiously, of the Third World. It is not clear how he hopes to achieve all these ambitious goals even when he becomes a nuclear power and the second richest oil producer after Saudi Arabia. But there may be little doubt that he intends to try and achieve at least the inner core of this grand scheme.

## NOTES

1. For details see Amatzia Baram, 'Qawmiyya and Wataniyya in Bathi Iraq: The Search for a New Balance', *Middle Eastern Studies*, 19, 2 (1983), pp. 188–200.
2. See, for example, Michel 'Aflaq, *Fi Sabil al-Ba'th* (Beirut: Dar al-Tali'a, 1974), p. 167; Saddam Hussein, 'A View of Religion and Heritage', *On History, Heritage and Religion* (Baghdad: Translation and Foreign Languages Publishing House, 1981), mainly pp. 24, 27–9. Also the internal party organ, *Al-Thawra Al-'Arabiyya*, (July 1980), pp. 13–18.
3. *Al-Jumhuriyya*, 15 January 1991.
4. *al-Thawra*, 10 October 1990; 17 September 1990.
5. Amatzia Baram, 'Re-Inventing Nationalism in Ba'thi Iraq', in *Princeton Papers*, 5 (1998), pp. 39–42.
6. For more details see Amatzia Baram, 'Neo-Tribalism in Ba'thi Iraq', *IJMES* 29 (1997), pp. 1–31.
7. For details see Amatzia Baram, *Building Toward Crisis: Saddam Hussain's Strategy for Survival* (Washington DC: The Washington Institute for Near East Policy, 1998), pp. 7–36 (hereafter cited as *Building Toward Crisis*).
8. A declaration by a Syrian parliamentarian; *al-Malaff al-Iraqi* (London), 54 (1996), p. 36. Reuters from Baghdad, 16 May 1996.
9. For example, an interview with Tariq 'Aziz, LBC Satellite TV [in Arabic] (Beirut), 2 January 2000, in FBIS-NES-DR, 4 January 2000. See also report of Iraqi officials leaving for Syria to open the interests section and information about mutual participation in international fairs in the two capitals and the opening of trade centers, *al-Ittihad* (Baghdad), 28 December (1999), p. 8; in FBIS-NES-DR JN2912131099, 29 December 1999.
10. US Energy Information Administration, Iraq, December 1999, p. 5; internet version < http://www.eia.doe.gov >.
11. See Egyptian denial of Iraqi reports that diplomatic relations will resume soon,

219

MENA [in Arabic], 24 November (1999); in FBIS-NES-DR NC2411190499, 24 November 1999.

12. See for example Mursi 'Ata Allah in *al-Ahram*, 18 November 1999 as reported by *Mid-East Mirror* 18 November (1999), saying Saddam Hussein was the first to impose his sanctions on his people, restricting their movements, speech and the way they thought.

13. See for example Foreign Minister 'Amr Musa: 'This [lifting sanctions] is not only an Egyptian demand but a general Arab demand'. Very inaccurately he also said: 'There are no reservations, either from Saudi Arabia or Kuwait'. Not surprisingly, Iraqi Foreign Minister Muhammad Sa'id al-Sahaf congratulated Musa on his position. See also Arab League Secretary General 'Ismat 'Abd al-Majid praising Saddam for his wish to engage in a 'quiet and rational dialogue to address past mistakes … [and] open a new page in Iraqi–Arab relations', Reuters, 13 September 1999.

14. Reported by David Nissman in *Iraq Report*, 2, 34 (1999).

15. *Al-Arab al-Yawm*, Amman, 24 January 2000, p. 14; Baghdad Iraq TV Network [in English] 24 January 2000; in FBIS-NES-DR, 25 January 2000.

16. The last exchange occurred in April 1998, when Iran returned 5,592 and Iraq 380 prisoners, see *New York Times*, 7 April (1998).

17. See for example an interview with Tariq 'Aziz, LBC Satellite TV [in Arabic] (Beirut), 2 January 2000; in FBIS-NES-DR, 4 January 2000.

18. See warning to Iraq by the Chief of Iran's Revolutionary Guards, news agencies from Tehran, 9 February 2000; from <kurdishmedia@hotmail.com>.

19. See for example, President Khatami inviting Saddam Hussein for a visit and Iranian parliamentarians calling for improved relations. *Mid-East Mirror*, 10 September (1999). For an agreement to allow 3,000 Iranian pilgrims to visit Karbala every week, see *IRNA* [in Persian] 12 November 1999; in FBIS-NES-DR LD1211192799, 12 November 1999. For three agreements on economic and trade co-operation, see BBC, 11 November 1999, in *Washington Kurdish Institute*, 15 November (1999); internet version, WKI@kurd.org.

20. See for example, *al-Ittihad* (Baghdad), 7 September (1999), p. 1; in FBIS-NES-DR MS0809131399, 8 September 1999; *Mid-East Mirror*, 10 September (1999).

21. See, for example, confirmed reports that Russian companies are selling spares for T-72 tanks and Mi-8 and Mi-24 helicopters, for which the UAE has no use, to companies in the UAE. These spares find their way to desperate customers, *Iran Defense Week*, 3 January (2000), p. 3. Also, see Shaykh Zayd Bin Sultan al-Nahyan, President of the UAE, calling for the lifting of the embargo, quoted in Baram, *Building Toward Crisis*. See also, Shaykh Muhammad Bin Rashid aal-Maktum, the UAE Minister of Defense calling upon Kuwait to give Iraq territory to build a harbor, as quoted by Kuwait's *al-Watan*, in *Iraq Report*, 3, 6 (2000).

22. Interviews with American officials, Washington, DC, December 1998.

23. See for example, Saddam Hussein's address to commanders, Iraq Satellite Channel TV [in Arabic], 2 September 1999; in FBIS-NES-DR, 2 September 1999.

24. See for example, *al-Iraq*, 7 September 1999 as reported by AFP, pointing out that Iraqis could: 'at a single stroke throw the al-Sabah monarchy into the waters of the Gulf.' The Kuwaiti criticism of Iraq: 'betrays their hallucinations

and aids the US–Zionist plot to divide the Arab and Islamic nation.' An official of the Ministry of Culture and Information on Baghdad Radio on 7 September accused Kuwait of 'using all their wicked methods to destroy any form of Arab solidarity' and calling the Kuwaiti regime 'the lowly ones.' Quoted by David Nissman *Iraq Report*, 2, 34 (1999). See an attack against both Kuwait and Saudi Arabia, stating that if they did not end their collaboration with the US they: 'will sustain further losses whether in terms of ... relations with the Americans, the way the Arab and Muslim masses look at you, the things history will write about you', Sami Mahdi in *al-Thawra*, 17 October (1999), p. 1.

25. See for example King Fahd's speech in the GCC twentieth Round of Foreign Ministers Summit: 'In our Gulf area the Iraqi regime still insists on its old stands and is still incapable of learning a single lesson of the painful past.' The Iraqi side replied by accusing Fahd of adopting 'the approach of treachery and forfeiting national and pan-Arab rights'. Reported on Baghdad Iraqi TV Network [in Arabic], 29 November 1999; on FBIS-NES-DR JN2911205099, 29 November 1999.

26. *AFP*, from Cairo, 13 September 1999.

27. For more details see Baram, *Building Toward Crisis*, pp. 109–22.

28. For example, the Russian Ambassador to Baghdad, Alexander Chevin, to *al-Jumhuriyya*, 27 November (1999), p. 3.

29. UNSC S/RES/1284 (1999), adopted by the SC at its 4084 meeting, 17 December 1999, internet version.

30. See for example Tariq 'Aziz, interview on Baghdad Radio of Iraq Network, 2 February 2000; in FBIS-NES-DR JN0202201800, 2 February 2000. Taha Yasin Ramadan, argued that no inspection at all would be tolerated any more because it served as cover for espionage (Baghdad Republic of Iraq Radio, 10 February 2000; in FBIS-NES-DR, 10 February 2000); but Deputy Foreign Minister Nizar Hamdun said Iraq might agree if major changes were introduced into the Resolution, *Iraq Report*, 3, 6, 11 February (2000).

31. For overtures to Syria, Jordan and Turkey to bust the embargo see Baram, *Building Toward Crisis*, pp. 87–96, 109–36.

32. For Russian ships involved see Steven Lee Myers, *New York Times*, 1 February (2000). For the foreign minister's demand that a Russian ship be immediately released and Iraqi meddling cease, see *Segodnya* (Moscow), 4 February 2000; in FBIS-NES-DR MS0402140900, 4 February 2000.

33. For a solid statistical analysis of child mortaility in Iraq see Richard Garfield, *Morbidity and Mortality among Iraqi Children from 1990 to 1998: Assessing the Impact of Economic Sanctions* (Goshen, IN: Institute for International Peace Studies, University of Notre Dame and the Fourth Freedom Forum, (1999).

34. *Ha-Aretz* (Tel Aviv), 17 February 2000. For more details see, 'The Political Scene' on MEES Website <http://www.mees.com>. (43,8), 21 February 2000.

# 10

## Living with a Nuclear Iran?[*]

### MICHAEL EISENSTADT

The nuclear status quo that has prevailed in the Middle East since the 1960s is eroding. Israel remains the sole – undeclared – nuclear-weapons state. But Iraq, having defied the United Nations (UN) for nearly a decade, retains its nuclear know-how, and has broken out of its International Atomic Energy Agency (IAEA) and UN Special Commission (UNSCOM) cage. And there are strong indications, meanwhile, that Iran is actively pursuing a nuclear option under the cover of its civilian nuclear program.[1] Iranian officials have, on several occasions, called for the development of nuclear weapons in order to counter the nuclear capabilities of Israel and the United States, while Iranian procurement activities since the late 1980s – particularly efforts to acquire fissile material, nuclear-research reactors and power plants and gas centrifuge enrichment technology – have raised suspicions that Iran's nuclear intentions are not strictly peaceful. Moreover, it seems implausible that Iran would go to the trouble and expense of producing the Shehab-3 missile (with a range of 1,300 km), developing the Shehab-4 (with an estimated range of 2,000 km), or drawing up plans for a Shehab-5 missile (with an expected range of 10,000 km), only to place a conventional high-explosive payload atop them.[2]

It appears that Iran is pursuing a nuclear option and that it may well be the next nuclear power in the Middle East. Iran's acquisition of nuclear weapons would transform the regional balance of power, and could alter the decision calculus of Iran's leadership, reorder political alignments in the region, and strike

[*] This article is reprinted with permission from *Survival*, 41, 3 (1999), pp. 124–48.

a severe blow to the international nuclear non-proliferation regime. Due to the volatility of Iranian politics, the clerical regime's involvement in terrorism, and Tehran's tense relations with several of its neighbors and the United States, a nuclear Iran would, at the very least, have a destabilizing impact in the Middle East. For these reasons, averting the emergence of a nuclear Iran will be a key interest of the United States and its allies in the coming years. Understanding Iran's motivations, the dilemmas it faces as it approaches the nuclear threshold, how nuclear weapons are likely to affect the conduct of the regime, and problems related to deterring a nuclear Iran, are thus crucial to devising a policy to dissuade or prevent Iran from crossing the nuclear threshold, and for managing the consequences of proliferation if it occurs.

## IRAN'S MOTIVES

In 1989, following its costly eight-year war with Iraq, Iran initiated a major program to rebuild, expand and modernize its ravaged armed forces. It was motivated by at least three factors: a desire to achieve self-reliance in all areas of national life, including the military arena; a determination to transform Iran into a regional power capable of projecting influence throughout and beyond the Middle East; and the need – after the war with Iraq – to strengthen its deterrent capability against various perceived threats in order to forestall new acts of aggression.

### Building Self-reliance

Revolutionary Iran has placed a strong emphasis on military self-reliance. Under the Shah, Iran depended on the United States and Britain for nearly all its arms. Following the 1979 revolution, Tehran was isolated internationally and faced Baghdad virtually alone during the Iran–Iraq War. Tehran's sense of isolation and abandonment was heightened by the apathetic international response to Iraq's use of chemical weapons in that war – an experience which has left deep wounds in the Iranian national

224

psyche to this day. In addition, a US-led arms embargo during the war greatly complicated Iran's efforts to replace its losses and sustain its war effort. The bitter legacy of the war has bred a determination in Iran that these experiences should not be repeated. Iran has thus sought to develop its own military industries, in order to reduce its dependence on foreign arms suppliers, to minimize the potential impact of future embargoes, and to create the foundation for a modern military, capable of dealing with a range of potential threats. In this context, Iran may see weapons of mass destruction (WMD) as a means of compensating for its military weakness and relative strategic isolation.

## Building Regional Power

Since 1979, Iran's foreign and defense policies have reflected the tension between two competing – although not necessarily contradictory – orientations: Islamic universalism and Persian nationalism. These have, at different times and in different places, exerted varying degrees of influence over Iranian policy. The Islamic tendency generally dominated in the 1980s; Persian nationalism took precedence in the 1990s.

Iran's clerical leaders believe that the Islamic Republic plays a key role in world affairs as the standard bearer of revolutionary Islam and the guardian of oppressed Muslims everywhere. Accordingly, they believe that the fate of the worldwide Islamic community depends on Iran's ability to transform itself into a military power that can defend and advance the interests of that community. This perception also leads Tehran to support radical Islamic movements in the Middle East and elsewhere, in order to undermine US influence, to make the regional and international environment more amenable to Iranian interests, and to burnish the regime's revolutionary Islamic credentials at home and abroad.

Most Iranians also believe that their country is a regional power by dint of geography, demography and resource endowments. Destiny dictates that Iran should be the dominant power in the Persian Gulf: it is the largest Gulf State; it has the longest coastline; and it has vital oil and gas interests there. This implies an ability to control the Gulf militarily and deny its use to others, to influence developments in the region, and to defend Iran's vital interests there against the United States, Iraq and Saudi Arabia.

There is a large gap, however, between the self-image and the aspirations of the regime, and the reality of Iran's military weakness. Tehran's efforts to expand and modernize its armed forces and enhance its military capabilities are intended to bridge this gap. Iran's financial problems, however, have prevented it from achieving its goal of building a large, capable military. Consequently, it has devoted much of its available resources to missiles and WMD, which potentially provide the biggest bang for Iran's limited defense bucks. In this context, nuclear weapons would transform Iran into a regional military power, provide it with the means to intimidate its neighbors, and enable it to play the role that its leaders believe is rightfully its due.

Other benefits of nuclear weapons might include:

- bolstering the standing of the regime in the eyes of the Iranian people and throughout the Arab and Muslim worlds;

- intimidating the Arab Gulf states and undermining their confidence in American security guarantees, in order to put an end to the US military presence in the Gulf;

- deterring Iraqi use of WMD on the battlefield or against Iranian towns or cities in the event of a new war;

- threatening US allies such as Israel, Turkey, Egypt or Saudi Arabia in order to gain leverage over Washington during a crisis or confrontation;

- deterring retaliation for attempts to disrupt oil shipments from the Gulf, or to block the Strait of Hormuz – although this is an option of last resort for Tehran, since it exports nearly all of its oil through the Strait; and

- intimidating Afghanistan or Azerbaijan during a crisis or war.

226

Nuclear weapons may also be the only way for Iran to become a military power without destroying its economy. While a nuclear-weapons program could cost billions, rebuilding its conventional military would cost tens of billions of dollars.[3]

## Building Deterrence

Iranian defense planning is also motivated by a desire to enhance its deterrent capability. At various times, revolutionary Iran has faced or at least perceived threats from Iraq, the Soviet Union, the United States, Israel and, more recently, Turkey, Afghanistan and Azerbaijan.

The defeat of Iraq in the 1991 Gulf War temporarily improved Iran's military situation. That war and its aftermath led to the dismantling of Iraq's known nuclear infrastructure, and to significant reductions in its missile force and chemical and biological weapons (CBW) capabilities. Iraq, however, still retains a significant conventional edge over Iran, a small number of operational al-Husayn missiles and a significant retained CBW capability; and might even be able to produce nuclear weapons in a matter of months were it to succeed in acquiring fissile material on the black market from the former Soviet Union or elsewhere. Iran thus probably sees its own missile and WMD capabilities as a counter to Iraq's retained and future capabilities in this area.

During the Cold War, the Soviet Union was the only neighboring country capable of invading and occupying large parts of Iran. Thus, the demise of the Soviet Union and the creation of a number of independent republics along Iran's northern border eliminated the only threat to its independence. However, this development created a whole new set of fears that instability in the Caucasus and Central Asia would spill over and destabilize the country, or undermine government control of peripheral regions. As a result, during the 1990s, Tehran worked with Moscow to ensure stability, and has acted with restraint in the Caucasus and Central Asia. Iran has eschewed activities – such as efforts to export the revolution – that could have angered Russia, its main source of arms and WMD-related technology. However, unlike Iraq, for example, which has used chemical weapons against its own population, Tehran does not appear to conceive of chemical or biological weapons as a means of dealing with the type of domestic unrest that could arise from instability in the Caucasus and Central Asia.

Since the 1991 Gulf War, the United States has reduced the size of its armed forces in a way that could limit America's future ability to intervene in the Gulf, particularly if it had to respond simultaneously to another crisis elsewhere in the world. This is potentially a net gain for Iran. Conversely, during the 1990s, the United States has dramatically augmented its forward presence in the Gulf. Iranian officials frequently express their discomfort at the American presence, particularly the naval presence, which they believe poses a direct threat to their country. More-over, Iranian officials believe – not without reason – that the United States is attempting to create an anti-Iranian bloc to their north and north-east. The annual military exercises with the Central Asian Peacekeeping Battalion (CENTRASBAT) – comprised of the military forces of Kazakhstan, Kyrgystan and Uzbekistan – is an example of increasing military co-operation with the countries in that region. The United States also con-tinues to encourage the construction of oil and gas pipelines that avoid Iran, while Tehran believed that Washington was support-ing the Taliban in Afghanistan. This perception was inaccurate and became rather obviously so after the 11 September 2001 terrorist attacks in New York led to a US vow to destroy the Taliban regime. Thus, Tehran fears what it perceives to be American efforts at encirclement, which are intended to harm its economy, reduce its diplomatic margin of manoeuvre and complicate its security environment.

Because Iraq's CBW capabilities did not deter the United States during the Gulf War, Tehran may believe that, in the event of military confrontation with Washington, only a nuclear capa-bility could enable it to avert defeat. This consideration may have been behind the 1993 comment by former Iranian Defense Minister Akbar Torkan:

> Can our air force ... take on the Americans, or our navy take on the American navy? If we put all our country's

budget into such a war we would have just burned our money. The way to go about dealing with such a threat requires a different solution entirely.[4]

Iran therefore probably sees its missile and WMD capabilities in general – and its efforts to acquire nuclear weapons in particular – as the key to dealing with potential threats from the United States.

Whereas Iraq and the Persian Gulf provided the main focus for Iran's foreign and defense policies in the immediate aftermath of the Iran–Iraq War, developments in Afghanistan have increasingly held the attention of Iran's leaders since the inauguration of Mohammed Khatami as President of the Islamic Republic in August 1997. Despite their mutual claims to be politically correct Islamist regimes, Iran viewed Afghanistan's Taliban government as an enemy. Tehran was not sorry to see that government targeted by an international coalition following the 11 September 2001 terrorist attacks on the United States by the Taliban's protected guest, Osama bin Laden. But Iran did not want to see US influence entrenched in Afghanistan either. Iran has long been indirectly involved in the protracted internal struggle in Afghanistan that followed the Soviet withdrawal in early 1989. Iran fears that the Pakistani-supported Taliban government could stir unrest among the two million Afghans in Iran, who provide much manual labor in large cities. It could also contribute to heightened Sunni–Shiite tensions in eastern Iran, where the Sunni minority constitutes one-third of the population. In addition, some Iranians suspect that a series of attacks by the opposition Mojahedin-e-Khalq organisation in 1998–99 may have originated from Afghanistan.

Relations with Azerbaijan have also become strained. Iran tacitly supported Armenia in its war with Azerbaijan – which ended with a shaky cease-fire in 1994. Furthermore, Tehran has long been concerned that an independent Azerbaijan might become a magnet for Iran's Azeris, who comprise about one-third of its population. These concerns have been reinforced by statements from senior Azerbaijani officials expressing a desire that some day 'northern' (independent) and 'southern' (Iranian)

Azerbaijan might be unified – the Azeri minority, however, is well integrated into Iranian society and the state, and is thus ambivalent towards the Azeri State to the north. More recently, calls by a senior Azerbaijani official for the North Atlantic Treaty Organization (NATO) or the United States to establish a base in Azerbaijan in order to counter the Russian presence in Armenia, have compounded Iranian concerns about encirclement by the United States. Senior Iranian officials fear that Azerbaijan is increasingly aligning itself with American and Israeli interests.[5]

Finally, Iranian decision-makers remember Israel's June 1981 air-strike on Iraq's Osiraq nuclear reactor, and have been alarmed by recent statements of senior Israeli military officials and politicians threatening to attack Iran's missile and nuclear infrastructure. Israel is in the process of acquiring arms – such as the F-15I strike aircraft, cruise-missile-capable diesel submarines, and extended-range Jericho missiles – that could enable it to make good on such threats. Moreover, as a result of growing military co-operation with Turkey, Israel now effectively has a presence on the Turkish border with Iran: it reportedly operates intelligence-collection facilities there, and Israeli reconnaissance or strike aircraft could over-fly Turkey *en route* to Iran. Iran probably believes that its missile and CBW capabilities provide a protective umbrella against Israeli attacks on its nascent nuclear program, and serves as a deterrent against anti-Iranian co-ordination between Israel and Turkey.

Iranian officials have usually justified the pursuit of nuclear weapons as a way to counter Israel's capabilities and redress Muslim weakness. In an October 1992 interview, then-Deputy President Ataollah Mohajerani stated that: 'because the enemy [Israel] has nuclear facilities, the Muslim states too should be equipped with the same capacity.'[6] Subsequently, Judiciary Chief Ayatollah Mohammad Yazdi declared in a June 1998 speech that:

> We are living at [a] time when the United States supports Israel which has the biggest arsenals of the mass destruction and nuclear weapons [and] an atomic power is needed in the world of Islam to create a balance in the region.[7]

What are the policy implications of this assessment? Iran is not pursuing nuclear weapons just to enhance its ability to deal with perceived threats. There are other powerful motives at work here, including the regime's drive for self-reliance and its desire to transform Iran into a regional power. So, even if Iran's security concerns could somehow be addressed through security assurances from the major powers, or the creation of a regional security system, such steps would probably not be sufficient to induce Iran to abandon WMD – and particularly its nuclear programs. Although the creation of some sort of regional security system is inherently desirable as a means of reducing tensions and enhancing stability, in the end there may not be much that the West can do to influence the entire range of motivations that underpin Iran's efforts to acquire nuclear weapons.

## CROSSING THE NUCLEAR THRESHOLD

As it weighs its nuclear options, Iran faces a number of dilemmas. To derive prestige and influence from the possession of nuclear weapons, or to deter potential adversaries, Iran would have to advertise that it has 'the Bomb.' To do so, however, would be to admit that it was in violation of its Nuclear Non-proliferation Treaty (NPT) commitments not to pursue nuclear weapons, and could expose Tehran to harsh sanctions and renewed international isolation – unless it were to withdraw from the NPT due to 'extraordinary events' – (a crisis or war) as allowed by the Treaty. Such a step could undermine years of painstaking efforts to rehabilitate the economy and to nurture ties with Russia, the European Union (EU) and the Arab World. Furthermore, it could spur the formation of an anti-Iranian coalition under Washington's aegis, and cause neighboring countries to redouble efforts to build up their own military capabilities.

For now, Iran's strategy seems to involve building up its civilian nuclear infrastructure while avoiding activities that could clearly violate its NPT commitments. However, Islamic Revolutionary Guard Corps (IRGC) Commander Yahya Rahim

Safavi's remarks, leaked from an April 1998 meeting with IRGC officers, have raised unsettling questions about the willingness of at least some conservative hardliners to adhere to Iran's arms-control commitments. In the middle of a tirade against the reformers around Khatami, Safavi reportedly asked his audience:

> Can we withstand America's threats and domineering attitude with a policy of détente? Can we foil dangers coming from America through dialogue between civilisations? Will we be able to protect the Islamic Republic from International Zionism by signing conventions to ban proliferation of chemical and nuclear weapons?[8]

Safavi's disparaging allusion to the NPT and the Chemical Weapons Convention (CWC) suggest an undercurrent in Iran which would like to ignore the country's arms-control obligations. The fact that it was Safavi who made these comments is particularly important. The IRGC is believed to be in charge of Iran's chemical, biological and nuclear weapons programs, as well as the country's missile forces. Safavi's options on these matters therefore carry great weight and are likely to have some – perhaps a decisive – impact on Iranian decision-making about the NPT (and CWC as well).

Safavi's comments reinforce suspicions that Iran is using its civilian nuclear program as a stepping-stone to a military program, while avoiding significant activities contrary to its NPT commitments that could result in harsh international sanctions and halt its procurement efforts. In this regard, Iran has three options:

- to create a civilian nuclear infrastructure capable of rapidly producing a nuclear weapon if the regional-threat environment were to change, without actually crossing the nuclear threshold;

- to use its civilian program to acquire the expertise and know-how required to embark on a clandestine parallel nuclear program once all the necessary building-blocks for a military program are in place, so that if the military program were discovered, a cut-off in foreign assistance would not disrupt these efforts;[9] and

- to create a clandestine, parallel weapons program concurrent with its efforts to build up its declared civilian nuclear infrastructure.

From Iran's perspective, all three options have drawbacks. In option one, the regional-threat environment could change very quickly; for example, if Iraq were to acquire fissile material from the former Soviet Union or if tensions in Afghanistan were to lead to a confrontation with Pakistan. For technical reasons, it simply may not be possible to create a rapid nuclear break-out capability. Thus, in the weeks or months between a decision to 'go nuclear' and the production of a nuclear weapon, Iran would face a window of vulnerability.[10] In option two, if a clandestine Iranian nuclear weapons program were discovered, Iran would face sanctions and censure – although it would eventually get a nuclear-weapons capability. In option three, if a clandestine parallel program were prematurely compromised, Iran would be censured, sanctioned and without a nuclear weapon – the worst of all worlds from Tehran's perspective. On the other hand, this option might provide the quickest route to a nuclear-weapons capability.

Because of the national-security risks Iran could face if it were to adhere strictly to its NPT commitments, Safavi's apparent call to ignore the NPT is likely to fall on sympathetic ears in Tehran – particularly among conservative hardliners who place little stock in Iran's ties to the broader international community. But matters are much more complicated for Khatami and his reform-minded allies. While these men are pragmatists, they are also Persian nationalists, interested in building a strong Iran. Missiles and WMD are probably the fastest route to this goal, as Iran lacks the money to fund a major conventional military build-up. In this light, it seems plausible that Khatami and his entourage would support the acquisition of such weapons.[11] Indeed, it should be remembered that it was Mohajerani, now Khatami's 'liberal' Minister of Culture and Islamic Guidance, who called on Iran in October 1992 to develop nuclear weapons to counter Israel's capabilities.[12] Conversely, the fact that Safavi said what he did indicates that there may be people in Iran – perhaps in the Foreign Ministry and elsewhere – pressing for Iran to adhere to its arms-control commitments. Clearly, it would be hard for a president who ran on a 'rule-of-law' platform, and who would like to reintegrate Iran into the international community, to justify the violation of international commitments and treaty obligations. Khatami might thus find it difficult to reconcile the two goals, though the matter may not be his to decide.

Domestic politics are also likely to influence any decision to cross the nuclear threshold. Some members of Iran's clerical leadership might believe that they could stand to gain *vis-à-vis* political rivals if Iran were to declare itself a nuclear-weapons state, or conduct a nuclear-weapons test. Iranian decision makers may also be encouraged by the favorable response in the Muslim world to Pakistan's May 1998 nuclear test. Indeed, such considerations might have been behind the timing of Iran's decision to test the Shehab-3 missile the following July.

A final factor that will affect Tehran's future nuclear posture is whether Iran obtains a nuclear capability through the diversion of small quantities of fissile material – probably from the former Soviet Union – or through the creation of a domestic fissile-material production capability. There will be strong – albeit different– incentives in such cases for Tehran to remain quiet about its nuclear capabilities.

The United States might not learn about an attempted diversion of fissile material until it is too late to prevent it. In fact, the United States might not find out about such an incident at all, unless Iran decides to announce it – presumably after it had produced a nuclear weapon. However, while it remains a member of the NPT, there are significant drawbacks to Iran declaring itself a nuclear-weapons state. As long as such disincentives remain, international support for the NPT regime remains solid, and there is no imminent threat to its security, Iran is unlikely to make such an announcement. Moreover, making such an announcement could scuttle opportunities for further diversions that could augment Iran's nuclear capabilities.

Alternatively, if Iran were to succeed in achieving a local fissile-material production capability, a declaration that it has the bomb, or a weapons test, could energize US efforts to disrupt Iranian procurement operations overseas, thereby hindering efforts to expand and upgrade its fissile-material-production capability. Moreover, Iranian decision-makers might fear that such a step could provoke Israeli or American strikes on facilities connected with its nuclear program.

For all these reasons, Tehran's stance towards its nascent nuclear stockpile is likely to be silence, coupled with officially-sanctioned efforts to encourage speculative reports in the foreign press about loose nukes making their way to Iran, in order to create ambiguity about its true nuclear capabilities. Meanwhile, Tehran is likely to use displays of its missile capabilities as a 'symbolic surrogate' for the full range of WMD capabilities it possesses, but which it cannot brandish – due to treaty obligations. In this way, Tehran probably hopes to increase its influence and leverage *vis-à-vis* its neighbors and adversaries. This may be one of the most important benefits Iran expects to obtain by acquiring nuclear weapons.

However, in the event of a crisis or war, all bets are off. In such circumstances, Iran might decide that an announcement or weapons test may be necessary, despite the drawbacks involved, to avert an even greater disaster. Revelations concerning Iraq's 'crash program' to build a bomb by diverting safeguarded reactor fuel following its August 1990 invasion of Kuwait, and North Korea's March 1993 threat to withdraw from the NPT rather than submit to a special inspection, demonstrate that states will violate their NPT commitments or withdraw from the Treaty when they believe that their vital interests are threatened. Because Iran is located in a conflict-prone region and has pursued anti-status quo policies that have put it at odds with several of its neighbors and the United States, it is more likely to find itself in such a situation than most other NPT member states.

## IMPLICATIONS OF A NUCLEAR IRAN

Arguments based on US, Soviet and Chinese experience during the Cold War – that the destructive potential of nuclear weapons and the logic of deterrence moderates the behavior of nuclear-weapons states, inclines their leaders towards caution and thereby enhances stability – are excessively sanguine and somewhat deterministic.[13] Such arguments are based on a selective reading of the historical record, ignore just how close the United States and the Soviet Union came to nuclear war during the 1962 Cuban missile crisis, and overlook contrary cases elsewhere. For instance, Iraq's increasingly assertive regional policies in 1989–90, and North Korea's willingness to engage in nuclear brinkmanship in 1993–94 almost certainly derived, at least in part, from the increased self-confidence that leaders of both countries drew from their growing missile and WMD arsenals. Furthermore, the fact that both India and Pakistan possess nuclear weapons did not prevent the two from coming to blows in Kashmir in May–July 1999.

In recent years, Iran has demonstrated a degree of caution and pragmatism in pursuing policy objectives befitting the country's military weakness and diplomatic isolation. The concern here is that the acquisition of nuclear weapons might radically alter the decision calculus of Iran's clerical leadership, and change this situation. Thus far, neither the acquisition of missiles nor CBW have derailed the general trend towards greater moderation in the foreign-policy arena. In the end, it is impossible to know in advance what impact the acquisition of nuclear weapons will have on Iranian policy. If the leadership reverts to the hands of hardline conservative clerics intent on pursuing a more activist and aggressive foreign policy, nuclear weapons will provide them with a powerful tool for doing so. A perpetuation of the current situation, in which the government is divided between conservative hardliners and moderate reformist politicians engaged in a bitter power struggle would also entail certain risks should Iran become a nuclear power threat. It is possible that in such circumstances, the power struggle might be limited to the domestic arena – as is currently the case. But the possibility that hardliners might sponsor terrorist attacks on Israeli or US interests overseas in order to discredit their domestic rivals, leading to a crisis with another nuclear-weapons state, must be treated seriously. On the other hand, should the moderate, reformist faction emerge ascendant, it seems likely that the trend towards pragmatism in the foreign-policy arena would continue, regardless of Iran's nuclear status. Even with moderate reformers in power, however, one should not expect an end to tensions, as such leaders are likely to pursue a nationalist agenda in the Persian Gulf and a rigid ideological approach towards Israel that will keep Iran at odds with its Arab neighbors, Israel and the United States.

The Cold War experience also showed that while nuclear-weapons states have often been unable to realize the military potential represented by these weapons, they were more often successful in using nuclear weapons as a means of exerting political influence. Tehran's ability to do so could be affected by its need to remain silent about, or to adopt an ambiguous posture towards, its nuclear capabilities. Much would also depend on how the United States would respond to an Iranian nuclear break-out, the timing of such an event (whether it occurs in peace time or during a crisis), and on domestic conditions in the country (which political faction is dominant in Tehran at the time).

How might Iran's neighbors respond to a nuclear break-out? They would have four basic options: tension-reduction and confidence-building measures; accommodation or appeasement; forge alliances with nuclear powers to reap the benefits of extended deterrence; or acquire an independent retaliatory capability (not necessarily nuclear).

Israel would probably send reassuring messages to Iran via third parties, as Jerusalem did when tensions with Iraq rose during 1989–90 in response to Baghdad's fears of an Israeli attack on its WMD facilities. Israel would also probably take steps to reduce further the increasingly thin veneer of ambiguity still surrounding its own nuclear capabilities, while seeking to deepen military co-operation with the United States. Most of the Gulf Co-operation Council (GCC) states would probably opt for a mixture of approaches. Kuwait, Qatar and Oman – whose relationship with Tehran in recent years has been correct, if not cordial – might put priority on improving relations with Tehran, while maintaining strong security links with the United

States as an insurance policy.[14] Bahrain and the United Arab Emirates (UAE) – whose relationship with Tehran has been strained – might put priority on deepening their security relationship with the United States, while nonetheless cautiously seeking to improve relations with Tehran. Saudi Arabia – which currently is in the process of mending relations with Tehran – is likely to move forward aggressively on parallel tracks, further intensifying contacts with Tehran, while enhancing security co-operation with the United States. And several of these countries might respond by developing a retaliatory capability and CBW – if they are not trying to do so already.[15]

For the states of the Caucasus and Central Asia, the Russian response to an Iranian nuclear break-out would be crucial. Indifference in Moscow could contribute to a perception of encirclement by a nuclear Russia and Iran that would increase the incentive of these states to forge security arrangements with outside powers. Azerbaijan might try to strengthen further its ties with the United States and Israel. At such a point, several countries in this region might also re-examine their WMD options.

The bottom line for the United States is that an Iranian nuclear break-out would probably deepen American involvement in the security of the eastern Mediterranean and Persian Gulf, and perhaps even in the Caucasus and Central Asia. It would complicate US power projection in the Persian Gulf, and raise the potential risks of a long-term US presence there. And it would challenge Washington to find ways to strengthen its deterrent capability and to reassure allies, without contributing to regional tensions. Finally, an Iranian nuclear break-out could have dire consequences for the NPT, raising questions about the future of nuclear arms control, and perhaps prompting other regional states to re-evaluate their WMD options.

## IRAN AND DETERRENCE

Because Shiite religious doctrine exalts the suffering and martyrdom of the faithful, and because religion plays a central role in the official ideology of the Islamic Republic, Iran is sometimes portrayed as an 'undeterrable' state driven by the absolute imperatives of religion, rather than by the pragmatic concerns of statecraft.[16] The impression has been reinforced by Iran's use of costly human-wave attacks during the Iran–Iraq War, its unnecessary prolongation of the fighting due to its pursuit of unrealistic war aims – for example, the overthrow of Saddam Hussein – and its support for groups such as the Lebanese Hizballah and the Palestinian Islamic Jihad which resort to such tactics as suicide bombings.

However, the perception of Iran as an irrational, undeterrable state with a high pain threshold is wrong. Iranian decision-makers are generally not inclined to rash action. Within the context of a relatively activist foreign and defense policy, they have generally sought to minimize risk by shunning direct confrontation and by acting through surrogates (such as the Lebanese Hizballah and Iraqi Dawa parties) or by means of stealth (Iranian small boat and mine operations against shipping in the Gulf during the Iran–Iraq War) in order to preserve deniability and create ambiguity about their intentions. Such behavior is evidence of an ability to gauge accurately the balance of power and to identify and circumvent the 'red lines' of its adversaries – a strong indicator of an ability to engage in rational calculation. Furthermore, Iranian officials seem to understand the logic and speak the language of deterrence. Shortly after the Shehab-3 missile test launch in July 1998, Defense Minister Ali Shamkani explained that, in order to increase Iran's deterrent capability:

> We have prepared ourselves to absorb the first strike so that it inflicts the least damage on us. We have, however, prepared a second strike which can decisively avenge the first one, while preventing a third strike against us.[17]

Tehran's conduct during the later stages of the Iran–Iraq War likewise demonstrated that Iran is not insensitive to costs. It is possible to argue that in the heady, optimistic, early days of the revolution – from the early to mid-1980s – Iran had a higher threshold for pain than did most other states. During the early years of the war, Tehran was willing to endure hardships, to make great sacrifices and incur heavy losses in support of the war effort – eschewing the opportunity for a cease-fire in 1982 to pursue the overthrow of the Ba'th regime in Baghdad and the export of the Revolution. But in its final years, popular support for the war with Iraq had waned: the population was demoralized and wearied by years of inconclusive fighting, making it increasingly difficult to attract volunteers for the front; and many clerics had come to the conclusion that the war was unwinnable.[18] This was not, as Ayatollah Khomeini was fond of saying: 'a nation of martyrs.' In fact, Khomeini was probably the only figure with the charisma and moral authority to inspire the Iranian people to sustain the level of sacrifice required to continue the war for eight years. The double blow embodied by the unsuccessful conclusion of the war in August 1988 and the death of Khomeini in June 1989 marked the end of the decade of revolutionary radicalism in Iranian politics. With respect to its ability to tolerate pain and absorb casualties, Iran has since become a much more 'normal' state.[19] Its cautious behavior during the 1991 uprising in Iraq and the 1998 crisis with Afghanistan that followed the Taliban victory provides perhaps the best proof that it is wary of stumbling into a costly quagmire for which there would be little or no public support. It will sooner compromise its Islamic ideological commitments and abandon endangered Shiite communities to their fate than risk Iranian national interests by entering into foreign adventures.

Such pragmatism is consistent with a basic principle of decision-making established by Khomeini shortly before his death. In a series of letters to then-President Ali Khamene'i and the Council of Guardians in December 1987 and January 1988, he affirmed the Islamic government's authority to destroy a mosque or suspend the observance of the five pillars of faith – the fundamentals of Muslim observance – if Iranian state interests so required. In so doing, he sanctioned the supremacy of state interests over both religion and the doctrine of the Revolution.[20] Ever since then, national interest has been the guiding principle of Iranian decision-making, whether with regard to social issues (such as birth control), the economy (foreign investment in the oil sector), or foreign and defense policy (restraint in pursuing efforts to export the revolution since the early 1990s).

This line of reasoning has interesting implications for Tehran's claim that it is not interested in acquiring WMD on religious grounds. Aside from the fact that strong circumstantial evidence – particularly Iranian procurement activities – would seem to contradict this argument, experience also shows that Iranian decision-making on critical policy issues is generally based on reasons of state, not religious doctrine or ideology.

The main problem posed by a nuclear Iran is thus not the putative 'irrationality' of the regime or its high threshold for pain. Rather, it is regime factionalism, which could make it difficult to establish a stable deterrent relationship with a nuclear Iran. Regime factionalism sometimes causes radical departures from established patterns of behavior, as different personalities, factions or branches of the government work at cross-purposes, act to subvert their rivals, or press the government to take actions inconsistent with its general policy line.[21] Accordingly, Iranian policy is often inconsistent and unpredictable. For instance:

- In November 1979, militant students stormed the US embassy at a time when moderates in the government were trying to re-establish normal ties with Washington after the Revolution.[22]

- In November 1986, opponents of efforts to improve ties with the United States leaked details to a Lebanese newspaper of what was to become known as the Iran–Contra affair, leading to the final collapse of efforts to establish an opening with the United States.[23]

- In February 1989, Khomeini issued a *fatwa* condemning writer Salman Rushdie to death, thereby undercutting months of painstaking efforts to mend relations with Europe by Parliament Speaker Ali Akbar Hashami Rafsanjani and allies in the Foreign Ministry.[24]

- In April 1992, Iran unilaterally seized control of Abu Musa

Island in the Persian Gulf, violating its 1971 agreement with the UAE in which it had agreed to share control of the island. This move, which inflamed Arab opinion, occurred at a time when Iran was trying to improve relations with its Arab Gulf neighbors.

- In March 1996, customs officials in Belgium thwarted an Iranian attempt to smuggle a large mortar and ammunition off of an Iranian merchant vessel in Antwerp, apparently for use against Iranian oppositionists in Germany. This incident marked a major departure from the pattern of curtailing attacks in the heart of Western Europe after 1992, because of the harmful impact of these operations on Iran's relations with France and Germany.[25]

The tug-of-war between different factions pursuing different agendas thus makes deterrence *vis-à-vis* Iran a difficult and uncertain proposition. Those seeking to undermine Khatami might engage in terrorism against US personnel or interests in order to embarrass and discredit him and perhaps prompt US retaliation, in the hope that this might halt the movement towards greater openness in Iran and bolster domestic support for their position. How does one establish a stable deterrent relationship in such a context?

Another concern is that old patterns of behavior might persist after Iran acquires a nuclear weapon, with elements of the regime continuing their involvement in conventional terrorism and efforts to export the Revolution. Iran's success thus far in obscuring its involvement in terrorism against the United States and other countries, and in avoiding retaliation or retribution, might lead some in Iran to believe that they can act again with impunity, or forestall retaliation by blaming the action on 'rogue elements.' In the new nuclear context such behavior would be risky and reckless. Attacks on US or Israeli personnel or interests by Iranian-supported groups might initiate a process of escalation that could lead to a nuclear crisis.

Finally, there is the issue of WMD terrorism. The fact that Iran or its agents have not yet employed CBW for terrorist purposes may indicate a normative threshold, or it may indicate

that, having achieved significant successes by means of conventional terrorism, Tehran and its surrogates perceive no need to
incur the risk that use of WMD would entail. Nonetheless,
because of the importance that Tehran has traditionally attached
to preserving deniability, Iran is likely to seek, when acting
against more powerful adversaries, a capability to deliver WMD
by non-traditional means – terrorist saboteurs, boats, or remotely
piloted aircraft. Because such methods offer the possibility of
covert delivery, they are likely to become important adjuncts
to more traditional delivery means such as missiles, and in
situations in which deniability is a critical consideration they are
likely to be the delivery means of choice.[26] The possibility of
deniable, covert delivery of nuclear weapons by Iran will pose a
major challenge for deterrence.

## POLICY OPTIONS FOR THE UNITED STATES
## AND ITS ALLIES

In order to assess current options for dealing with Iran's nuclear
program, it is necessary to evaluate the policies that the United
States and some of its key allies – the states of the EU and the
GCC – have pursued against Iran until now. For most of the past
20 years, the United States, the EU and the GCC have regarded
the Islamic Republic with suspicion and distrust, though
differing over the nature and magnitude of the threat posed by
Iran, and how to respond to it.

All three have had bitter and difficult experiences dealing
with the Islamic Republic. Europe has had to endure repeated
bouts of Iranian-sponsored terrorism on its soil in the 1980s and
early 1990s. The GCC has had to deal with Iranian attempts to
subvert several of its members in the 1980s; while in the 1990s
the Iranian Navy has regularly held provocative maneuvers in
the Persian Gulf, calculated to intimidate its Arab neighbors.[27]
The UAE is also involved in a long-standing territorial dispute
with Iran over three islands currently held by Iran. As for the
United States, American diplomats were held hostage in Tehran
for more than a year during the early days of the Revolution,

while Americans were the target of Iranian-inspired terrorists in the 1980s. US warships upholding freedom of navigation in the Persian Gulf were damaged by Iranian mines and clashed with Iranian warships towards the end of the Iran–Iraq War in the late 1980s. Iran has also quietly worked to undermine American-sponsored peace talks between Israel and its Arab neighbors in the 1990s.

However, differing in terms of their proximity to Iran and their place in the world, the United States, the EU and the GCC have parted in the way they have defined the threat from Iran and how they have responded to it. For the EU, Iran mainly poses a threat of terrorism on its soil. For the GCC, Iran poses a threat to the stability and territorial integrity of its members. By contrast, the United States has tended to see Iran as a geo-strategic threat, due to Tehran's efforts to overthrow friendly governments, obstruct efforts to resolve the Arab–Israeli conflict and develop long-range missiles and WMD.

The United States and the EU have pursued similar objectives *vis-à-vis* Tehran. They have sought to manage the threat that Tehran posed to their interests, and to promote stability in the Middle East and Persian Gulf by influencing Iran to cease its involvement in terrorism, its support for groups opposed to the Arab–Israeli peace process, and its efforts to acquire WMD. To these the EU added the issue of human rights – embodied by the Salman Rushdie affair – which topped its list of concerns.[28] The GCC states have pursued a more circumscribed agenda: defusing potential Iranian threats to their security by engaging Tehran, while acquiring and maintaining an American security umbrella. However, the steps taken by the United States, the EU and the GCC to realize these complementary, often overlapping objectives, have been very different.

US policy towards the Islamic Republic had, until recently, relied almost exclusively on sticks.[29] Confronting a regime that worked consistently to undermine US interests in the Middle East, Washington sought to contain Iran in the 1980s by denying it access to arms and technology that could enhance its military capabilities. In the 1990s economic sanctions were introduced to reduce Iran's income and press it to abandon policies that ran

counter to American interests.[30] The United States also spent a
great deal of time and energy trying to convince other countries
to do the same. This effort yielded mixed results overall, although
scoring some important achievements. The May 1997 election
of Khatami, however, raised hopes that Iranian policies might
soon change, thereby facilitating more normal relations between
Washington and Tehran. The United States subsequently adjusted
its policy to incorporate a more balanced mix of carrots and
sticks. While sanctions and efforts to deny Iran arms and technology continue, the United States has also proposed to Tehran
a 'road map' leading to normalization.[31]

By contrast, EU policy towards the Islamic Republic has relied
almost entirely on carrots. The EU was involved from December
1992 to April 1997 in a largely unsuccessful effort to engage Iran
in a 'critical dialogue' to bolster the position of moderates in the
regime and thereby alter Iranian policy. The EU believed that
the dialogue was itself the major incentive for 'good behavior'
by Tehran, and it eschewed economic sanctions as a policy
instrument, which would have involved foregoing billions of
dollars worth of trade. Thus, while EU officials presented critical
dialogue as a good-faith effort to influence Iranian policy for the
better, many critics saw critical dialogue as a means of insulating
trade with Iran from politics, and an insurance policy against
Iranian terror. A major setback for EU–Iran relations occurred
in April 1997 when a German court implicated Iran's top
leadership in the 1992 murder of four Iranian dissidents in
Berlin. The critical dialogue was permanently broken off and the
EU recalled its ambassadors from Iran. This setback, however,
proved short-lived. The ambassadors returned in November
1997 and the dialogue resumed in July 1998, but in a different
format and with an agenda that emphasized economic co-
operation between the two parties, in order to bolster Iran's flag-
ging economy and thereby strengthen the position of Khatami
and his allies.[32]

Few, if any, of the GCC states have embraced the US approach
to Iran. Most of the smaller Gulf states see no point in anta-
gonising their large neighbor, which they consider a potential
counterbalance to Iraqi power and Saudi influence. Kuwait,

Bahrain, the UAE and Saudi Arabia have significant Shiite populations, and fear Iran's ability to meddle in their internal affairs. Furthermore, the UAE – namely, Dubai – conducts a thriving trade with Iran that is important to its economy and which it does not want disrupted. And, fearing that it could get caught in the middle of a US–Iran clash should evidence point to an Iranian role in the June 1996 Khobar Tower bombing, Saudi Arabia under the stewardship of Crown Prince Abdallah, has been working assiduously to improve ties with Tehran – this led the UAE in June 1999 to criticize sharply Saudi Arabia for its *rapprochement* with Iran absent settlement of the dispute over the three islands. Thus, for political, economic and security reasons, nearly all the GCC countries have moved to fend off potential Iranian threats by pursuing policies of political or economic engagement with Tehran – even if they remain wary of Iran's intentions. Cognizant of the imperatives of power and geography that drive these policies, Washington has reconciled itself to the independent approach of its GCC allies – who have nonetheless been very supportive of the US military presence in the region, which serves to curb both Iraqi and Iranian adventurism.

How successful have the divergent policies of the United States, the EU and the GCC states been? Neither the United States nor the EU can claim much success in changing specific Iranian policies through either political engagement or economic pressure. Tehran has not ceased its involvement in terrorism,[33] its support for opponents of the Arab–Israeli peace process, or its efforts to acquire WMD, nor has the human-rights situation in Iran improved – in fact, in some ways it has deteriorated in the past year or two.[34] Meanwhile, the EU and Iran succeeded to some degree in their shared goal of insulating trade from the vagaries of politics, while the GCC states can claim a degree of success in deflecting potential threats from Iran through a complex balancing act involving both Tehran and Washington.

The United States has had a fair degree of success in defining the agenda relating to Iran in consultations with its allies, and in convincing many to take steps that served to advance US policy objectives. Due in large part to US prompting in the

1980s, America's European allies imposed tight restrictions on the transfer of many types of dual-use technology to Iran, while banning the transfer of arms and nuclear technology outright.[35] The United States has also achieved a degree of success in pressing its European allies and multilateral lending institutions such as the World Bank and the International Monetary Fund (IMF) not to extend new concessional loans or credits to Iran – although these efforts have been aided by Iran's economic problems. By contrast, US efforts to urge Russia, North Korea and China to adopt restrictions on arms and technology transfers to Iran have met with only partial success. In recent years, Russia has been Iran's main source of conventional arms, missile technology and civilian nuclear technology. China has been also an important source of the conventional arms, missile technology and technology for Iran's CBW and civilian nuclear programs. And North Korea has been an important source of missile and missile-production technology. Russia has agreed, however, not to conclude any new arms deals, to halt all conventional-weapons transfers after September 1999, and to limit civilian nuclear co-operation with Iran – although co-operation in the missile field shows no signs of abating. China likewise has agreed not to transfer any more advanced anti-ship missiles and to halt the transfer of civilian nuclear technology to Iran after current contracts are fulfilled.[36] It remains to be seen, however, whether the souring of US relations with Russia and China as a result of NATO's war in Yugoslavia will undermine these achievements.

US policy towards Iran can claim one key, unambiguous achievement: success in halting and delaying Iran's efforts to expand and modernize its armed forces and enhance its WMD capabilities, through strategies of arms and technology denial, and economic sanctions.[37]

US pressure, diplomatic demarches and interdiction operations have thwarted several major conventional arms deals and countless smaller ones. They have cut off Iran from Western arms and technology sources, forcing it to rely on less advanced suppliers such as North Korea, China and Russia. Moreover, they have hindered procurement of spare parts for its armed forces, thereby making it more difficult for Tehran to maintain its existing force structure. These constraints may have made Iran more careful to avoid a confrontation with the United States that could lead to losses it knows it could neither absorb nor afford to replace. US efforts were also instrumental in thwarting a large number of prospective deals concerning technologies useful for the development of WMD, particularly in the civilian nuclear arena – although in many of these cases the United States could not have succeeded without the help and co-operation of friendly intelligence services and governments in Europe and elsewhere. For instance:

- Germany repeatedly refused Iranian requests, starting in 1984, to complete the Bushehr nuclear power plant begun by the Shah;

- Argentina refused to supply Iran with nuclear-fuel fabrication and reprocessing technology and a 20–30-Megawatt (MWt) research reactor in 1987;

- China refused to supply Iran with a 30-MWt research reactor in 1990 and a uranium hexafluoride conversion plant in 1998;

- India refused to supply Iran with a 10-MWt research reactor in 1991; and

- Russia refused to transfer a gas centrifuge-enrichment facility or a 330-MWt research reactor in 1995 that it had previously promised to Iran.[38]

Sanctions have also been an important policy tool. Iran's economic woes, which have been exacerbated by US sanctions, have forced Tehran to pare back its military expenditures dramatically. Iran's economy is a shambles, due to low oil prices, rapid population growth, the lingering costs of its war with Iraq, government mismanagement and corruption and a large short-term debt.[39] These economic problems have forced Tehran to cut military procurement by more than half since 1989. Following the Iran–Iraq War, Iran's Majlis (parliament) announced plans to spend $2 billion a year over five years for weapons purchases. Actual spending, however, has fallen far short of this target.[40]

Accordingly, in the period 1989–96, the actual numbers of weapons obtained by Iran also fell far short, in most categories, of its acquisition goals. Thus, while Tehran had been hoping to obtain some 1,000–1,500 tanks, it acquired about 225; of 250–500 infantry fighting vehicles, it acquired about 80; and of 100–200 aircraft, it acquired about 65. The only areas in which Iranian procurement objectives may have been met were in field artillery and warships – it acquired 320 artillery pieces and 13 warships.[41]

Lacking the funds to sustain a major, across-the-board military build-up, Iran has had to content itself with selectively enhancing its military capabilities. The shortfall in Iranian arms spending has therefore had a significant impact on the balance of power in the Persian Gulf. With an extra $1–2 billion a year, Iran would have been able to add many more weapons to its inventory, complicating US defense planning. This shortfall has also forced Tehran to delay or deter efforts to acquire conventional arms and WMD-related technologies.

Thus, while the United States has not succeeded in influencing Tehran to change its policies, it has succeeded – often with the help of others – in denying it the means to carry them out. By helping to deprive Iran of the resources it could have otherwise used for a military build-up, American sanctions have contributed to the security of the United States and its allies – however much the latter might dislike sanctions.[42] Because Russia and North Korea continue to sell Iran arms and technologies needed to produce missiles and WMD for largely financial reasons, measures such as sanctions that hinder Tehran's ability to raise the hard currency needed for these purchases should remain a key element of US policy towards Iran. Moreover, sanctions should remain in place until Iran halts its efforts to acquire WMD, its involvement in terrorism and its support for violent opponents of the Arab–Israeli peace process – either unilaterally or as part of a deal with the United States.

If they cannot agree on a common overall approach to Iran, the United States, the EU and the GCC states should, at least, agree to make clear to Tehran that it will pay a very high political and economic price – in the form of diplomatic isolation and severe economic sanctions – should it cross the nuclear threshold in violation of its NPT commitments. Deterring Iran from following the nuclear route will require continued US leadership on this issue, and a recognition that America's EU and GCC allies have an important role to play in shaping Iranian expectations and structuring Tehran's framework of incentives. EU and GCC representatives should not miss an opportunity in meetings with their Iranian counterparts to stress the potential costs of such a decision by Tehran. Likewise, the stance of the international community towards Iranian compliance with its CWC obligations will have important implications for Tehran's nuclear decision calculus. If Iran is able to cheat on its obligations under the CWC, it might be tempted to do likewise with the NPT.[43]

Even if the United States and its allies are unable to halt Iran's development of long-range missiles and nuclear weapons, efforts to delay these programs are important. First, when Iran and the United States hold official talks some day, it might be easier for Tehran to trade away capabilities under development than to abandon capabilities that already exist, in return for the easing or lifting of sanctions by Washington. Iran has been able to create only 350,000 jobs annually for the 800,000 young men – not to mention the women – joining the labor force each year. It will need tens of billions of dollars in foreign investment in the coming years to create jobs for these people and thereby avoid economic turmoil, and possibly political unrest. Iran badly needs the investment capital that US sanctions and pressure on third parties impedes. Washington's ability to help Iran mitigate its financial problems by easing or lifting sanctions provides it with a great deal of leverage over Tehran, and could set the stage for a 'Grand Bargain' wherein Tehran abandons its nuclear program in return for sanctions-relief and assistance in developing non-nuclear power sources.

Second, it buys time for the United States and its allies to develop countermeasures to Iranian capabilities. For instance, in 1993–94, US-orchestrated multilateral pressure on North Korea discouraged Pyongyang from transferring the Nodong-1 missile to Iran, forcing Tehran instead to take the more roundabout route of building the Shehab-3 missile – which is based on the Nodong-1 – using production technology supplied by North Korea. That five-year delay provided the time for Israel to develop its US-funded Arrow anti-missile system. The Arrow system is expected to be partially operational by the end of 1999, at about the same time that the Shehab-3 is expected to enter operational service. Further delays in the Iranian program might likewise provide the United States and its allies with additional time to improve their theater-missile-defense capabilities and for the United States to develop a national-missile-defense system.

Finally, it is a hedge against the possibility of a more aggressive foreign and defense policy should hardline conservative clerics gain control over all the major centers of power in Tehran in the future. In such a situation, the hardliners will have fewer means at their disposal with which to pursue their objectives. Conversely, should the trend towards pragmatism and moderation in Iranian politics continue, American efforts could succeed in postponing Iran's development of longer-range missiles and nuclear weapons until the time that more moderate political elements are more firmly ensconced in Tehran. In this case, it is possible that they may decide, for a variety of reasons, to abandon Iran's long-range missile and nuclear-weapons programs. But if they continue these programs, it is better that the country be in the hands of relatively moderate reformers among Iran's clerical leadership than in the grips of conservative hardliners. Although both groups are committed to pursuing nationalistic policies in the Persian Gulf, and rigid ideological policies towards the Arab–Israeli conflict, the reformers may be less inclined to adventurism and less likely to rely on terrorism and subversion to achieve their goals. In this way, the potentially destabilizing impact of a nuclear Iran might be mitigated.

This means that efforts to deal with nuclear proliferation by Iran should not only rely on traditional tools such as export controls, arms-control regimes and sanctions, but also on efforts to encourage the evolution in Iranian society towards greater openness and moderation. The United States and its allies have a limited degree of influence over domestic developments in Iran, although they can shape the context in which these events occur and perhaps indirectly influence their outcome. Exactly how to do this is a continuing source of disagreement between the United States and its allies. Resolving this debate in a way that maintains comity among the allies while advancing a common interest – deterring Iran from crossing the nuclear threshold – will pose one of the most important challenges for the United States and its allies in the coming years.

## NOTES

1. For the evidence pointing in the direction of an Iranian nuclear-weapons program, see Andrew Koch and Jeanette Wolf, 'Iran's Nuclear Procurement Program: How Close to the Bomb?', *The Nonproliferation Review* (1997), pp. 123–35; David Albright, 'Iran', in David Albright, Frans Berkhout and William Walker (eds), *Plutonium and Highly Enriched Uranium 1996: World Inventories, Capabilities, and Policies* (New York: Oxford University Press/ SIPRI, 1997), pp. 352–63; Michael Eisenstadt, *Iranian Military Power: Capabilities and Intentions* (Washington DC: The Washington Institute for Near East Policy, 1996), pp. 9–25; and David Albright, 'An Iranian Bomb?', *Bulletin of the Atomic Scientists*, July–August 1995, pp. 21–6.
2. The Shehab-3 has been tested only once, in July 1998, while the Shehab-4 is expected to be ready for its first test launch in 2–5 years. The Shehab-5 is believed to exist only on the drawing board at this time. For more on the Shehab family of missiles, see Steven J. Zaloga, 'Third World Ballistic Missiles', *World Missile Briefing* (Fairfax, VA: Teal Group, August 1999); Clifford Beal, 'Iran's Shehab-4 is Soviet SS-4, says US Intelligence', *Jane's Defense Weekly*, 17 February 1999, p. 5; and Donald H. Rumsfeld, *Report of the Commission to Assess the Ballistic Missile Threat to the United States: Executive Summary* (Washington DC: Government Printing Office, 1998), pp. 12–13.
3. Conventional arms are extraordinarily expensive: a tank may cost $1–3 million and a combat aircraft $25–50 million; while a warship may cost anything from $50 million for a fast-attack craft, to $500 million for a modern frigate. Thus, creating a large modern military could cost tens of billions of dollars. By contrast, a well-planned, well-managed nuclear program might cost only a few billion dollars.
4. *Financial Times*, 8 February (1993), p. 4.
5. *Washington Times*, 27 January (1999), p. A12.
6. *Washington Post*, 17 November (1992), p. A30.
7. IRNA, 5 June 1998.
8. AFP, 29 April 1998; Reuters, 30 April 1998. Safavi also bitterly complained that as a result of the press and public freedoms instituted by Khatami and his supporters: 'Liberals have taken over our universities and our youth are now chanting "Death to Dictatorship …"' In response, he threatened to: 'root out counter-revolutionaries wherever they are … to cut the throats of some and cut off the tongues of others,' adding that, 'our sword is our tongue …

we will name these cowards.' *Iran Brief*, 4 May (1998), p. 5.

9. In the first and second options, Iran could engage in nuclear weapons related research and development work under the cover of a defensive program ostensibly intended to provide an understanding of the nature of the nuclear threat posed by Iraq, Israel and the US (in much the way that Sweden concealed its investigation of a nuclear option in the late 1950s and early 1960s in its own 'defensive program'). Iran could conceivably make progress in weapons design without unambiguously violating its NPT commitments, and probably with a very low likelihood of getting caught. For more on the Swedish 'defensive program,' see Paul M. Cole, 'Atomic Bombast: Nuclear Weapon Decision-Making in Sweden, 1946–72,' *Washington Quarterly* (Spring 1997), pp. 233–51.

10. This is clearly the lesson Iraq learned during the Gulf War. After its August 1990 invasion of Kuwait, Iraq initiated a 'crash program' to produce one or two nuclear weapons within about eight months, using diverted safeguarded reactor fuel. The outbreak of the Gulf War in January 1991 pre-empted these plans, which were running behind schedule anyway. This experience under-scored the importance of possessing a 'nuclear force in being.' Being a 'threshold' or virtual nuclear-weapons state may not, in some circumstance, provide a hedge against disaster.

11. A key official responsible for procurement for Iran's biological weapons program is a scientific adviser to Khatami. *New York Times*, 8 December (1998), p. A1.

12. *Washington Post*, 17 November (1992), p. A30.

13. For instance, see Shahram Chubin, 'Does Iran Want Nuclear Weapons?' *Survival*, 37, 1 (1995), pp. 97–8, 100.

14. In fact, one can argue that the Gulf Co-operation Council States will feel more comfortable dealing with Iran *because* they retain an American security umbrella.

15. Saudi Arabia and the United Arab Emirates have already acquired ballistic missiles (Chinese CSS-2s and Soviet Scud-Bs, respectively) and it may be that the UAE is interested in the Anglo-French Black Shahine air-launched cruise missile in order to augment its retaliatory capability.

16. The concept of 'undetterable' states was popularized by the late US Secretary of Defense Les Aspin, and continues to enjoy some currency among defense analysts. See Secretary of Defense Les Aspin, remarks to the Committee on International Security and Arms Control, National Academy of Sciences, Washington DC, 7 December 1993.

17. Interview with Defense Minister Admiral Ali Shamkani on Tehran IRIB Television Second Program, 30 July 1998; translated in FBIS-NES-98-217, 5 August 1998.

18. Shaul Bakhash, *The Reign of the Ayatollahs: Iran and the Islamic Revolution* (New York: Basic Books, 1990), p. 273 (hereafter cited as *Reign of the Ayatollahs*).

19. Even the Lebanese Hizballah movement, which shares Tehran's general ideological framework and which is notorious for its use of suicide bombers, has proven responsive to religious-ideological constraints and sensitive to losses in its ranks. In the mid-1980s, Lebanese Shiite clerics placed a conditional ban on suicide bombings, fearing that the fine line between 'self-

martyrdom' in combat (as they call it) which they permitted, and suicide – which is prohibited by Islamic law – was being crossed by many young recruits and their overzealous controllers. Martin Kramer, 'Sacrifice and "Self-Martyrdom" in Shiite Lebanon,' in M. Kramer (ed.), *Arab Awakening and Islamic Revival: The Politics of Ideas in the Middle East* (New Brunswick: Transaction Publishers, 1996), pp. 231–43. Since then, the Hizballah has generally eschewed suicide operations, and relied mainly on conventional guerilla tactics in its war against Israeli troops in south Lebanon, It has, moreover, changed its tactics in recent years in order to reduce casualties among its forces, generally abandoning costly frontal assaults on well-defended positions held by the Israeli army and its local allies in south Lebanon, in favor of less risky tactics: remote-controlled bombs, mortar fire and long-range ambushes of Israeli troops. *Jerusalem Post*, 28 October (1995), p. 7.

20. David Menashri, *Revolution at a Crossroads: Iran's Domestic Politics and Regional Ambitions* (Washington, DC: The Washington Institute for Near East Policy, 1997), p. 8.

21. Sharough Akhavi, 'Elite Factionalism in the Islamic Republic of Iran,' *The Middle East Journal*, 41, 2 (1987), pp. 181–201.

22. Gary Sick, *All Fall Down: America's Tragic Encounter with Iran* (New York: Random House, 1985), pp. 186–90.

23. John Tower, *Tower Commission Report* (New York: Times Books, 1987), pp. 51, 434–5.

24. Bakhash, *Reign of the Ayatollahs*, pp. 279–80.

25. *New York Times*, 1 May (1996), p. A8.

26. However, even in the missile arena, Iran is seeking the option of deniable delivery. Iran reportedly test-launched a short-range ballistic missile from a barge in the Caspian Sea in early 1998. Basing short-range ballistic missiles on merchant ships could enable Iran to hit targets currently out of missile range (such as the United States) while maintaining deniability, since a merchant vessel used to launch a missile might be able to blend in with the normal maritime traffic in the area immediately after launch and thereby avoid detection. See K. Scott McMahon, 'Ship-Based Missiles Surface as Potential Terror Weapon,' *Defense News*, 15 March (1999), p. 27; *Iran News*, 8 March (1999), p. 1.

27. There is apparently reason to believe that these efforts continued, albeit at greatly reduced levels, through the mid-1990s in Bahrain and elsewhere in the Gulf region: *Washington Post*, 8 January (1998), p. A28.

28. There were also differences in the degree of emphasis the United States and EU placed on these various issues. While the United States placed more-or-less equal emphasis on all three, the states of the EU generally gave precedence to human rights and terrorism.

29. This is not for a lack of efforts to engage Iran. Twice Washington has tried to engage 'moderates' in Tehran – in 1979 and 1985–86 – and twice it has been burned. Following the 1979 Islamic evolution, the United States tried to engage moderates in Tehran, and senior US and Iranian officials met at the UN and in Algiers in late 1979. Radicals succeeded in sabotaging these efforts by seizing the American embassy in November 1979. Moreover, the Iran–Contra scandal was initially conceived as an opening to moderates in Tehran. This effort exploded in the faces of its American architects when Iranian

254

opponents of the initiative leaked details to a Lebanese paper in November 1986. For this reason, US officials are wary of policy approaches predicated on supporting one faction in Tehran against another, as advocated by many members of the EU and the GCC.

30. Critics of US policy towards Iran in the 1990s often claimed that it was driven by domestic politics or Israeli concerns. While no doubt both factors played a role in the formulation of American policy, they did not drive the policy of containment, which had powerful supporters in America's foreign policy and national-security bureaucracies.

31. Secretary of State Madeleine Albright, speech before the Asia Society, 17 June 1998.

32. For background on the 'critical dialogue' policy, see Johannes Reissner, 'Europe, the United States, and the Persian Gulf', in Robert D. Blackwill and Michael Sturmer (eds), *Allies Divided: Transatlantic Policies for the Greater Middle East* (Cambridge, MA: MIT Press, 1997), pp. 138–40.

33. Tehran has, however, become more careful in selecting targets and venues for terrorism. The locus of its activities shifted during the 1990s from the politically sensitive heart of Europe (particularly France and Germany) to the Middle East (Iraq) and South Asia (Pakistan) where such attacks barely make news in the West. This does show that Tehran is sensitive to the political and economic costs of its involvement in terrorism, which has had a harmful impact on its relations with countries such as France and Germany.

34. Although speech and press freedoms have increased since Khatami's election, attacks on those exercising these freedoms – particularly intellectuals and political activists – have also increased (these include a rash of 'disappearances' and murders attributed to the Intelligence Ministry). Moreover, the number of prisoners executed for various crimes has grown sharply in recent years, while persecution of members of the Bahai faith has intensified: see Maurice Copithorne, 'Report on the Situation of Human Rights in the Islamic Republic of Iran,' United Nations Economic and Social Council, Commission on Human Rights, E/CN.4/1999/32, 28 December 1998.

35. See, for instance, Peter Burleigh, 'Lessons of "Operation Staunch" for Future Conflicts', in Eric H. Arnett (ed.), *Lessons of the Iran–Iraq War: Mediation and Conflict Resolution* (Washington, DC: American Association for the Advancement of Science, 1990), pp. 9–14.

36. At least some of these successes can be attributed to Iran's inability to pay for these items, rather than any reluctance on the part of suppliers to provide them. For instance, Chinese officials relate privately that the reason China agreed to stop deliveries of advanced anti-ship missiles to Iran was that Tehran owed Beijing hundreds of millions of dollars for missiles and missile boats and was way behind in its payments. In this case, economic pressure on Tehran was a more effective way to staunch arms transfers than inducements to the Chinese (which included offers of access to US civilian nuclear technology).

37. The following assessment draws heavily on Patrick Clawson and Michael Eisenstadt, 'Opportunities and Challenges for US Policy', in Patrick Clawson (ed.), *Iran Under Khatami: A Political, Economic, and Military Assessment* (Washington, DC: The Washington Institute for Near East Policy, 1998), pp. 99–114.

38. There are, however, persistent rumors that negotiations between Russia and

Iran concerning the gas centrifuge facility and research reactor are continuing: *Ha'aretz* Internet Edition, 18 February (1998); see: <http://www.3.haaretz. co.il/eng/scripts/open.asp?datee=2/18/98>; *Washington Times*, 7 May (1998), p. A1.

39. Thus, although sanctions were clearly not at the root of Iran's economic problems, they undoubtedly contributed to them, while the lack of US investment over the past two decades has imposed substantial opportunity costs on Iran for its policies. For detailed assessments of the impact of US sanctions, see Jahangir Amuzegar, 'Iran's Economy and the US Sanctions,' *Middle East Journal*, 51, 2 (1997), pp. 185–99; 'Islamic Republic of Iran', in *United Nations General Assembly, Human Rights and Unilateral Coercive Measures: Reports of the Secretary General*, A/53/293, 28 August 1998, pp. 4–7.

40. According to Iran Central Bank figures, actual spending on arms imports reached $1.625 billion in 1989–90; $1.6 billion in 1990–91; $1.678 billion in 1991–92; $808 million in 1992–93; and $850 million in 1993–94 – the last year Tehran published such figures (International Monetary Fund, *Islamic Republic of Iran: Recent Economic Developments*, 19 September 1995, p. 74, and 5 October 1993, p. 38). These figures are roughly consistent with US government estimates that Iranian foreign-exchange expenditures on arms dropped from a high of $2 billion in 1991 to less than $1 billion in 1997 (Bruce Riedel, *US Policy in the Gulf: Five Years of Dual Containment*, The Washington Institute for Near East Policy, Policy Watch No. 315, 8 May 1998, p. 2).

41. Figures for arms transfers are derived largely from the UN Register of Conventional Arms, 1992 through 1996.

42. Some critics claim that by denying Iran the ability to build an effective conventional military, US policy – particularly sanctions – has forced Tehran down the proliferation path since WMD provide the biggest 'bang' for their very limited 'bucks.' However, Iranian efforts to acquire WMD date to the mid-1980s, long before the most punishing US sanctions – of 1995 and 1996 – and they were developed initially in response to the war with Iraq and to the latter's WMD programs. Thus, US policy simply ensured that Iran had fewer resources available to pursue options it was pursuing anyway.

43. Iran submitted an initial declaration concerning its chemical weapon (CW) capabilities to the Organization for the Prevention of Chemical Warfare (OPCW) in the Hague in November 1998. According to the senior diplomat heading the Iranian delegation to the OPCW, Iran developed a CW 'capability' during the Iran–Iraq War for purposes of 'deterrence,' but relied on 'diplomacy as the sole mechanism to stop [the use of CW] by its adversary.' Following the war 'the decision to develop chemical weapons capabilities was reversed and the process was terminated' (Statement by H.E. Ambassador Mohammad R. Alborzi, Director General of the Ministry of Foreign Affairs and Head of Delegation of the Islamic Republic of Iran to the Third Session of the Conference of the State Parties of the Chemical Weapons Convention, The Hague, Netherlands, 16–20 November 1998). It has not yet been possible to assess the declaration for accuracy and completeness.

# 11

# Iran and Weapons of Mass Destruction

## SETH CARUS

Iran's Shehab-3 missile, a 17-ton medium-range ballistic missile (MRBM) able to carry a 1.2-ton payload with a range estimated at 1,300 km,[1] became operational following a successful test launch around 20 February 2000.[2] The Shehab-3 was first test-fired in August 1998. Yet only 18 months before an earlier test, a senior US intelligence official had told Congress that it might take Iran as long as ten years to acquire a missile with such a long range.[3] Following the 1998 launch, the US government recognized that: 'the Shehab 3 significantly alters the military equation in the Middle East by giving Tehran the capability to strike targets in Israel, Saudi Arabia and most of Turkey.'[4]

Iran's development of the Shehab-3 is significant for two reasons. First, it gives Iran a delivery system able to strike every important US ally in the region. Second, it was clearly designed as a delivery system for weapons of mass destruction. Iran has been developing nuclear, biological and chemical (NBC) weapons since the early 1980s, during Iran's long war with Iraq. But the pace of development significantly accelerated in the early 1990s.

Iran's weapons program significantly affects the strategic environment in the entire Middle East. In addition to undermining international non-proliferation norms, these programs pose a direct military threat to US interests and allies in the region and to US military forces deployed there. The Iranians appear to have accelerated their work on NBC weapons and associated delivery systems in recent years. While some analysts believe that Iran would use its NBC weapons and missiles only

257

if the regime's survival were in question, the limited available evidence calls that thesis into question. Iran's storage of chemical weapons on Abu Musa, an island in the Persian Gulf off the coast of Dubai, suggests that Tehran would use such weapons long before the regime's security was in doubt.[5] By merely possessing these weapons or by threatening to use them, Iran could also use them to gain leverage over neighboring states.

## NUCLEAR, BIOLOGICAL AND CHEMICAL WEAPONS PROGRAMS

The development of NBC weapons and delivery systems has strong support in Iran, as George Tenet, Director of the Central Intelligence Agency (CIA), noted in testimony to Congress in early 1999: '[Iran's] reformists and conservatives agree on at least one thing: weapons of mass destruction are a necessary component of defense and a high priority.'[6]

Contrary to the view of some analysts, there is no evidence indicating that the growing influence of relative moderates in Iran would reduce support for these programs. Indeed, it appears that the greater influence of technocrats is enhancing the programs by making possible the appointment of individuals selected more for their technical expertise than for their religious or political affiliations. For these reasons, even if the radicals lose influence in Tehran, there is no reason to believe that the Islamic Republic will constrain development of NBC weapons.

Iran's progress in developing NBC capabilities varies considerably from program to program. The chemical weapons program, for example, appears considerably more advanced than its nuclear or biological counterparts. Fortunately, a lack of money, difficulties in integrating complex programs, and constraints imposed by Western technology transfer controls have slowed the programs. Although Iran has made considerable progress in developing ballistic missiles, it is less clear that it has developed missile delivery systems for its existing chemical or biological agents. Nevertheless, unless significant changes occur in Iran, it is only a matter of time before Iran has an effective NBC arsenal.

## Nuclear Weapons

Since the early 1980s, US officials have worried that the clerical regime in Tehran was bent on acquiring the infrastructure to build nuclear weapons. These concerns became more acute in the early 1990s. A 1997 Arms Control and Disarmament Agency concluded: 'Although Iran's rudimentary program has apparently met with limited success so far, the US believes Iran has not abandoned its efforts to expand its nuclear infrastructure to support nuclear weapons development.'[7] In early 1999, CIA director Tenet testified that Iran: 'seems to be pushing its [nuclear] program forward.'[8]

Numerous estimates, many unduly pessimistic, have been made by various governments regarding the time Iran needed to acquire nuclear weapons, often suggesting that this would happen by the year 2000. The most credible estimate was provided in January 1995 by US Secretary of Defense William Perry and Israeli Prime Minister Yitzhak Rabin, who estimated that Iran would need 7–15 years to acquire a nuclear weapons capability, implying acquisition between 2002 and 2010.[9] In contrast, General Anthony C. Zinni, Chief of the US Central Command, and thus responsible for US military forces in the Middle East, believes that Iran will acquire a nuclear weapon within a few years.[10]

Nevertheless, the Iranian effort to acquire nuclear weapons has been hampered by an inadequate technical base. According to the US Defense Department: 'At this stage, Iran's scientific and technical base remains insufficient to support major nuclear programs. The Iranians recognize their dependence on foreign assistance and are encouraging younger Iranians to study abroad to gain needed technical assistance.'[11]

Despite considerable efforts since 1996, then, there is little public evidence to suggest that Iran has made more than limited progress in developing nuclear weapons. Iran still might require 7–15 years to produce a weapon, or achieve this goal only between 2006 and 2014. Certainly, though, it is difficult to predict when Iran will cross the nuclear threshold.

Iran could acquire nuclear weapons in one of several ways. It could attempt to steal a weapon from the former Soviet arsenal now located in one of the successor states.[12] Iran could also acquire fissile material from the former Soviet Union. Such highly enriched uranium or plutonium suitable for use in making atomic bombs would allow the Iranians to field a crude nuclear weapon much faster.[13] It has been estimated that Iran could then produce a fission bomb between 9 and 36 months.[14]

Finally, Iran could create the infrastructure needed to produce fissile material on its own. In this case, the time needed to develop a weapon would grow considerably. This process would also be more easily detected because of the size and complexity of the associated facilities and the unique signatures of the chemicals used. Evidence shows that Iran has explored developing capabilities to produce both highly-enriched uranium and plutonium, each of which requires a considerably different infrastructure.

While the Russians are currently building the VVER-1000 reactor at Bushier, this type of reactor is considered poorly suited to plutonium production. Russia has also promised that the reactor will be subject to inspection by the International Atomic Energy Agency (IAEA) and that spent fuel would be returned to Russia.[15] Should Iran decide to break these agreements, it could extract plutonium from the spent fuel only by building reprocessing plants. Although the Iranians tried to obtain such a facility from Russia, there are no reports that it has succeeded. Thus, while the US government officials are concerned that acquiring this reactor will help Iranian scientists improve their skills, Tehran would need another reactor better suited to plutonium production.

Responding to US government efforts to block its enhancement of nuclear capabilities, Iran tried to find countries willing to supply the technology but found few such opportunities. Consequently, by the early 1990s, Iran was largely limited to two principal suppliers of nuclear technology, China and Russia. A Department of Defense report noted: 'Chinese and Russian supply policies are key to Iran's success.'[16]

In response to US pressure, Iran has taken the unusual step of allowing the IAEA to conduct relatively intrusive inspections of its nuclear infrastructure. The IAEA has detected no violations of Iran's Nuclear Non-Proliferation Treaty (NPT) commitments. Although some experts discount the IAEA conclusions, most believe that Iran is so early in the process of developing nuclear weapons that it has little need to hide its activities.[17]

## Biological Weapons

Iran already has an offensive biological weapons program and may have produced small quantities of biological agent.[18] It is unclear from the available information when US experts believe that Iran will have a more serious biological agent dissemination capability.

There is relatively little public information about Iran's biological weapons program. During the 1980s, an Iranian scientist made repeated efforts to acquire different strains of a fungus that produces mycotoxins from Canadian and later Dutch facilities.[19] According to a December 1998 *New York Times* report, Iran attempted to hire scientists in the former Soviet biological weapons program, the world's largest and most sophisticated. At least some of these scientists have accepted the Iranian offers, although it remains unclear how many or what expertise they provide.[20] Given Iranian ties to Russian expertise, Iran might adopt agents developed by the former Soviet program, such as Marburg, smallpox, plague and tularemia.[21] At the same time, the Iranians are trying to reduce their dependence on foreign technology and assistance.

## Chemical Weapons

Iran started its chemical weapons program in 1983 and produced its first agent in 1984, during the Iran–Iraq War and in response to Iraq's efforts. In 1996, the US Defense Department estimated that cumulative production had reached at least: 'several hundred tons of blister, blood, and choking agents.'[22] One source claims that the Iranians might have as much as 2,000 tons of chemical agent, possibly including nerve agent.[23] More authoritatively, General Anthony Zinni reported that Iran: 'may have produced several thousand tons of chemical agents to date.'[24] According to Middle East defense analyst Michael Eisenstadt: 'Iran has the most active chemical warfare program in the developing world.'[25]

Iran is also working to enhance the sophistication of its chemical program. It is trying to develop nerve agents, including VX, the most advanced agent to enter the inventories of the United States and the Soviet Union.[26] The US government has suggested that Iran possesses stockpiles of chemical-filled artillery shells and bombs.[27] Persistent reports that Iran may possess chemical warheads for its SCUD missiles have never been confirmed.[28]

The effectiveness of Iran's existing chemical weapons arsenal is uncertain. Iran apparently relies heavily on hydrogen cyanide which is highly toxic but not an effective battlefield weapon.[29] One estimate suggests that 20 tons of hydrogen cyanide is necessary to equal the military effectiveness of one ton of sarin nerve agent.[30]

The Iranians have signed onto the Chemical Weapons Convention (CWC), under whose terms they will be forced to eliminate existing stocks of chemical weapons and dismantle chemical production facilities. The Defense Department, however, doubts Tehran's sincerity and believes that Iran: 'continues to upgrade and expand its chemical warfare production infrastructure and munitions arsenal.'[31]

Recent reports that Iraq may be acquiring from Russia a new type of chemical agent, known as Novichok agents, should raise concerns that Iran may do the same.[32] The Soviet Union reportedly developed the Novichok agents in order to evade the controls imposed by the CWC. Although prohibited by the treaty, these agents are not specifically mentioned in the annexes to the convention. Russian scientists estimated that one Novichok agent was 5–8 times more lethal than VX, the most dangerous nerve agent that the United States ever developed.[33]

## LONG-RANGE DELIVERY SYSTEMS

Essential to the effectiveness of an NBC weapon is the delivery system that transports it to the intended target. The delivery system must be capable of carrying the weapon's weight, have sufficient range to reach the intended target and possess enough accuracy to allow the weapon to do significant damage. For tactical applications, field artillery can be used, and Iran is believed to possess such munitions for at least its chemical agents. To strike targets at longer ranges, however, Iran needs to rely on either long range aircraft, such as its Soviet-supplied Su-24 strike aircraft, or surface-to-surface missiles.

### BALLISTIC MISSILES: A GROWING CAPABILITY

The Iranians first began to acquire ballistic missiles in the mid-1980s, when the Libyans reportedly provided about 30 Soviet-built SCUD-C missiles with a 300-km range. Since then, Iran has acquired additional missiles from North Korea and China, and has received assistance for indigenous development from China, North Korea and Russia.

According to the International Institute for Strategic Studies, Iran has more than 400 surface-to-surface missiles: including about 25 CSS-8 launchers with 200 missiles, and about ten SCUD launchers with 210 SCUD-B and SCUD-C missiles.[34] These missiles have sufficient range to hit targets in Iraq and the other states bordering the Persian Gulf. They cannot strike targets very far into Saudi Arabia, and are unable to reach Israel. In addition, the missiles are relatively inaccurate.[35]

Iran's efforts to develop a region-wide missile capability took a big step forward with the 1998 test launch of the Shehab-3. The United States believes that Russian technology has played a critical part in the development of the Shehab-3, though the missile itself is based on the North Korean No Dong.[36] In late 1999, a senior US defense official reported that Iran was experiencing problems with the missile and had several unsuccessful tests.[37] However, in early 2000, the Iranians conducted another successful test launch of a Shehab-3, using one of a dozen North Korean rocket motors supplied to Tehran in early 1999.[38]

Iran is also believed to be working on more advanced systems. The Shehab-4 appears to be an intermediate-range ballistic missile (IRBM) with a range of 2,000 km. In contrast, it appears that the Shehab-5 will be a 10,000-km-range intercontinental-range ballistic missile (ICBM).[39]

Significantly, the US intelligence community is no longer confident about how long it will take Iran to develop an ICBM.

> If Iran follows a development time line similar to that demonstrated with the Shehab-3, which included significant foreign assistance, it would take Iran many years to develop a 9,000–10,000-km range ICBM capable of reaching the United States. But Iran could significantly shorten the acquisition time – and warning time – by purchasing key components or entire systems from potential sellers such a North Korea.[40]

The US intelligence community's evolving views on Iran's chance of acquiring ICBMs are reflected in the unclassified version of a National Intelligence Estimate released in September 1999. According to the testimony of the National Intelligence Officer responsible for the report, North Korea is the most likely country to acquire an ICBM. He added that: 'Iran is the next hostile country most capable of testing an ICBM capable of delivering a weapon to the United States during the next 15 years.' Other assessments of Iranian missile capabilities include the following:

- Iran could test an ICBM that could deliver a several-hundred-kilogram payload to many parts of the United States in the latter half of the next decade, using Russian technology and assistance.

- Iran could pursue a Taepo Dong-type ICBM and could test a Taepo Dong-1 or Taepo Dong-2-type ICBM, possibly with North Korean assistance, in the next few years.

- Iran is likely to test a space launch vehicle (SLV) by 2010 that – once developed – could be converted into an ICBM capable of delivering a several-hundred-kilogram payload to the United States.

Beyond that, analysts differ on the likely timing of Iran's first flight test of an ICBM that could threaten the United States. Assessments include:

- Likely before 2010 and very likely before 2015 – noting that a space launch vehicle (SLV) with ICBM capabilities will probably be tested within the next few years.
- No more than an even chance by 2010 and a better than even chance by 2015.
- Less than an even chance by 2015.[41]

Given the available information, it is probably prudent to assume that Iran will possess a missile capable of striking US cities by 2010.

The key problem for the Iranian ballistic missile program is the development of warhead designs to permit effective delivery of NBC weapons. As the Iranians develop longer-range systems, the need for more sophisticated warheads grows. A warhead suitable for use in a short-range missile such as the SCUD-B, which flies at a relatively low speed and does not leave the atmosphere, is unlikely to be useful in an ICBM missile. To deliver effective biological and chemical weapons, Iran must develop warheads capable of delivering cluster munitions. The United States and Soviet Union are known to have developed such munitions and thus could be a source for such arms, if Moscow ignores US pleas not to do so.[42]

## CRUISE MISSILES: THE NEXT STAGE?

The Iranians also have an interest in cruise missiles – unmanned aircraft-like missiles with a self-contained guidance system. Using modern satellite navigation systems, cruise missiles can attain accuracies of less than 20 m and can carry nuclear, biological, or chemical weapons.[43]

Recently, Iran took a step forward in its efforts to develop cruise missile capabilities. According to the *Washington Post*, US intelligence experts believe that Iran can now produce the C-802 anti-ship cruise missile, a Chinese system based on the French Exocet anti-ship missile.[44] If these reports are correct, Iran could adapt this system for delivering biological and chemical weapons against neighboring states. To reach more distant targets, it would need to develop a different system.[45]

## US POLICY OPTIONS

What steps can be taken to halt or constrain Iran's efforts to develop weapons of mass destruction? US government efforts over nearly two decades working to stop Iran's NBC-acquisition programs have been largely successful. Consequently, Iran's capabilities have been slowed and reduced. Still, it is highly unlikely that such programs will stop or roll back Iran's weapons programs. Thus, the United States needs to prepare to deal with the implications of NBC weapons in Iranian hands.

Any country committed to acquiring NBC weapons will eventually obtain them. Non-proliferation efforts, however, are critical for several reasons. First, they drive up the cost of programs, inevitably reducing the size of a country's weapons arsenal. Second, prevention programs reduce the sophistication of capabilities because the Iranians cannot necessarily obtain needed technology from the best sources. Finally, non-proliferation efforts impose delays.

Thus, US policies have yielded significant benefits and should not be abandoned once Iran actually begins to acquire NBC weapons, since Tehran would try continually to upgrade and obtain larger quantities of arms: to replace hydrogen cyanide and mustard gas with agents like VX, and to secure longer-range missiles.

What this suggests, however, is that non-proliferation programs cannot be the only component of a reaction toward Iran's

NBC programs. Deterrence strategies must reduce Iran's readiness to employ NBC weapons. US assurances must persuade allies and friends in the region of a real commitment to their security.

## EXPLOITING IRANIAN VULNERABILITIES

Reviewing Iran's NBC and missile development programs suggests that the Iranians have two weaknesses that can be exploited as the United States continues to develop its responses. First, Iran remains dependent on foreign technology and expertise, especially in program management and systems integration. Second, the Iranians have limited financial resources, which prevents them from establishing massive parallel programs the way Iraq did during the 1980s. Thus, they cannot compensate for delays or increased costs imposed by US interference simply by throwing more money at the problem.

## ARMS CONTROL

The framework for US efforts to constrain Iran is the non-proliferation regime created over many years through the negotiation of multilateral arms control treaties. The NPT is intended to halt the spread of nuclear weapons by controlling sensitive technologies associated with their development. The NPT's focus has traditionally been on the nuclear fuel cycle to prevent a country from building the infrastructure needed to produce fissionable material. The problem is that there are alternative ways to acquire fissile material, especially given the disarray in the former Soviet Union. Thus, even if the IAEA mechanisms are highly effective – a dubious proposition – Iran still possesses alternative routes.

Two treaties form the basis for arms control in the area of biological weapons. The Biological Weapons Convention (BWC) prohibits the possession or production of biological weapons, while the 1926 Geneva Protocol prohibits use of biological weapons. The BWC provides no inspection or verification system, but there is no reason to believe that even a well-designed verification system would detect a well-hidden biological weapons program. Therefore, the main utility of the BWC is to provide the international norm that justifies US concerns for Iran's illegal efforts to develop biological weapons.

Finally, there is the CWC. As previously noted, Iran must eliminate its chemical weapons capabilities to comply with its CWC obligations. Iran has admitted to past possession of chemical weapons production facilities but does not admit to any current possession of weapons.[46] It appears that Tehran will try to evade the treaties restrictions and retain chemical weapons and associated production capabilities.

While these treaties themselves may not prevent Iran from acquiring NBC capabilities, they can provide the basis for bilateral and multilateral diplomatic initiatives.

When the Soviet Union collapsed, US officials recognized that there was a high risk that expertise, technology and sensitive materials critical to the development of NBC weapons could assist proliferating countries like Iran. Therefore, the Co-operative Threat Reduction initiative was launched. Although these efforts have chemical and biological components, the primary focus has been the security of former Soviet nuclear technology.

## EXPORT CONTROLS

Iranian efforts to develop NBC weapons and delivery systems depend heavily on foreign assistance. Iran's nuclear weapons program appears to rely on assistance from China and Russia; its chemical weapons program on support from China; its biological weapons program on Russian help; and its missile program on a combination of Russian, Chinese and North Korean support. The salience of external support is evident in a US Department of Defense statement about Iran's chemical weapons program:

'China is an important supplier of technologies and equipment for Iran's chemical warfare program. Therefore, Chinese supply policies will be key to whether Tehran attains its long-term goal of independent production for these weapons.'[47] This suggests that eliminating foreign support for Iran's weapons programs would slow development, reduce sophistication and increase costs.

The Clinton administration has pressured China, Russia and North Korea to end state-supported proliferation activities and to curtail illicit exports. The record of accomplishment, unfortunately, is extremely uneven. North Korea clearly views missile sales as a source of badly needed foreign exchange, and has made it quite clear that it will continue its sales. Similarly, there are severe doubts about the willingness of China and Russia to stop all but the most flagrant exports. Russia particularly has expressed a desire to prevent Iran from acquiring NBC weapons and their associated delivery means. But, in practice, Moscow has shown limited willingness to identify and act against those responsible for exporting Russian technology to Iran.

Two problems suggest that it will be impossible to rely on export controls to halt technology transfers. First, despite considerable pressure from Congress, the Clinton administration has not been willing to impose significant penalties on China or Russia for on-going efforts to support Iran's weapons programs. Although these views may be justified by a broader view of the US strategic interests, they do little to ensure that Iran does not develop NBC weapons.

Second, even countries that support US non-proliferation objectives often engage in trade with Iran contrary to US wishes. This is a clear lesson of the French willingness to sell Microturbo engines to Tehran, ostensibly as power generators, even though the equipment might be helping Iran develop an indigenous production capability for cruise missiles. If it is difficult to reach agreement with a NATO partner, the prospects of reaching agreement with countries that have radically different views of their national interest is even less likely.

## TRADE RESTRICTIONS

In particular, the US Congress has sought to exploit Iran's need for investments. A focal point of this effort was the 1996 Iran and Libya Sanctions Act (ILSA). In May 1998, the administration, however, agreed to waive sanctions for oil and gas investments in Iran, effectively gutting the act. Secretary of State Madeleine Albright justified this action: 'Among other factors, I considered the significant, enhanced co-operation we have achieved with the European Union and Russia in accomplishing ILSA's primary objective of inhibiting Iran's ability to develop weapons of mass destruction and support of terorism.'[48]

European countries objected to ILSA as imposing sanctions on entities outside the legal jurisdiction of the United States. Moreover, the Europeans prefer a policy of engagement toward Tehran, rather than one focusing on sanctions. As a practical matter, ILSA had only a limited impact. In general, the Iranians have been hindered more by their own unfriendly policies toward investment than by US sanctions legislation. Indeed, a study by the Economist Intelligence Unit ranked Iran 59 of 60 countries in terms of their attractiveness to foreign investors.[49]

## COUNTER-PROLIFERATION

Another main component of an effective US strategy is the Department of Defense's Counterproliferation Initiative. This effort was started in the early days of the Clinton Administration because of Secretary of Defense Les Aspin's strong views that non-proliferation efforts might fail and, as a result, the US military might be forced to fight an adversary armed with NBC weapons. As originally conceived, the Counterproliferation Initiative focused on the need to have a balanced military response to allow the United States to defeat an NBC-armed adversary.

## THEATER MISSILE DEFENSES

Active defenses are a critical element of efforts to defeat NBC weapons. Because the most likely delivery system for these weapons are ballistic and cruise missiles, the US military needs robust theater missile defense systems. The importance of the missile defenses was highlighted during the 1991 Gulf War, when Patriot missile batteries, despite their incomplete effectiveness, helped nullify the strategic advantage that the Iraqis gained from their missile attacks against Israel and Saudi Arabia.

Because of the Gulf War experience, Israel increased its commitment to missile defenses and to the Arrow missile program. The first of three Arrow batteries became operational in March 2000. Unfortunately for Israel, Iranian missiles pose an even tougher challenge for Israel than the Iraqi missiles. The farther a ballistic missile flies, the higher its speed on re-entry, and the harder it is for a missile defense system to intercept it. Thus, Israel appears interested in developing a Boost Phase Intercept weapon, designed to destroy a ballistic missile just after launch or a launcher immediately after it has fired a missile. The Israeli program appears to rely on remotely-piloted vehicles, which would have to be flown into Iranian territory, a daunting technical challenge. The United States needs to work with Israel to ensure that it has the capabilities needed to defend against Iranian missiles.


## CHEMICAL AND BIOLOGICAL DEFENSES

After the end of the Gulf War, the Department of Defense determined that the US military lacked adequate chemical and biological defenses. Consequently, considerable effort has been made to solve this problem by equipment to detect chemical and biological agents, protective garments and gas, and decontaminating materials to eliminate hazardous substances.

Israel is the only country in the region that has a significant capability in this area. In addition, it is one of the few countries anywhere in the world that provides such protection for its civilian population. As a result, Israel is probably better prepared as a nation to deal with this threat than virtually any other country, including the United States.

## CONSEQUENCE MANAGEMENT

As a result of the Clinton administration's concern that US cities may be increasingly vulnerable to chemical and biological terrorism,[50] the United States is devoting considerable resources to develop programs to deal with casualties and to clean up contaminated areas. While Israel already has considerable capability to conduct such operations, other US allies in the region have far less ability to do so. The United States needs to work with them to ensure that they are not vulnerable to chemical and biological weapons use. The anthrax attacks on the US government and other targets in the autumn of 2001 are certain to accelerate these efforts.

## CONCLUSION

The United States probably cannot stop Iran from acquiring NBC weapons, so long as the Iranians remain willing to pay the political and economic costs of pursuing such programs. But there is a great deal the United States can do to constrain Iranian capabilities that will reduce the risks posed by Iranian NBC capabilities to US military forces, friends and allies in the region. Three administrations have pursued policies aimed at preventing the Iranians from acquiring NBC weapons and missile delivery systems. Although they have not prevented Iran from making progress, these policies have slowed the Iranian programs, increased the financial cost and limited the size and sophistication of Iranian capabilities.

The United States must take an active role in assisting Middle Eastern countries to develop responses to the threat posed by NBC weapons, with requirements varying for each country. The United States needs to continue to co-operate with Israel in missile defenses, and extend that effort to the arena of consequence management. Other countries, especially the six GCC states, need more direct US help. Where appropriate, the United States needs to ensure missile defenses are available, either by selling them or by deploying US-manned systems. Moreover, the United States needs to work with the GCC countries to enhance their chemical and biological defense and consequence management capabilities.

Finally, the United States must continue to pursue a strategy combining multilateral, bilateral and unilateral activities. The United States cannot deal with this problem by itself, and needs the support of governments around the world. At the same time, the United States cannot allow itself to be captured by those in the international community who believe that consensus is more important than results, going it alone when necessary to protect national interests, despite criticism from others.

## NOTES

1. Tehran IRNA [in English], 1722 GMT 4 August 1998, FBIS.
2. Steve Rodan, 'Iran Completes Shehab-3 Development', *Ha'aretz*, 12 March (2000), as carried by Foreign Broadcast Information Service's on-line database.
3. Statement by Acting Director of Central Intelligence, George J. Tenet, before the Senate Select Committee on Intelligence, hearing on Current and Projected National Security Threats To The United States, 5 February 1997, as found at <http://www.cia.gov>. He stated: 'in less than ten years probably Iran will have longer range missiles that will enable it to target most of Saudi Arabia and Israel.'
4. Robert D. Walpole, National Intelligence Officer for Strategic and Nuclear Programs, 'North Korea's Taepo Dong Launch and Some Implications on the Ballistic Missile Threat to the United States', Center for Strategic and International Studies, 8 December 1998, as found at <http://www.cia.gov>.
5. Ralph Perry, 'Iran Rejects Chemical Weapons Charge', *United Press International*, 23 March (1995).
6. Statement of the Director of Central Intelligence George J. Tenet, as prepared for delivery before the Senate Armed Services Committee hearing on Current and Projected National Security Threats, 2 February 1999, as found at <http://www.cia.gov>.
7. Arms Control and Disarmament Agency, *Adherence to and Compliance with Arms Control*, 1997, as found at <http://www.acda.gov>.

8. Statement of the Director of Central Intelligence George J. Tenet, as prepared for delivery before the Senate Armed Services Committee hearing on Current and Projected National Security Threats, 2 February 1999, as found at <http://www.cia.gov>.

9. *New York Times*, 10 January (1995), p. A10.

10. *Aviation Week & Space Technology*, 13 December (1999), p. 33.

11. Office of the Secretary of Defense, *Proliferation: Threat and Response* (Washington, DC: Government Printing Office, April 1996), p. 14 (hereafter cited as *Proliferation*).

12. Michael Eisenstadt, *Iranian Military Power: Capabilities and Intentions* (Washington, DC: Washington Institute for Near East Policy, 1996), p. 24 (hereafter cited as *Iranian Military Power*); and Anthony H. Cordesman and Ahmed S. Hashim, *Iran: Dilemmas of Dual Containment* (Boulder, CO: Westview Press, 1997), p. 306 (hereafter cited as *Iran*).

13. Eisenstadt, *Iranian Military Power*, p. 16.

14. Cordesman and Hashim, *Iran*, p. 306.

15. Cordesman and Hashim, *Iran*, pp. 299–301; and Eisenstadt, *Iranian Military Capabilities*, pp. 19–21.

16. Office of the Secretary of Defense, *Proliferation* (November 1997), p. 25.

17. Cordesman and Hashim, *Iran*, pp. 299–301.

18. Office of the Secretary of Defense, *Proliferation* (November 1997), p. 27.

19. Don Sutton, 'Harmful Fungi Requested by Iranian, Scientist Says', *Globe and Mail* (Toronto), 14 August (1989), p. A1, as cited in Ron Purver, *Chemical and Biological Terrorism: The Threat According to the Open Literature* (Ottawa: Canadian Security Intelligence Service, 1995), p. 35.

20. Judith Miller and William J. Broad, 'Bio-Weapons in Mind, Iranians Lure Needy Ex-Soviet Scientists', *New York Times*, 8 December (1998), pp. A1, A12.

21. For a discussion of the former Soviet program, see Ken Alibek with Stephen Handelman, *Biohazard* (New York: Random House, 1999).

22. Office of the Secretary of Defense, *Proliferation* (April 1996), p. 15.

23. Andrew Rathmell, 'Chemical Weapons in the Middle East: Lessons from Iraq', *Jane's Intelligence Review*, December 1995. Eisenstadt, *Iranian Military Power*, p. 26, suggests that Iran can produce several hundred tons of agent per year.

24. Statement of General Anthony C. Zinni Commander in Chief US Central Command before the House Armed Services Committee, 11 March 1999, as found at <http://www.house.gov/hasc/>.

25. Eisenstadt, *Iranian Military Power*, p. 26.

26. Office of the Secretary of Defense, *Proliferation* (November 1997), p. 27.

27. Office of the Secretary of Defense, *Proliferation* (November 1997), p. 27.

28. Cordesman and Hashim, *Iran*, p. 292; and Eisenstadt, *Iranian Military Power*, p. 26.

29. Office of the Secretary of Defense, *Proliferation* (April 1996), p. 15. For the First World War experience with hydrogen cyanide, see L.F. Haber, *The Poisonous Cloud: Chemical Warfare in the First World War* (Oxford: Clarendon Press, 1986), and Augustin Prentiss, *Chemicals in War: A Treatise on Chemical Warfare* (New York: McGraw-Hill Book Company, 1937), pp. 171–4. World War Two research is discussed in Stanford Moore and Marshall Gates, 'Hydrogen Cyanide and Cyanogen Chloride', in Division 9, National Defense

Research Committee, Office of Scientific Research and Development (ed.), *Chemical Warfare Agents and Related Chemical Problems*, Parts I–II (Washington, DC: 1946), pp. 7–16.

30. Office of the Secretary of Defense, *Proliferation* (November 1997), p. 27.
31. Office of the Secretary of Defense, *Proliferation* (April 1966), p. 16.
32. Richard Z. Chesnoff with Douglas Pasternak, 'Mystery at a Pesticide Plant', *US News and World Report*, 25 October (1999).
33. Judith Miller, 'US and Uzbeks Agree on Chemical Arms Plant Cleanup', *New York Times*, 25 May (1999); and Jonathan Tucker, 'Converting Former Soviet Chemical Plants', *Nonproliferation Review* (1999), pp. 78–89. Tucker's article provides considerable detail on the program to develop the Novichok agents.
34. International Institute for Strategic Studies, *The Military Balance, 1998/99* (London: Oxford University Press/for the International Institute for Strategic Studies, 1998), p. 127.
35. 'DRC Receives Iranian "Scud" Missiles', *Jane's Defense Weekly*, 1 December (1999).
36. Statement for the Record to the Senate Foreign Relations Committee on Foreign Missile Developments and the Ballistic Missile Threat to the United States Through 2015 by Robert D. Walpole, National Intelligence Officer for Strategic and Nuclear Programs, 16 September 1999, as found at <http://www.cia.gov>.
37. *Aviation Week & Space Technology*, 13 December (1999), p. 33.
38. Bill Gertz, 'N. Korea Sells Iran Missile Engines', *Washington Times*, 9 February (2000), p. 1.
39. *Aviation Week & Space Technology*, 13 December (1999), p. 33.
40. Statement of the Director of Central Intelligence George J. Tenet, as prepared for delivery before the Senate Armed Services Committee hearing on Current and Projected National Security Threats, 2 February 1999, as found at <http://www.cia.gov>.
41. Statement for the Record to the Senate Foreign Relations Committee on Foreign Missile Developments and the Ballistic Missile Threat to the United States Through 2015 by Robert D. Walpole, National Intelligence Officer for Strategic and Nuclear Programs, 16 September 1999, as found at <http://www.cia.gov>.
42. Alibek and Handelman, *Biohazard*, pp. 5–8.
43. This discussion of cruise missile technologies is based on W. Seth Carus, *Cruise Missile Proliferation in the 1990s* (Westport, CT: Praeger, 1992).
44. John Mintz, 'Tracking Arms: a Study in Smoke', *Washington Post*, 3 April (1999), pp. A3–A4.
45. Aaron Karp, 'Lessons of Iranian Missile Programs for U.S. Nonproliferation Policy', *Nonproliferation Review*, Spring–Summer (1998), p. 20, discusses the possibilities of Iran developing cruise missile systems.
46. 'News Chronology', *CBW Conventions Bulletin*, 46, 1999, p. 25, includes Iran in a list of nine countries – China, France, India, Iran, Japan, Russia, the UK, the USA and one other – that have declared production sites as of 31 August 1999. It is not on the list of four states that have admitted to possession of chemical weapons – US, Russia, India and 'one other' (the one other is presumably the same one in the previous list). On 17 November 1998, the Director General of the Iranian Foreign Ministry admitted that Iran possessed

chemical weapons at the end of the Iran–Iraq War, but said: 'Following the establishment of cease fire, the decision to develop chemical weapons capabilities was reversed and the process was terminated.' See 'News Chronology', *CBW Conventions Bulletin*, 43, 1999, p. 20.

47. Office of the Secretary of Defense, *Proliferation* (November 1997), p. 27.
48. Secretary of State Madeleine K. Albright, Statement on 'Iran and Libya Sanctions Act (ILSA): Decision in the South Pars Case', London, United Kingdom, 18 May 1998, as released by the Office of the Spokesman US Department of State, as found on the Department of State web site, <http://www.state.gov>.
49. Keith Weissman, 'Iran Failing to Attract Foreign Investment', *Near East Report*, 12 July 1999, as found at <http://www.aipac.org>.
50. See George Tenet's speech with commentary by Barry Rubin published in *MERIA Journal*, 4, 2 (2000), pp. 54–5. Also, see <http://meria.biu.ac.il>.

# 12

# The Internal Struggle over Iran's Future

## ABBAS SAMII

During most of the 1980s – after some purges and due to the Iran–Iraq War's unifying effect – Iran seemed set on a thorough-going Islamist transformation following the dictates of the revolution's leader, Ayatollah Ruhollah Musavi-Khomeini. By the mid-1990s, however, two factions waged a major struggle over their very different visions of the country's future. This chapter uses two case studies – the media's changing role and the 2000 parliamentary elections – to show each side's supporters and views, as well as its prospects for implementing these policies or gaining full power to run Iran.

Among those seeking to reform the system and bring it to a greater degree of participatory democracy are political parties, pressure groups and student organizations identified with the May 1997 election of President Hojatoleslam Seyyed Muhammad Khatami-Ardakani. This grouping is also called the Second of Khordad movement, after the date of Khatami's election. These 'reformists' have the formal powers of several executive branch organizations at their disposal. In this chapter's context, the most relevant are the ministries of Interior and of Islamic Culture and Guidance. The most significant instruments for the reformists, however, are the newspapers identified with them, because they have the power to mobilize opinion and voice the aspirations of the almost 70 percent of the electorate that elected Khatami.

On the side of those wanting to maintain the status quo or even roll back the reforms implemented since 1997 are other pressure groups and student organizations. Conservative and hardline publications project their views and opinions. The official Islamic Republic of Iran broadcasting system is also firmly on the conservative side and is frequently criticized for its biased coverage of news events.

Equally, hardliners control many of the legal institutions that make, implement, and execute laws. The parliament passed press laws in July 1999 and May 2000 and restricted the activities of reformist journalists and publications. The courts prosecute and close down reformist publications. Law enforcement forces make little, if any, effort to prosecute hardline vigilante actions against reformist publications.

## PRESS LAW

Hardline forces' manipulation of the media laws worked to the disadvantage of the reformists. Tough – but also unclear – laws limited what the press could report or say. Minister of Islamic Culture and Guidance Ataollah Mohajerani said:

> The existence of red lines in the press is not a hidden and unknown fact and any managing director should observe his limits in this connection because this is the law and not individual preferences that draw borders of the press.[1]

People in journalism and publishing, however, frequently complained that the rules are vague. In an interview with Radio Free Europe/Radio Liberty's Persian Service, Ali Nazari, managing editor of *Arzesh* magazine, said: 'Every time the press in Iran is warned by officials, we are told that we have crossed a red line, although no one has bothered to tell us where that red line is.' He continued: 'When *Tous* and *Jameah* were closed down [in 1998], they gave the same explanation: that these two publications crossed the red line.'[2]

Under the guise of clarifying these limits, a revision of the press law was proposed in the parliament in October–November 1998. Mohajerani argued that while there were some ambiguities in the current law, they were tolerable and the passage of a new law was unnecessary.[3]

Journalists were particularly unhappy with the proposed amendment. A letter from the Press Association said: 'Tabling bills which are restrictive and which undermine freedom would not only not make the press [corps] law-abiding, but would place them under [a] monopoly by a few people and drive society towards samizdats and other methods.'[4] *Neshat* reporter Minoo Badii said: 'To attain a civil society and achieve political development we need to have numerous newspapers and publications, [but] if you look at the proposal to amend the press law you will see that it would restrict this trend.'[5] Even President Khatami was critical of the proposed press law. Speaking to an audience of judicial officials, Khatami said a jury should hear all press cases.[6]

A hint as to how the parliament would vote came when 228 parliamentarians signed a declaring that: 'Like the leader, they too sense the cultural inroad of the enemy in the form of a plot for transformation and overthrow of the system ... [and] ... will spare no effort to foil such a conspiracy.'[7] Parliament approved the draft bill on 7 July 1998. Of 215 deputies present, 125 voted for the draft, which was approved on an open ballot.

The law says that a complaint against a publication can be filed for an unlimited period. In other words, there is no statute of limitations. Part of the bill calls for a reporter to be held responsible for what he or she writes, whereas final responsibility rested with the publication's director or chief editor. Granting of press accreditation was made more restrictive. The bill said that a Qom seminarian and the head of the Islamic Propagation Organization would serve on the Press Supervisory Board. Also, the bill said Revolutionary Courts are qualified to hear press offenses, whereas Article 168 of the constitution only permits press courts to do so.

Just a day before the voting on the press bill, a copy of an October 1998 proposal for drastic revisions to the press laws by Deputy Minister of Intelligence and Security Said Emami was published by a reformist newspaper. Emami complained that journalists' activities would: 'cause security problems for the Islamic Republic of Iran.' Whereas the current press law amendment only held license-holders and managing directors responsible for what appeared in publications, Emami wrote, the writers themselves must be confronted: 'individually, using the law, in order to ban them from writing or publishing.'[8]

Emami proposed the drafting of a bill that would: 'lend legality to the security measures.' He wrote: 'The bill must include the professional nature of the work and eligibility for it.' This meant that writers and translators would require licenses. Emami proposed a special disciplinary court to judge press offenses. Emami wrote: 'In this way, associations that are acceptable to us can be strengthened and hostile elements driven away.'

In January 1999, Emami was arrested for his part in the late-1998 murders of writers and dissident political figures. It would seem that he was implementing part of the plan proposed in his letter. But little was known about Emami's letter until after his death in June, when he allegedly committed suicide while in custody. And the newspaper that published the letter was shut down less than a month later.

News about Emami's proposed press law was one of the sparks that led to the massive disturbances of July 1999. Parliament, therefore, postponed acting on it, leading to speculation that the new parliament could overturn it. But in late April 2000, a little more than a month before the new parliament was inaugurated, a new, tough press law was passed.[9] The new law permits Revolutionary Courts to prosecute press cases and prohibits the reappearance of banned publications coming out under a new name. The new law prohibits criticism of the constitution and it makes journalists, as well as publications' directors, liable for what appears in the press.

PRESS CLOSURES

Throughout 1999, conservative figures blamed the press for the country's problems. Iranian Revolutionary Guards Corps (IRGC) General Yahya Rahim Safavi said: 'The influence of the anti-revolutionary elements in the country's press should be stopped.'[10] Four senior ayatollahs wrote to President Muhammad Khatami, asking him to confront the press's: 'violation of religious principles, efforts to undermine Islamic belief, and distortion of ethics.'[11] A Friday Prayer leader in Tehran warned newspapers: 'You may think you can write whatever you wish today. You may boast about your action because you defamed this or that person, but when we are dead and buried in our graves, we shall be together again.'[12] A Source of Emulation advised that: 'The press must always protect the religious and revolutionary environ- ment in our society.[13] But, he complained: 'The press had deviated from its path.' He went on to condemn newspapers that repeat statements heard on foreign radios: 'I do not at all consider news- papers and publications which write things with the aim of pleasing America and Israel to be friends of the revolution, the state, or Islam.'

The efforts to strengthen the press laws were ominous, there- fore, but in such an environment the judiciary seemed to have little trouble closing publications under the existing laws. To look at the issue purely in terms of hardliners *versus* reformists, or conservatives *versus* pro-Khatami moderates, however, would be overly simplified. By examining five of the more significant cases in 1999, one sees that only twice – in the cases of *Salam* and *Khordad* – was the issue so clear-cut. The cases of *Zan*, *Hoviat-i Khish*, *Neshat* and many others demonstrate the com- plex factors involved in silencing Iran's more outspoken media.

On 7 July 1999, the daily newspaper *Salam* was closed and its Editor-in-Chief, Abbas Abdi, was arrested on the basis of a complaint from the Ministry of Intelligence and Security (MOIS). The complaint stemmed from a 6 July *Salam* report about a MOIS plan to restrict the press. The MOIS said that the *Salam* report was false; the MOIS had no such plan and the letter cited by *Salam* was a fake.[14] But, the MOIS dropped the complaint against Abdi and he was released.

It was too late, though. An 8 July student demonstration against the *Salam* closure and the press bill, catalyzed by anger over the earlier arrest of students protesting the detention of officials from a weekly magazine, *Hoviat-i Khish*, escalated into some of the worst violence in the Islamic republic's history.

The Managing Director of *Salam*, Hojatoleslam Muhammad Asqar Musavi-Khoeniha, was tried by the Special Court for the

Clergy on 25 July 1999. He faced charges of spreading fabrications, disturbing public opinion and publishing classified documents. This latter charge referred to the MOIS plan for a crackdown on the reformist press. The report about the plan was published the day before parliament approved the new press law.

Khoeniha was found guilty and sentenced to a three-and-a-half-year jail term and a flogging. Due to his revolutionary background, however, the sentence was suspended and Khoeniha was fined instead. He was banned from publishing activities for three years, and Salam was banned for five years.[15] Meanwhile, the Islamic Revolution Court in Qom started hearings against Abdi on the basis of complaints that he insulted a mob chanting: 'Death to America' by calling them 'thugs.'

Actions against Salam were politically driven. By restricting Khoeniha and Abdi's media access, hardliners eliminated some of the institutional support for the Second of Khordad movement. Khoeniha is a co-founder of the pro-Khatami student group called the Office for Strengthening Unity, which is a member of the Second of Khordad movement. Khoeniha also is a leader of the Students Following the Line of the Imam, the organization that occupied the US Embassy in 1979 and held the American hostages. Abdi is a member of the latter group, and he is a founder of Khatami's Islamic Iran Participation Party. Leaders of the Office for Strengthening Unity, such as Ebrahim Asgharzadeh, are also one-time members of the Students Following the Line of the Imam.

Application of the law in this case clearly showed political–factional motivations. Hardline publications – the weekly *Javan* and the dailies *Kayhan* and *Jomhuri-yi-Islami* – printed copies of a letter from 24 Islamic Revolution Guard Corps commanders to Khatami in which they threatened to take the law into their own hands if the president did not act against the demonstrators.[16] The Islamic Culture and Guidance Ministry sent written warnings to these publications' managing editors for publishing a classified document.[17] But that was all that happened.

Hearings before the Special Court for the Clergy in the case of *Khordad* Managing Editor Hojatoleslam Abdallah Nuri got underway on 30 October. This case, more so than that of *Salam* and Musavi-Khoeniha, was based on the publication's pro-Khatami leanings. Nuri served as Khatami's Interior Minister until his June 1998 interpellation. He was elected to Tehran municipal council in February 1999, and after announcing his intention to run for the legislature he was seen as a possible speaker of the parliament.

Nuri faced charges of publishing reports that insulted officials and institutions of the system, reporting lies and waging a propaganda war against the system, insulting Father of the Revolution Ayatollah Ruhollah Khomeini and his views, publishing reports contrary to religious principles and insulting religious sanctities. Other charges included backing ties with America, promoting dissident cleric Ayatollah Hussein-Ali Montazeri's political views and urging recognition of Israel.[18] The contents of *Khordad*, the Special Court for the Clergy's special prosecutor said: 'smack of conspiracy and hostility.'

Nuri's defense undermined many long-standing hardline values with clear logic, and the Tehran media covered the case extensively. While this may have earned him popular support, it did not help Nuri's case. The prosecutor in the case, Hojatoleslam Muhammad Ebrahim Nikunam, said that the more Nuri talks: 'We realize that our opinion about him was right and his guilt becomes more certain.'[19] The jury found Nuri guilty on 15 of the infractions and recommended against any leniency in sentencing. He was sentenced on 27 November to five years in prison and barred from journalistic activities for five years after that.

The *Salam* and *Khordad* cases were obvious attempts to eliminate reformist newspapers and to limit the influence of reformist political figures. Reasons for the closures of *Zan*, *Hoviat-i Khish* and *Neshat* were also factionally related. Their closures were not, however, related to their relationship with Khatami or their reformist tendencies.

The Judiciary closed Tehran's daily newspaper *Zan* on 6 April. It was punished for publishing a cartoon ridiculing the current Iranian interpretation of the principle of 'blood money' – in Iran, the compensation one must pay to a murdered woman's family is less than that which must be paid to a murdered man's family. Tehran Islamic Revolutionary Court Judge Hojatoleslam

Gholamhussein Rahbarpour also cited publication of a letter from the ex-Empress of Iran.

The case against *Zan* was not so much an attack on a Second of Khordad publication, although Faezeh Hashemi herself is a Khatami supporter. There was resentment over her apparent personal ambition. It was also an attempt to lessen the influence of Hashemi's father, Expediency Council head Ayatollah Ali-Akbar Hashemi-Rafsanjani. He is identified as the leader – in loose terms – of the Executives of Construction Party that is connected with Khatami's successful election campaign. In addition, there is a great deal of resentment over the cronyism, nepotism and corruption associated with him.

On 16 June the Revolutionary Court detained the weekly publication *Hoviat-i Khish*'s Editor-in-Chief, Heshmatollah Tabarzadi, and Director, Hussein Kashani. Tabarzadi's real crime, it seems, was his role as a leader of the Islamic Union of Students and Graduates, a more radical student group. The 8 July student demonstrations were catalyzed by the arrest two days earlier of students who gathered to protest Tabarzadi and Kashani's detentions. The Revolutionary Court judge later said that members of the Islamic Union of Students and Graduates were being prosecuted for their parts in the July demonstrations.[20]

The 5 September closure of *Neshat* was also politically motivated, although the charges brought against it did not indicate this clearly. The paper was closed on the orders of Press Court Judge Hojatoleslam Said Mortazavi after a complaint from the public prosecutor. The charges against the daily stemmed from its publication of an open letter urging Supreme Leader Ayatollah Ali Khamenei to distance himself from hardliners, as well as two articles criticizing capital punishment.

From the very beginning, *Neshat* seemed destined for a bad end. Its staff consisted of personnel from the previously banned *Tous* and *Jameah* newspapers. In April, just three months after getting its license, Managing Director Latif Safari had to appear before the Tehran Revolutionary Court on charges of questioning the Islamic Revolution and supporting the monarchy.[21]

On 18 August complaints were filed against *Neshat* by the Law Enforcement Forces, state broadcasting, the state prosecutor,

Qom's Special Court for the Clergy, the Islamic Open University and some Majlis deputies. *Neshat*'s Managing Director had to appear in court, as did *Neshat* columnist Ebrahim Nabavi.[22] When *Neshat* was banned on 5 September the Tehran Justice Department pointed out that: 'repeated summons and bails [*sic*] have proved ineffective in preventing the daily from repeating its offense.'[23]

And once again, the law was unevenly applied. *Neshat* officials apologized for any offense the articles might have caused,[24] but they were not forgiven. When *Qods* was charged with offending two sources of emulation, however, it published an apology and the Press Supervisory Board only issued a written warning.[25]

Despite conservative criticism, and despite the press closures, new publications kept emerging, often using the same facilities and personnel of a just-closed publication, and they covered most aspects of Iranian politics. Parliament, furthermore, postponed voting on the proposed press law.

By the beginning of the year 2000, therefore, there was reason to believe that the press was in for a respite. But in early-January the managing directors of several reformist newspapers – *Iran, Hamshahri, Akhbar-i Eqtesad, Mosharekat, Manateq-i Azad, Sobh-i Imruz, Aftab-i Imruz, Asr-i Azadigan, Fath* and *Arya* – wrote a letter to President Khatami indicating their concern about the pressure facing them.[26] The letter stated that the newspapers' involvement in politics is in order to practice democracy and not because they are against the government. The same point applies when they expose cases of official corruption. Nowadays, the letter said, the prohibition of vice and the promotion of virtue are societal duties, and this is what the press is doing. The signatories indicated their resentment at being accused of harming national security, when all they are doing is asking questions.

Harassment of people in journalism also continued but, again, those affiliated with reformist publications faced greater problems. On one hand, Said Hajjarian of *Sobh-i Imruz*, as well as Yadollah Eslami of *Fath* and Ghafur Garshasebi of *Asr-i Azadigan* were summoned by the Press Court on 16 January for having reprinted an interview with Ayatollah Hussein-Ali Montazeri that appeared in a British newspaper. On the other hand, the trial of Hussein Shariatmadari of the hardline *Kayhan* newspaper on charges that included defamation, publishing state secrets and upsetting the public was postponed several times. And the hearing of Abdolhamid Mohtashem of the hardline *Yalisarat Al-Hussein*, who was to face complaints brought by Muhammad Salamati and Behzad Nabavi of the Mujahidin of the Islamic Revolution Organization, was postponed.

In March and April the situation took a turn for the worse. At that time, Supreme Leader Ayatollah Ali Khamenei gave several sermons and speeches that were critical of advocates of reform and of the reformist press specifically.

In one sermon, Khamenei complained about unnamed promoters of 'Americanized reforms' and seemed to indicate that they were acceptable targets of violence.[27] And in another, he said that the West first attacked Iran via its radio stations, but now it is building a 'stronghold' in Iran. He said the press is creating anxiety, discord and pessimism:

> It seems as if 10 or 15 newspapers are being directed from the same center to publish articles with similar headlines. They make mountains out of molehills ... kill the hope among the youth ... weaken the people's trust ... offend and insult.

The Supreme Leader added that President Muhammad Khatami is unhappy with the press too: 'We are trying to stop the enemy from realizing his propaganda conspiracy.'[28]

Such statements inspired the IRGC to say that:

> If necessary, our enemies, be they small or large, will feel the reverberating impact of the hammer of the Islamic revolution on their skulls and the impact will be so strong that they will never be able to engage in hatching plots or committing crimes.[29]

Then the new press law was passed. In just one week, 16 publications were closed, and, by mid-June, 19 publications were closed. And this time, it was quite clear that the closures, with one exception, related to the publications' criticism of the hard-liners and support for reformist causes:

- *Aftab-i Imruz* strongly supports the reformist movement and is critical of the conservatives.

- *Arya* is identified with the Freedom Movement (Nihzat-i Azadi).

- *Asr-i Azadigan* is the successor to the banned dailies, *Jameah*, *Tus* and *Neshat*.

- *Bamdad-i No* is a reformist daily formerly known as *Iran Vij*.

- *Bayan* is the daily published by Hojatoleslam Ali-Akbar Mohtashemi-Pur, an ally of President Khatami.

- *Fath* succeeded Khatami-ally Hojatoleslam Abdallah Nuri's *Khordad* daily.

- *Guzarish-i Ruz* is linked with Heshmatollah Tabarzadi, leader of the more radical student group, the Islamic Union of Students and Graduates.

- *Ham-Mihan* is former Tehran Mayor Gholamhussein Karbaschi's daily.

- *Manateq-i Azad* is a moderate daily linked with the free trade zones.

- *Mellat*, a daily intended to reflect reformist and conservative views, was closed after its first print run.

- *Mosharekat* is the Islamic Iran Participation Party's daily.

- *Payam-i Azadi* is considered part of the radical reformist fringe and its Managing Editor is Davud Bahrami Minavoshani.

- *Sobh-i Imruz*, Said Hajjarian's daily, is identified with the pro-Khatami Second of Khordad front.

- *Ava*, a weekly from Najafabad, publishes views expounded by the popular Ayatollah Hussein-Ali Montazeri-Najafabadi.

- *Aban* is a moderate pro-Khatami weekly.

- *Arzesh* is a pro-reform weekly.

- *Jebheh* is a hardline weekly identified with the Ansar-i Hizballah.

- *Payam-i Hajar* is a weekly reflecting national religious views.

- *Iran-i Farda* is the monthly of Ezzatollah Sahabi, who is identified with the national religious movement.

Despite these closures, many newspapers and publications continued to function. Some of these were the most hardline ones, such as *Kayhan, Resalat* and *Jomhuri-yi Islami*. Some of the more moderate ones still operate as well, including *Iran* – affiliated with the official Islamic Republic News Agency – and *Hamshahri* – affiliated with Tehran municipality and the Executives of Construction Party.

After the initial closures, an unnamed judiciary official explained that a committee formed to investigate the press concluded that: 'despite frequent warnings given to them, they continued with their anti-Islamic and anti-revolutionary activities,' and 'the tone of material in those papers had brought smiles to the faces of the enemies of the Islamic Republic and hurt the feelings of devout Muslims at home and even the leader of the Islamic revolution.' The judiciary official warned that: 'we are also trying to detect the foreign links of some of these newspapers.'[30]

Unlike the previous July, when the closures of *Salam* and *Hoviat-i Khish* triggered violent demonstrations, the reaction to the mass press closures was more subdued, due to calls for calm from the Office for Strengthening Unity, the main pro-Khatami student group. There were peaceful protests against the newspapers closures, however, in Tehran, Hamedan, Bandar Abbas, Mashhad, Sanandaj and Kashan – a 28 April demonstration at Tehran's Shahid Beheshti University turned violent until intervention by the Law Enforcement Forces and the Basij Resistance Forces.

Heshmatollah Tabarzadi, Director of the banned publications *Guzarish-i Ruz* and *Hoviat-i Khish* – banned in summer 1999 – and leader of the Islamic Union of Students and Graduates, said that the students want to avoid unrest. He explained: 'Every society has its own threshold for bearing with oppression and force, they will be patient up to a point. Last year they were patient and they are not scared now. They want to maintain unity and order.'[31] Khatami's comments on the press closures and the general atmosphere were indirect and open to interpretation. During one speech, he said: 'The political tendencies and groups, by relying on religious sanctities and everything which is held in respect and honor by the people, take unfair advantage of the situation to enhance factional interests and specific [political] tendencies.'[32] A few days later, Khatami said that: 'the Iranian people are revolutionary and will remain revolutionary. They want a religious and Islamic state and no one can hinder the nation's process of reforms.'[33]

## ISLAMIC CULTURE AND GUIDANCE MINISTER ATAOLLAH MOHAJERANI

Publications are licensed by the Islamic Culture and Guidance Ministry, but the judiciary is authorized to close them. The same day that *Neshat* was closed, Judiciary Chief Ayatollah Mahmud Hashemi-Shahrudi met with Islamic Culture and Guidance Minister Ataollah Mohajerani. Hashemi-Shahrudi said the ministry should: 'render useless any grounds for attacks against the principles and basic tenets of the system.'[34] The Judiciary Chief told Mohajerani that if his ministry did its job, the judiciary's intervention would be unnecessary.

Mohajerani's position has never looked solid. He was seen as weaker than Interior Minister Hojatoleslam Abdallah Nuri – interpolated in Summer 1998 – and he had done more to irritate the hardliners, imposing press controls too slowly for their liking. Weakening Mohajerani's position even further, Supreme Leader Ayatollah Ali Khamenei criticized him openly several times.[35] Mohajerani wrote that he would rather resign than abandon his beliefs.[36]

Symbolically, Mohajerani's departure would have been harmful to Khatami, because he was Minister of Islamic Culture and Guidance until he was forced to resign in 1992. On 21 April 1999, 31 parliamentarians submitted a motion for Mohajerani's removal. The motion said Mohajerani had not restrained the press sufficiently and had questioned the judiciary's performance. He had advocated separation of religion and politics, as well as establishment of relations with the United States. Mohajerani was also guilty of founding the writers' association. 'The Ministry failed to support intellectual and cultural movies and instead films were produced with the aim of making profits' and fewer movies about the Sacred Defense – Iran–Iraq War – were produced. Finally, he was accused of misappropriating funds deposited for the minor pilgrimage to Mecca.[37]

Waging a successful defense on 31 April and 1 May, Mohajerani was not removed. In the Majlis session, which was broadcast live, Mohajerani survived the motion by 135 to 121, with 7 abstentions. At that point it seemed that the Majlis was taking a popular stance and siding with the reformists, perhaps thinking the issue was one on which votes would be cast in the pending election. Thus, it appeared that the body and its large block of independent members were turning away from its conservative tendencies.

Even after the closure of Neshat, Mohajerani did not abandon his principles. The Islamic Culture and Guidance Ministry said the newspaper's closure did not fall within legal bounds.[38] It then permitted Neshat to take over the dormant license of Akhbar and resume publication of Akhbar-i Eqtesad, employing Neshat staff.

In late-September and October, there were renewed protests against Mohajerani over a play about the 12th Imam that was published in an Amir Kabir University student magazine called Mowj. There were demands for the firing and/or execution of Mohajerani in January and February 2000 in reaction to a cartoon that ridiculed Ayatollah Muhammad Taqi Mesbah-Yazdi.[39] Participants in rallies marking the revolution's 21st anniversary – on 11 February – in Qom, Karaj, Orumieh and Shahr-i Kord demonstrated against Mohajerani, and anti-Mohajerani slogans were displayed in Nahavand, which Mohajerani was scheduled to visit.[40]

After the numerous press closures in April 2000, some observers suggested that Mohajerani should resign in protest.

Indeed, only days before the mass closure was announced, a meeting between Mohajerani and 22 publishers and chief editors, as well as Iranian Republic National Assembly (IRNA) officials, was held. At this meeting, Mohajerani said: 'If pressures are exerted to close down the newspapers, then I would be forced into becoming an instrument for closing them or resigning, in that case I would prefer to tender my resignation.'[41]

Journalist Ahmad Zeydabadi told RFE/RL's Persian Service a protest resignation by Mohajerani would not be enough to stop conservative attacks. Zeydabadi explained that:

> If Mr Mohajerani were to resign there would be no signi-
> ficant effect or reaction to such an action. It might even
> encourage those people to go more on the offensive. I think
> if things move toward the dismantling or loss of everything
> [the reformists] have gained so far, Mr Mohajerani should
> harmonize his actions with Mr Khatami and I think Mr
> Khatami has to step aside. I think this would be more appro-
> priate than Mr Mohajerani's resignation.[42]

## STATE BROADCASTING

Radio and television already had a powerful role in opinion-making because newspapers and print media have a limited circulation outside the main cities. The closure of so many publications only increased this advantage. And because Iran has no private broadcasting, state media was placed in a particularly strong position. Islamic Republic of Iran Broadcasting (IRIB), however, is criticized for being one-sided. One newspaper commented that IRIB: 'broadcasts only the sound and pictures of a particular class and disseminates the opinions of a limited group of people in Iran.' IRIB reporters always go to the same sources, and the broadcasters do not represent the nation. IRIB's activities explain the popularity of foreign radio services, the daily noted:

> Considering the limitations of literacy and the even greater
> limitation in their access to the press, people will turn to

Voice of America, the BBC and Radio Free Europe, which can be heard in the most remote villages with two-band radios.[43]

For example, IRIB coverage of the 1997 presidential election gave preferential coverage to the heavily favored conservation candidate, Hojatoleslam Ali-Akbar Nateq-Nuri. On the other hand, its coverage of his chief rival, Khatami, was less frequent and much less favorable. A daily from Rasht claimed that IRIB directed 'propaganda attacks' against Khatami. The daily continued: 'They called him a "liberal" and even hinted he was against the Vilayat-i Faqih,' the concept of a ruling clerical spiritual guide for the country promulgated by Ayatollah Ruhollah Khomeini.[44]

Serious unhappiness with IRIB and its director, Ali Larijani, resumed in January 1999.[45] At that time, a guest on the 'Cheraq' program said Khatami's allies were behind the murders of intellectuals, dissidents and journalists the previous autumn. Eighty-eight members of parliament sent a letter to Supreme Leader Ayatollah Ali Khamenei requesting reforms in the IRIB. In the letter they complained that state broadcasting was not impartial and: 'instead of safeguarding national interests, is evidently backing a certain faction.' The parliamentarians wrote that such behavior will: 'encourage tension, discredit the important media to the people, and ultimately deal fatal blows to our holy Islamic system.'[46]

And in March 1999, IRIB was criticized for its coverage of Khatami's trip to Italy. Although the President's speech at the European International University in Florence was broadcast live, the applause after the speech was not broadcast in its entirety. This, and the fact that the speech was not rebroadcast, nor was it mentioned in news reports the next day, showed the IRIB has an anti-Khatami bias, claimed a newspaper.[47]

The April 1999 motion to remove Mohajerani brought renewed criticism of IRIB. For example, Editor Abbas Abdi said that if the parliament wants to fire Mohajerani for what is in newspapers, then it should launch a military attack against IRIB. Abdi said the Islamic Culture and Guidance Ministry does not produce the newspapers, whereas IRIB produces what it broadcasts. He continued: 'All the unethical materials and pictures published by newspapers are still less than the unethical programs broadcast by the TV only during the week.'[48]

It is for such reasons that Iranians turn to foreign Persian-language radio broadcasts. The Iranian government, already critical of foreign radio broadcasts into Iran, tried to control outside commentary on the February 2000 parliamentary elections by jamming short-wave broadcasts by Radio Free Europe/Radio Liberty's Persian Service, the British Broadcasting Corporation and the Voice of America. It would do so either by direct bubble-type interference or by over-riding the foreign broadcasts with the Arabic Service of the Voice of the Islamic Republic of Iran – on the western and southern borders – and the Dari Service of the Voice of the Islamic Republic of Iran – on the eastern and northeastern borders.[49]

Under such circumstances, Interior Minister Hojatoleslam Abdolvahed Musavi-Lari was forced to urge IRIB to be impartial in its election coverage.[50] Apparently IRIB did not heed this suggestion, because Second of Khordad movement spokesman Behzad Nabavi and secretary of the Militant Clerics Association (Majma-yi Ruhaniyun-i Mobarez) Hojatoleslam Mehdi Mahdavi-Karrubi complained that IRIB's pre-election coverage was insufficient.[51]

And in April 2000, state television broadcast a heavily edited video of Iranians' comments at a conference in Berlin. This broadcast was used as a pretext for arresting several of the conference's participants, and it sparked strong reactions. One cleric suggested: 'Kill them [reformists] wherever you find them' and 'If the enemy does not attack you, you should attack them.'[52] Another warned: 'Those who go on about reformism are, in fact, trying to revive the traditions of apostates of 2,500 years ago in Iran's Islamic society'[53] – the penalty for apostasy is death.

The broadcast also earned IRIB more criticism. President Khatami said: 'I did not in any way agree with what the Voice and Vision had done, that is, to raise an issue in such a manner, and contribute towards provoking sensitivities of the people.'[54] Khatami went on to say: 'This was not the right thing to do. I do not accuse it of having been a criminal act or prompted by cliquish motives. But, I do not approve the action.' Minister of Science, Research and Technology Mustafa Moin-Najafabadi said the IRIB is involved in: 'the burgeoning of mistrust and discrepancy in society as well as giving cause for disappointing the youths.'[55]

Pro-reform newspapers also criticized IRIB's broadcast and accused it of ulterior motives. One said that the broadcast was part of:

> a clear and ongoing scenario based on which there is sup-posed to be obstacles thrown in the path of reform, progress, and even national security and unity. Through this method they want to ensure that the interests and political desires of a political oligarchy is saved.[56]

Even the closure of 19 publications did not enhance IRIB's popularity. Shopkeepers said that the demand for short-wave receivers in Iran increased after the press closures.[57]

## ELECTION LAWS AND THEIR IMPACT

It was not just strengthened press laws and restrictions that favored the hardliners. Use of vague existing election-related laws and creation of new, stricter, laws also seemed to favor hardliners in the period leading up to the 2000 parliamentary election. The Iranian constitution's Article 99, which states: 'The Guardians Council has the responsibility of supervising the elections of the Assembly of Experts for Leadership, the President of the Republic, the Islamic Consultative Assembly, and the direct recourse to popular opinion and referenda,' was a particularly acute issue. Questions over the meaning and inter-pretation of 'supervision' were hotly debated in 1999, as the law was used to disqualify about 600 potential candidates in what had come to be a highly politicized process. Perhaps what reflec-ted this most strongly was President Khatami's apology to disqualified candidates during a 8 February speech.[58]

In August 1999, the parliament approved an amendment to the electoral law that said: 'The Guardians Council will have the supervisory task in every stage of the parliamentary elections. This supervision will be expedient and comprehensive in every election related to the Majlis.'[59] Moderate parliamentarians tried to modify this by introducing a bill that said candidates must be given the legal reason for disqualification, so they would have a greater chance to appeal. But the Guardians Council, which must endorse all legislation, rejected this measure, because: 'in some cases the explanation could create corruption and destroy an individual's reputation.'[60]

The other body with responsibility for elections is the Interior Ministry. Its chief, Hojatoleslam Abdolvahed Musavi-Lari, complained that: 'the Guardians Council is responsible for supervision and the Ministry of Interior is responsible for administration. Any move which damages the separation of responsibilities or puts the supervisor in place of the administrator is contrary to the constitution.'[61] Musavi-Lari added that the government tried to reach an understanding with the parliament and the Guardians Council on the election law: 'but unfortunately the Guardians Council rejected the single article that was supposed to be the basis of the agreement.'[62] At the end of September, parliament concluded its discussions on the draft election law and eliminated Article 60, which gave the Guardians Council authority to: 'disqualify any candidate for the Majlis who commits any type of offense – or any offense which may affect the outcome of the election – and declare the election null and void.'[63]

The Guardians Council continued to increase its powers, declaring in January that it is not sufficient for parliamentary candidates to be Muslims, they also must show commitment to Islam. This did not go over well, and a government-run newspaper said that judging a person's faith and religion 'is entirely in the hands of Almighty God.'[64] Thirty-two prominent Iranian political figures sent an open letter urging Khatami to ensure that the parliamentary election is not rigged.[65]

Other aspects of the electoral laws caused problems. In January, hardline parliamentarians proposed eliminating second-round run-offs, suggesting that anybody who gains a plurality should win, whereas under then-current laws the winner had to gain at least one-third of the votes. A walkout occurred and a quorum could not be formed when deputies objected to the proposal. After a closed-door session the next day, a compromise was reached in which it was decided that whoever earned a minimum 25 percent of the vote would win, and in case of a second round, the winner just needed to gain a majority.

By 18 December, about 6,860 Iranians, including 504 women and 35 non-Muslims, registered as candidates for the February parliamentary elections. Five parliamentary seats are reserved for non-Muslims. Within ten days, 401 candidates had been rejected.[66]

Candidates' eligibility, in terms of their persona, political and ideological backgrounds, was investigated initially by commissions in each constituency. The work of these commissions had to be endorsed by supervisory councils that fielded the grievances of disqualified candidates. The supervisory councils endorsed or reversed the decisions of the local commissions on the basis of evidence offered by the rejected candidate. And the supervisory councils had the option of explaining their decisions in cases where doing so will not have (unexplained) 'unwelcome consequences.'[67]

Many candidates were rejected on the basis of Article 28 of the election law, which calls for 'belief in and practical commitment to Islam and the Islamic Republic system' and loyalty to the constitution and the Vilayat-i Faqih (Guardianship of the Supreme Jurisconsult). Others were rejected, per Article 30, because they had worked to strengthen the monarchy in the past or had acted against the theocracy more recently.[68]

The Guardians Council announced on 27 January that its investigation of appeals was complete, and it confirmed the rejection of 600 candidates – out of an original total of 758 – and two days later it announced that 669 candidates were rejected, with 192 candidacies being reinstated and 99 new candidates being disapproved.[69]

The Guardians Council spokesman explained that:

> [Candidates] were rejected because legally their files were imperfect. The reasons for the rejection of most of the

candidates ... were that they did not have the educational qualifications, were not old enough or had not resigned their posts – only in those professions which they were legally obliged to resign. Some of them did resign, but their employers did not accept their resignation within the deadline ... The rejection of a candidate did not mean he [or she] was not worthy. We just observed the law.

Possibly predicting complaints, the Guardians Council spokesman said: 'The council does not favor any particular faction or individuals. And when the final results are announced, the people will definitely make a fair judgment.'[70]

People were complaining already. Hojatoleslam Hadi Khamenei, Secretary-General of the Reformist Groups Following The Imam's Line, said: 'Some people, feeling a sense of religious duty, permit themselves to step beyond the bounds of the law when vetting candidates.'[71] The head of Iran's election headquarters said that some of the candidates were not even told why they were disqualified, and he wondered why those whose candidacy was approved in previous elections were rejected this time.[72] Most of the rejected candidates were identified as reformists, while others were fairly outspoken opponents of the system.[73]

President Khatami also voiced unhappiness with 'advisory supervision' at this time. As if to reassure any hardliners, Khatami said during a meeting with students that: 'even if we leave this society alone and do not place supervision or conditions over it, the choice of most of the people would be religion, independence, and honor.'[74] In an added warning, he said: 'We should refrain from useless pressure and strictness, which are called for neither by religion nor by law.'

A few days later, Khatami restated these themes, while urging people to vote. He said that the public still wants Islam, but it is: 'an Islam that has respect for these people ... [one] that wants to see the establishment of a popular government and to have the people decide for themselves and determine their own destiny.' Turning to advisory supervision and its critics, Khatami remarked that: 'Some people may like this law, some people may not like this law, but the right thing for us to do is to respect the law.' Khatami added that: 'no right should be trampled, neither the right of the voter, nor the rights of the people being elected.'[75]

The Guardians Council announced its ultimate list of 576 rejected candidates on 7 February. 'The list sent by the Guardian Council to the election headquarters, dated the eighteenth of Bahman [7 February], is final and should form the basis for action.'[76] But a week later it was reported that the Guardians Council was trying to reject more candidates.[77] Campaigning officially started on 10 February, and two days before the election the Interior Ministry announced that there was a total of 6,083 candidates running for parliament. The same day, the Interior Ministry announced that 890 candidates had withdrawn, which would bring the total to 5,193.[78]

The Guardians Council announced on 15 February that all disqualified candidates were provided with written explanations. Those who appealed got a fair hearing and were shown the relevant documents, except in cases where: 'this had to be done for legal reasons and for the sake of safeguarding the rights of third persons or the country's interest.'[79]

## THE PARLIAMENTARY ELECTION

By the time of the parliamentary election, there were some 111 licensed political parties in Iran. This included groups with primarily political orientations, as well as those that had more single-issue orientations, such as the Armenian See in Tehran or the Society of Assyrians in Orumieh. Parties and factions were more significant in the major cities, where voters had to choose from large lists of candidates and ideological considerations were more relevant in their selections. The ideological groupings could effectively be classified as reformists and conservatives.

The reformist Second of Khordad coalition included 18 groups. The major ones were:

- Executives of Construction Party (ECP). A party with a strong technocratic core that was formed by associates of former President Ali Akbar Hashemi-Rafsanjani, including his brother Muhammad, Tehran Mayor Gholamhussein Karbaschi, and 16 ministers and vice presidents.

- Islamic Iran Participation Party (IIPP). This organization was founded in Autumn 1998 as a pro-Khatami party by former members of the Executives of Construction Party and the Tehran Militant Clergy Association, as well as Students Following the Imam's Line member Abbas Abdi.

- Islamic Labor Party. This party announced its formation in February 1999, and its initial platform was described as 'protecting the rights of the workers and laborers.' Spokeswoman Soheila Jelodarzadeh also is an advocate of women's issues. Founding members were part of the Workers House (Khaneh-yi Kargar), which supported Khatami's presidential bid.

- Militant Clerics Association (Majma-yi Ruhaniyun-i Mobarez). This group's leadership is Hojatoleslams Mehdi Mahdavi-Karrubi, Muhammad Asqar Musavi-Khoeniha and Ali Akbar Ashtiani. This group broke away from the original Tehran Militant Clergy Association (Jameh-yi Ruhaniyat-i Mobarez-i Tehran), and it is now considered the left-leaning clergy association. Dissatisfied with what it saw as manipulation of the system, it ran no candidates for several years. In October 1996, the group resumed its political activities.

- Mujahidin of the Islamic Revolution Organization. This group is led by former Minister of Heavy Industry Behzad Nabavi-Tabrizi and Muhammad Salamati. Much of its membership consists of ex-Mujahidin Khalq Organization members. It dissolved in the early 1980s but re-emerged in the late 1990s. The group advocates government intervention in the economy and in development.

- Office for Strengthening Unity. This loose grouping of pro-Khatami Islamist associations is comprised mainly of student groups. It was the most active of the university-affiliated ones, and it has gotten into physical confrontations with the hardline Ansar-i Hizballah. Its leaders include Amir Mir-Damadi and Ebrahim Asgharzadeh.

Other reformist groups are the Islamic Solidarity Party and the Groups Following the Imam's Line.

There are a number of conservative political groups, too, although there were fewer of them fielding candidate lists and there was greater unity in these lists:

- Islamic Coalition Association. Led by Habibollah Asgaroladi-Mosalman, this group was formed as a coalition of grass-roots, local Islamic clubs, and a joint venture of conservative bazaaris and clerics. Interwoven with the Resalat Foundation, it supports the Supreme Leadership. It supported parliamentary speaker Hojatoleslam Ali Akbar Nateq-Nouri in the 1997 presidential election. The ICA absorbed members of the anti-Bahai Hojattieh Society when it ceased its activities in 1983.

- Tehran Militant Clergy Association (Jameh-yi Ruhaniyat-i Mobarez-i Tehran). This group originated in 1936, and it was active in the 1963 riots in Iran. It supported Nateq-Nouri in the 1997 presidential election. Members favor a market economy, and are very conservative culturally. This group strongly supports Supreme Leader Ayatollah Ali Khamenei and the doctrine that ultimate decision-making power should rest with the Leadership.

Not only did the coalitions field different candidate lists, there was an overlap in candidates of the reformist and conservative factions. Some Executives of Construction candidates, for example, also appeared on the Islamic Coalition Association and Tehran Militant Clergy Association lists. Such a confusing situation, therefore, ensured that the newspapers had a very important role to play in keeping voters informed.

By law, the campaigning period lasted just one week, from 9 February to 16 February. But press coverage of electoral issues had started much earlier, and as was indicated earlier, many of the newspapers are *de facto* party organs. Party officials, furthermore, traveled the country to address 'meetings' well before the official campaigning began. Also, the news coverage given to officials in office doubled as a platform for campaigning.

Expediency Council chairman Hojatoleslam Ali-Akbar Hashemi-Rafsanjani was one of the most flagrant in his attempts to appeal to voters as a reformist. When the JRM criticized President Khatami at the end of September, Rafsanjani distanced himself from the organization; 'an informed source' said that Rafsanjani, 'had long since discontinued his organic links' with the group and 'in a distant past' he only 'routinely and sporadically' met some of its members.[80]

The next major event in Rafsanjani's candidacy was the release from prison of former Tehran Mayor Gholamhussein Karbaschi, who was imprisoned in early 1999 on corruption charges. A commentator opined that Rafsanjani would like to get the credit for Karbaschi's release, while a reformist newspaper claimed that Rafsanjani actually wrote Karbaschi's appeal for clemency.[81] A parliamentarian predicted that Karbaschi's release would bring the Second of Khordad movement and the ECP closer together.[82] Known as a king-maker (shah-saz) for his part in engineering Khatami's presidential victory, one newspaper asked whom Karbaschi would coronate this time.[83] Yet, the former mayor stayed silent during the campaign period, though he spoke out on Rafsanjani's behalf after the election.[84]

As a substitute Friday Prayer leader, Rafsanjani was in a strong position to discuss campaign issues, because the Tehran Friday Prayers are normally carried by state broadcasting. He used this platform to call his critics 'sanctimonious extremists' who are acting: 'just for the sake of gaining a few votes from the people or the uninformed young people.'[85] Rafsanjani later suggested that people who were once insiders (khodi) were now at odds with the revolution and sought: 'refuge in foreign powers and global arrogance.'[86] He added that the so-called reformists are actually extremists: 'You wouldn't imagine how much I suffered in trying to curb their excesses – hangings, trials, and confiscation of private property – in the early years of the revolution.'[87]

Rafsanjani seemed to garner the most attention because his candidacy was so controversial. But other candidates and parties also engaged in early campaigning. Expediency Council secretary Mohsen Rezai, for example, suddenly became a great fan of the Second of Khordad movement, calling it a 'golden page' in Iranian history.[88] Ebrahim Asgharzadeh of the OSU was 'beaten up and seriously injured' when he visited Rasht, a provincial capital, in January.[89] The IIPP's Muhammad Reza Khatami got off lightly when he went to Rasht the next month, because protestors only jeered him.[90]

In Khuzestan, home to many Iranians of Arab origin and where ethnic sentiments have been a political issue in the past: 'Some of the candidates and their supporters [were] involved in inciting nationalist feelings and provoking ethnic tendencies among the people to obtain votes.'[91] There also were reports of election unrest in Tabriz and Ardabil, which have large populations of ethnic Azeris, because the authorities refused to allow the registration of an Azeri nationalist figure.[92]

Once the campaign was officially under way, there were physical attacks on candidates throughout the country. Other candidates were arrested, and rallies turned into ruckuses. In addition to the sensational violence, the election campaign featured serious debate over issues such as limiting judicial power, addressing the 1998 serial killings of political dissidents, liberalizing the economy and improving relations with the United States.

The reformists employed Western campaigning strategies and techniques, recognizing that old methods would not work on the younger generation. Campaign slogans shifted away from ideology and revolutionary commitment. The ECP emphasized 'Security, Prosperity, and Freedom' and the IIPP called for 'Iran for all Iranians.' Slogans promoting the 'Twenty-ninth of Bahman' (18 February) as another 'Second of Khordad' gained currency. Reformist candidates often described their academic qualifications or technical experience in promising to build a better future and spoke of themes such as economic reforms, pluralism, greater individual freedom and the equality of all citizens before the law. Reformists were usually pictured as smiling, like President Khatami, and sporting designer stubble – a two- or three-day beard long enough to meet theological requirements but not long enough to look like a cleric.

The conservatives also changed their approach, a little. Two of the main conservative bodies – the Tehran Militant Clergy

Association (Jameh-yi Ruhaniyat-i Mobarez-i Tehran, JRM) and the Coalition of the Line of the Imam and Leader – emphasized 'understanding' in their slogans. In their speeches, however, conservatives most often spoke of their religious qualifications as they promised to maintain the original values of the revolution. Their speeches stressed spiritual integrity and faith in theocracy. In their campaign posters the conservatives did not smile, in line with a dictum by the revolution's founder, Ayatollah Ruhollah Musavi-Khomeini, that anyone who smiles is smiling at Satan. The rationale is that true Shiites are grieving over the seventh-century martyrdom of Imam Hussein.

State officials and religious figures urged the public to vote in the days before the election, although they gave different reasons to do so. Supreme Leader Ayatollah Khamenei told prospective Hajj candidates in an address broadcast by state radio that they would participate wholeheartedly in the election, because 'elections symbolize the people's participation and restoration of their rights.'[93] Saying that voting is both a right and a duty, he added that: 'it is important what percentage of people who could vote take part in the elections and vote.' He urged the public to vote for candidates who are: 'able to stand up to coercion, scare-mongering, excessiveness and avarice of world powers, and assess the problems of the country and the nation.'

Some of President Khatami's get-out-the-vote speeches seemed factionally-oriented. In a speech marking the revolution's anniversary, he urged people to elect candidates who will not oppose the executive branch's policies.[94] Khatami said:

> The government will be able to take more confident steps to serve you, if it were to enjoy the co-operation of a qualified parliament and a parliament which carefully scrutinizes the behavior and decisions of the executive officials and the judicial authority.

On election day, polling stations were supposed to be open for a maximum of 12 hours, but the Interior Ministry reported that turnout was so large that voters who had arrived before the deadline and were still standing in line were allowed to vote anyway. In light of the final reported turnout of 69 percent, it seems more likely that the polls were kept open in the hope that somebody would show up. The Guardians Council had rejected efforts to computerize the counting system, so all votes were counted by hand. It took only a few hours to get the results in the smaller constituencies, but in Tehran it took three months – see below.

Within two days of the election it was clear that reformists had won many of the 290 legislative seats and conservatives had fared badly. By 26 February the numbers were 148 reformists, 37 conservatives, 35 independents and five religious minorities.

Run-offs for 52 seats were held on 5 May in the 66 constituencies where no candidate attracted 25 percent of the votes. Eligible to vote were those who voted in the same constituencies in the first round or who did not participate in the first round. By the next day, reformists were claiming a sweeping victory. Behzad Nabavi, spokesman for the reformist Second of Khordad front, said that 71.2 percent of the elected candidates were reformists, 15.15 percent were conservatives and the remainder were independents. Nabavi broke this down as 47 reformists, ten conservatives and nine independents.[95]

## REVERSALS AND DELAYS

Hardliners in the government did not intend to make it easy for the reformist forces. One way in which they created obstacles was by having the Guardians Council disallow reformist electoral victories in 13 constituencies. Members of the public reacted to this by staging a number of demonstrations, several of which turned violent.

Also, the Guardians Council delayed announcing the results of the Tehran election, claiming a recount was needed because major discrepancies were being discovered. Observers believed that any discrepancies were not substantial enough to make a real difference in the final result. Rather, they thought the Guardians Council was trying to find a way to improve Hashemi-Rafsanjani's standing. He had finished 30th out of the top 30 candidates. This was good enough to earn him a seat in the parliament, but it dashed any hopes that he would be chosen as speaker, and it was generally humiliating for the man who had served as speaker of parliament before, and who had also been president for two terms.

The delays caused uneasiness in Tehran. A conservative parliamentarian said that: 'only the cancellation of the Tehran elections could clean the shame of the election officials.'[96] Student-leader Heshmatollah Tabarzadi, on the other hand, warned that: 'If the Guardians Council annuls Tehran election results, we will definitely break silence and take to the streets in protest – and to defend our constitutional and legitimate rights.'[97] Also, the Tehran bazaar almost came to a standstill, with the near elimination of larger transactions – from ten million rials upward – and fears of bankruptcy for smaller traders.[98]

The Guardians Council announced the final results for Tehran on 20 May, on instructions from the Supreme Leader. Twenty-eight out of 30 of the final winners were announced, with Hashemi-Rafsanjani moving from last to 20th place and another conservative candidate – Gholamali Haded-Adal – winning a place.

Although announcing the Tehran results may have been intended to quell criticism, it had the opposite effect. Two demonstrations in Tehran became violent.[99] A senior cleric also denounced the delay in announcing the results and the improvement in Hashemi-Rafsanjani's standing. He said that:

> After recounting the votes, a person was moved upward from the 30th to the 20th place. God forbid, the people are not stupid. They understand these matters. The Guardian Council, by respecting the people's rights, should clarify the issue. This is why we say that the country needs reforms.[100]

Hashemi-Rafsanjani announced on 25 May, just two days before the opening session of the new parliament, that he would not take his seat. 'In spite of my request to the supervisory and executive officials to take steps to remove any doubt and ambiguity and to discover all the facts ...' Rafsanjani said, 'there are still certain doubts and ambiguities concerning the results of elections in Tehran. Such ambiguities can be used as a pretext by the enemies of the Iranian nation and cause disunity among forces committed to the Islamic system.'[101] Rafsanjani went on to explain that this made it difficult for him to:

> Discharge my duties and responsibilities in a proper manner and to make efforts in the cause of national consensus and to reinforce the reconstruction of the country, which has been one of the major and important aims of my partici- pation in the political process.[102]

### COUP D'ÉTAT?

The press battles and the parliamentary election provided the outside observer with the clearest view of Iran's factional con- flict. But underneath this was the omnipresent threat of violence and even a hardline coup with the IRGC serving as its vanguard. Hints of this had come in April 1998, when IRGC chief Yahya Rahim-Safavi said: 'We seek to tear out the roots of counter- revolution wherever they may be. We should cut the neck of some of them. We will cut the tongues of others.'[103] Two months later, Safavi said that: 'The Guards ... have identified many of the elements of these groups ... They have at this time left them free to set up their groups and newspapers but we will go after them when the time is ripe.'[104] Safavi warned: 'The fruit has to be picked when it is ripe. That fruit is unripe now. We will pick it ... when it turns ripe.' Safavi was also quoted as saying that: 'We have thrown a stone inside the nest of snakes which have received blows from our revolution, and are giving them time to stick their heads out.'

Such concerns were renewed in July 1999. At that time 24 IRGC commanders sent a letter to President Khatami in which he was warned that the unrest was due to his policies, and if he did not act, the IRGC would take matters into its own hands.[105] The IRGC officials first issued subtle warnings:

We can see the footprints of the enemy in the afore-mentioned incidents and we can hear its drunken cackle. You should understand this today because tomorrow is too late … look at foreign media and radios. Can you not hear their joyful music?

Then they came to the point: 'Our patience has run out. We cannot tolerate this situation any longer if it is not dealt with.'

The results of the parliamentary election only increased fears that a coup might occur. Less than a month after the parliamentary election, reformist ideologue Said Hajjarian was shot by men with links to the IRGC.[106] In April, several IRGC commanders, as well as 'some conservative religious scholars and some members of the Assembly of Experts,' approached Supreme Leader Ayatollah Ali Khamenei, expressed their concern about the system's future, and threatened to act against the reformists.[107] They urged Khamenei to cancel the election results and extend the current term of parliament by another year. Khamenei rejected all these suggestions and warned of a civil war if the IRGC acted.

Fueling fears about an IRGC coup was its aggressive 16 April statement that: 'enemies … will feel the reverberating impact of the hammer of the Islamic revolution on their skulls.' In Tehran, this was called Statement Number 0, in the belief that Statement Number 1 would be the announcement of a coup. The reformist Mujahidin of the Islamic Revolution Organization warned that the hardline 'Power Mafia' was trying to manipulate the IRGC to achieve its own ends: 'the Power Mafia intends to turn this popular force into a suppressive entity to confront the nation.'[108] After its proud history in the war with Iraq, they continued, the IRGC might be reduced to the level of: 'jack-booted soldiers of the third world who seek to increase their power through suppression of writers, by banning newspapers and through fear and intimidation.'

At the end of April reports of an IRGC 'crisis headquarters,' which also was part of the supposed coup plan, emerged.[109] Details of this plan included the arrest and prosecution of reformists and labeling them as foreign agents, closing reformist publications to interrupt the flow of information, and con-vincing Supreme Leader Ayatollah Ali Khamenei of the danger to the system. Other steps included disrupting the Tehran bazaar and the seminaries to provoke senior clerics, silencing intellectuals, and using terror against Khatami supporters.


CONCLUSION

In the end, nothing came of the fears about a coup, and Iran's sixth parliament was inaugurated uneventfully on 27 May 2000. Initially, it seemed that its first steps would be to address economic issues, which would have the greatest impact on the voters' day-to-day lives.[110] Such an approach would make sense in a country with an estimated 25 percent inflation rate, where unemployment is officially at 16 percent and is estimated to be at least 25 percent, and where those who are employed often go unpaid for months. Such economic improvements would reduce dependence on government subsidies, drug abuse and social volatility. Indeed, the new Speaker of Parliament, Hojatoleslam Mehdi Mahdavi-Karrubi, said the parliament's priorities would be: 'economic issues and issues that affect the people's lives, employment and unemployment, creating a secure environment for investment and eliminating problematic areas in the law.'[111]

When debate on new legislation began, however, the first subject was reform of the restrictive press law, and there were indications that the next subject for discussion would be the election laws. Karrubi said that: 'the parliament must propose new laws governing press freedom,' and he added a few days later: 'We are sure our people are after freedom of expression.'[112] Karrubi also proposed changes to the election law, specifically mentioning the Guardians Council and its 'excessive' oversight powers. Karrubi added: 'God willing, we will remove obstacles so that in future elections people will have more room to maneuver … so that they can take part in a climate of opposing viewpoints.'[113]

Yet the reformist newspapers remained closed, and there was little indication on when, or even if, they would re-open.

These events show the complex reality of domestic Iranian politics. The two factions contend fiercely, though so far non-violently over Iran's future path. Public opinion and elections tend to favor the reformists. Yet the hardliners manage to find ways to invoke their preferences, slowing or stopping reformist measures, harassing the expression of reformist opinion, and holding onto large elements of state power. Personal conflicts and the interest of sub-factions also play an important role in the distribution of power and the occurrence of conflicts.

For some time, the picture should remain one of de facto compromise among the two factions, which will often mean deadlock over implementing any changes. The tide of support for reformism has seemed high, yet its ultimate triumph will not come easily or quickly.

## NOTES

1. Islamic Republic News Agency (IRNA), 20 September 1999.
2. *RFE/RL Iran Report*, 2, 15 (12 April 1999).
3. IRNA, 29 September and 29 November 1998.
4. *Jomhuri-yi Islamic*, 8 June (1999).
5. Islamic Republic of Iran Broadcasting (IRIB), 5 July 1999.
6. IRNA, 27 June 1999.
7. *RFE/RL Iran Report*, 2, 23 (7 June 1999).
8. *Salam*, 6 July (1999).
9. *Kayhan*, 29 April (2000).
10. *RFE/RL Iran Report*, 2, 17 (26 April 1999).
11. *Jomhuri-yi Islami* and *Kayhan*, 19 April (1999).
12. Ayatollah Muhammad Emami-Kashani, cited by the Voice of the Islamic Republic of Iran, Network 1, 10 September 1999.
13. Grand Ayatollah Muhammad Fazel-Movahedi-Lankarani, cited by the Vision of the Islamic Republic Network 1, 20 December 1999.
14. *Kayhan*, 7 July (1999).
15. IRNA, 4 August (1999).
16. *Jomhuri-yi Islami*, 19 July (1999).
17. IRNA, 21 July 1999.
18. *Hamshahri*, 12 October (1999).
19. *Sobh-i Imruz*, 11 November (1999).
20. Islamic Revolutionary Court Judge Gholamhussein Rahbarpour, cited by *Jomhuri-yi Islami*, 12 September (1999).
21. *Qods*, 18 April (1999).
22. *Sobhi-i Imruz*, 24 August (1999).
23. IRNA, 5 September 1999.
24. *Neshat*, 2 September (1999).

25. IRNA, 9 August 1999.
26. *Hamshahri*, 12 January (2000).
27. Tehran Friday prayer sermon, the Voice of the Islamic Republic of Iran, 14 April 2000.
28. Live speech by Ayatollah Ali Khamenei, to a group of young people in Tehran, the Voice of the Islamic Republic of Iran, 20 April 2000.
29. Vision of the Islamic Republic of Iran, Network 1, 16 April 2000.
30. *Tehran Times*, 25 April (2000).
31. *RFE/RL Iran Report*, 3, 17 (2000).
32. Vision of the Islamic Republic of Iran, Network 1, 23 April 2000.
33. IRNA, 29 April (2000).
34. IRNA, 5 September 1999.
35. See, for example, *Jomhouri-yi Islami*, 6 April (1999).
36. *Ettelatt*, 8 April (1999).
37. IRNA, 21 April 1999.
38. IRNA, 7 September 1999.
39. Nikahang Kosar drew cartoons that ridiculed Mesbah-Yazdi's claim – 25 January 2000 – that a former director of the Central Intelligence Agency had come to Iran and given money to reformist publications and individuals. Mesbah-Yazdi went on to say that this money was in addition to the $20 million that was previously dedicated to overthrowing the Iranian regime, as reported by Asr-i Azadigan on 27 January. There was more to this nefarious plot, according to Mesbah-Yazdi: 'The CIA has also invited our country's journalists to go to America in order to brainwash them and let them have a good time, so to speak.'
40. *Mosharekat*, 12 February (2000).
41. IRNA, 22 April 2000.
42. *RFE/RL Iran Report*, 3, 17 (2000).
43. Suleiman Kiai, *Sobh-i Imruz*, 29 March (2000).
44. *Khabar va Nazar*, 18 January (1999).
45. For an analysis of the politically powerful Larijani family, see Muhammad Quchani, 'The Larijani Brothers', *Asr-e Azadigan*, 22 April (2000).
46. *Zan*, 20 January (1999).
47. *Iran*, 14 March (1999).
48. *Khordad*, 25 April (1999).
49. Mr Nemati, Director of the Islamic Republic of Iran Broadcasting's communications department, rejected reports that foreign radio broadcasts were being jammed. 'Those who make such allegations on the eve of the elections intend to create tension and discord,' he told *Asr-i Azadigan* on 17 February 2000.
50. IRNA, 14 February (2000).
51. *Fath*, 15 February (2000).
52. Former Guardians Council member Ayatollah Abolqasem Khazali, cited by *Sobh-i Imruz*, 19 April 2000.
53. Ayatollah Taqi Mesbah-Yazdi, cited by *Fath*, 18 April (2000).
54. Speech by President Muhammad Khatami to inaugurate the new Ministry of Science, Research, and Technology in Tehran, Vision of the Islamic Republic of Iran, on 22 April 2000. On Network 1, 23 April 2000.
55. IRNA, 2 May (2000).

56. *Fath*, 20 April (2000).
57. Kar va Kargar, cited by *Iran Daily*, 2 May (2000).
58. *Mosharekat*, 9 February (2000).
59. Voice of the Islamic Republic of Iran, Network 1, 12 August 1999.
60. *Sobh-i Imruz*, 21 September (1999).
61. *Khordad*, 20 September (1999).
62. IRNA, 24 September (1999).
63. Vision of the Islamic Republic of Iran, Network 1, 28 September 1999.
64. *Iran*, 5 January (2000).
65. IRNA, 4 January 2000. Among the letter's signatories were the Secretary-General of the Militant Clerics Association, Hojatoleslam Mehdi Mahdavi-Karrubi; Hojatoleslam Muhammad Asqar Musavi-Khoeniha; parliamentarian and Secretary-General of the Islamic Assembly of Women, Fatemeh Karrubi; Islamic Labor Party founder Soheila Jelodarzadeh; and former Khatami adviser Seyyed Mehdi Imam-Jamarani.
66. Vision of the Islamic Republic of Iran, Network 1, 28 December 1999.
67. *Iran News*, 20 December (1999).
68. IRNA, 29 December 1999.
69. Ayatollah Reza Ostadi, quoted by the Voice of the Islamic Republic of Iran, Network 1, 27 January 2000. Voice of the Islamic Republic of Iran, Network 1, 29 January 2000.
70. Ayatollah Reza Ostadi, quoted by the Voice of the Islamic Republic of Iran, Network 1, 27 January 2000.
71. *Sobh-i Imruz*, 25 January (2000).
72. Interior Ministry Deputy for Socio-Political Affairs Mustafa Tajzadeh, quoted by IRNA, 2 February 2000. Forty people who had served in previous parliaments were rejected this time, according to *Mosharekat*, 13 January (2000).
73. Muhammad Rezai-Babadi, Tehran Deputy Governor for Political and Security Affairs, and Head of the Tehran Province Election Headquarters, quoted in *Iran*, 31 January (2000). Among the former group were Islamic Iran Participation Party (IIPP) founders Abbas Abdi and Ali Reza Farzad. And among the latter group were Heshmatollah Tabarzadi, Director of the banned Hoviat-i Khish and leader of the Islamic Union of Students and Graduates, and nationalist-religious figures like Ezattolah Sahabi, Habibollah Peyman, and Ebrahim Yazdi of the banned – but tolerated – Freedom Movement.
74. Voice of the Islamic Republic of Iran, Network 1, 25 January 2000.
75. Voice of the Islamic Republic of Iran, Network 1, 31 January 2000. The regime cites voter participation as a mark of its legitimacy, so a boycott of any sort could undermine such claims. It is possible, therefore, that Khatami urged voter participation in order to avoid such an embarrassment. This interpretation finds support in Supreme Leader Ayatollah Ali Khamenei's warning that: 'the enemy is trying to prevent people from massively participating in the parliamentary elections so as to claim that people have distanced themselves from the revolution and system'. Through their massive participation, Khamenei said, the Iranian people will 'slap America's face.' IRNA, 2 February 2000.
76. Vision of the Islamic Republic of Iran, Network 1, 8 February 2000.
77. Interior Minister Musavi-Lari, cited by *Hamshahri*, 14 February (2000).
78. IRNA, 16 February 2000.

79. Vision of the Islamic Republic of Iran, Network 1, 15 February 2000.
80. IRNA, 29 September 1999.
81. Professor Sadeq Zibakalam, interview with RFE/RL's Persian Service, 26 January 2000. *Aftab-i Imruz*, 22 January 2000. Karbaschi told *Newsweek* on 10 February 2000 that Rafsanjani had consistently defended him, and he served as the intermediary in getting Karbaschi released.
82. Parliamentarian Muhammad Baqer Zakeri, quoted by *Arya*, 26 January (2000).
83. *Iran-i Vij*, 26 January (2000).
84. *Mosharekat*, 23 February (2000).
85. First sermon, Voice of the Islamic Republic of Iran, Network 1, 21 January 2000.
86. Voice of the Islamic Republic of Iran, Network 1, 26 January 2000.
87. *Iran*, 26 January (2000). Rafsanjani did not name names, but he was referring to individuals like Ayatollah Sadeq Khalkhali (the 'Hanging Judge' who toyed with the corpses of American soldiers killed in the 1979 hostage rescue mission) and hostage-takers like Abbas Abdi (now a member of the IIPP) and Ebrahim Asgharzdeh (now the leader of the Office for Strengthening Unity).
88. IRNA, 29 January 2000.
89. *Sobh-i Imruz*, 5 January (2000).
90. *Iran Daily*, 8 February (2000).
91. *Jomhuri-yi Islami*, 3 February (2000).
92. The United Azerbaijan Movement, cited by Baku's Turan news agency, 28 January 2000. The National Liberation Movement of Southern Azerbaijan, cited by *Azadlyg*, 25 January (2000). The nationalist figure often cited by Azerbaijani irredentists is Mahmudali Chehragani. See A.W. Samii, 'Ethnic Issues in Iran–Azerbaijan Relations', *Caspian Crossroads*, 4, 3 (1999). One hundred and twenty candidates ran for Tabriz's six seats. Two reformist candidates, one of them an incumbent, won in the first round of voting in Tabriz, but run-offs will be required for the four remaining seats. Rather than the apathy suggested by Azerbaijani sources, the week of campaigning was 'hectic'; Robin Allen, 'Tabriz Gripped by Election Fever as Iranian's Prepare to Vote', *Financial Times*, 18 February (2000).
93. IRIB, 15 February (2000).
94. Vision of the Islamic Republic of Iran, Network 1, 11 February 2000.
95. IRNA, 6 May 2000.
96. Muhammad Javad Larijani, cited by *Iran*, 7 May (2000).
97. *Associated Press*, 13 May 2000.
98. *Ham-Mihan'*, 7 May (2000).
99. At the first rally, people at Tehran University protested against the Guardians Council's actions and objected to Hashemi-Rafsanjani's enduring presence on the political scene, chanting 'Hashemi, Hashemi, let go of the country'; Associated Press, 22 May 2000. The second rally was organized by members of Heshmatollah Tabarzadi's more radical student organization; Reuters, 24 May 2000. The pro-regime Iranian Students News Agency reported that the latter event was 'broken up by a group called "Ansar-i Hizbullah".'
100. Ayatollah Muhammad Abai-Khorasani, Secretary of the Qom Association of Seminary Students and Lecturers – Majmae-yi Mudarisin va Muhaqiqin-i Howzeh-yi Elmieh-yi Qom – cited by *Iran*, 24 May (2000).

101. Vision of the Islamic Republic of Iran, Network 2, 25 May 2000.
102. Vision of the Islamic Republic of Iran, Network 2, 25 May 2000.
103. *Jameah*, 29 April (1998). Safavi added: 'Our sword is our tongue. We will expose ... these cowards,' leading to speculation that he was not making physical threats. The IRGC then issued a statement, published in the *Kayhan*, on 3 May: 'What has been said in certain newpapers and used by certain political currents to sensitize the atmosphere is a distorted and defective version of a secret and private conversation among the Guards commanders on security issues'. The statement warned that the information had been leaked 'without due attention to the classified and security nature of the exchanges,' which were held in Qom. 'It was maliciously forged with no regard to moral, legal and security considerations.'
104. *Hamshahri*, 4 June (1998).
105. The 12 July letter was reproduced in the 19 July (1999) issues of *Jomhuri-yi Islami* and *Kayhan*.
106. *RFE/RL Iran Report*, 3, 12 (2000); 13 (2000); 14 (2000); 3, 18 (2000); and 3, 21 (2000).
107. *Asharq al-Awsat*, 18 April (2000).
108. *Iran*, 19 April (2000).
109. Reuters, 26 April 2000.
110. Jahangir Amuzegar, 'Prospects for Iran's Post-election Economy,' *Middle East Economic Survey*, XLIII, 13 (2000). Vahe Petrossian, 'Iran: It's the Economy', *Middle East Economic Digest*, 27 June (2000).
111. Tehran Voice of the Islamic Republic of Iran Radio, 30 May 2000.
112. *Time Europe*, 6 June (2000). Reuters, 11 June 2000.
113. Reuters, 11 June 2000.

# Index

315